FAITH AND
IDEOLOGIES

Faith and Ideologies is
Volume I of Jesus of Nazareth Yesterday and Today

FAITH AND IDEOLOGIES

JUAN LUIS SEGUNDO

*Translated from the Spanish
by John Drury*

ORBIS BOOKS
Maryknoll, New York

DOVE COMMUNICATIONS
Melbourne, Australia

SHEED AND WARD
London, England

Originally published as *El hombre de hoy ante Jesus de Nazaret*, Volume 1, *Fe e ideologia*, copyright © 1982 by Ediciones Cristiandad, S.L., Huesca, 30-32, Madrid, Spain

English translation copyright © 1984 by Orbis Books, Maryknoll, NY 10545
Published in the United States of America by Orbis Books, Maryknoll, NY 10545
Published in Australia by Dove Communications, Box 316, Blackburn, Victoria 3130, Australia
Published in Great Britain by Sheed and Ward, Ltd., 2 Creechurch Lane, London, England

Manufactured in the United States of America

Some of this material was presented, in substantially different form, as the subject of the Edward Cadbury Lectures given by Juan Luis Segundo at the University of Birmingham, England, in the academic session 1979/80.

Library of Congress Cataloging in Publication Data

Segundo, Juan Luis
  Faith and ideologies.

  Translation of: El hombre de hoy ante Jesus de Nazaret.
  Includes bibliographical references and indexes.
  1. Faith. 2. Ideology. I. Title.
BV4637.S3813   1984   234'.2   83-19386
ISBN 0-88344-127-6 (pbk.)

DOVE/ISBN 0-85924-298-6
SHEED AND WARD/ISBN 0-7220-3518-7

To R.A.,
to whom I am indebted for the idea of this book
as well as for many more important things

Contents

Author's Note

Part One of this book is essential for an understanding of the rest of the work. I want the vocabulary to be as strict as possible and the meaning of terms to be fully recognized and respected. In this way readers will be able to see clearly how my arguments unfold and are linked together.

For this reason I have added a series of clarifying REMARKS at the end of the first four chapters, before the Notes proper. The REMARKS follow the text of the chapters, and thus they constitute a more compact articulation of the points presented in the main part of each chapter. They can be read separately, but they are also cross-referenced to the chapter to show exactly where they fit in.

Readers may find the REMARKS a bit dry and difficult, but I think their content will help my readers to follow my methodological approach and to familiarize themselves with the heart and core of this work. In any case I hope the REMARKS will help readers to grasp my argument better and thus to form a more considered judgment of the whole book.

Abbreviations

CEPAL   Comisión Económica para America Latina.

GS   *Gaudium et spes*. Vatican II. Pastoral Constitution on the Church in the Modern World. November 21, 1964.

MED   Second General Conference of Latin American Bishops (Medellín, Colombia, 1968). Official English edition edited by Louis Michael Colonnese, Latin America Division of the United States Catholic Conference, Washington, D.C.: *The Church in the Present-Day Transformation of Latin America in the Light of the Council;* Vol. I, Position Papers; Vol. II, Conclusions.

Part One

DIFFERENTIATING TERMS

CHAPTER I

Toward a New Statement
of the Problem

It may prove fruitful to begin by expressing doubts about a formulation that is very much in vogue today. According to this popular view, a radical division is set up between those human beings who have "faith" on the one hand, and those who structure their lives around some "ideology" on the other hand. And then there is a further group of people who do not seem to adhere to either alternative, so their lives cannot be neatly classified.

Given this basic formulation, it is perfectly logical for people to assume that faith and ideologies, being alternatives, oppose and exclude each other; and that this is true even when the opposition between them is silent and oblique rather than frontal and explicit.

But why have doubts about a formulation that enjoys so much popularity and almost sociological status? To begin to show the reasonableness of such doubts, I think it would be wise to start with a phenomenological analysis rather than a definition. For the fact is that many definitions are currently used to provide artificial solutions to problems, despite the complexity of existence.

I. Two Basic Anthropological Dimensions

A literary example will help us to break ground for our analysis. I have in mind the play by Albert Camus entitled *Caligula*, but I want the reader to realize that my intention here is not to interpret the mind or intention of the author in writing this extraordinary play. Prescinding from whatever his literary intention may have been, I want to reflect on the problem posed to each one of us by the adventure undertaken by Caligula in this play.

3

Caligula's Problem

The problem that torments Caligula is the difficulty that a human being seems to have in attaining happiness (see REMARK A, p. 20). Caligula, the Roman emperor, believes that at the end of their lives few human beings have the sensation of being happy; and he thinks this is due to the fact that in practice no one manages to reach the goal he or she has set out for themselves. The question, then, is: Why is this negative balance-sheet on the totality of an individual's existence such a general phenomenon? Caligula's conclusion is one with great logic to it. It is that human beings do not arrive at the goal they set for themselves; and they do not do so because they are distracted on route. They are not sufficiently serious and iron-willed in structuring what they do. Their actions, enticed by secondary aims and ends, are dispersed. The whole problem would be solved if human beings were logical in placing all in the service of the end or goal that they have chosen for their existence as a whole.

Now Caligula is an emperor, a predestined human being who does not need anyone or anything, thanks to his power. Thus he proposes to set himself up as a universal example of the proper logic and to give the gift of happiness to human beings by showing them the proper way to it.

But he must go to the root of the problem. He knows that he will not be able to attain a goal that will give meaning to his existence, or even take the first step towards that goal, without a prior step. He must first gear himself completely to the inner logic that will make him invulnerable to the distractions that lead all other human beings off the right track. And Caligula knows that all the failings of logic in this domain come from affectivity: the emotions. It is that which drives human beings to follow after secondary finalities and expend precious energy on them.

If Caligula seeks to be free, then he cannot be tied to other persons by affection. So through the play we see him systematically breaking down his emotional ties. Rights, loyalty, friendship, love: all are sacrificed to the pitiless logic of becoming truly free. A perfect freedom rises into view on the horizon; and beyond that it seems that happiness is within one's reach, whatever might be the goal that one is pursuing.

But the denouement of the play shows us that this freedom quite literally has no object any longer. In destroying his affectivity, Caligula has also destroyed the source of the values that could give meaning to this freedom. His freedom is now prepared to choose with complete logic, but it no longer has anything to choose; and death comes as an additional sign of this *impasse*. With this iron logic the road to happiness seems even more tightly closed than it was before. Caligula has not taken even a single step towards it.

As I indicated above, I am not interested here in a literary analysis. Though the author may have had some other intention, his character Caligula takes us by the hand and, through the steps described above, leads us through some of the essential data involved in an existential analysis of the possibilities and dimensions relating to human happiness (see REMARK B, p. 21).

Value, Meaning, and Faith

I think there are two conclusions to be drawn from this play: one direct, the other indirect. The first conclusion relates exclusively to freedom insofar as it is free will. The second has to do with determining the value-structure that one can give to existence.

Insofar as free will is concerned, it is obvious that when we apply it to the attainment of some value—or happiness, which sums up all of them—every option which is positive (in intent) becomes limiting (in its result). In other words, to choose one path is to close ourselves off to other paths. (Even Caligula's prior choice of being free closes off the possibility of taking a different option or pathway later.) If we choose to attain a certain value experientially and to go through the mediations necessary to arrive at it, that means we decide to remain forever unfamiliar with the experiences that were waiting for us on other potential roads which we did not take. If a person decides to be a doctor, for example, that means that he or she will never acquire direct, empirical knowledge of the satisfactions and displeasures which are part of an engineer's life. And the same holds true in every case. Our freedom, insofar as it is free will, is something like money: when we buy one thing, we necessarily lose at the same time the possibility of buying everything else.

André Gide has elaborated this theme in his literary works. In *Les nourritures terrestres* he writes: "The large quantity of this remainder would always be preferable to any one unit."[1] The only problem is that there is no system which permits us to choose the "remainder" rather than one given thing. That is how our free will is constituted, and that is our human condition.

Thus when Caligula thought he was preparing himself for any pathway whatsoever, he was in reality already choosing one pathway—the most unsatisfactory of all; and there was no chance for him to backtrack. Here we have the first essential datum in our analysis. Insofar as human beings are dealing with complex values rather than immediate sensations, values that oblige us to employ slow and costly means, they can only travel one road, strictly speaking. Thus, if they could look back over it from the end-point of their life, they would see it whole and entire as a single, unique pathway which opened up one possibility for them while simultaneously closing off all other possibilities—i.e., all those that never became part of their actual experience (see REMARK C.1, p. 22).

The second consequence, as I indicated above, relates to the necessity and the possibilities that a human being has to give a meaning-structure to his or her existence. It is obvious, as Caligula himself surmises, that such a structure is necessary if the quest for some value (or happiness) is to be effective. Our activity must be structured if it is not to be diluted and to suffer from a partial or total loss of effectiveness. But what exactly are our possibilities in this area? Obviously we will never be able to choose a pathway knowing beforehand *from actual experience* just exactly how satisfying it is. Here again

Gide, preoccupied with this sort of problem, draws the conclusion from his earlier thought and expresses his doubts as follows: "To give oneself direction in life, is it necessary to set one's eyes on an objective? I have debated this question through the whole night. In what am I to invest this force that I feel in me? How am I to summon up what is best in me? By dedicating myself to some specific end? . . . If I were even sure that I were giving preference to the best in me, then I would choose it over all the rest. But I do not even succeed in knowing what is best in me."[2]

Here we have the whole problem facing all human beings. If we must give an operative and efficacious logic to our actions, how are we to establish one goal above all the rest? That is the question. But it is obvious that this goal cannot be really known as the satisfactory one ahead of time by any empirical means. Therefore every human being must *take a chance* on life, choosing as his or her supreme goal something whose value is not known in a personal, experiential way.

This is the second consequence, more indirect perhaps, that can be deduced from an existential analysis of *Caligula*. We cannot jump to the end of life to see what is worth the trouble to realize in action and then, with this certain knowledge in mind, go back to the beginning and resolve to do it (see REMARK C.2, p. 22).

Now if that is the case, and there is no doubt that it is, then experience readily reveals something that may be quite disconcerting at first glance. This enormous and fundamental difficulty, which paralyzes the heroes of a Camus or a Gide, does not seem to hinder or paralyze the vast majority of human beings. What is more, the lives of the majority of human beings do not seem chaotic to us despite this fact. The people we know in real life have their own personalities. And the proof is that to a large extent we can foresee their reactions in our daily dealings with them. What, then, is the source of that logic?

Here again experience will show us that only through the experiences of others is it possible for us to have an idea of a satisfactory pathway or choice in any positive way. (Right now I will not go into the epistemological problem connected with this fact, exploring in detail the epistemological ways in which each human being relates himself or herself to the experiences of others. That will be examined later on.) Thus experience points up clearly the basic solidarity of the human species. Experiences of effectively realized values are conveyed to us by our fellow human beings. Before we have these experiences ourselves, we perceive their value and their possibilities for satisfaction in and through the experience of others. Thus, faced with the necessary limitedness of our lives, we all are dependent on each other.[3]

The fact is that the valuational structure of every human life depends on the *referential witnesses* in whom we believe. In countless ways, most of them not explicit, these witnesses tell us of the satisfaction that goes with the realization of some value. In one way or another, all of them without exception compel the infantile human being not to let itself be guided by immediately experienced satisfactions, to trust that it will obtain unsuspected satisfactions of a far superior sort by going through annoying mediations. The obligation to study is a good example—leaving aside possible deviations—as is also job-training of any sort.[4]

So the human person known to us has a cognitive and valuational dimension that is necessarily social. And the latter does not result from some alleged contract that is meant to overcome a prior individualistic stage; it is there from the very beginning with each new generation. To debate which comes first here, the individual or society, would of course be equivalent to debating the old question of the chicken or the egg. The thing I want to point up here is the fact that in human beings even individualism is a social posture that results from society (see REMARK C.3, p. 24).

Furthermore, to say society here is to say *faith*. After all, what are we to call a universal, unfailing tendency to fill the gaps in our own experience with the borrowed experience of others? Of course I am not using the term "faith" here in a specifically religious sense. At this point in our reflection faith shows up before us as an absolutely universal dimension of the human being (see REMARK C.4, p. 25).

Action, Means, and Efficacy

Our analysis must now proceed to point up a second anthropological dimension alongside faith. It is, in other words, another element that is necessarily part and parcel of every human life. And since its relations with faith, in the sense just described, are very close, it will not be easy to distinguish it from faith. At first glance it would seem to be nothing more than the extension of faith. I do not want to rush ahead too fast, however, so let us get back to the problem where we left it in Section I.

If we look at the activity of any human being, we will notice that some values seem to be superior to others. The values form a "scale" that can be verified implicitly. For example, a given person values loyalty more than money, or vice-versa. Now we saw above that human beings, once they get beyond their first few steps in life, cannot be guided by their own immediate experience of the satisfaction to be derived from their first act of loyalty or from their first $100 bill. Hence we must conclude that their preference for one or the other of these two "values" derives from an act of faith. It is through the complete lives of other human beings that have been dedicated to loyalty or money that a given person perceives and accepts the notion—without any direct personal experience—that one of these values or ultimate satisfactions surpasses the other.

Thus every option, every act of preferring one thing to another, involves the implementation of a faith. Extending this to all the acts of "preference" in a human life, we can say that faith *structures* a whole life around some specific meaning. Life is valued, is considered meaningful, to the extent that concrete valuations converge towards that which has been chosen as the culminating thing in terms of value, of what ought to be.

In other words, faith starts off by teaching us which value is the one to which we can "entrust" our whole life; but then we also have to structure the rest of it. We must then learn what other values are conducive to the primary value, and to what extent they are; what price we can pay for a given partial achievement of our aim, and what price is so high that it would mean the destruction of the very goal we are seeking.

This brings us into the whole problem-complex dealing with means. We see that faith gradually shifts from what we might call questions of "conscience" to what we might call questions of "method." The first set of questions involves the logic connected with the value that has been chosen as the absolute; the latter set of questions involves the logic connected with effectiveness in using available means.

We also see that this second logic differs from the first on a very important point. It is obvious that our freedom is not creative, strictly speaking. To attain its values, our freedom uses natural and artificial mechanisms as mediations. Digestion and the clock will serve as examples here. The charactcristic feature of these mechanisms is that they have their own internal logic, and that we must respect that logic if we want them to function properly, to be efficacious. The natural or artificial workings of things are ignorant of our motivations, of the value-structure and meaning-structure that we have freely given to our lives. They function with their own proper dynamics and the latter determines their efficacy, prescinding completely from the ultimate aim we have in mind when we set them in motion or simply utilize their operation.

The greatest problem associated with freedom, then, is the fact that we, in order to realize values, must "learn" methods which in themselves are independent of those values. In a certain sense, then, we must submit to them without submitting completely. And there is no doubt that we are here faced with two different dynamisms that must be combined into one. For it is obviously a fact that we as human beings can have the same guiding value and yet accept or reject existing methods, criticize them, or even find better ones. We may take any one of the courses just mentioned without changing our final aim one whit.

At first glance it might seem that this latter aspect dealing with methods is merely a prolongation or extension of the first aspect having to do with meaning and our scale of values. But if we look closely, we will find that there is a *radical* difference between the two, as I have already noted: whereas our scale of values depends entirely on ourselves, judgment about our "methods" depends on factors that escape us. I can establish a very specific goal for myself: e.g., driving in a nail. But in choosing between possible tools—which is to say, in choosing the "method" to use—I must pay attention to the objective difference in effectiveness that various tools possess for my purpose. I must consider the potential effectiveness of such tools as a hammer or a pliers (see REMARK C.5, p. 26).

We can do the same thing, starting from the other end as it were. We can consider the attitude of a human being towards failure, analyzing it in a way that will be illuminating for our purposes. Clearly if a failure is on a fairly large scale, that is to say, if it affects a major portion of our life or activity, it gives rise to a twofold line of criticism. I can study my failure in terms of effectiveness, and I can study it in terms of meaning or value. But however much the two types of study intermingle in a given situation, they have little or nothing in common. They follow very different courses.

Analysis of my failure in terms of effectiveness presumes that I, without changing my system of values, could possibly have chosen a more effective method to obtain what I was seeking. Analysis of my failure in terms of meaning is more subtle, but equally universal. It involves asking myself whether there is not some value in the very fact of failure when one holds my particular scale of values: or, to put it another way, it means asking whether failure itself was not a price worth paying in order to achieve a higher end, and in the end this would come down to saying that it was not such a failure after all. The martyr for a cause, for example, certainly did not want to die. From this point of view the death that must be suffered by the martyr is a kind of failure which poses a problem to the person involved. Perhaps that person could have achieved his or her ideal without dying. In that case his or her activity is devoid of effectiveness, and dying is an awkward and stupid thing which hardly deserves the name of martyrdom. If, on the other hand, the person involved could not save his or her life without renouncing their basic ideal or sacrificing it to some extent, then dying itself ceases to be a failure and becomes a duty: i.e., something that must be done, a value. And it is a value which, together with everything that has been done previously, converges towards the value which has been chosen as the basic one.

Another example may be even more useful for us here because it shows even more clearly the mechanisms we use, often in an unwittingly illogical way, to combine the dimension of efficacy and that of meaning. Let us consider the political arena. In the face of an election defeat, it is likely that the defeated candidate will elaborate two lines of thinking more or less simultaneously. On the one hand the candidate will ask himself or herself whether good use was made of all the available means, compatible with his or her aims, to win the support of the masses. On the other hand he or she will probably emphasize a "valuational" explanation of the defeat: he or she did not win because undoubtedly the masses are at the mercy of the first demagogue who appears on the scene; thus the election defeat proves the purity of his or her intentions and methods. In other words, viewing the matter in the light of one's absolute value, the very meaning of one's political activity, one prefers to lose this way than to win another way.

What is this? Is it rationalization, justification or sublimation of a failure, or a valuation that goes deeper than mere opportunism or success at any price? Here the authenticity of each human being comes into play. But the point I want to bring out is the necessary presence of two sets of criteria relating to two different and complementary dimensions. Both are in fact necessary. If someone considers failures solely from the viewpoint of efficacy, that person will end up paying any price (in value) to obtain whatever is desired. If someone considers failures solely from the viewpoint of their possible value, in the end that will turn every inept, ignorant, or lazy person into a hero or martyr; ineffectiveness will be canonized.

I should point out here that I chose the moment of failure as the example for our analysis here because it is normally accompanied by a certain period of criticism. We could say the same things about success. The difference lies in the fact that success does not ordinarily lead to such reflections (see REMARK C.6, p. 26).

However difficult it may be, both of these two radical dimensions of human activity must be taken into account as fundamentally distinct yet equally necessary. For only that approach can serve as a solid foundation for the maturity and freedom that a human being can achieve in life.

II. The Development of These Dimensions in Human Beings

In the analysis undertaken so far, we have as it were taken a cross-section of the flow of life in the existence of an adult. I think the same points will become much clearer if we now study the matter genetically. By that I mean that we will examine how the structures of meaning and efficacy under consideration here begin to take shape in a human being.

In the Young Child

Meaning-structure does exist in the life of a small child, of course, but on a very elementary level. It is elementary in two senses. First, the satisfactions which direct the activity of the small child are initially those inscribed instinctively on the memory of the species; to that extent they are part of what is most basic and elemental in the human being. Secondly, even when the small child learns to postpone simple, immediate satisfactions for other more complex ones that are promised in the long run, it does not do this by introducing conscious aims or goals into its activity; on a much more elemental level the child is taught, under pain of evident dissatisfactions, to move away from obedience to instinct. In reality the child is taught to adapt its conduct to a somewhat more evolved instinct: i.e., the security placed in the "methods" taught by the adult persons who are rearing and taking care of it.

Here it is difficult to talk about "faith" in the sense that I have been using it so far. The fact is that the values which structure the activity of parents (for example), and which are transmitted to their little children, are not even perceived, much less imitated and adopted, in any conscious, personal way.

The latter step takes place only much later. The child, using what we call its "reason," gradually learns to identify certain complicated valuational structures. It grasps something, if not all, of the implicit (and sometimes explicit) scale of values held by its parents or educators. And normally it has "faith" in what it perceives. This is the stage when such people as parents or teachers seem to the child to have satisfactory answers for all the problems of life. Their assumed omniscience deserves the tribute of "faith": i.e., of subordinating one's conduct to canons which are no longer decreed by simple, immediate satisfaction but rather by the comprehension of a certain system of means and ends (however limited it may be at the child's age).

In terms of what follows, it is worth noting here that children also learn to name the object of their "faith" in abstract form. And they do so in accordance with the name that the adults give to the value-structure that they claim to be the key to their own conduct and the reason behind the orders they impart to the child they are rearing. It is not surprising, then, that a small child might call itself a Christian, a Buddhist, an atheist, a liberal, or a Marxist. For that is the label which those in whom it has "faith" apply to themselves when they attempt to explain why they are acting in this or that manner. Later we will have occasion to examine the confusions that arise from this fact. Right now we shall simply state the fact itself.

In the Adolescent

The picture changes noticeably in adolescence. The very discovery of the ego or self is synonymous with a search for one's own identity in a structure of meaning or values. Because one is unique and the center of one's own existence, it is logical to think about the meaning that ought to be given to one's existence. Hence adolescence is the stage of establishing the ideal.

At the same time it is a stage of criticism in more than one sense. The childish faith placed in parents and educators falls apart in large measure. One discovers that they are far from being omniscient; that they have problems as everyone else does, and no solutions for many of these problems; and that as referential witnesses of meanings and values, they are puny figures when compared with the great personages of past or present history.

Note that I said that faith in one's early referential witnesses falls apart "in large measure." For the fact, easily verifiable, is that adolescents, however critical of parents and educators they may be, cannot easily free themselves from the whole sum-total of (inchoative) value-experiences realized under the guidance of those elders. Many rebellions which seem to be total, or which are said to be total, are still strongly bound up, even if only in a negative sense, with the values whose logic was experienced in countless unconscious ways during infancy and early childhood.

In any case there still remains for the adolescent the problem of finding a new "faith," one that will be its own. And here again the adolescent cannot solicit a system of values from anyone except another human being. Even when he or she combines values deriving from two or more persons, the adolescent must "believe" in the satisfaction that these values are supposed to produce; and the adolescent "believes" because he or she sees that satisfaction reflected in the referential witnesses, even without having experienced it personally.

At this stage of life, when "faith" is fluid and remains subject to the discovery of new persons and personages who are "creditable" or worthy of faith, something else normally happens at the same time. The adolescent is also introduced into a different world: the world of objective techniques, of knowing how to do things. Prior to this time these techniques were inculcated in an impersonal manner. In other words, they came across in the interplay of artificial satisfactions or dissatisfactions (i.e., rewards and punishments), or else they were bound up with the "faith" invested in the values and "methods" of others—parents, for example.

So the adolescent discovers that values and methods belong to two very different worlds. In due time the disappearance of rewards and punishments helps him or her to make this fundamental distinction; indeed his or her task as a human being will be precisely to make those two different realms complementary. Like all human beings, adolescents submit to the thankless realm of methods and objective techniques. They must learn how to practice a trade or profession, to put away savings, and so forth. And there is no way of knowing what the outcome will be. But at this point they no longer operate *directly* on "faith." To be sure, through "faith" they continue to prefer one valuational structure to countless others. But insofar as methods are concerned, they judge them in terms of their efficacy and their internal consistency with the aims sought. At the very least, the adolescent makes a start in that direction and thus ceases to be a little child.

But the adolescent is also an apprentice in learning about methods, so he or she does not yet know the objective dimension of their efficacy. As a result, the adolescent may act just like the little child, applying the labels used by the referential witnesses of his or her faith, the words they utter when they try to name their value-structure or the methods that lead them to it.

For example, an adolescent might idealize the historical figure of Christ on the one hand, or that of Che Guevara on the other. In one instance the adolescent would say that he or she was a Christian, more than likely, and in the other that he or she was a Marxist. Yet these labels would probably not be grasped solidly in any objective sense. In one case it would be the human image of Jesus and his life that would count, that would prompt the teenager to say that he or she was a Christian. Objective fidelity to the message and the demands of Jesus would be a secondary matter at best. Jesus' claim to be the Messiah or the Son of God would not be perceived as very relevant, even though it is precisely that claim and acceptance of it that permits people to call themselves Christians—objectively speaking. The same holds true in the case of Che Guevara. The solidity of Che Guevara's analysis of the revolutionary situation in Bolivia would probably not be the big thing in the teenager's adulation of him. Yet it would be that sort of analysis, rather than individual heroism or self-sacrifice, that would objectively allow someone to say that he or she was a Marxist.

But undoubtedly it is something else that clearly marks off this adolescent stage from a corresponding state in the mature life of the human being. And that something else is the fluidity of the adolescent's "faith." The fact is that adolescents have not burned their bridges behind them. Their free will is wider, precisely because they have made less use of it so far. All doors are open to them, or so they think, insofar as values are concerned. Adults, on the other hand, are much more conditioned by the options they have already made, the roads they have already taken. This "fluidity" of adolescent faith has its good points and bad points. On the one hand it is still open to new and greater ideals, to new referential witnesses to happiness. On the other hand, since the world still lies open before it, it is able, and in fact tempted, to change its "faith" when it confronts the first setback, the first serious failure of efficacy in its choice of some method to achieve its ideal.

In the Adult

How does this change when we come to the mature adult? Can adults divest themselves of "faith," in the sense I have been using the term, to move on to some rational, scientific, objective, valuational structure? We have already seen that this is impossible by very definition. And it should be remembered that we arrived at that conclusion from an analysis of adult experience. How, in fact, are we to know what we can ask of life before we have lived out all possible values *to the end*? And how could we possibly go back from there to choose objectively on the basis of our own personal experience? So adulthood does not differ from childhood or adolescence in the sense that it represents a transition from subjective "faith" to some sort of objectivity conferred by science, scholarly knowledge, or reason. It is not at all true that adults move in some valuational direction knowing ahead of time from experience or some verifiable calculus what to expect at the end of the road.

In reality, the difference lies in two facts that any analysis of real-life experience will make plain.

The *first* fact is this: As "faith" becomes less fluid and more established, as it tends to "structure" a person's whole existence more than was the case when that person had all roads open to him or her, the person devotes less and less attention to that faith and more to the problems bound up with methods. The person has burned his or her bridges, as it were, by choosing some value as supreme. The attainment of this value within a world of nature and a culture that are complicated and often hostile is itself a complex task. So the person is compelled to greater objectivity, to pay greater heed to reality and the prices that must be paid in it.

I noted above that it becomes harder and harder for adults to change their "faith." That will seem quite logical when we realize that they have already expended enormous amounts of energy to achieve certain values. By choosing one road, they have found many other roads closed off to them. And even when they can "make a break" with their past life, they know that they have much less energy left to attain something satisfactory on some new course.

This helps to explain the tendency that I mentioned in Section I of this chapter, and that we do not find in adolescence, unconscious defense against criticism. As we saw, failures and the resistance of reality to our desires are so many alarm sirens. They raise questions, be it about the "faith" we have already chosen or about the "methods" employed. And since it is impossible or extremely difficult to change one's faith at some point in adult life, there is a growing temptation to rationalize or idealize our failures. In other words, we are tempted to transform them from something negative into something positive insofar as they relate to the meaning-structure we have chosen.

That is another way of saying that the mature human being rarely calls his or her faith into question. Instead we manipulate our own acquaintance with reality so that the latter loses its critical-minded character. We have a thousand techniques to evade this confrontation, this potential for criticism. And this is precisely the thing, the fact, that I would like to stress here because it is most important for what follows. "Faith," conceived as a meaning-structure and a valuational structure, does not simply inform us about what we ought to do; in the life of the adult at least, it is also a crucial factor in deciding how that adult perceives reality. Faith, in other words, is not simply the way in which we endow our perception with some value; it is also a cognitive principle which enables us to see certain things rather than other equally obvious things.

The *second* fact is equally well known, and it has to do with the adult's growth in the systematized knowledge of methods and techniques which we call "experience." Here I am using the word in the ordinary sense, not in some specialized philosophical sense. Now let us leave aside the point that this solidified and self-justificatory "faith" is used as an argument against the idealism of younger people. The fact still remains that the adult possesses greater, and frequently a more complex and profound, awareness of the objective conditioning elements to which the search for values is subjected.

At the same time adult people frequently re-examine their "faith" to certify—and often force—its compatibility with the price they have had to pay in the face of resistance from nature or society to their values.

In any case we find a greater dose of objectivity in the "faith" of the adult. But the "faith" itself, of course, persists. For example, those who believe in Jesus Christ may now ask who he was, what he really said historically, and what criteria they can or should use to determine that. The important point here is that this new emphasis on "orthodoxy," on the objective Jesus, whether it is used to accept or reject faith in him, leaves intact the phenomenon of "faith" as an anthropological dimension.

For example, some people may decide that the supreme value lies in the social combination of justice and freedom. Exasperated by the resistance offered by the facts of history, these people may examine more closely the "orthodoxy" of economic liberalism, its objective limitations and possibilities. But it is not this "orthodoxy" that will determine their "faith." Even when their study reveals the possible contradiction between reality and the search for a certain value through certain methods, they will still be faced with the question as to whether it is not worth failing in the quest for certain ideals rather than succeeding without them. "Faith" continues to be "faith," however much we may pretend to present it in terms of some "orthodox," rational, or scientific position.

Let me offer an example from a different front. It is surely correct to say that an adult criminal will be more concerned than a juvenile delinquent about the probability of going to prison for some crime. We can even imagine some statistical study "proving" to him, in as scientific a way as possible, that he has one chance in a thousand of staying out of prison for the rest of his life if he continues on his present course. It is very likely that he himself would point to this scientific proof to explain his change of "faith," should he decide to go straight in society's terms. But it is no less certain that scientific analysis has offered him only a conditional proposition: "If you want this, then you must do or accept that." The same calculus might just as well lead him to accept prison for the very same reasons.

In the last analysis neither ignorance nor scientific knowledge will decide what values I decide to entrust my life to, what values I will choose to make the keystone of my life (see REMARK C.7, p. 27). And values, remember, are conveyed through persons.

III. Three Specifications

Before I conclude this chapter and pick up my analysis in the next chapter, I want to add three specifications. They deal mainly with the terminology that I have been using so far, and that I will continue to use in future chapters.

My Choice of Terms: Faith and Ideology

First of all, I have used the word "faith" to describe the first anthropological dimension. And I have put the word in quotes so that the reader might understand that it is not to be given the religious import that is often attached to it. In the following pages of this book I will try to justify the use of the term "faith" more precisely and convincingly, granting that it may give rise to superficial misunderstanding because of its "religious" use. At this point it should simply be clear to the reader that in talking about "faith" I am simply talking about an *anthropological* dimension, a dimension as universal as the human species itself whether religion be involved or not. So from here on, I shall omit the quotation marks around the term.

But now we see that there is a *lacuna*, a gap, in my terminology. What name am I to give to the second dimension about which I have been speaking (see REMARK C.8, p. 27)? I have talked about "efficacy" or "effectiveness," but these clarifying words refer more to the result than to the realm in question or the mechanisms that constitute it. So for this realm, which is also anthropological, I propose to use the term *ideology*. And I do this knowing full well that definitions do not solve problems and are, in the last analysis, arbitrary. If we choose, we can introduce a new use for some word. That use can be explained and justified without even offering any explicit definition. The content that we systematically give to the word will take the place of a definition.

But if some innovation in terminology is not to cause confusion, it should have some meaningful tie-in with current, ordinary language even while it fills some gap in the latter. In later chapters I will try to show that such in fact is the case with my use of the word "ideology."

Right now I will simply pick up the thread of this chapter. I shall use the term "ideology" for all systems of means, be they natural or artificial, that are used to attain some end or goal. I could also say, and the second specification below will bring this point out, that ideology is the systematic aggregate of all that we wish for in a *hypothetical* rather than an absolute way. In other words, it is every system of means.[5]

Why do I choose to use the term "ideology" for the realm of means that I have been talking about? Without going into any detailed discussion, which will be the subject of subsequent chapters, I would simply say that my reason is an etymological one. Contrary to the sometimes subjective connotations put on the word "idea," the original Greek word (*idea*) refers to the visible form or look of things: i.e., my perception of the objective realm. Ideology, then, would be the systematization of my perception of the real. Every technique, every methodology, every science, everything that proposes to be effective and to master facts, is part of an objective *experience* of a system by which we believe we have grasped the real, however precarious our knowledge may be.

Thus ideology connotes—and here ordinary language agrees—a vision of things that claims to be objective: i.e., nonvaluational. Even Marx's pejorative use of the term lies in the fact that ideologies claim such objectivity when in fact they do not possess it. Why? Because they are always in the service of certain interests that distort our perception of the real. But he uses the term precisely because our common understanding of it is that it stands outside the realm of values.

Let me put it another way, sticking with ordinary language usage. While we are subjectively determined by the values that we *choose*, we are objectively affected by the natural or artificial conditionings which we *see* or perceive (Greek *idein*), and which we are obliged to work with. This is the main reason why I have chosen the term "ideology" to describe the second anthropological dimension under discussion. In later chapters I will again consider why it is preferable to certain possible alternatives.

The Problem of Values

The *second* specification I want to make here also has to do with terminology, and specifically with the word "value" that I have been using.

We must realize what we are doing here. While we may have no alternative but to use the term, we must realize that we are at the borderline-limits of conceptual language and its possibilities. We all know what a value is, but we cannot define the word without succumbing to tautologies. It is useless to say that value is what makes things or persons desirable. It is equally useless to say that value is the reason or motive for our preferences and options. And all that is useless because the definitions tell us no more than the word itself did in the first place. If we did not already know what a value is, we would not know what a preference or a motive is.

The difficulty intensifies, or at least becomes more obvious, when we try to *name* values. Here an illuminating paradox might be introduced: It is virtually impossible for any human being to express, in conceptual terms, the value to which he or she has subordinated every other aspect of his or her life—presuming the options taken have been logical. We sometimes try to do it by naming some virtue: e.g., justice or loyalty. But people would regard us as strange or incomprehensible if we were to specify such a view by saying that we wanted to be virtuous. The fact is that a "virtue" is not a value, even though it presupposes the latter. Neither is a vice, though it too always presupposes some value; otherwise no one would ever be given to vice. And if we leave aside the virtue-vice dichotomy, what exactly do we mean when we say that some person has devoted his or her life to seeking money or power or whatever in the way of things or circumstances?

We could go on and on indefinitely showing the failure of all attempts, like that of Max Scheler for example, to systematize the realm of "values" conceptually. But here I would prefer to concentrate on two conclusions that are inescapable and that relate to our purpose.

First of all, we know from actual experience, if not from conceptualizing, what "value" means. One of the simplest and most meaningful expressions in ordinary language, and one which has great relevance for our activity, is: "It's *worth* the trouble." That justifies the use of the term "worth" or "value" here and in what follows.

Secondly, the term "value" is a highly abstract term. Indeed it "abstracts" from real life in three different ways.

The first abstraction lies in the fact that we talk about "value" without noticing that our motivations do not relate to things but to *persons* in the concrete. In the last analysis money, power, friendship, justice, and so forth, are so many abstract ways of saying how we affect persons. It is persons that really interest us. The proof lies in the fact that human beings seeking "justice" are not left twiddling their thumbs when they manage to attain it. (Indeed the very "attainment" of it is an abstraction vis-à-vis concrete persons.) They will continue to be interested in the persons for whom they have attained justice. In the concrete, justice was a way or means of relating positively or negatively to certain persons, however privileged and special a way it might be.

The second abstraction is this: Even when we primarily focus on persons rather than on things, the *plurality* of values does not correspond to any concrete reality. We do not choose between pre-established "values," such as the true, the good, the beautiful, or the useful. While choosing and the plurality of "chooseable" objects may go hand in hand, the plurality itself is framed within the context of a larger fundamental unity, which of course is very complex. All of us simultaneously seek for our own fulfillment and that of the beings we love, choosing among the diverse forms or possibilities of this single, unique "value." What we call "values" are nothing else but different abstract forms, more or less stabilized, within the framework of developing or transforming one single, unique energy and achieving fulfillment.[6]

The third abstraction lies in the fact that we leave aside the role of *imagination* in these various forms by which our energy is stabilized. We do not concretely choose between values, but between imagined representations of possible satisfactions. We do not opt for the "virtue" or the "value" of peace; we opt for our imagined picture of the satisfaction we would get from knowing that those we loved dearly were living in a situation of peace or greater peace. And then we put an abstract name on this prospective piece of imagining. It is the role of imagination which logically explains why a human being often operates in a very complicated way with what we might call a scale of values. Human beings will not implement the same "values" in dealing with different types of people, for example. Yet they will be consistent with the concrete image and ideal that their imagination fashioned, while still regarding different people in different ways.

The above remarks should make clear why it is both necessary and difficult to talk about values in a precise way.

Now I should like to talk about "absolute value," which will only increase the difficulty and the necessity of being precise. For on the level of "values" as lived out by concrete human beings, the simple fact is that we cannot avoid using the adjective "absolute."

I have no intention of entering the confused and trackless wastes surrounding the philosophical use of the term. In using the term "absolute" here, I am sticking to its etymology. Thus "absolute" means "not tied to anything else," "unconditioned."

The question whether we can, strictly speaking, talk about an "absolute being" is a highly complicated one. Certainly we can say that we do not experience unconditioned things, beings, facts, or events on the plane of everyday reality. But even in the most humble human life, on the other hand, we do encounter an absolute in the realm of value. We are always "preferring" something or other; and that means that we are choosing, that we are exercising our freedom. So there has to be something that we "prefer" for itself, not as a means or condition for some other person or thing. Here we have the "absolute" as a value. In other words, every value-structure, however elementary it may be, must be crowned by something that is not a means towards something else, that turns everything else into a means towards it. So we can say that every meaning-structure of human life is composed of things that a human being wills *hypothetically* (i.e., insofar as they help him or her to get something else), and of something that he or she wills *absolutely* (i.e., for its own sake).

The reader can see that here "absolute" has nothing to do with something infinite, perfect, or metaphysical. The way in which the simplest or most superficial human being conceives happiness is that person's "absolute." That is the sense in which I shall use the term "absolute" here.

An example may help to clarify my use of the term "absolute," and also to clarify the points I was trying to bring out in the previous specification. Though it is no longer in fashion, it was once fairly common for people to commit suicide when they fell into bankruptcy. We might often hear people make the superficial judgment that "honor" was the supreme value on whose altar debtors immolated themselves when they could not pay their creditors. So should we say that "honor" was the absolute value for those who committed suicide? Definitely not, because all the normal, day-to-day exertions of those people, all their efforts and attention, were aimed at acquiring money, not honor. Closer analysis will reveal to us that the business people in question did not commit suicide on the altar of some abstraction, but rather in view of certain persons. The act of suicide may have been prompted by egotism: the person in question might have considered it impossible to endure the shame involved, or his pride might have made it impossible for him to endure the blow to his self-image. And if suicide seemed more important than mere living in terms of that self-image, then the person would accept the former. On the other hand the act of suicide might be prompted by altruistic motives: the person involved might want to maintain his family's good name, and it might have seemed impossible to preserve that name and still go on living.

In other words, it is almost impossible for us to define in conceptual terms the absolute value underlying such an act in the life of a person who performs it in a way consistent with his or her scale of values. We have to point to motives that are often unconscious, to the understanding of certain social roles, or to various groups of persons who have an impact on the case, each in their own way. Only a different language, one which is not conceptual but which often is clearer, will enable us to "understand" or "comprehend" the absolute values of other people in terms of their actions. And the point is that the imagination plays a decisive role both in the formation and the understanding of this language.

Labels and Meaning-Structures

We come, finally, to the *third* specification. The preceding discussion has pointed up two universal anthropological dimensions: faith and ideology. All human beings without exception—however sublime or ignoble their values may be, and however ignorant or knowledgeable they may prove to be in handling their actions—present us with this complex constellation which makes every human life both mysterious and penetrable at the same time.

We have also seen that both "faith" and "ideologies" are communicated by some human beings to others. Despite the enormous diversity of the panorama so afforded us, there are certain vital structures which seem to be repeated to some extent in each epoch. The fact that these structures are given names helps to ensure this, or is a result of this. "Christianity," "liberalism," "Marxism," "materialism," and "scientism" are examples of what I am talking about here.

Now if my previous remarks make any sense, then the fact is that those labels often introduce confusion. In sociology all those "isms" are frequently labelled "ideologies." Sometimes a distinction may be made between "religions" and "ideologies," but that only increases the confusion. For to use that distinction is to turn something that is accidental, anthropologically speaking, into something decisive: i.e., whether people relate their values to a God or not.

If readers have taken note of what was said above, they will realize that God never constitutes the concrete origin of the values which dominate a human life, and also that people frequently give the name "God" precisely to the representation or personification of the values that they have chosen for themselves.

Thus, for example, people assume that Christianity, being a "religion," is a faith whereas Marxism, being a-religious, is an "ideology." But to do this is to fall into a serious confusion. After all, can one have a Christian "faith" without ideologies: i.e., without methods conditioned by the changing reality of history that are designed to enable him or her to implement certain values which are judged to be essential to the Christian? And, looking at the other end of the spectrum, we can raise a similar question in the case of the Marxist or the liberal. Can a Marxist or a liberal explain his or her existence solely in terms of some science, without admitting that every science is in the service of certain values that have been decided upon from outside science itself? Althusser, for example, appeals to Theory with a capital T. (The word "theory," by the way, comes from the Greek verb *theorein*, which means "to see.") But isn't every theory in the service of certain values determined from outside theory itself? So what exactly is the "faith" of a Marxist or a liberal and where does it come from? Is materialism a "faith" or a theory of the real with scientific pretensions or implications?

The specific point I want to make here is to warn the reader against the misunderstandings that derive from labels and "isms." First of all, most of the meaning-structures of human lives have no labels and cannot be catalogued. Secondly, even those that can be catalogued somehow often leave aside the problem that concerns us here: i.e., the distinction to be made between "faith" and "ideology" and the complementarity between the two; or, if you prefer, the determination of value on the one hand, and the determination of efficacy on the other.

Remarks

REMARK A (see p. 4). The word "happiness" could mislead readers, if they think that I am applying it to something specific or concrete. That is not the case. I am starting off from *the basic, undeniable fact* that every human being is moved by a quest for *satisfaction*. The reader might ask: Satisfaction of what? But that very question is not pertinent at this initial stage. Here I am simply referring to the fact that in our lives all of us are always comparing possible "satisfactions" and "pleasurable sensations or experiences" of every type. This work of comparison takes place long before we think about cataloguing these satisfactions as (e.g.) instinctual or deliberate, direct or sublimated, material or spiritual. From early childhood on, we are in the habit of mixing all kinds of satisfaction, delight, or pleasure in a common bowl. We want to compare them in their unique, general character as "satisfactions," so that we can then decide which one is more satisfying. So we compare things as unlike each other as martyrdom and sexual intercourse, the miser's hoarding of money and the suffering of the masochist, and eating oysters versus sacrificing oneself for a more just society. An interesting problem is explaining how we can "compare" things that are so different and perhaps even contradictory. But that we do make such comparisons is a basic fact. It is to the credit of great thinkers that they have discovered or pointed up this fact.

The later Freud, for example, said that all satisfaction derived from what he called the "libido." He was not at all trying, against all evidence, to reduce all pleasure to sexuality—unless this is a mere tautology because one starts out in principle by calling all pleasure sexual. Instead, at the price of great abstraction, Freud establishes one, single principle for comparing all pleasure or satisfaction. That principle goes in two directions. Recessively it turns back towards immediate satisfaction, towards death (*Thanatos*). Progressively, it moves forward towards mediated satisfactions, synthesizing ever vaster units (*Eros*).

Just as people have spoken disparagingly of Freud's pansexualism, so the popular image of the Epicurean is that of a sensual human being. In reality Epicureanism was one of the most original and profound efforts of ancient anthropology. It sought to compare all the varieties of possible satisfaction with the available energy of the human being in order to organize human life in the most fulfilling (or satisfying, or happy) way possible.

These two attempts (of Freud and Epicureanism), to which I am not here subscribing at all, were combatted in the name of other theories. These latter claimed to know *a priori* what happiness consisted in, either through the study of nature (Stoicism) or through the revelation of divine rewards. So they believed they were relieved of the necessity of comparing satisfactions and choosing between them. The use of the term "happiness" here, then, could lead readers into error if they do not take note of the observations made here.

REMARK B (see p. 4). Some readers may be a bit confused by my reference to Camus's *Caligula*, or the way it is used in my analysis. The character by that name in the play explicitly poses the question of *happiness* to himself, and it seems to him that human beings are not able to attain it. But in the course of his career, Caligula *actually* is trying to solve a prior problem, the problem of *freedom* (or liberty). In other words, he does not so much consider, if at all, what goal he is to choose, or how to choose it, or how he is to compare the satisfactions which different courses may provide him with. Instead he decides to go down a difficult road which is *prior* and, we could say, *neutral* with respect to any specific goal. He wants to be free, so that he will then be able to follow any path whatsoever without succumbing to inconsistencies.

However, Caligula encounters *two* surprises. The *first* surprise is that even the adventure of being free, like any other in quest of a specified goal, tends to close off avenues rather than opening them up. This is the first fact, which I shall here call *the structure of liberty*, or of free will. The *second* surprise has to do with limits upon the individual. Caligula chooses to be free, and considers this as the basic, *preliminary* choice. But whether that course is neutral or not, the fact remains that human beings do not have the time or energy to go down some *preparatory*, exploratory road first and then choose some definitive one. Only once do they travel to the very limits of their life, there to gain or lose a goal that was or was not worth the trouble. So when Caligula is ready at the end to choose a goal, his life comes to an end. This is the second fact that hits him as a surprise: *It is impossible for the individual to explore the possibilities of existence ahead of time in an empirical way.*

REMARK C.1 (see p. 5). Starting off from the basic fact noted in Remark A, we now come to the *first decisive fact* or reality in our analysis: the structure of human liberty, or human free will. To put it briefly, we could say that *freedom is gradually and steadily lost as we use it.* Insofar as we use our freedom and make choices, we are taking a certain road or moving towards a certain kind of satisfaction; thus we are losing the possibility of *ourselves* experiencing the other types of satisfaction which other roads might bring to us. Hence it becomes increasingly difficult for us to "compare" satisfactions which are gradually and definitively moving outside the pale of our own personal possibilities for experience.

The same thing holds true for Gide's characters. Sometimes they refuse to opt for one road in order to remain free and available for the different (immediate) satisfactions that life offers them on whatever track. But in reality they, too, are making choices by not choosing. At the very least they are closing themselves off from the road that leads to *mediate* satisfactions: i.e., those which call for long mediations, habits, periods of apprenticeship, and structures. So though they might think they do, in fact they too do not escape this dimension of loss involved in human freedom that we are examining here.

REMARK C.2 (see p. 6). This is *the second decisive fact* revealed by our analysis: *the impossibility*, faced by every human being, *of experientially exploring* the limits of human possibilities insofar as satisfactions are concerned. And this impossibility shows up at the very moment when he or she necessarily must decide—because of the structure of human liberty as described in Remark C.1. To put it another way, the human being must compare things—specifically, various possible satisfactions. But human beings must always do this comparing in a half-blind way, for they do not know from *their own* personal experience what satisfactions await them at the end of each road.

Not enough attention has been paid to the fact that the human individual who opts for a certain road in life is always operating with *transcendent data*: i.e., data relating to things which he or she cannot personally experience and which, in that sense, are beyond him or her. Here I am not referring to things or beings which transcend this world, which are situated "above and beyond" the latter: e.g., metaphysical entities such as God, destiny, and so forth. Even when we are talking about things that "a" human being can, or could, experience, the sum-total of them all *transcends* the experiential possibilities of any given individual.

Thus, by way of example, *every single one* of the experiences of a new doctor, a new engineer, or a new lawyer is nontranscendent, immanent (in the metaphysical sense), and hence within the reach of a human being. But when we view those experiences *as an aggregate*, that aggregate transcends the experiential possibilities of any normal human being. This is an important point for my analysis because it means that the human being must seek out those data—which are necessary for any option whatsoever, so that one can compare them and then choose one pathway over another—in a different way than he or she acquires ordinary experiential data.

When one tries to analyze experiential reality as I am trying to do here, moving step by step, one finds it interesting to "demythologize" statements that are currently in vogue. Consider, for example, the following view that is central to the Freudian conception of culture: i.e., "man's discovery that sexual (genital) love afforded him the strongest experience of satisfaction, and in fact provided him with the prototype of all happiness. . . ."[7]

Strictly speaking, Freud is talking about a comparison which is *experientially impossible*. One of the terms of the comparison can certainly be known experientially: i.e., genital sexual love. But what about the other? The other term of the comparison is nothing less than all the experiences of satisfaction that can be provided by human existence. Who, on the basis of his or her own experience, knows all these possibilities and is thus able to make an empirical comparison? Up to a certain point any human being can certainly compare the intensity or quality of one immediate satisfaction—sexual love in this case—with another obtained through long effort, provided that memory does not fail him or her. But even in this case we face two basic limitations. First of all, framed in the human realm and considered in all its own temporal density, the genital sexual act itself is not an immediate experience. It presupposes decisive mediations if the resultant satisfaction, even on the physical level, is to be intense and gratifying. It is not an act; it is a *process*, a trip. So I cannot even say that I possess from experience the first term of the comparison. What I possess is a particular experience of satisfaction, not something that can be measured in the general terms Freud employs: i.e., "the strongest experience of satisfaction." Indeed Freud himself notes that his comparison is valid "for a great number of people."[8] But what about the rest? If the comparison yields the experiential results indicated by Freud, how could there be people who have consciously sought out greater satisfactions by other pathways at certain stages in their lives, or possibly throughout their lives? How could they have sacrificed wholly or to some extent what Freud calls "the strongest experience of satisfaction"? If Freud's hypothesis for explaining this situation is that these people have been deceived by cultural factors, that very fact would suffice to prove that the experience mentioned by him is not, and cannot be called, experiential in the scientific sense of that word. Of course one could give another, more acceptable meaning to the "experience" of which Freud speaks. Here I am simply warning the reader against a specific and fairly widespread way of interpreting it.

In addition, the real impossibility of experientially making the comparison in question is echoed in Freud's own remarks. With his usual honesty he writes: "It seems certain that we do not feel comfortable in our present-day civilization, but it is *very difficult to form an opinion whether and in what degree men of an earlier age felt happier.* . . . We shall always tend . . . to place ourselves, with our own wants and sensibilities, in *their* conditions, and then to examine what occasions we should find in them for experiencing happiness or unhappiness. This method of looking at things, which seems objective . . . is, of course, the most subjective possible, since it puts one's own mental states in the place of any others, unknown though they may be. *Happiness, however, is something essentially subjective*" (my italics).[9]

REMARK C.3 (see p. 7). Here we establish the *third decisive fact* in our analysis: i.e., the *social structure* of experience, which is necessary for the use of freedom. This follows from the first two facts noted above, and it is readily observable. To compare satisfactions which we do not yet possess, and which we will never possess simultaneously, we must accept data given to us by *other persons*. Thus the data come to us socially. The most decisive data for our lives are acquired through the lives of others and must be *believed in*; we must have *faith* in some people and not in others.

Though there is a certain resemblance, we must not confuse this fact with another one: i.e., that even in the realm of objective information, we receive from society the vast majority of data with which we operate without having had direct personal experience of that data. Here I am talking about the acceptance of other people's valuations, of testimony to satisfactions inextricably bound up with those people.

So we could say that the data with which we choose our most basic orientations do not come from our own (experiential) memory but from the memory of the (human) species. We accede to that memory insofar as we explicitly or unconsciously put our trust in certain persons who convey those data to us through their subjective lives. So on the one hand we have *transcendent data*—because that data can never be given within *one* specific complex of experience. And that data correspond, on the other hand, to a *type of knowledge* that should be labelled *faith*, taking the latter term in a social, secular sense.

REMARK C.4 (see p. 7). In the light of the three basic facts brought out by our previous analysis, we now come to our first conclusion: *faith*, understood in the broadest, secular sense, is an *indispensable component*, a dimension, of every human life. It is an anthropological dimension. Contrary to what we might have assumed, every human being needs referential witnesses to articulate his or her realm of values; and we cannot help but give the designation, *faith*, to the criterion which prompts them to accept or reject those witnesses (and the latter's testimony about various possible satisfactions). The religious aura of the word does not interest us here. As I pointed out in the chapter, I am referring to a certain type of knowledge (and its criteria). In other words, I am referring to the fact that it is based, not on any direct or scientifically verifiable experience, but on witnesses provided by society.

To clarify this first conclusion, it might be well to bring together here various points scattered throughout the chapter which have a bearing on it:

a. What we call "faith" in the religious sense is a particular instance subsumed under this more universal anthropological dimension of faith. In religious faith, too, we have human referential witnesses (see pp. 10f.). But if that is the case, then from an anthropological standpoint it is not proper to set up a meaning-based division between "believers" and "nonbelievers" (the latter presumably being scientific and rational), since both groups base their values-structure on a type of knowledge that we must call *faith*.

b. The function of anthropological faith is to *structure* existence in a meaningful way. To express this, I have used various terms as synonyms: valuational structure, meaning-structure, values-structure, meaning of life, and so forth. It is a *structure* in the two senses of that word: (1) because it brings order into the complex realm of values—with its means, its primary and secondary ends, etc. (hence the synonymous term, "scale of values"); and (2) because it serves as a mechanism which enables people to classify happenings and events, in a largely unconscious but nevertheless effective way, in accordance with the values they have accepted and hierarchized. It saves energy for us since we do not start off every line of deliberation from scratch, and often do not deliberate at all (see pp. 7–8). It is very difficult to express this "structure" in words and concepts, but it is easy enough for our fellow human beings to perceive it. Thanks to it, they can identify us and they know how to relate differently to each human individual (see pp. 6 and 18–19).

c. Anthropological faith is characterized by the fact that it hierarchizes what we call "values," arriving ultimately at one to which it subordinates all the rest. We call that one value "absolute," not because it is actually realized or because it is an absolute being, but because that value as such, in the life of the person who chose it, is not subordinated to, or conditioned by, any other value. All other values are subordinated to it (see pp. 17f.).

d. We human beings have all the trouble in the world trying to express in a precise conceptual way what we *believe in*. (I say "believe in" because the data-items transcend our direct experience yet give direction to our lives.) It is very difficult to formulate, except perhaps in symbolic terms, something that functions as a structure in unconscious, almost mechanical terms. That may well be one of the reasons why human beings reflect so little on it (see p. 10). Even the word "value" used here is a convenient abstraction for something that is much more concrete, complex, and personalized (see pp. 17f.).

REMARK C.5 (see p. 8). Here we discover a *fourth basic fact*: the *objective structure of reality*. After we have compared values and shown a preference for certain ones, and after we have structured our lives accordingly *in principle* (and *subjectively*, since individuals have different preferences), we must then turn our preferences and choices into reality. To be effective in doing that, we must *objectively* (truly) know reality so that we will be able to *make use of it*. Whatever our theory of knowledge may be—realism, idealism, materialism, etc.—the first and foremost cognitive problem for human beings is governed by a utilitarian criterion. We want and need to know things in such a way that we will be able to exert influence on the objects of our knowledge.

Unlike our values (which are essentially *ours* because they derive from a decision each one of us makes), reality and the procedures for using and managing it are *universal* in principle. We exchange data about these matters with other people, even though we may then put this information in the service of very different aims and values. At first glance efficacy (or effectiveness) might seem to be a mere prolongation of our freedom, of the meaning-structure we have chosen; it might seem to be our idea of what ought to be turning into what is. But in fact efficacy includes a *new* element: i.e., the structure of reality itself, which holds true for all and which is neutral vis-à-vis the values we want it to serve.

We could go further here and say that this neutrality is in fact resistance. For when we use a mechanism of reality to serve some value, we are plucking it away from its own proper dynamism (which knows nothing of this value or any other). Hence all the great problems of our civilization can be summed up as one problem: i.e., What is the best and most economical way to combine the meaning of existence with the know-how to manipulate reality?

REMARK C.6 (see p. 10). Some human experiences are more likely than others to pose the whole problem of the dualism and the complementarity of meaning and efficacy. In this section of the chapter, I analyze the experience of *failure*. For tightly hierarchized societies such as present-day socialist ones, Adam Schaff offers a parallel analysis of the experience connected with one's *responsibility* to obey certain orders or not.

All these experiences confront us with a *fifth basic and decisive fact*: Meaning and efficacy are two *different but complementary human dimensions*. In its own field of operation, each of these anthropological dimensions tends to overlook the other, or to regard the other as a mere derivative of itself. Each, in other words, tends to set itself up as the one and only criterion. When that is done, and it is, we end up with inhuman results. On the one hand we may give in to what is natural and impersonal in us—instincts, passions, habits, routines, convenience—and thus turn ourselves into nothing more than another thing. On the other hand we may rationalize, idealize, or give reasons to justify our inability to realize our values so that we may feel at ease with our conscience; in the last analysis, the impersonality of the latter result looks very similar to that of the first approach.

REMARK C.7 (see p. 15). In Section II of this chapter I am doing nothing more than examining the same five basic facts in *the growth and development of a human being from childhood to adulthood.* I am considering from a different standpoint the structure of freedom, the limits of all individual experience of satisfactions, the social structure of the valuational experience, the objectivity that conditions the realization of our chosen values, and the difference and complementarity existing between our values-structure and efficacy.

REMARK C.8 (see p. 15). On the basis of the five basic facts considered previously, we now come to a *second conclusion*: i.e., that *besides faith* there is *a second anthropological dimension*, which I call ideology. This conclusion and my reasons for using the term "ideology" will be considered in more detail in subsequent chapters. The point I want to bring out right now is that a second anthropological dimension does exist and that it is both different from, and complementary to, the dimension of faith.

Right now let me bring together several points that are scattered around in Chapter I (and Chapter IV). They will help me to clarify and spell out my second conclusion:

a. I am going to use the word *ideology* for all human knowledge about *efficacy* (or *effectiveness*). The human knowledge in question deals with what will happen in the face of certain conditions or circumstances, or with the conditions one must satisfy if one wants certain results. (Efficacy and predictability are identified in the concrete.) This type of knowledge always arises in subordination to values, or to satisfactions (see pp. 15–16).

b. So understood, an *ideology* never provides us with a meaning-structure (or, a scale of values, a life-meaning). We do find cases where the word "ideology" is applied to a system which includes both a meaning-structure and an efficacy-system designed to realize the values embodied in the former. Thus liberalism and Marxism are called "ideologies," for example. In such cases I would apply my different terminology to point out that there are really two elements in those "ideologies," two different but complementary elements. Some features derive from what I would call anthropological *faith*, while others relate to a systematization of objective knowledge about efficacy that I would call *ideology*. In short, the systems which many people call "ideologies" are really shaped by two different but complementary ways of knowing, whether they realize it or not (see pp. 19–20).

c. Understood in the sense proposed here, an *ideology* must always strive to become as scientific and as rational as possible. It must do all it can to foresee conditions and circumstances, in line with the state of knowledge in a given age. Note the implications of this point. I have applied the term "ideology" to systems of efficacy valid in any age. Thus in past ages, and even in our own, magic rites would fall under this rubric. Nevertheless, there has been ongoing progress in predictability (a synonym for efficacy), and hence in being able to provide better guarantees. This point will be considered in greater detail in Chaper IV.

d. In principle *ideology*, as I define it here, does not determine the meaning-structure or the values-structure of a human life; it is the other way around (see pp. 14–15). In other words, a value is never chosen as the dominant one simply because it is *realizable*. On the contrary, human beings will seek out methods that are effective in terms of the values they appreciate most (see Chapter IV, Section I). Experience shows us that no one can reasonably claim to have replaced *faith* with *ideology* in seeking to determine the basic values of his or her life. For such values will always depend on referential witnesses to satisfactions, on people in whom one believes.

Further on we will consider how the difficulty or impossibility of realizing certain ideals can lead us unwittingly to change them (or to do so indirectly by inconsistency or bad faith). But even in such a case we will merely have changed our referential witnesses, our faith.

NOTES

1. André Gide, *Les nourritures terrestres*, p. 73; cited by Archambault in the article entitled "Amoralisme," *Dictionnaire de Sociologie*, col. 649. A little later in the same work of Gide, Ménalque exclaims: "The necessity of choosing was always intolerable to me" (*Les nourritures terrestres*, p. 77).

2. André Gide, *Los monedros falsos*, Spanish trans. (Buenos Aires: Poseidon, 1949), pp. 348–349; Eng. trans., *The Counterfeiters: With Journal of the Counterfeiters* (New York: Knopf, 1951; Random, Vintage, 1973).

3. It is worth pointing out that in general this social dimension of human experiences of freedom has not been elaborated by the major proponents of existential or phenomenological analysis. Thus it is with some reason that we now hear the accusation that such analysis is the individualistic expression of a bourgeois society in the process of falling apart. But I would like to make two points to forestall possible misunderstandings here.

First of all, the flaw does not come from the *method* itself. It is not as if any existential or phenomenological analysis which starts with the individual is doomed to end up with an individualistic view of existence. Secondly, the rejection of the social dimension in Sartre's existential analysis derives from an *a priori* notion of freedom that he imposes on the facts he analyzes. His notion is that freedom is all the more worthwhile and authentic, the less conditioned it is (see Adam Schaff, *La filosofía del hombre*, Spanish trans. [Buenos Aires: Lautaro, 1964], pp. 30f.). Since the social dimension—as well as the natural essence of the human being and the universe—is a conditioning factor, Sartre—at least the early Sartre—tries to break free of it. He seems to imagine that a human being would be all the more human insofar as it could derive its most original options from itself alone as if it were the first human individual. Here we may also detect traces of an ongoing distortion that is to be found in any philosophy which has not given up its fascination for the individual *cogito* of Descartes and his successors. To any such philosophy the individual *cogito* still seems to be the most pristine and secure point of departure.

4. This obligation to go through nonpleasurable mediations in order to obtain what I call "mediate" satisfactions means that every culture must be "repressive." In other words, every culture must set restraints on satisfactions of the immediate type. But of course this does not relieve us of the task of analyzing whether the cultures with which we are familiar do not impose unnecessary repression (see Herbert Marcuse, *Eros and Civilization* [New York: Random, Vintage, 1962], pp. 32, 34, and *passim* on "surplus-repression").

Freud, who extolls the gratifying capacity of immediate satisfaction, acknowledges that he sees no alternative to the repression enforced by cultural training. Making no such distinction as Marcuse does between necessary and surplus-repression, Freud refers to such repression as the "reality principle" (see Freud's works, *Beyond the Pleasure Principle*, new ed., trans. James Strachey [New York: Liveright, 1970] and *Civilization and Its Discontents*, ed. and trans. James Strachey [New York: Norton, 1962]).

5. Of course there are certain problems involved in applying the term "ideology" to this type of knowledge, and I shall consider those problems later. Here I simply want to point out that my choice of terms is not a mere whim, a lexicon exclusive to this work. In his work cited earlier (*La filosofía del hombre*), Adam Schaff reports an incident which we will examine more fully later. Attending a student discussion supposedly about "ideological themes," he tells us that the students indulged in the "tasteless joke" of annoying him with questions concerning ethics, and about the *meaning of life* in particular. Thus Schaff sets up a radical difference between "ideological" questions and questions dealing with the "meaning of life." The first set of questions presumably can be discussed and solved independently of the latter. Schaff does not deny the validity of questions dealing with the meaning of life, but he was upset to see the students trying to inject them into an "ideological" discussion. Here I use the term "faith" for all issues dealing with the meaning of life or ethics. As Schaff points out, the whole question of responsibility comes up on this level.

6. Since Freud's day we have come a long way towards being certain that there exists only one basic value or energy, one that is in continuity with instinctual life and *bipolar* as the latter is. In other words, love—which Freud prefers to call *libido* in consideration of its source—can move in two opposite directions. One direction is positive, and Freud calls it *Eros*. The other is negative, and Freud calls it *Thanatos*. If all the energy we possess comes from a common biological source, as it is logical to assume, then all its embodiments, however sublime they may be, will belong to this common trunk. Love as self-giving (*Agape*) is not an exception to this fact, as Marcuse rightly observes, despite the teachings of a theology that did not think in evolutionary terms: "The notion that Eros and Agape may after all be one and the same—not that Eros is Agape but that Agape is Eros—may sound strange after almost two thousand years of theology" (*Eros and Civilization* [Boston: Beacon, 1955], p. 192). Using a basic epistemological principle which he applies to all evolution, Teilhard de Chardin makes clear that such a view does not at all represent a *reduction* of the spiritual to the material, or of the conscious to the unconscious: "In the world,

nothing could ever burst forth as final across the different thresholds successively traversed by evolution (however critical they may be) which has not already existed in an obscure and primordial way'' (*The Phenomenon of Man*, Eng. trans. [New York: Harper Torchbook, 1961], p. 71).

7. Freud, *Civilization and Its Discontents*, p. 48.

8. Ibid.

9. Ibid., p. 36.

CHAPTER II

Faith—Trust—Religion

In this second chapter we might well be tempted to move right along to one of the most crucial problems facing human beings today. That problem has to do with maintaining or ensuring consistency between the faith that they profess and the ideologies they fashion or adopt to flesh out their faith. But a prior problem, hinted at in the first chapter, rises to the surface when we try to identify more concretely the terms which must be reconciled if people are to lead a consistent, harmonious life.

The points discussed and the examples adduced in the previous chapter should at least have made clear the two anthropological functions associated with my key terms, faith and ideology—or, meaning and efficacy respectively. Yet as soon as one attempts to offer a concrete example of a faith or of an ideology, one runs into ambiguities. Consider what we call Christianity, for example. Rarely if ever does that term in the concrete refer solely to a faith. It is accompanied by, and fleshed out in, ideologies that are not specifically Christian. Indeed in some cases it may simply be replaced by such ideologies, as we shall see later. On the other hand we also find that in most cases ideologies which are openly recognized as such—e.g., liberalism, Marxism, Nazism—do not dovetail with the term ideology as I have analyzed it. Implicitly, if not explicitly, they are structured by elements that I have called anthropological faith, even though those elements may not be recognized as such.

Now one of the most convenient ways to evade this confusion would be to give up my terminology and accept the usual terminology which breeds these commonplaces and confusions. I grant you that no terminology can solve a real-life problem. The reader who has familiarized himself or herself with the way I formulated the problem in the previous chapter will recognize that I do not propose to use a mere change in terminology to untangle the knot created by such profound and intricate human data. But at the same time one must admit that an adequate terminology, a terminology that resonantly echoes the deeper reaches of human language, is a big help in trying to formulate a problem more clearly and solidly. Hence it is logically a big help in trying to find better solutions.

I would be only too willing to change my terms, faith and ideology, for other synonymous or equivalent ones that are more in use. But I find that every attempt to get closer to the usual language employed in these matters leads to adverse consequences for the new formulation of the issues that I am seeking to offer here. In a way that is not surprising, because the misunderstandings in this area have become commonplaces in our culture.

So at the risk of boring readers who have grasped the basic points presented in Chapter I, and who may even have accepted them and now want to see where they lead, I want to return to further discussion of my terminology as compared with that of other people. I hope that this discussion, even though slightly repetitive, will open up new horizons (see REMARK A, p. 50). I will begin with faith.

I. Pannenberg's Fundamental Trust

Do I or do I not have faith? In the previous chapter I made clear my disagreement with the commonplace view which divides human beings into believers and nonbelievers—or, religious people and atheists. The essential thing does not lie there, I would insist. Here my analysis seems to agree with other current views that regard "faith" or some synonymous term as an anthropological dimension rather than a phenomenon restricted to some group of "believers."

Despite this seeming convergence of views, I will try to show that the "faith" which some authors speak about in this connection would be better expressed by such terms as "trust" or "religion" and also that certain key elements in my analysis seem to justify the use of the term "faith" more for my own position.

Here is a passage written by the German theologian, Wolfhart Pannenberg:

> Actually, faith as a vital act is synonymous with trust, a trust that has to do with the fundamental and basic moments in any human life. Like any such moment in life, this trust extends beyond the boundaries of any Christian avowal. . . . The trust we need to live does not extend solely to specific circumstances, things, and persons; going beyond them, it leads us to trust in the undetermined. . . . So we can say that above and beyond any conditioned trust that we place in the circumstances, things, and persons among which our life moves, there is a deeper, unconditioned trust by which we live. But even this unconditioned trust, for all its openness and unconditionality, is a trust in something where any human being is concerned. It is always concentrated in a person or a thing. In the first stages of infancy, this pristine trust is

bound up with father and mother. Later it must be freed from them, but it still remains the basic condition for the formation of a healthy personality. Under normal circumstances, most human beings reflect little on the foundation of this fundamental trust which constitutes the bulwark or support of their lives. Normally we do not consider the object of our fundamental trust. The latter is not shaken or even called into question. . . . Where do we place the ultimate concern of our heart? What do we trust in ultimately? This is the most serious question that a human being can ask himself or herself. "The faith and trust of the heart make . . . both God and idols." That is one of Luther's enduring statements.[1]

Similarities

This long citation is justifiable, I think, because it will enable us to spell out certain important points about my formulation of the issue and to differentiate them from the approach that talks about "fundamental trust."

To begin with, note that faith and trust seem to be used as synonyms throughout the passage cited, though the latter term is preferred in Pannenberg's elaboration of his point. There is good reason for that preference, as we shall see.

Another point is worth noting. Clearly moving along the same lines that I do, Pannenberg is talking about an anthropological dimension rather than a specifically religious act. It is the human being as such who needs an "unconditioned" or "fundamental" trust, and who always finds some such trust, however well or badly placed. Normally this trust is first placed in one's parents; then it moves on from them (see REMARK B.1, p. 51).

Differences

It is from here on that I would begin to differ from Pannenberg's terminology. The first problem is that the faith or trust mentioned by him does not seem to be the total meaning-structure which is different for each human life, but rather what he himself calls a "bulwark" (or support). Viewed in this light, it would seem that the trust mentioned in Pannenberg's passage refers to that common something which enables a human being to overcome the fear that would prevent him or her from facing up to circumstances, using things, and relating to persons. That is why at various points Pannenberg indiscriminately mentions "circumstances, things, and persons" as the object of this fundamental trust.

My formulation is not contradictory, but it is different. As I see it, faith (or unconditioned trust, if you will), insofar as it is the meaning-structure of *each* human being, cannot have as its object reality: i.e., the whole complex of circumstances, things, and persons. It can only have certain specific persons as its object. Pannenberg may be unwittingly alluding to this fact when he writes that in infancy one's fundamental trust is bound up with one's parents. For if it was a question of some mere "bulwark" for every action, the relationship to parents is not relevant. The baby left to itself will have a more superficial and immediatist system of values, but it will have the same "fundamental trust."

For our purposes here, I will also not go into any long discussion as to whether money—a typical thing in these analyses—is really a "thing" or a value. Even if we were to call it a "value," it would be anthropologically impossible to talk about an unlimited trust in money. At best one can have a certain amount of trust in what money provides, and we visualize and "believe" it when we see it embodied in the satisfactions exemplified by people who possess money. As a "thing," money can never inspire unconditioned trust. Such trust must always be "conditioned" by satisfying human situations connected with money and located in persons. And the same can be said for "circumstances": e.g., victory or success (see REMARK B.2, p. 51).

So leaving aside the hazards of translation with respect to Pannenberg's citation, I would say that the important difference in our analyses lies in the shadings which separate ordinary usage of the terms "faith" and "trust." And I would say that in the case of my analysis, these shadings tip the scales in favor of using the term "faith." It seems to me that in the lexicon of the ordinary person the term "faith" has a far more personal cast than does the term "trust." And my phenomenological analysis has brought out the fact that there are no circumstances or things "of value" unless value shows itself through some personal relationship. This should help the reader to see more clearly that the faith I am talking about is each and every meaning-structure of a human life rather than the vital "bulwark" (or support) that a human being needs to act at all. Lack of "faith" would disorientate a human being; lack of "trust" would paralyze him or her. Or, to put it another way, lack of "faith" would paralyze a person through disorientation whereas lack of "trust" would paralyze a person with timidity or atony—two very different things (see REMARK B.3, p. 52).

II. Tracy's Religion

Besides helping us to weigh the respective advantages of using "faith" or "trust" to designate the anthropological dimension discussed in my previous chapter, Pannenberg's passage is a convenient introduction to a current of modern thought which replaces my word "faith" with the word "religion" in order to designate the anthropological dimension under discussion. This is done frequently, not without certain reasons.

Right off I might object that people are only multiplying linguistic confusion and misunderstanding when they try to pin the label of "religious" on human beings who have explicitly rejected any established religion or have openly espoused atheism. But they might well respond: "Physician, cure thyself!'' They could point out that the same sore point can be found in my attempt to attribute an anthropological dimension to "faith" when many human beings profess to being "nonbelievers."

In self-defense I could point out that up to now I have used the word "faith" solely in a general human context, referring to the faith that one human being has in another human being insofar as his or her values-structure or meaning-structure for life is concerned—whether it be religious or not. I could also claim that the accusation is really offbase since the word "faith," unlike the word "religion," does obviously have a nonreligious use.

However, such rebuttals only touch the surface of the problem here. In my opinion, the current of thought about which I am speaking here, and which is particularly evident in Anglo-Saxon culture, has far more serious disadvantages. Let me say right off what I think the problem is. My hypothesis is that the intention implicit in the tendency is to make "religion" the anthropological dimension I designate by the term "faith" in order to minimize the differences between religious *dogmas* and their different socio-political consequences, attack the growing influence of secularism, and displace the essential question whether Christianity, as the fonts present it to us, is or is not a "religion" like any other.

We can follow this current of thought in the interesting book by David Tracy entitled *Blessed Rage for Order*. Tracy starts with the definition of religion formulated by a sociologist, Clifford Geertz. Religion is:

1. a system of symbols which acts to
2. establish powerful, pervasive, and long-lasting moods and motivations in men by
3. formulating conceptions of a general order of existence, and
4. clothing these conceptions with such an aura of factuality that
5. the moods and motivations seem uniquely realistic.[2]

But Tracy is too clever not to see the unsuitability of taking a wide variety of religious phenomena, which are completely different and often contradictory in nature, and throwing them all into one basket. On the other hand he is much less sensitive to the important fact that all these elements can likewise be found outside the religious sphere: in such ideologies as liberalism, Marxism, and fascism. Be that as it may, Tracy prefers to disregard the effort to include all the constitutive elements of the religious realm under one definition. He chooses to focus on one basic (or fundamental) human element which, he says, is ordinarily associated with the word "religion" and which enables us to set aside all the other diverse elements and concentrate on an anthropological dimension that is very similar to, if not identical with, that of Pannenberg. This is how Tracy describes the element:

Employed in our common discourse, "religion" usually means a perspective which expresses a dominating interest in certain universal and elemental features of human existence as those features bear on the human desire for liberation and authentic existence. Such features can be analyzed as both expressive of certain "limits-to" our ordinary experience (e.g., finitude, contingency, or radical transcience) and disclosive of certain fundamental structures of our existence beyond (or, alternatively, grounding to) that ordinary experience (e.g., our fundamental trust in the worthwhileness of existence, our basic belief in order and value).[3]

Corresponding to the limits-to, and logically parallel to them, are the limits-of which Tracy mentions, and which include our "fundamental trust" and our "basic belief." In the very next paragraph of his book, the word "belief" is explicitly replaced with my term "faith":

We can often both experience and articulate the "limits-to" aspect of the religious perspective. On such occasions, we may also find the ability occasionally to speak, more often to "show" or "disclose" the horizon, ground, or "limit-of" such language and experience. In either case, we need to reflect upon both the explicit limits-to our ordinary experience (the everyday and the scientific, the moral, aesthetic, and political) and the implicitly disclosed dimension which functions as limit-of or ground to (e.g., *fundamental* faith or trust) our more ordinary ways of being-in-the-world.[4]

Similarities

The reader can see that in this fairly esoteric passage Tracy presents a view of certain features that are similar to those in my own analysis and that I have subsumed under the term "faith" (see REMARK C.1, p. 52).

First of all, Tracy writes about an anthropological dimension which he calls "faith" or "fundamental trust," because it is the necessary basis of all sorts of everyday experiences. Secondly, Tracy, like me, locates this dimension at the very limits of every human being's existence. His terms, "limits-to" and "limits-of," connote that every human being must face up to our limited supplies of energy; hence every human being must make an "imaginary" trip to the limits of his or her existence in order to give it meaning. Tracy also agrees with my view that conceptual language is not the most suitable language to convey this reality, which he designates "limit-of" and which I have called the object of our "faith": i.e., our valuational structure. The most appropriate language is symbolic language, which does not so much conceptualize as re-present and evoke this experience of value (see REMARK C.2, p. 52).

Differences

Despite these points of agreement, it is obvious that Tracy is much closer to Pannenberg's analysis than he is to mine. This is evident right off from his preferential use of the term "trust," which is much more suited to designate the basic support or "bulwark" of existence to which Pannenberg refers. This thrust is confirmed when we see Tracy indicating that the object of basic trust is not any specific meaning-structure but the more general fact of the "worthwhileness of existence," or such abstract, indeterminate terms as "order" and "value." My analysis, by contrast, stressed the necessity of each human being *deciding*, through faith, what exactly is worthwhile in existence, what value or order he or she can entrust their whole life to. At the risk of jumping ahead to conclusions and arguments, I would go so far as to say that Tracy's formulation seems a-critical precisely to the extent that it is generalizing.

Some readers might think that the analyses of Pannenberg and Tracy merely stress a different but no less real element than my analysis does. They might feel that the two types of analysis can go hand in hand so long as we do not equate the use of certain terms whose contents are different, and particularly the term "faith." But in fact my criticism is far more radical, as I indicated above.

To stay with the above two examples of analysis, I must ask myself wherein lies Tracy's (if not Pannenberg's) interest in linking up the anthropological dimension of fundamental trust with "religion." The answer is clear to anyone who reads Tracy's book, and it flows from the premises set forth above. Human beings are divided up into those who have, and those who have not, succeeded in explicating the religious dimension of their existence—with approval going to the former of course. For anyone who stops to ponder the "limit-of" his or her existence and somehow manages to name it, names the absolute, or God, and affirms his existence and necessity even if he or she does not realize it.[5]

My readers will recall that this is not the real, relevant line of demarcation according to my analysis. The only radical definition, as I see it, depends on the scale of values that human beings choose, not on whether they are believers or not (see REMARK C.3, p. 53). In Tracy's formulation, however, this radicalness disappears from sight in two respects that are typical of our "Christian, Western civilization." By stressing what is explicitly religious, by trying to turn "religion" (which is always explicit in common discourse) into an anthropological dimension, the terminology of Tracy and others creates a twofold misunderstanding which has the most serious consequences.

First of all, this divinizing terminology tends to minimize the all-too-human components that enter into our conception of the "god" which religion handles so explicitly and so vaguely. Almost throughout Tracy's book, the unquestioned assumption seems to be that we need only mention God as the "limit-of" existence to elevate the latter to a certain degree of value, cognitive value at least, since it is assumed that in enunciating the noun one knows who or what one is dealing with. Thus the important thing seems to be "religion," not *what sort of* religion *exactly*. Here Tracy seems to adapt his thinking to a tendency that is particularly strong in the Anglo-Saxon world, and especially so in the United States. The tendency is for people to regard themselves as "religious," as if that connoted some value common to any and every sort of "dogmatic" affiliation which one might prefer in the concrete.[6]

Secondly, this approach situates religion on the plane of fundamental values. It thus loses sight of the fact that the most common and perhaps primitive function of explicit and recordable religions has been "ideological" in my sense of the term (as explained in Chapter I). In other words, they have served as *instruments* for any and every class of values. So when one identifies the religion to which one belongs, one is usually identifying certain procedures or methods for obtaining pre-established values rather than the gamut or structure of those values (see REMARK C.4, p. 53).

To explore these two crucial points, let us consider a basic question that arises from all we have said so far: Does the explicit religion we profess help us to identify our "faith" (in the anthropological sense), that is to say, our meaning-structure? There are serious reasons for answering "no" to that question. One reason is derived from the sociology of religion, the other from the Christian message itself.

Concrete experience immediately suggests that different values-structures would logically call for distinct religions by way of explanation, or at least for different ways of viewing "religion." Thus, to identify or express their anthropological faith, believers would have to begin by identifying the God in whom they believe, the God whose revelation supposedly determines the values that they hold as absolute. (Indeed they would have to start off here by writing "god" in small letters, and that in itself is the problem.)

Now this first step in what is supposed to be a "religious" identification of anthropological faith has been greatly confused for centuries by a cultural fact. All the different divine names which flourished in antiquity have been brought together under one noun: God. It serves as a proper name (of the Christian God, the Jewish God, and the Muslim God), and at the same time as a common noun designating any divinity regarded as such in other cultures distant in time or space from us.

We can assume that in ages of what we call idolatry or polytheism the identification of one's anthropological faith through the identification of the deity who was the object of worship and religious faith must have been much more definite and conclusive. A specialist in primitive religions such as Gerhard von Rad writes: "People in antiquity had no doubt that human life was mysteriously surrounded and determined by divine power. But this conviction was by no means a comforting one, when man did not know what kind of a deity he was specifically dealing with, that is, when he did not know *its name* and was without the possibility of invoking it and gaining its interest for himself and his need. The deity must first 'cause his name to be invoked' (Exod. 20:24) within the human field, otherwise men were quite unable to invoke him" (my italics).[7] And this memorial or remembrance in the realm of human existence is precisely what sociology and common discourse call "religion." In his book on the phenomenology of religion, Gerardus van der Leeuw tells us that use of the divine name "forces the figures to stay and guarantees that the human being always finds it again. The number of these numina is boundless."[8]

This fact seems to be confirmed both by exegesis of the Judeo-Christian Bible and by religious phenomenology past and present. It leads us to the logical conclusion that, in many cases at least, the divine "name" and the "religion" associated with it do not at all designate the "faith" which gives value-structure to life; instead they designate an "instrument," a method, by which to attain values that have been fixed beforehand and that are independent of the god who is adopted and adored. In other words, perhaps in most instances with which we are acquainted, the religious realm is an instrumental, essentially "ideological" realm as I defined that term in Chapter I; it is definitely not the realm of "faith," as I mean it.

Here is an example from our own day. In terms of the meaning-structure of existence, the horoscope and astrology in general, so much in vogue in our supposedly secularized age, are obvious instances of ideology, not of faith. People have "faith" in their horoscope as they have "faith" in a brand of automobile or in a hammer. The only difference is that in the case of the horoscope the instrumentality is the residue of an age-old magical outlook by which people sought to conquer the uncertainty of life. But the fact that the instrument is old or ill-chosen for the purpose does not change it into something else; it still remains an instrument. In common discourse, of course, the horoscope can and should be regarded as a religious datum; but it has nothing to do with the faith we are considering here as an anthropological dimension.

Seen from this strict point of view, the Christian faith of people who structure the meaning of their lives in accordance with what they understand to be the supreme values conveyed by divine revelation in Jesus Christ has nothing to do with the Christian "faith" of those who receive a sacrament or take part in a Catholic procession in order to feel more secure before God or to obtain a "grace."

When we try to get "religious" vocabulary to function as an anthropological dimension, it becomes particularly confusing. To consider the matter solely from this first point of view that I have been discussing, religious vocabulary confuses entirely distinct phenomena—both for the human sciences as well as for theoretical and practical theology. To put it more concretely, it confuses the plane of meaning, which can find expression and realization in religious or nonreligious terms, with the plane of efficacy, where human beings ever since they have been around have sought magical or supernatural effects when scientific techniques or stratagems seemed inadequate or were nonexistent (see REMARK C.5, p. 53).

I would like to add something here, a serious assertion about a possible misunderstanding. People who make the mistake of thinking that the religious realm as such has to do necessarily, or for the most part, with the plane of meaning, in other words, people who thus absolutize the religious because it is "religious" and hence has to do with the "Absolute" do nothing less than close themselves off to an understanding of the Christian gospel itself.

For the problem that we have just considered in pretty abstract terms was, in much more concrete terms, the core of the polemic that divided Jesus from the authorities in his own "religion." In the next section, which really serves as a commentary on this one, I should like to make this point in greater detail.

III. Jesus' Polemic against Religion

Sociologically speaking, we must remember certain points about the New Testament community. It was only later (see Acts 2:46 and *passim*), and after a period of institutional hardening and persecution, that Jesus' disciples came to realize that they no longer were part of the Jewish religion, that they were not simply even a heretical "sect" of Judaism, as Paul put it in Jerusalem (Acts 24:14). In this connection one can compare the differences between Matthew 9:16–17 and Luke 5:33–38, taking note of the fact that the final redaction of these Gospels seems to date from somewhere between A.D. 70 and 75. That Jesus did not intend "Christianity" to compete with the Jewish religion, that he saw it as the culmination of the latter's inner evolution, seems clear from a critical study of the Gospels. It seems particularly clear from a study of Matthew's Gospel, which may well be closest to the overall thought and language of the historical Jesus.

Here we shall leave aside another question that is of no little interest: Were the prophets of the Old Testament stressing the same central point that Jesus was? There certainly seems to be a similarity of outlook when we read such passages as the following one from Trito-Isaiah:

> . . . they seek me daily,
>   and delight to know my ways,
> as if they were a nation that did righteousness
>   and did *not forsake the ordinance* of their God;
> they ask of me righteous judgments,
>   they delight to draw near to God.
> "Why have we fasted, and thou seest it not?
>   Why have we humbled ourselves, and thou takest no knowledge of
>   it?"
> Behold, in the day of your fast you seek your own pleasure,
>   and oppress all your workers.
> Behold, you fast only to quarrel and to fight
>   and to hit with wicked fist.
> Fasting like yours this day
>   will not make your voice to be heard on high.
> Is such the fast that I choose,
>   a day for a man to humble himself?
> Is it to bow down his head like a rush,
>   and to spread sackcloth and ashes under him?
> Will you call this a fast,
>   and a day acceptable to the Lord?

Is not this the fast that I choose:
>to loose the bonds of wickedness,
>to undo the thongs of the yoke,
to let the oppressed go free,
>and to break every yoke?
Is it not to share your bread with the hungry,
>and bring the homeless poor into your house;
when you see the naked, to cover him,
>and not to hide yourself from your own flesh?
Then shall your light break forth like the dawn,
>and your healing shall spring up speedily;
your righteousness shall go before you,
>the glory of the Lord shall be your rear guard.
Then you shall call, and the Lord will answer;
>you shall cry, and he will say, Here I am [Isa. 58:2–9, my italics].

This passage certainly seems to relativize something any sociologist would call "religious": i.e., fasting. It seems to diminish its value in favor of something that is much more "secular" or "profane": i.e., just social relationships vis-à-vis the oppressed. But in this passage the two things are classified as the righteousness and will of God. They are described in terms that are still religious. One could conclude that a more authentic, orthodox religion would give first place to the matter that truly deserved it *within the overall framework of religious criteria.*

Be that as it may,[9] this point becomes central in the polemics between Jesus on the one hand and the scribes and Pharisees on the other. And it is expressed in terms that are much more explicit and radical because they are nonreligious. So we learn from the Gospel of Mark, which is commonly recognized as one of the two sources for the three synoptic Gospels.

Obeying Religious Commandments versus Doing Good

One of the first major disputes has to do with keeping the sabbath. People see Jesus' disciples picking off stalks of grain on the sabbath. To justify their action, Jesus cites the historical incident of David and his men. Being hungry, they went into the temple and ate the holy bread which only the priests were permitted to eat. What is interesting right off in Mark's account is that Jesus does not justify the action of his disciples by alluding to the fact that they are with him or that he has given them permission. He simply cites the action of David and his companions. This fact takes on added significance when we realize that nothing in Mark's account suggests the disciples of Jesus are in such dire need as David and his men had been. It is not an exceptional case justified by an emergency. Jesus is trying to establish a scale of values. And if one of the terms is the religious value of the sabbath, the other term is a value that is obviously not religious.[10]

Thus, in Mark's account, Jesus' conclusion is a radical one. It is the sabbath that is relative, human welfare that is absolute: "The sabbath was made *for man*, not man for the sabbath" (Mark 2:27; my italics). It is not the religious dignity of Jesus but that basic fact which makes him lord of the sabbath (Mark 2:28). That is why his disciples are justified in what they are doing.

Now anyone who uses that line of argument must go one step further, a step that is ordinarily not considered. In saying that the criterion for using the sabbath is that the latter is made for the human being, one is assuming that one knows *previously* what is good for the human being. In other words, one's understanding of the human being is prior to, and independent of, religious prescriptions. Such an outlook runs counter to the more common arrangement of values, and it certainly runs counter to the standards being used by the religious authorities of Jesus' milieu, the Pharisees.[11]

Thus everything of a "religious" nature points to God. But the God of Jesus, paradoxically enough, points to human beings, their needs and their values. This explains the unexpected conclusion in the Letter of James, when it seeks to define religion that is pure and undefiled: "To go to the help of orphans and widows in their distress . . ." (James 1:27).

Accustomed to reading this passage in a habitually Christian context, we automatically rob it of its force. Instead of reading what is in the text, we tend to read it as if it said: "Christianity pure and undefiled is to help orphans and widows when they need it." We assume that the text is warning us about the danger of not carrying our faith to its ultimate consequences insofar as practice is concerned. But in strict logic we should read the passage somewhat as follows: "Any and all religion that leads to offering help to orphans and widows is pure and undefiled."

What we have here is the criterion for judging when a religion is correct. Here again, as in the Markan passage, the "religious" realm is obviously relativized. Everything that ordinary language regards as religion is allocated to the instrumental, functional level. It has no value *in itself*. It is dislodged from its ordinary status as the ultimate criterion.

Let us go back to Mark's Gospel again. Immediately after the sabbath incident discussed above, we find Jesus in the synagogue healing a man with a withered hand (Mark 3:1–5). But first he poses a question which, for very logical reasons, will go unanswered by the religious experts of Israel. Their "religion" enabled them to know beforehand what one was permitted or not permitted to do on the sabbath. Precisely because of their religious training, they were prepared to clear up all queries on that matter. But Jesus poses a different question, one that sounds really odd not only to the Pharisees but even to our supposedly Christian ears: "Is it permitted to do good or to do evil on the sabbath?" (Mark 3:4).

The question goes unanswered because it makes no sense to Jesus' interlocutors. For this question, even more clearly than the case of David cited earlier, presupposes that human *good* and *evil* can and should be determined before resorting to the religious realm, since they are independent of that realm. Saving or destroying a life, healing a withered hand, and like actions are values which, in Jesus' mind, are clearer than those deriving from religious prescriptions about the sabbath, even though such prescriptions may be based on the Bible. As criteria, they are also superior to such religious prescriptions.

It is also worth noting that the Markan account does not suggest at all that the religious experts gave a negative response to Jesus' question, and hence to the permissibility of curing the man with the withered hand. The account simply says that they remained silent. Why? No doubt because they would have formulated the whole issue differently. They would tend to give priority to the religious criterion over any that might arise from asking what is good or evil for a human being. And why would they tend to do that? Perhaps because they absolutized the religious element, perhaps because they felt that in the Bible Yahweh himself seems to spell out what should and should not be done on the sabbath, or perhaps because they distrusted the ambiguity inherent in any criterion that would propose to establish what is good or evil for a human being within the complex reality of history.

Whatever the underlying reasons for the attitude of the Pharisees, the evangelist characterizes it as "obstinate stupidity," hardheartedness. Jesus is deeply grieved and angered by it (Mark 3:5). Here again literary criticism would tell us that the word "heart" (in the Greek text) probably did not refer to emotion and sentiment as it does for us today. But it would certainly include sensitivity and the emotions because "heart," as a biblical metaphor, tended to signify the source of human criteria and decisions. Its connotations would include intelligent understanding, sensitivity, and affection. Thus "hardness of heart" refers to lying in practice and to bad faith. It means using criteria which lead to twisted judgments that do not pay heed to the reality before one's eyes. We find the same idea expressed in the First Letter of John:

> But if a man has enough to live on, and yet when he *sees* his brother in need *shuts up his heart* against him, how can it be said that the divine love dwells in him? . . . But if a man says "I love God," while hating his brother, he is a *liar*. If he does not love the brother whom he has *seen*, it cannot be that he loves God whom he has not seen [1 John 3:17 and 4:20; my italics].[12]

From where does a human being, particularly one who claims to be "religious," derive his or her value-criteria? This is the central issue in Jesus' argument with his opponents. And in Mark's account we see Jesus subordinating "religious" criteria to those which arise from a sense of responsibility in the face of the visible needs of one's fellow human beings. Religious criteria are merely functional. As such, they must be *judged* by higher criteria that are valid in themselves.

We thus move from ceremonial prescriptions to morality guided by religious precepts. And we shall see that in Jesus' eyes a religious "law" cannot give value *in itself* to any category of human acts. We shall see that it is the intended project of a human being towards his or her fellow humans that constitutes the one and only criterion, however hazardous, for determining the "law," the will of God. That project, in other words, is the one and only criterion for spelling out what is good *in itself*.

This is the core of the polemics that occupies most of Chapter 7 in Mark's Gospel. Once again Jesus' disciples are accused of not heeding religious prescriptions. This time the prescriptions have to do with what is pure and impure. In justifying his disciples, Jesus addresses himself first to the scribes and Pharisees (Mark 7:1–13), then to the crowd of listeners (verses 14–16), and finally to his own disciples (verses 17–23).

A key point in the debate is the fact that Jesus' opponents appeal to "tradition," religious "tradition," in condemning his disciples. By contrast, Jesus begins his arguments by making a distinction between the commandments of God and religious traditions. He refers to the latter as "human" traditions (verse 8): i.e., traditions created by human beings. Using an example, he goes on to show that it is not a matter simply of a distinction but rather of a real alternative choice between two possibilities. His adversaries utilize their religious traditions concerning gifts for the temple to evade God's commandment to honor one's father and mother (verses 9–12).

The choice between human traditions and divine commandments obviously implies the establishment of a scale of values, even though both criteria appear to be religious ones on the surface. Jesus further complicates the choice by citing a passage of Isaiah (Isa. 29:13) in which human religious traditions are likened to a religion of the *lips*, whereas the commandments of God are likened to a religion of the *heart*. In other words, we again have an accusation of bad faith, for which religion serves as instrument and justification.

Of course some will say that there is another kind of "religion" which is not manipulated, one in which the "heart" is in conformity with God's commandment. That is certainly true. But what is the criterion for finding this conformity: the pre-existing commandment or the dictate of the heart? Jesus' remarks to the people and his subsequent explanation to his disciples as to what is pure and impure will answer this question for us. His answer here will dovetail with his remarks in the passages studied above, and it will sound no less paradoxical to our religious ears.

Jesus again sets up a contrast between lips and heart, but in this case they are nonreligious metaphors. Here they point to the *source* of moral criteria. The lips become the "mouth," which metaphorically signifies the invasion of the insides by *outside* criteria. By contrast, the "heart" signifies the criteria that reside in the intended project of a person whereby what is *inside* him or her is to be realized outside (verses 14–23). Here Matthew and Mark tell us that Jesus attached moral relevance only to the latter kind of criteria: "Nothing that goes from outside into a man can defile him. . . . It is what comes out of a man that defiles him (Mark 7:18, 20; Matt. 15:18–19).[13]

What is it, then, that comes from the "outside," that enters the "mouth"? Jesus is not talking about the mouth, and hence food, in any literal sense. This is obvious from the contrasting term: what comes from the inside. Jesus is not talking about one's intention in eating but about such completely independent things (begging Freud's pardon) as fornication, avarice, murder, and so forth. In talking about what comes from "outside" human beings with a label of pure or impure already on it, Jesus is clearly referring to the precepts of religious law. He is referring to religious norms which determine what is licit and what is not even before considering what a human being intends to do in using something. Jesus himself takes a very different stand, with respect to adultery for example. He implicitly but clearly suggests that an act of adultery does not consist in some specific or specifiable use of sexual relations in itself, but rather in the result of a person's intended project. Only that project gives the act its moral dimension of adultery. Only the projects of human beings make them pure or impure, moral or immoral. And from the list of sins he cites, it is obvious that *all* human failings are subsumed under this perspective.

Any and all legislation, however religious it may be, remains external to human beings if it comes before the determination of their project. As such, it comes from "outside" them; and, according to Jesus, not even God can determine the morality of a human being from "outside." Whenever people have tried to make such "outside" determinations, within Christianity or outside it, they have in fact been devising a religious prescription that is "human" in its origin; they have been indulging in a religion of the "lips" rather than a religion of the "heart."

On the other hand a criterion which stems from a sensitive human heart, however hard and risky it may be to establish it, rises above any religious consideration. It is superior to the latter as a criterion, insofar as religion often tries to establish moral legislation. St. Paul points to one's understanding and acceptance of this point as proof that one has truly moved from the Old Testament to the new situation he repeatedly describes as the "freedom of Christ."[14] In this connection Mark takes a decisive step further when he adds: "Thus he declared all foods clean" (Mark 7:19).[15]

This statement, probably formulated and appreciated some time after Jesus' actual preaching, no longer scandalizes us. It is clear that its anti-religious import was lost once people began to worship Jesus himself. It is only when people made Jesus the founder of still another "religion" and began to worship him as God that they ceased to see anything abnormal in his utterance. For here he is making clean foods that Yahweh himself had declared unclean from time immemorial—according to the traditions gathered together in the Bible.

We have lost sight of the radical thrust of Jesus' line of argument. He began by making a distinction between divine commandments and religious traditions invented by human beings. Then he equated a religion of the heart with the observance of the divine commandments, and a religion of the lips with the observance of human religious traditions. Finally, following the force and the logic of "outside" and "inside" as metaphors, he ended up including even the divine commandments—or what had been regarded as such up to that time—under the category of "outside" things.

Thus the basic criterion of Christian morality is to be found in the features of a person's intended project, in what the heart bids a person do in the face of the needs of his or her fellow humans. Following the logic of this view perfectly, the Johannine writer will later tell us that the only commandment Jesus gave to his disciples was, paradoxically enough, a nonreligious one: "As I have loved you, so you are to love one another" (John 13:34). This is the commandment *of God*, this is "religion" pure and undefiled: something which does not appear to be religion and which is not justified as such, something which is grounded in values that an alien observer would call simply "human."

Religious Authority versus Human Criteria

There is another dimension of the "religious" realm, as ordinary language uses that term, and it is closely bound up with the ceremonial and legalist dimension that we have just examined. This other dimension is the interpretation of actual events in which the presence and direction of God's will is discovered. It is the same moral dimension, if you will, but in this case we take a shortcut and arrive at it without going by way of general principles. Of course the very possibility of God's *revealing* a "law" to human beings presupposes that human beings can recognize moments of revelation, can separate the latter from the process of natural causality as well as from other forms of opposing or evil "religious" causality.

The point here is that this dimension of the "religious" realm is attacked just as radically by Jesus. At least it is attacked to the extent that religious criteria try to oppose or take priority over criteria deriving from human values—which is to say, deriving from the historical sensitivity that enables us to see such human values.

Mark will again be our guide (Mark 3:22–30), though the passage is in all three synoptic Gospels. And even though Mark's account may be the source, in this case Jesus' argument with the scribes is not set in its logical context in the second Gospel. Matthew (12:22) and Luke (11:14) make it clear that Jesus was curing a mute, and Matthew adds that he was also blind. In the cultural context of Jesus' time and place, curing such a person meant "casting out a demon."

The scribes who are present try to interpret the phenomenon of curing, which they cannot deny, in "religious" terms. From that standpoint it is obvious to them that both God and the chief demon possess the power that can account for the result obtained by Jesus. And so, by way of hypothesis or conclusion, the scribes say: "He drives out the devils by the prince of devils" (Mark 3:22).

Jesus' counter-argument is well known, but its full implications are far from understood. Jesus accepts the hypothesis of his opponents. What will happen if the prince of devils begins to cast out devils? Clearly a kingdom or a house divided against itself cannot stand: "If Satan is in rebellion against himself, he is divided and cannot stand; and that is the end of him" (Mark 3:26). Here we find Jesus' whole argument. If the kingdom of Satan is dividing and falling apart, that can only benefit people and help to establish the kingdom of God. So why bother about any such "religious" interpretation of what is happening? Are you going to reject the kingdom of God because it will come into being through the defeat or stupidity of Satan?

In other words, Jesus here distinguishes between two kinds of historical criteria. One criterion seeks to establish the religious power or authority, be it positive or negative, that lies behind the cure. The other criterion is concerned solely with what is actually and effectively good for human beings. If someone is cured, says Jesus, God always comes off the winner. The welfare of human beings is always God's cause and God's work. Once again the more human criterion, the less "religious" criterion, is the more divine one.[16]

But there is more to it. Jesus is not denouncing a simple error. He is denouncing the scribes for bad faith. He is saying that whenever people lose sight of the functional, derivative significance of the "religious" realm—its ideological character, in my terminology—they are more or less consciously evading their human responsibility before God. It is the same "hardness of heart" we saw earlier, when people chose to follow religious regulations rather than to concern themselves with the "good" of the sick man, or to use "human" religious traditions to evade the divine commandment about honoring one's parents. God's commandment, ultimately, is to love human beings.

The same point is stressed again by Jesus in his remarks to his disciples. They are scandalized when the scribes accuse Jesus of being a henchman of Beelzebub, the prince of demons; they feel such an accusation is blasphemy. Jesus takes the opportunity, and picks up this religious term, to clear up another mistaken view about the proper hierarchy of criteria (Mark 3:28-30). Blasphemy is a most serious religious category having to do with speaking ill of God, sacred things, or sacred persons. Jesus explains that there are all kinds and degrees of blasphemy, that speaking ill of God may or may not be pardonable, depending on the circumstances. Specifically, he says that blasphemy against the Son of Man and all sorts of blasphemy will be forgiven, but not blasphemy against the Holy Spirit.

The whole context of the incident suggests that the attitude of Jesus' opponents is gravely wrong because it represents blasphemy against the Holy Spirit, not because it is blasphemy against himself as we might think at first glance. And contrary to our usual exegesis, it is the category of blasphemy against the Holy Spirit that is clear, not that of blasphemy against the Son of Man. Indeed once we examine the context and see what blasphemy against the Holy Spirit means, we can then figure out what Jesus means when he says that speaking ill of the Son of Man is pardonable.

In the Bible the Spirit of God is God himself operating with all his power. It is the absolute value perceived through the events produced by its force. What, then, is blasphemy against the Holy Spirit, against the power of God in action? Such blasphemy consists in refusing—for selfish and self-interested reasons—to see God at work in events where human beings (e.g., the mute and the ill) recover their full human capability in some respect.

That is the sin committed by Jesus' opponents. It would be pardonable for them to prefer another kind of human help to that offered by the Son of Man if their goals were the same. What is not pardonable[17] is using religious speculations as a way of evading and disclaiming what God is actually accomplishing in reality, particularly when the results are right before their eyes.

I would offer one final remark on this incident. The notion of an unpardonable sin is the negative counterpart of the absolute value. It is the other direction that a human being can take. To phrase the issues raised by Jesus in my terminology, I would say that wanting to know the religious agent at work is an "ideological" question while regarding or not regarding the cure of a human being as the work of God is a question of "faith." Every addition of fuller humanity is an issue that falls under the latter category.

Jesus, then, teaches us that the "religious" realm can falsify the interpretation of historical happenings. This teaching is completed in a passage of Mark's Gospel: "Then the Pharisees came out and engaged him in discussion. To test him they asked for a sign from heaven. He sighed deeply to himself, and said, 'Why does this generation ask for a sign? I tell you this: no sign shall be given to this generation' " (Mark 8:11–12).

The other synoptic Gospels have attached even more importance to this particular point than does Mark. They add details that are relevant to our discussion here.

First of all, they provide us with the context, which is absent in Mark's Gospel. In general, Luke's Gospel tries to find more "logical" contexts for the teachings of Jesus, even if that means disregarding the more likely chronology. In this case Luke's Gospel associates the request for a sign from heaven with the reaction of people to Jesus' cure of the mute discussed above: "But some of them said, 'It is by Beelzebub, prince of devils, that he drives the devils out.' Others, by the way of a test, demanded of him a *sign from heaven*" (Luke 11:15–16). It is clear that the author of Luke's Gospel saw the same basic problem, the same basic issue, at stake here.

Secondly, both Matthew's Gospel and Luke's Gospel add coloring to Jesus' refusal to offer a sign (a "sign from heaven," according to Luke). According to both Gospels, Jesus has actually offered signs comparable to, and even greater than, those of Jonah to the people of Nineveh and of Solomon to the queen of the South. So both Matthew and Luke slightly alter the words in Mark's Gospel: "The only sign that will be given is . . ." (Luke 11:29 f; Matt. 12:39–40).

It is worth noting that while the challenge hurled at Jesus may mention the phrase, there is no explicit indication in the response that the sign offered by

Jesus, like that of Jonah or Solomon, is "from heaven." Indeed everything points to the fact that it is not, which would explain the no voiced in Mark's Gospel. When asked for a sign from heaven, Jesus always replied with a clear no. But he also indicated that he had given clear enough signs for anyone who was not overly concerned with heavenly signs. The fact is that the sign of Jonah, while not a sign "from heaven," was enough to be recognized as such by the Ninevites and so was the sign of Solomon for the queen of the South. All the more reason, then, that the signs of Jesus should be enough for his contemporaries, who will be judged far more severely on the basis of the signs offered them.[18]

So what exactly was the "sign" of Jonah to the Ninevites or the sign of Solomon to the queen of the South? Here we must note another important point. Both the Ninevites and the queen of the South were pagans. Even more significantly, they continued to be pagans after having seen the sign and repented (Matt. 12:41; Luke 11:32). To people versed in the Bible at least, it was evident that it did not register any mass conversion of Nineveh or the South to the "religion" of Israel. The conversion praised by Jesus here is specifically a conversion in conduct, not a change in religion. In one case there was a decrease in unjust violence; in the other, an increase in wisdom. The case of Nineveh is the clearer one. Jonah told the Ninevites that their city would be destroyed in forty days. This provoked a crisis of meaning for them. The Ninevites had enough historical sensitivity to believe that such destruction would indeed be bound to take place, that it fitted in with those values that ought to be absolute. Their change in conduct was the result. Similarly, the sensitivity of the queen of the South prompted her to use all the means at her disposal to increase her wisdom by profiting from that of Solomon.[19]

Put simply, then, the point is that in the eyes of Jesus the "religious" realm is not one where guarantees and certitudes from above spare human beings the effort of applying to events the "human" criteria which serve and suffice for any and every other sort of activity. Indeed, as we shall see in the next chapter, Jesus goes further and accuses his opponents, who are the epitome of orthodoxy, of idolatry on this point. Why? Because the god from whom they seek such supernatural criteria is not the God revealed to them by the prophets and Jesus himself. For the latter God does not want to be sought out by any other criteria than those which human beings use to orientate themselves in history.

That is why Jesus breathes a sigh of discouragement, according to Mark. It also explains the shocking and radical question which ends the debate in Luke's Gospel: "Why can you not judge for yourselves what is the right course?" (Luke 12:57). There could hardly be a more scandalous question put to the Jewish people. For up to that time God had seemingly decreed that they judge what is right by having recourse to their sacred scriptures, to the priests and Levites, and, should doubt persist, to the sacred use of the *urim* and the *thummim* (see for example 1 Sam. 14:41).

I could go on citing other lesser passages in Mark's Gospel that continue this central issue in the message of Jesus.[20] For the sake of brevity I will not. But it should be clear by now that this synoptic source of Jesus' words and deeds[21] stresses Jesus' polemics with "religion," the latter being understood in its most obvious and ordinary sociological sense. Indeed Mark's Gospel makes this polemics the key to recognizing Jesus and his original brand of prophetism (see REMARK D, p. 54).

Now while this basic attack of Jesus against the explicitly religious realm does go far beyond the concrete case of his own contemporary religion, it clearly does not directly attack what David Tracy calls religion: i.e., a dimension common to all human existence whereby we tend to seek out values as if the latter did not have the iron-clad limits which experience brings home to us. But if Jesus does not attack religion in the latter sense directly, he does make clear a couple of things. First of all, it is clear that in reality the "religious" realm is generally a realm of *instrumentality* rather than a realm of value-structure. Secondly, it is clear that the "divine" character attributed to this instrumentality, however unwittingly, constitutes one of the most serious dangers facing human life. The danger is that human beings will refuse or fail to give meaning to their own lives by creating, through anthropological faith, a values-structure—with all the risks that entails. In attacking the religion he found around him, the founder of Christianity was attacking the fact that it was an "ideology" rather than a "faith"—to use my terminology. What is more, it was an ideology which, by virtue of its divine, absolutized categories, was particularly well equipped to pass itself off as "faith." Thus, in the last analysis, it was a symptom and tool of "bad faith," of hypocrisy.

But isn't there any other conception of the "religious" realm which comes closer to Jesus' own position? Isn't there one which comes closer to what David Tracy calls "religion" and what I call anthropological "faith"? This is the basic question we shall consider in the next chapter.

Remarks

REMARK A (see p. 32). It might seem that we have done enough to clarify the two anthropological dimensions examined in Chapter I. But when we look at ordinary language and its use of the terms I have proposed here, we often find that it disagrees with the content of my terms or replaces them with other terms to suit itself. This may seem to be a matter of chance to many readers. But my hypothesis, which underlies the discussion in Chapters II, III, and IV of this book, is that the vagueness and equivocal cast of ordinary terminology betrays the fact that its users have not undertaken the analysis I am making here.

So now I am going to consider other people's terms that are used as substitutes for mine, and that might seem to be close to mine at first glance. I hope this discussion will further clarify the two basic anthropological dimensions discussed in Chapter I, and also their relationship with other basic structures of human life and activity.

Thus, under the guise of a discussion of terminology, I will really be continuing my analysis. I will begin with the first dimension, that of meaning; then I will move on to the second dimension, that of efficacy. In this chapter I will focus on the first dimension and consider two terms that are proposed as substitutes for my term "faith." One is "trust." The other is "religion." In this chapter I shall consider only the first and most basic meaning of the latter term.

REMARK B.1 (see p. 33). Pannenberg's passage offers the first potential substitute or replacement for what I have called anthropological "faith." His term is "fundamental trust." In this REMARK I will indicate the *points of contact* between his term and mine:

a. His term refers to a real *anthropological dimension*, a precondition if human life and activity are to be possible at all. Its absence would lead immediately to paralysis and existential (even if not biological) death.

b. Despite his remark about trust being bound up with one's father and mother in infancy, Pannenberg is talking about an "unconditioned trust." It keeps us moving and searching despite personal flaws and failures. This formulation agrees with mine because it *clearly moves beyond the plane of efficacy*. It also talks about "the heart . . . God and idols," and so it too refers to the plane of meaning and value as my notion of anthropological faith does.

c. Pannenberg's trust is *unconditioned* or *absolute*, as is my faith. Everything else depends on it. No value or mediation has meaning without it.

d. Even though it is not clear why it is so important to know in whom or what this trust is placed, Pannenberg says that "this is the most serious question a human being can ask himself or herself." And just as I indicated in the case of anthropological faith, Pannenberg notes that it is difficult for human beings to *reflect explicitly* on the object of their fundamental trust or formulate it in conceptual terms.

REMARK B.2 (see p. 34). However, there are important *differences* between Pannenberg's term and mine. So his "fundamental trust" is not synonymous with my anthropological "faith." Let me indicate two basic differences here:

a. Pannenberg's "trust" is not a dimension that *brings persons into relationship with each other*. For the same reason, and to the same extent, it is not a *social dimension* of valuation that is part and parcel of every human life. Though the terms "trust" and "faith" are close to each other in common usage, the former refers more to an individual's vital tonus whereas the latter refers more to a specific relationship between persons. This is true even though some people may use them indiscriminately as synonyms. The very fact that Pannenberg talks indiscriminately about "circumstances, persons, and things" in describing the object of trust indicates that he is not talking about "believing" in some specific personal testimony.

b. Thus Pannenberg's fundamental trust does not enable us to know *what concrete values* a person believes in. It does not tell us the values-structure that each human being gives to his or her life. Rather, it is a basic quality common to all human values-structures. It is more akin to the basic biological energy that conditions all sorts of activity.

REMARK B.3 (see p. 34). My *conclusion*, then, is that Pannenberg's term, "fundamental trust," will not do as a synonym for my term "faith." It does refer to an anthropological dimension. But it refers to a dimension that is *prior* to the structuring of human activity into faith and ideologies. The latter sort of structuring tells us *how an individual human life organizes* the basic energy available to all human beings. Pannenberg's "trust," by contrast, would seem to be the conscious expression of the basic energy itself, insofar as a human being feels its presence as a vague impulse to act in ordinary circumstances or its absence at moments of crisis. Further on in this volume I shall consider the impact of this prior dimension, or its failings, on faith and ideologies.

REMARK C.1 (see p. 36). Tracy's text and the overall thrust of his book offer us a second potential substitute or synonym for my term "faith." It is the term "religion" as Tracy himself describes and defines it.

First of all, I shall examine the points of contact and the differences between Tracy's term and mine, just as I did with Pannenberg. But then a *second* task awaits us, which I will begin in this chapter and continue in the next chapter. For unlike Pannenberg's term "trust," the term "religion" has two fairly technical meanings besides the meaning Tracy gives it. Since those other two meanings are fairly common and well known, we cannot disregard them when we are trying to establish a proper teminology. Besides, they would only create confusion if we equated them unthinkingly either with Tracy's analysis or my own.

REMARK C.2 (see p. 36). First I will indicate the *points of contact* between Tracy's term "religion" and my term "faith." Three features are worth noting in this respect:

a. Tracy himself uses the terms "faith" and "trust" as synonyms for the term "religion." Moreover, his "religion," like my "faith," reveals its character as a *general anthropological dimension* only through a phenomenological analysis. Otherwise it, too, remains implicit. Thus the average person may say that he or she does not have "faith" or does not have "religion."

b. The key point in Tracy's analysis is that human beings, despite the "limits-to" their empirical existence, are always acting *as if* such limits did not exist. Thus, through their values and their searching, they establish something beyond those limits: Tracy's "limits-of." They may give any name they wish to this "limit-of"; but it cannot be denied that one of the most commonly used names for this "limit-of" is God and that the corresponding attitude is called "religion."

c. This basic "religious" region is very hard to conceptualize. (See the definition which Tracy cites without fully adopting it as his own on p. 35 of this volume). And it is best expressed in symbolic terms.

REMARK C.3 (see p. 37). Insofar as the *differences* between my "faith" and Tracy's "religion" are concerned, we must make a distinction here as I indicated above. Firstly, there are the differences stemming from *the reality which Tracy himself describes.* Secondly, there are differences stemming more indirectly from current uses of the word "religion." In this REMARK I shall consider the first set of differences:

a. Like Pannenberg's "trust," Tracy's "religion" is not a *personal* relationship within this world, and hence it is not *social.* It refers to something even more basic than the distinction between faith and ideology, something that prompts people to seek out values *as if* they had no limits even when experience tells us that they do. This something makes existence, order, and values seem real and worthwhile. But it, unlike my "faith," does not spell out concretely *what sort of* existence, order, and values are worthwhile.

b. It is very difficult to talk meaningfully about an *implicit* religion since the word "religion" normally designates an explicit reality with dogmas, rites, and symbols. Only people who name and worship the Absolute can be called "religious" without ambiguity. But Tracy uses a linguistic term referring to the explicit plane ("religion") to describe a basic, universal anthropological dimension. In so doing, he hinders any analysis of this basic dimension in the "religious" nonbeliever. And whether he means to or not, he thereby helps to foster the mistaken idea that the basic division between human beings is the one between "religious" believers and nonbelievers. It is also worth noting that when our analysis discovers the *faith* implicit in some specific values-structure, it is discovering a *fact*; but when it discovers "religion," it must go one step further and show that the facts *entail* this "religious" dimension.

REMARK C.4 (see p. 38). There are also differences stemming from the use of the word "religion" in our culture, as I indicated. Here I am not referring simply to ordinary usage but also to technical and scientific usages.

It is not a matter simply of comparing terms and picking the best one, as I have indicated. What I want to do here is to understand the reality of what I call "faith" as clearly as possible and to clearly distinguish it from other realities. In this particular case I want to clearly distinguish it from the reality that is commonly called "religion."

Now both the history and the sociology of religion, as well as the relationship of the biblical prophets and Jesus to "religion," will bring out the first difference between anthropological faith and religion. That is the difference discussed in the rest of this chapter. A second difference will be discussed in the next chapter.

REMARK C.5 (see p. 39). The history and sociology of religion, of highly developed as well as primitive religions, points up the following elements in religion that differ from my conception of anthropological faith:

a. People with very different or even opposed values practice the same religion. In it they seek supernatural means that will effectively realize their different values.

b. People usually choose between different religions more for reasons of efficacy than because of different values-structures. In the last analysis people who are called "religious," or who call themselves "religious," generally see religion primarily as a set of *means*. For them it lies on the plane of *efficacy*. And usually it is some sort of magical efficacy that came before scientific efficacy in the course of human evolution. That is why I think it is wrong to identify religion with anthropological faith. For, as I have defined the latter term, it specifies the realm of values and their proper hierarchy, not the realm of means and efficacy.

REMARK D (see p. 50). This long analysis of the attitude of Jesus towards the "religious" realm of his day is meant to make a specific point here. Even such highly developed religions as the Judaism of Jesus' day and the sociological Christianity that followed the period of persecutions do not correspond to what Tracy calls "religion" as an anthropological dimension. In fact, they are poles apart from "religion" in that sense.

I am not saying this to attack Tracy's line of thought right now, nor even to reject his terminology as offbase. I simply want to point up the misunderstandings that can arise when one tries to use a term like "religion" to designate the human being's basic confidence in ultimate values. For the term "religion" usually designates the refusal of human beings to face up to the task of structuring the ultimate values in which they believe. Consider the characteristics of the "religion" that Jesus attacks:

a. It replaces the choice between doing good or harm to human beings (a meaning-structure) with ritual rules that are, or have been made, independent of these values. On the other hand, those ritual rules seem to be endowed with a divine character. Such, for example, is the observance of the sabbath.

b. It replaces moral criteria based upon choosing between values in history with rules that are independent of any such valuation but that are supposedly backed up by divine commandments: e.g., rules about what is pure and impure.

c. It replaces historical sensitivity in judging events with a demand for ahistorical divine criteria: e.g., the hypothesis that Jesus' cures are dependent on the help of Beelzebub or the demand for signs from heaven.

This "religious" flight from the realm of meaning, which we have been examining in Mark's Gospel, basically entails the sacralization of instruments without regard for the ends they are supposed to serve. This process gives deep assurance to human beings. The point I want to make here is that it is closely bound up with the pole of instinctual energy that Freud calls Thanatos, the "death instinct" (see Note 6 of Chapter I in this volume). Contrary to what is sometimes thought, the death instinct does not so much entail aggression against other people (wishing to kill them) as regression towards the inorganic state, towards death. Human beings are tempted to evade complications and difficulties, to focus on immediate satisfactions, and to long for the security of the womb. Hence it is a "conservative" aspect of instinct, and this is what led Freud to discover it.

Now of course this death instinct threatens human beings through *some sort of* mediating factor which they accept in order to realize their values. But the instrument has its own laws, and it is easier for human beings to give in to it than to control it in trying to make it serve their ego interests.

"Religion," in the sense we have been considering it, greatly facilitates this regression. For it endows the instrument with an aura of sacredness and with a supernatural, infallible kind of efficacy as opposed to historical efficacy. It is disturbing to me that people's reflections on "popular religion" or the religion of the "common people" do not take into account this danger that was *stressed so much by Jesus himself*. I am not saying this is the only criterion involved in the issue, but it disturbs me that it is not mentioned at all.

NOTES

1. Wolfhart Pannenberg, *La fe de los Apóstoles*, Spanish trans. (Salamanca: Sígueme, 1974), pp. 15-16.

It is worth noting that the phrase of Luther cited by Pannenberg does not, strictly speaking, apply to what Pannenberg calls "fundamental trust." It really applies to the anthropological faith that I am talking about, the faith whereby we concretely choose the value (God) or antivalue (some idol) to which we are going to dedicate our lives.

2. David Tracy, *Blessed Rage for Order: The New Pluralism in Theology* (New York: Seabury Press, 1975), p. 92.

3. Ibid., p. 93.

4. Ibid. Let me give a little concrete example that will illustrate what Tracy is trying to say in such dry, theoretical terms. Imagine an old woman over seventy sitting in a beginners' class in philosophy. There is no prospect of a degree or a job ahead of her. The only thing prompting her to take the course is the desire for knowledge. Then some other student in the class, a young person, decides to "reason" with her. After all, in a few years she will be dead. She will never be able to solve the intricate philosophical problems of life or get deeply into them. So why should she bother to go to class at all?

What the young student does not realize, however, is that his situation is not really very different. Even if he has fifty years of life ahead of him, what do they mean over against the infinite expanse of knowledge itself? Couldn't one echo the remark of one of Zola's characters: "Since no one will ever know everything, why seek to know more?" (*Le Docteur Pascal* [Paris: Fasquelle, 1963], p. 127). The remark in the novel, however, is part of an argument *ex absurdo*.

But if the young student and the old woman are seeking some value for its own sake rather than some utilitarian goal, then both are making the same unreasonable wager. They are acting *as if* the obvious limitations of existence did not exist, as if they could abolish finiteness and install the absolute in the course of their activity.

5. Tracy, *Blessed Rage for Order*, pp. 183-184 and 187.

6. This supposition is based on my experience with the university milieu in North America insofar as religion is concerned, taking into account the fact that Tracy is addressing that audience. But even if that explains Tracy's initial choice of the term "religion," it should be pointed out that Tracy hedges as he proceeds. He notes that his vocabulary, specifically the term "God" in this instance, is valid "for the Christian religion at least" (p. 148). And not even for all of that.

7. Gerhard von Rad, *Old Testament Theology*, 2 vols., Eng. trans. (New York: Harper & Row, 1962), vol. 1, p. 182.

8. Cited in ibid., p. 135.

9. I am not knowledgeable enough to decide for certain whether every great religion has some hard core of resistance to being used as a holy instrument, in the bad sense meant here. E. Lévinas tries to prove this in the case of Talmudic Judaism. In an interesting article he considers when one is permitted to erase the divine name in a parchment in order to write some (secular) text over it. See his article in the anthology, *Il nome de Dio*, Archivio di Filosofia (Padua: Cedam, 1967).

10. Matthew is usually more cautious than Mark. In this case it is worth noting that Matthew (12:1-8) does not draw the same conclusion from this episode. Besides citing the David incident, he immediately adds another instance of the violation of the sabbath: the work of the priests in the temple on the sabbath (12:5). In so doing, he destroys the point of the argument, the contrast between secular human needs and religious observances. For the work of the priests, though an exception, is still religious whereas the hunger of David and his companions was not. Thus the conclusion to be drawn from Jesus' words in this Gospel is that religious laws allow for reasonable "exceptions," not only in view of human needs but also in view of a scale of values that is strictly religious. Typically enough, Matthew sees Jesus as "sovereign over the sabbath" because in religious terms he is above the temple, the place of divine worship, and hence is the supreme reason for the religious value of the day consecrated to God (Matt. 12:5-6). As I indicated, Mark 2:23-28 is much more radical, besides being more likely closer to Jesus' actual words.

11. It should be pointed out that Matthew, despite his usual caution, lets slip the basis for drawing the same conclusion that Mark's Gospel does. After citing the work of the priests on the sabbath as an example of an exception, he quotes a passage from the Book of Hosea that is important for his Gospel: "I require mercy, not sacrifice" (Matt. 12:7; Hos. 6:6). Here we would do well to cite the full verse of Hosea: "Loyalty is my desire, not sacrifice, not whole-offerings but the knowledge of God" (Hos. 6:6).

Obviously this passage goes far beyond the case of priests working in the temple on the sabbath and even far beyond the case of David. Instead of referring to certain exceptions permitted by an emergency, it establishes a general principle, a scale of values: "I desire this, not that." And then it suggests that "this" is what is "knowledge of God," not "that."

Now we know that in biblical terminology "knowledge" denotes intimacy, not just objective knowledge; but it obviously includes the latter even though it goes beyond that. It is also clear that "not knowing God" is synonymous with idolatry. We shall see further on that this notion is important for our subject here. But it should already be clear that human beings know God and practice right religion only insofar as they give chief value to the needs of human beings in their more secular aspect. And this holds true always.

12. In his book *Jesus of Nazareth*, Eng. trans. (Maryknoll, N.Y.: Orbis Books,

1979), J. Comblin points out that in the Gospels Jesus does not appear as a person who practices the Jewish religion in the technical sense of that term. He does not go to the temple and the annual feasts to participate in the formal worship but to preach. He does not urge his disciples to perform conventional acts of piety, and they must come to him to ask for some little form of prayer; and so forth. Then Comblin adds this point: "More surprising yet is the fact that Jesus did not found a cult himself. He did not organize a new manner of adoring God, of giving him homage or presenting gifts and supplications to him" (p. 96). So why do we continue to present Jesus as the founder of the "Christian religion"?

13. Readers of Matthew's Gospel may find it somewhat difficult to see that Jesus uses both terms, mouth and heart, as metaphors for the *source* of moral criteria. This is particularly true with regard to the word "mouth." Pure and impure were associated mainly with dietary prescriptions in Jesus' day, and Matthew was slow to notice that the term "mouth" meant much more than our receiving apparatus for food. But thanks to a stylistic device—"What *comes out* of the mouth has *its origins* in the heart"—even Matthew is forced to arrive at the same moral dimension that Mark does. "Wicked thoughts, murder, adultery, fornication, theft, perjury, slander—these all proceed from the heart; and these are the things that defile a man" (Matt. 15:19; see Mark 7:21-23).

14. See also Acts 11:1-18.

15. Matthew does not draw such conclusions. He is content to establish the premises, to transmit the words of Jesus as he finds them in the written source he is using. Mark certainly goes much further, even though he does not perceive, or choose to formulate, these conclusions in their more universal dimension as Paul does.

16. The teaching goes deeper when Jesus explains why casting out a demon—i.e., curing a human being—occupies a key place in God's total plan to bring his reign into human history. Jesus shows that the situation in which he finds human beings is not what it should be. Humanity is oppressed under a power that exercises dominion over it. That will continue until this power, this "strong man," is displaced by another that is even stronger. Then Jesus makes it clear that this is precisely what is happening in his activity because those once possessed are now free, and the mute are recovering their speech. The "strong man" who had been enslaving human beings is being beaten.

There are no indifferent actions or halfway compromises, and this ensures the validity of the historical criterion. And there can be no doubts, precisely because there is no question of identifying *a priori* which of the "strong men" is at work. That is clear from the results, the actions themselves, since the new "strong man" does not enslave people as the former one did. The strength of the newcomer is designed to free human beings, not subject them.

It follows, then, that historical sensitivity, however little it may be religious, must perceive the change. Mark's version clearly implies that the victory of the new "strong man" does really signify human liberation. But the point is even more obvious in Luke's account, which completes the image contained in the Markan source. Luke tells us that the victorious new "strong man" does not seek to subjugate his prey but rather to "divide the plunder" (Luke 11:22). Clearly he is going to divide them with human beings, those who had formerly been despoiled. Sight or speech is restored to the liberated human being.

This basically discredits the pretension of Jesus' opponents. Confronted with the change in the situation of a human being, they attached the most importance to determining who exactly was the "religious" agent behind the change even before examining the change itself and its value for the human being affected by it.

17. If a human being does not repent. Much ink has been spilled trying to determine the curious sin "against the Holy Spirit" that would infallibly lead a human being to final impenitence. Here Jesus is simply pointing out the criterion of divine judgment and its intimate connection with what we do in real life to other human beings. Matthaean and Lucan passages (Matt. 25:31f.; Luke 10:29f.) express a similar point in different terms: i.e., that it is an unpardonable sin in God's eyes to do harm to one's neighbor.

18. Matthew typically takes the opportunity to make Jonah a christological figure and hence to make Jesus the fulfillment of an Old Testament prophecy. As Jonah was in the belly of the whale for three days, so Jesus was three days in the heart of the earth before being resurrected (Matt. 12:40). Was this the sign of Jonah to which Jesus is alluding? The continuation of the argument in Matthew, as well as the parallel text in Luke, proves that it was not. The matter is obvious in any case because Jonah did not point out any such thing to the Ninevites. Yet they saw some sign in him because they were converted by his "preaching." This is even more obvious in the case of the queen of the South and her reaction to Solomon. Not even Matthew can find any way to connect Solomon with Jesus' resurrection or some other central event in his life.

19. Matthew associates what seems to be a new and different request for a sign—and this time he adds "from heaven"—with a charge of hypocrisy that Jesus makes against his opponents (according to Luke too):

> The Pharisees and Sadducees came, and to test him they asked him to show them a sign from heaven. His answer was: "In the evening you say, 'It will be fine weather, for the sky is red.' And in the morning you say, 'It will be stormy today; the sky is red and lowering.' You know how to interpret the sky; can you not interpret the signs of the times? It is a wicked generation that asks for a sign; and the only sign that will be given it is the sign of Jonah." So he went off and left them [Matt. 16:1–4; see Luke 12:14–57].

Here, then, we have another line of argument which leads Jesus to say no once again to a "religiously" based request for "heavenly" criteria to be used in judging historical events. In this case the event in question is the meaning of Jesus himself. Here Jesus argues that it is hypocrisy (Luke's account) or maliciousness (Matthew's account) to seek criteria and guarantees that are surer and more certain than those which suffice for the other affairs of life.

20. It is enough to say that this perspective sheds light on other passages of Mark's Gospel. Mark 2:18–19 is a good example, I think. Fasting for "religious" reasons is inappropriate when one is living through a period of real joy. And the test does not indicate explicitly whether the joyful period in question is "religious" or not.

21. We could make a parallel study of the other synoptic source, which scripture scholars refer to as the Q document. It allegedly contains the *logia*, the scattered sayings and teachings of Jesus. Why talk about Q? For readers not familiar with scriptural exegesis, this source is posited, among other reasons, because the Gospel of Mark is considerably shorter than that of Matthew and Luke. The latter two Gospels also present a fair amount of shared material (e.g., the Beatitudes) that is not con-

tained in Mark. So the assumption is that they had before them another written source about Jesus besides Mark's Gospel.

Now here is what some scholars think the Q document contained insofar as the Beatitudes are concerned:

> Blessed are the poor because theirs is the kingdom of heaven.
> Blessed are those who weep because they will laugh.
> Blessed are the hungry because they will have their fill.

Now, supposing the validity of this source, I would like to point out that we see traces of the same relativization in this version. The people declared blessed are the poor, the hungry, and the weeping. No preference on God's part for people with "religious" qualities is mentioned. Indeed in the Gospel of John (7:49), Jesus takes note of the fact that they are held by the Pharisees in *religious* discredit: "As for this rabble, which cares nothing for the Law, a curse is on them."

God's preference for these people is based on a criterion that any sincere, straightforward person can understand: they are the people most in need of justice and love. This "secular" reason is the one that enables us to determine whom a "faithful" God, in complete harmony with the loving heart of a human being, is going to favor with his reign.

CHAPTER III

Faith—Religion—Dogmas

In this chapter I will continue the close examination of terminology, and of alternative terms to mine, which I began in the previous chapter. I have been trying to show that appropriate terminology helps us to frame problems better even though it does not solve them for us. And even though our more careful use of terms may not have an impact on ordinary language, close study of the content we unwittingly inject into everyday terms should prove beneficial.

Let us sum up where we are. We have been talking about an anthropological dimension that structures the meaning of every human life. Taking note of the radically social character of this dimension, I have called it "faith." In the last chapter I tried to show that the term "trust" would not be a suitable replacement for my word "faith." I also began to deal with the task of showing that the term "religion" is not a satisfactory substitute either. By considering our concrete experience of what is commonly called the "religious" realm and by examining the sources of one of the "world religions" (Christianity), we saw that use of the term "religion" (as an anthropological dimension) raises more serious problems than it solves.

My line of argument presented us with an undeniable fact: i.e., that religion frequently designates a merely instrumental realm which is manipulated by values prior to, and independent of, religion itself. In short, religion designates an "ideological" realm, in the sense that I defined "ideological" in Chapter I. We shall deal more with that point in later chapters (see REMARK A.1, p. 78).

An additional problem with the word "religion," one stressed in many different ways by the gospel message, is that the term "religion" throws a cloak of "sacredness" over this realm of instruments, thereby confusing it with the realm of meaningfulness and serving as one of the most consistent sources of bad faith on the part of human beings. It enables them to evade other values that would call for their attention and responsible action if they looked at reality around them with a heart open to the needs of their fellow humans, i.e., to the principal source of meaning-structures insofar as human beings are concerned.

Since my analysis is being made within the cultural coordinates of what is known as the Christian West, I called attention to the fact that today Christianity frequently presents the very same features which Jesus felt obliged to denounce and which prevented the representatives of the Jewish religion from giving him recognition.

The early Christian community clearly presented a very different face to the world. Under the impact of Jesus' criticisms of "religion," it was so obviously a "lay" structure that Christians were frequently accused of being atheists. Today it is easier for us to say that than to really picture it. But the first Christians avoided applying sacred terms to their meeting places or ceremonies. They also expressly and deliberately used secular appellations for their authorities. They called them "elders," "overseers," and "ministers" whereas their contemporaries referred to their equivalent authorities as "priests" or "pontiffs." [1]

If we today want to picture what Jesus' curious community seemed to be like, we would do better to imagine a community of the Masonic type. His community did not seek to be one more religion, even though it used its own specific symbols, gestures, and ceremonies. In principle, it was open to all cults at the start. Only gradually and indirectly was it driven by its own intrinsic exigencies to part company with other existing religions. And it did so, not to found another new religion, but for the sake of human values that were incompatible with the practices of other existing religions. In the Christian community spontaneous expressions of worship, religious charisms, were strictly subordinated to anything and everything that could benefit fellow members of the community and those outside the community as well.

All this meant that the community was a kind of counterculture. Hence its attitudes were minority attitudes. Its resistance to "religion" was embodied in small groups and entailed great difficulty, even as resistance to consumptionism does today. Very soon however, here and there in the early Church there began to reappear the mass-oriented features that Jesus had criticized in the "religious" mindset of the Jews: e.g., the tendency to seek security in divine laws,[2] the tendency to subordinate the "secular" criteria of love to the incipient ceremonies and authorities of the new community,[3] and the assumption that what is permitted and forbidden can be determined a priori by appealing vertically to heaven.[4] When the Church did acquire or accept mass-oriented dimensions, religious features once again invaded all its language, symbolism, ritual, and morality. That story we know, for it is still ours today.

But the Christian message and its radical criticism of the "religious" could not be completely silenced. In various ways, however fragmentary, it would resurface in every age because Christians continued to read the same gospel message. Serious and sincere efforts would be made to get down to its substance and live its message.

This brings us to the second crucial point of our problem, to which I alluded earlier: the concept or revelation of God as the source of meaning and a values-structure. I said earlier that the ordinary religious realm is "ideological," or instrumental. But if we examine the so-called "universal religions," we see that they always or almost always give rise to a phenomenon that cannot be reduced merely to an instrumental function in the service of pre-established values. In talking about God, in filling this concept with images relative to human life and trying to understand it with complete sincerity, religion too becomes a vehicle of value and meaning to some extent. And this would apply to the Christian religion as well (see REMARK A.2, p. 79).

Even though Jesus did not found a "religion," he did relate everything to God; and this, too, we call *religion*. Jesus was a religious human being if by religion we mean this permanent, disinterested, and deep relationship with God. This use of the word "religion" is just as unavoidable as the first use discussed in the previous chapter, even though it designates phenomena that are less frequently encountered. And since it is so close in content to what I have designated by the word "faith" as an anthropological dimension, we must ask what its exact relationship with my term might be. Is it a faith that is radically different from my "faith," one that is based on witnesses of a qualitatively different order?

I. Misunderstandings about Religious Faith

Right at the start we must preclude a persistent misunderstanding. It is the notion that in naming the God of any religion we are naming the values that structure every human life and that we are doing so directly because God's self-revelation is equivalent to the revelation of the highest values.

Now this particular misunderstanding is fairly well grounded in a terminology that has become commonplace, as I indicated in Chapter I. It has to do with the notion of something unconditioned, or absolute, and the way people tend to equate the Absolute with God.

We saw that faith is the anthropological dimension associated with the overall meaning of life for each human being. In a certain sense that is equivalent to saying that faith, insofar as its content is concerned, is akin to a scale of values; or that it is the basis of such a scale of values. To put it in more concrete existential terms, we can say that a scale of values indicates what price a human being is willing to pay for what he or she esteems and desires. By the same token, it also indicates what price a person is not willing to pay in the realm of mediating factors because that price would sacrifice part of the "unconditioned" sector, the sector that is not up for sale at any price and that cannot be made conditional for the sake of anything else.

Now, as we noted in Chapter I, "unconditioned" and "absolute" are synonyms. In ordinary language, of course, the word "absolute" is used more with reference to decisions than to factual realities. But another notion tends to sneak in here, especially when we try to shift to a more refined, philosophical type of language. We tend uncritically to adopt the old axiom that the order of values and the order of beings are identical. The more something is perfect in being, the more valuable it is. Therefore a conditioned being could not possibly have anything absolute about it. And since the only being whose reality is absolute would be God, the word "absolute" is reserved for divine values when one is trying to speak correctly and strictly. By the same token, it is ruled out for human beings, even though everyday experience shows us that human beings do place absolute value on things or persons they know to be imperfect and perishable.

In short, ordinary educated language has turned "Absolute" and "God" into synonyms. One of the worst mistakes resulting from this equation is the assumption that nonbelievers, people who do not have faith in God—or, to use another common expression, people who do not have faith—are human beings destitute of any absolute. One erroneously imagines that their scale of values will topple as soon as Dame Fortune ceases to smile on them. Why? Because supposedly their scale of values is not attached to anything at its upper extreme.

I indicated that such a view makes no sense at all. One cannot help but admit that every scale of values implies some value that is not conditioned by the rest. One must also admit that possessing a scale of values is a universal anthropological dimension. So one is also forced to admit that something in the decisions of every human being is really absolute and unconditioned in the strict sense.

Now one could argue, as Tracy does, that once human beings perceive the limits to their existence, they somehow pass them and affirm something beyond them. Even if they do not use the word "God," their very lives bear witness, even if only implicitly, that they have an absolute, unconditioned trust in "the worthwhileness of existence, . . . order and value."[5] But what we are trying to find out here is whether and how people reach the "religious" conviction that *this* concrete life and *this* particular order or value justify all the mediations, however painful they may be, which are used to realize them. In other words, the question is: What relationship does the conviction of the absolute value of a *specific* meaning-structure have with God and his revelation (see REMARK B.1, p. 79)?

This formulation of the question necessarily forces us to analyze what takes place when our anthropological "faith," without ceasing to be "faith" and without turning into faith in sets of instruments, becomes *religious* faith in the proper sense. How is a human meaning-structure related to God? To answer this question, we shall first deal with it in negative terms, consulting our experience. Then we shall turn to the Christian sources to deal with it in positive terms.

The Gods behind Values

Insofar as the first approach is concerned—i.e., consulting our real-life experience—our response can go in either one of two directions: (1) a faith is related to God when it abandons human witnesses to entrust the question of values to a divine revelation; or (2) a faith is related to God when it looks at a particular series of human witnesses and sees a certain quality which it attributes to God, whether logically or not.

The first approach is the most common one in the analysis of faith. It has become the classic approach in theology manuals. They state that religious faith, properly so called, consists in setting aside human witnesses to rely on the authority of the revealing or self-revealing God.[6] Here, by contrast, I shall try to show that only the second approach does justice to our experience.

Let me start with this assertion: If "relying on the authority of God" presumes that our meaning-structure *no longer depends on human witnesses*, that it depends solely on what God himself has revealed as worthy of belief, then we must assert that no such faith is to be found ever.

We are forced to admit the following fact: Since God does not enter the bounds of our sense-experience, any revelation by God—be it about values or about the human witnesses who are to be believed as divine messengers— must be perceived and transmitted through human testimony.[7] It is people like ourselves who have lived through certain historical happenings as the "revelation" of God and thereby sought to mark those happenings off from ordinary events. There is no doubt that the disciples of Jesus, insofar as they were able to spell out what they had grasped about him, perceived that Jesus (rather than the religious authorities of Israel, for example) was the vehicle for a revelation about God, about the values that God himself was elevating to the level of the absolute. Despite that fact, or rather precisely because of it, each one of us today must have *faith* in the disciples of Jesus. And we must do so, not just because they were eyewitnesses—i.e., because the concrete events are transmitted to us by them—but also because it was their evaluational judgment of those events that is a decisive element insofar as "faith" vis-à-vis Jesus is concerned.

Let us consider an imaginary case and strip it down to its minimal components. Let us assume at the start that Jesus said that he was God himself made human, hence a directly divine revelation. Let us further assume that we ourselves, thanks to better techniques than those now available to us, could see and hear Jesus directly as he was—without the intermediaries who interpreted him and then described him in speech and writing. What does the gospel message itself say about our possibilities for accepting this "revelation" and defining our values by it? It tells us precisely what we have just seen in the previous chapter: that Jesus was recognized as the revelation of God only by those people who *already* had those values.

Let no one think that this assertion is something odd and unheard-of. This aspect of our experience is so well known that it has become a Gordian knot in every theological treatise on faith. The fact is that faith must be a rational act—or a reasonable act, if you prefer—rather than a blind decision of will. Moreover, Jesus' own arguments to prove that he was God's envoy were obviously meant to give rational grounding for faith in him since he himself made it clear that they made his listeners responsible. Herein lies the issue for theology. If Jesus himself refused to give signs from heaven, then God himself had to decide for whom Jesus' arguments or signs were really that and for whom they were not. In other words, the gratuitousness of faith consisted in the fact that God gave some people the "eyes of faith" to consider the signs or arguments of Jesus, to perceive their importance, and to accept the force of such proofs. To be quite logical then, we must say that faith had to precede faith.

This leads us inescapably to the same conclusion that we had already arrived at: i.e., that the values upheld by human beings enabled them to see in Jesus the revelation *of a God* who in effect declared those very same values to be his own divine, absolute values (see REMARK B.2, p.79).

Thus we must say the same thing about supposedly "revelatory" historical events that we said about a more general issue. Both then and now, believing "in God" has been of little importance because the problem of religious faith does not lie in accepting or denying God's existence—or, if you prefer, God's *presence* at this or that point in history. The problem lies—if I may be permitted to put it this way—in *being in agreement with God*. In the face of some potential revelation, the first valid question is not whether *God* is present or not, but rather *what* God could be present there and whether that is acceptable or not.

Nicholas Berdyaev once made the pointed observation that the problem of God did not consist so much in establishing God's existence as in "justifying it," by which he meant judging it before the tribunal of our values.[8]

Further on I shall consider that question in terms of the God of the Gospels. Right now we are examining it in terms of our own experience. And we shall see that Berdyaev is right. We have a hard time freeing ourselves from the spurious logic which tells us that we must first determine whether something exists or is present before we can pass judgment on it. In this particular case at least, we shall see that such logic is totally fallacious.

The existence of those beings who populate our sense experience, be it helpful or harmful, clearly forces itself upon us as a *datum*. Such is not the case when a *line of reasoning,* one that is not merely tautological, forces us to admit some reality beyond the bounds of any possible experiential verification. In the latter case we know that a risk is involved in our reasoning. Will our reasonings be valid once they have crossed beyond the boundaries of their natural application to the sense realm? Once such a risk is there, once we are not compelled to admit something on the basis of experience itself, or of experience aided by reason, then we are forced to consider whether the risk is "worthwhile." Thus, even on the level of *cognition*, the order of *values* becomes a determining factor vis-à-vis the realm of data. With a great deal of reasonableness we will accept certain arguments because they tend to confirm, deepen, and expand our own values.

Just as we tend to bypass some "insignificant" person as if we did not see him or her, so we do not stop to ponder arguments designed to prove the existence of God so long as we picture God as opposed to our values. The supposition that we first accept God and then ask God what values we are to cultivate is nothing but an absurd cliché. We have been conned into believing that by an objectivist and objectified philosophy which, as we noted earlier, maintains that the order of values coincides with the order of beings; that the former go hand in hand with the greatness, power, and perfection of the latter. Even the most minimal spiritual experience gives the lie to any such idea.

That being the case, there will be as many *gods* as there are values structures among human beings. So what decisive importance is there in arriving at a "religious" level, if the latter term evokes nothing more than a false generality? Isn't that as vague as saying that every human being has his or her own values-system and meaning-structure and that some value in it is an unconditioned one which conditions all the others?

The Heterodoxy of Believers

This relativization of the alternative between religion and atheism is crystal clear in such ecclesiastical passages as section 19 of Vatican II's Pastoral Constitution *Gaudium et spes*. I am not citing it here because it is a statement by the Roman Catholic magisterium. I cite it here because it is one more example, from a noteworthy source, of the same sort of analysis of atheism that I have been presenting here:

> Hence believers can have more than a little to do with the birth of atheism. To the extent that they neglect their own training in the faith, or teach erroneous doctrine, or are deficient in their religious, moral, or social life, they must be said to conceal rather than reveal the authentic face of God and religion.[9]

The first thing that strikes our attention in this passage is the fact that never has the official Church so frankly acknowledged the social character involved in the acceptance of God. Traditional apologetics seemed to assume that each individual, when confronted with certain arguments, would or would not arrive at the conclusion that God did indeed exist and that he had been revealed in certain events or through certain messengers in human history. In the above passage from *Gaudium et spes*, however, it is clear that human beings share responsibility *in common* for the "god" they convey to others. Otherwise, why would doctrinal errors and the conduct of Christians "have more than a little to do with the birth of atheism"?

The assumption in the conciliar text, unheard-of in earlier days, is that Christians, even in their efforts to propagate their faith, are *responsible* for the denial of God on the sociological level—as if to say that those around them did not have a more expeditious way to fashion an idea of God for themselves, that nonbelievers on their own could not use the dictionary or whatever to arrive at a clear and satisfactory idea of what was meant by the word "God" spoken by Christians.

A second point in the conciliar text is also worth noting. It seems that the authentic face of God can be concealed, and God himself rejected, because believers "are deficient in their religious, moral, or social life." Notice the underlying supposition: even though believers may use correct definitions that enable other human beings to identify God in the order of beings, it is the order of values that ultimately decides whether God is or is not to be rejected.

Now if we connect the two above points we find that the social responsibility for atheism lies in the fact that there are as many "gods" or "idols" as there are values-systems embodied in the conduct of human beings. Two people may recite the same creed and yet, through their significantly opposite lines of conduct, get across to other people the correct idea that they are hearkening back to different deities. Why? Because in naming "God," a values-structure does it much more clearly and radically than any conceptual content does. On the plane of beings, and indeed in our dictionaries, we may get beyond polytheism by using one noun ("God") for all the divine appellations, but the plurality of deities still surfaces in all its radical decisiveness on the plane of values. That is why, as the conciliar passage tells us, the "god" rejected by nonbelievers is often not the genuine God.

There is a third point worth noting in the conciliar text. Without saying so explicitly, the conciliar passage assumes that when it comes to accepting or rejecting God, the ultimate, decisive court of appeal is a set of pre-existing values. It is not God who tells neutral observers what values they are to cultivate. If that were the case, then Christian conduct would not force anyone to reject God, no matter how wrongheaded such conduct might be. But the point is, as the conciliar text implies, that the values already cultivated by sincere Christians are what decide whether the god about which Christians speak in their actions is a false deity or the true God.

Looking at the conciliar text, we simply cannot evade the following question: Is it possible that Christians, despite their wrongheaded religious, moral, and social conduct, *believe in the true God?* Is it possible that they still have a clear and correct picture of God, even though they conceal his face from others? The logical and obvious answer, disconcerting as it may be, is *no.*

Christians, of course, are only human, and so their conduct will not always be positively in line with the values they associate with their God. In such cases there still is the possibility of repentance, which is a critical part of human conduct and which, in many different observable ways, also gives expression to the values we are seeking to cultivate. It re-establishes the coherence between conduct and values that had been lost.

But our "no" answer to the above question is still disconcerting, for when the cause of atheism is attributed to the conduct of Christians—as it is in the conciliar text—the assumption is that these Christians have remained loyal to the orthodox creed as it finds expression in suitable formulas. After all, no one would worry about the future of belief in God if counterproductive lines of conduct could be clearly identified with religious heterodoxy.[10]

There is a fourth point in the conciliar text which might seem to contradict the preceding remarks at first glance. The conciliar text implies that Christians, in carrying out the social side of their religious responsibilities, possess criteria in their own religious faith which will enable them to discover and implement the values that are consistent with the true God. In other words, Christians are not supposed to operate with some principle of "methodic doubt." It is not as if they, like non-Christians, must base their witness solely on their own moral sincerity.

So suggests the conciliar document. But why should that be the case? I shall try to answer that question in Section II of this chapter. I shall try to show that this fourth point leads us to the second approach mentioned on page 64. I shall also try to show that the fourth point when combined with the three preceding comments on the conciliar document, demolishes the first approach discussed above as a way of handling our problem (see REMARK B.3, p. 80).

The God of Metaphysics

Before we proceed to Section II, however, I would like once again to consider some observations made by David Tracy in *Blessed Rage for Order*. Readers will recall that Tracy proposed to invest the term "religion" with a basic anthropological dimension. In my last chapter I tried to bring out the first problem entailed in that approach, to show why my term "faith" should not be replaced by Tracy's term "religion." The problem is that the term "religion," in its ordinary sociological sense, tends to designate a realm of instruments, a realm that is "ideological" in my sense of that word; this particular realm of instruments is especially dangerous, according to Jesus, because of the absolute, sacred overtones that tend to cluster around it.

In this chapter I began by tackling the issue from a different standpoint, examining another possible meaning of the term "religion." In this case "religion" referred to the same thing that my anthropological term "faith" did: i.e., to the specification of a set of values. But then we saw that "religion," when used in that sense, was a false generalization. With its reference to a God, it was nothing more than a linguistic trap. For when religion can rightly be viewed as a cause of atheism, it is obvious that many misunderstandings have been allowed to crop up along the way.

Doesn't Tracy take this into account? In my opinion, the trajectory of his thinking in *Blessed Rage for Order* is instructive on this point. It will, in fact, confirm what we have just been talking about.

First of all, we note that Tracy, strictly speaking, does not carry his argument about "religion" being a synonym for "fundamental faith" beyond the bounds of the Christian religion. That in itself bodes ill for a supposedly universal anthropological dimension, of course. But the point here is that Tracy thinks that his use of terminology will fit the Christian religion at least. Here is what he says about the word "God": "Given the prior analysis of religious language and experience, it seems fair to conclude that, for the

Christian religion at least, the word "God" has a primary use or function to refer to the objective ground in reality itself for those limit-experiences of a final confidence and trust disclosed in Christian God-language."[11]

But even this limited affirmation has its price. For it assumes that the term "God" possesses the same content within the confines of the Christian religion "at least." Nothing could be more open to question, however. As we saw in our analysis of the passage in *Gaudium et spes*, this unity of content does not at all dovetail with concrete experience.

We should not be surprised to find that this statement by Tracy comes in a chapter entitled: "The Question of God: Metaphysics Revisited."[12] For the fact is that only *metaphysics*, not Christian theology or Christian experience, can achieve conceptual unity where an irreducible plurality exists. I do not wish to pass judgment on the possibility of metaphysics here. But I would point out that all the definitions of God we find in dictionaries are metaphysical ones and that those very definitions are the basis of the misunderstanding which prevents us from detecting, among other things, one of the major sources of atheism.

Tracy does not completely overlook this fact, since he advocates a *new* metaphysics: "A new set of metaphysical categories was developed to replace those of classical rationalisms, empiricisms, and transcendental methods. A firm grasp of those central categories is crucial for any understanding of the new theism."[13] Presumably it is also crucial for understanding the way Tracy uses the term "religion." For on that depends the assertion that we can give oneness of meaning, within Christianity at least, to the term "God."

Supporting the view I upheld above, Tracy also shows how a central assertion of the Christian message—i.e., that God is love—was systematically reduced to naught in theological thought and the average Christian mentality by the various versions of traditional metaphysics. The latter always ended up conceiving the perfection of a being in terms of self-sufficiency and hence of immutability and inaccessibility.

With the new metaphysical categories endorsed by Tracy, both the Protestant and the Catholic traditions "could find articulate and coherent conceptual expression through a metaphysics whose crowning exemplification is precisely an eminently social, temporal, related—in a word, loving—God."[14]

Please allow me to make a few remarks about such results, while leaving aside the question of metaphysics itself and its use. My main point would be the uselessness of employing metaphysics *here*. There is no point in revisiting metaphysics to talk about God when we possess an equally symbolic language that has already been articulated by Christian revelation. Indeed that language has been reformulated in countless different ways, and it has likewise been contradicted in countless different ways by patterns of conduct claiming to be Christian.

The only advantage in a recourse to metaphysics would be to be able to make use of some general concept of God and hence of religion. But what do we find in Tracy's case? At the end of his experiment he has left aside the pagan concept of God, that of non-Christian religions, and even the classical concept of God in both Protestant and Catholic theology. To remain faithful to his own logic, he must reject as inconsistent the concepts of God that come from classical forms of metaphysics and their derived theologies. Why, when all is said and done, does one opt for Tracy's "loving God"? Because one is a sincerely good human being, or because one finds in the First Letter of John that " God is love"? In either case we see clearly how useless and prejudicial it is to use the term "religion" as a substitute for the universal anthropological dimension that I have chosen to call "faith." The false generality of the term "religion," insofar as it claims to be an anthropological dimension, has been made clear through our analysis of the false generality of the term "God" vis-à-vis the decisive realm of meaningfulness (see REMARK B.4, p. 81).

If I feel that so far the term "faith" seems to be the most suitable designation for a concrete anthropological dimension, it is because even so-called "religious faith" must allow itself to be judged by that dimension insofar as value is concerned.

But I said above that there might be another approach whereby a "religious faith" could become a source of values: i.e., pass judgment on the latter somehow. We shall consider that approach in Section II and see where it leads us.

II. The Two Elements of Religious Faith

When does a concrete faith in human witnesses become "religious" faith in the strict sense?

In the previous section we saw the problems connected with the classical answer to that question. The classical answer was that religious faith begins when faith based on human witnesses moves on to find support solely in the witness and authority of God. The reasons proffered in Section I of this chapter have hopefully made it clear that any such claim is belied by experience.

I tried to show what happened when one *claimed* to believe in the testimony of a revealing God but, in fact, continued to make one's own values the decisive court of appeal for accepting or rejecting any such "revelation." So we are left with the main question: When I say that I believe in a divine revelation, does my statement have no meaning whatsoever? Or are there authentic cases of "religious" faith? If there are, what goes to make up this specific "faith" that is different from "faith" as a general, anthropological dimension?

The Message of Jesus as an Example

Here again I think we would do well to introduce an example from the same source that revealed the antireligious polemic of Jesus to us: i.e. Mark's Gospel. According to that Gospel, at the start of his public ministry Jesus addressed the following message to the crowds in Galilee: "The time has come;

the kingdom of God is upon you; repent, and believe the Gospel'' (Mark 1:15).

We will take this simply as an example of the way in which a ''faith'' in the broadest human sense becomes ''religious'' faith and specifies basic values in the person who accepts it. Let us see what really happens in such a case.

First of all, it is obvious that Jesus is appealing to a religious faith and that the latter does not constitute a mere set of instruments. He mentions God, and the faith demanded by him is connected with the proximity of the supreme religious event: i.e., the establishment of the divine will on earth. It is nothing less than the answer to the appeal: ''Thy kingdom come, thy will be done on earth'' (Matt. 6:10).

Secondly, the assumption is that this faith, with its religious content, should alter, and in some radical way, the scale of values of those who listen to his preaching. That is the precise meaning of the Greek word *metanoia*, which is normally translated as ''conversion.'' The term ''conversion'' will occupy our attention further on, again on the same basic anthropological plane, because it, like the word ''faith,'' is not exclusively confined to the realm of religious terminology. In any case the point here is that the correct translation of *metanoia* is ''change of mind,'' of criteria and values. Thus it directly and explicitly alludes to a change in meaning-structure, in ''faith'' as I have been using the term. It is perfectly clear that the evangelists understand it in that sense. We can see that in the explanation which both Jesus and John the Baptist give to *metanoia* on the plane of moral criteria and attitudes. Paul and his school are just as clear on this point. In talking about ''conversion,'' the Pauline writers use the radical image of the ''old man'' who must die to make room for the ''new man.'' According to the Letter to the Ephesians, that means a fresh spiritual way of thinking, a renewal of the mind (see Eph. 4:23; 4:17ff.). Attitudes that were once judged positively must now be regarded as negative things, and vice versa (see Eph. 4:28).

These first two elements are crystal clear. They show that the authors of the New Testament were certain that the preaching of Jesus was a summons to a religious faith in the fullest sense of the word: i.e., a faith as the source of a (new) meaning-structure.

But there is something curious about this which we do not often think about even though we should. If the biblical texts are a faithful summary of the preaching of Jesus and John the Baptist, it seems at first glance that something is missing in that preaching. No sort of reason or argument is offered to induce that faith, even though the faith in question is supposed to do nothing less than transform the meaning-structure of people's lives.

Closer analysis, however, will show that this is not the case. For implicitly but clearly we find two converging lines of argument in the three phrases: ''The time has come, the kingdom of God is upon you; . . . believe the Gospel.'' When it comes to faith, of course, one should not expect a logical demonstration, but neither can one call for an act of blind submission, as we shall see.

To put it briefly, the two converging lines of argument are constituted:

(1) by certain facts that are decisive for pre-existing values; hence the reference to a gospel, a piece of "good news" having to do with the nearness of an event; and (2) by an appeal to a unified and somehow identified series of previous witnesses; hence the mention of the "kingdom of God" and the time being close. Let us consider each of these two points.

Jesus makes clear that the news he is proclaiming, the news of the nearness of God's reign, is a "gospel," a piece of "good" news. Then, completely in line with what we saw earlier, he appeals to values pre-existing in his listeners. Only vis-à-vis the latter can a piece of news, however divine it may claim to be, be declared "good." After all, the nearness of the kingdom could hardly be regarded as good news by those whom Jesus said would be made wretched by it: "Alas for you who are rich . . . who are well fed now . . . who laugh now" (Luke 6:24-25).

Yet the strange thing is that we are still faced with an antinomy because those who have "faith" in the news as a "good" must still undergo conversion. There must be a change in their meaning-structure, in their attitude. So we seem to be faced with two curious alternatives. If, on the other hand, the news is supposed to be regarded as something *good in itself* vis-à-vis the already existing values of human beings—because that judgment comes from God, let's say—then that would invert the order of criteria to which we saw Jesus appealing.

The only logical escape from this antinomy lies in assuming that we human beings have an eye for more than one scale of values, even though one of them does in fact rule our actions. Such in fact is the case, as experience will confirm.

I noted earlier that the best way to define a scale of values lies in the question which we often ask ourselves and which we always answer somehow in our activity: i.e., is this worthwhile? To make it specific: is it worth trying to earn more and more money if that means I must give up all chance of enjoying a normal family life?

I also said earlier, and I still maintain it here, that our answer to such a question comes from a comparison of values. But this does not operate in abstract terms; it is done within the economy of energy that governs every human life. In this case, for example, one would compare the concrete benefits of money with the concrete benefits of a normal family life.

Transcendent Data

It should be clear, however, that we have merely touched the surface of the issue. Declaring one value to be superior to another is not an arbitrary, subjective matter of mere preferences. Nor would the experiences of other people suffice to resolve the question. Knowing whether some specific value is worthwhile or not will depend on what could be called *transcendent data*. To put it another way: just as we cannot enjoy direct experience of the satisfaction a given value can provide once it has been realized to the ultimate limits of human possibilities, so neither can direct experience provide the data required to complete the comparison between values about which I have just been talking. And yet what may happen beyond verifiable experience will be decisive for that comparison.

So Jesus' preaching assumes that many of his listeners would be inclined to change their behavior completely if they could really believe in this datum: i.e., that the kingdom of God is at hand. If, on the other hand, the arrival of the kingdom were to be estimated in terms of Greek calends (i.e., a time that will never come), then Jesus would know perfectly well that a different scale of values would strike people as more reasonable and satisfactory.

Thus Jesus offers a "reason" why a different meaning-structure should come to the forefront and replace the prevailing one in his listeners' minds. This other meaning-structure is already present in his listeners even though it is not the dominant one; it is attractive to them but held under wraps by other considerations. Thus, in terms of the hypothesis he evokes, "good news" and "conversion" are not incompatible.

The fact is that every human being possesses a store of "utopias." They are meaning-structures that would come to occupy first place *if* reality were not what it is or seems to be. But here again we must remember that the total possibilities of reality exceed the limits of direct experience and verification.

I call such data "transcendent" because they do in fact transcend all concrete experience. They are not destined to fill out experience from within or to be accepted as data where gaps in scientific knowledge exist. And yet they are decisive for the acceptance or rejection of specific values because they have to do with the possibilities for satisfaction which those values can or cannot provide.

I should add here that the message of Jesus furnishes a multitude of such data, at least as his disciples saw it. The fact that God is love, for example, makes certain things rather than others *worthwhile* (1 John 4:11–20). The fact that the Father raised Jesus from the dead also makes certain things worthwhile. It would be foolish to maintain that particular meaning-structure if the "datum" were wrong. As Paul put it, we would be "of all men most to be pitied" (1 Cor. 15:19). The fact that the Christian God shows no favoritism means that we should not show partiality (James 2:1–9). This point, too, means that certain values are worthwhile while other values contradict the *presuppositions* of the Christian faith. Numerous other examples could be cited here.

Now before I move on to the second element required for a simply human faith to be "religious" faith, let us make sure that we have a firm hold on some of the central points connected with the first element we have just been examining.

The first point is that on the human level values are not chosen or preferred unless some noninstrumental conception is part of that decision. In this case the conception has to do with the ultimate possibilities (or limits) of the universe and the human being. In that sense every values-structure contains at least one transcendent datum.[15]

The second point is that no scientific reasons exist for or against those limit-possibilities. By their very nature they escape experimental verification. If they are consistent in themselves, science can only say that they lie outside its field of action and its critieria.

The third point is that, despite the above, language not only can but must use some such expression as "data"; otherwise an area that is decisive for values-structures would lack adequate means of expression and communication. The fact that these special "data" have been unduly mixed up with data derived from observation or scientific calculations, especially in past ages, should not lead us to reject a consistent and necessary idiom.

The fourth point is that the faith which embraces those transcendent data does not in any way belie the primacy of the human valuational criteria pre-existing in the person who believes. Anthropological faith is not displaced. Only by building on the latter can we develop faith in the transcendent data. Thus it still remains irrelevant whether this faith is accepted explicitly or not, whether we consciously cross this overall limit of experience. Much more decisive is the matter of determining what values or what meaning-structure those transcendent data support, correct, develop, or deepen. What matters is their potential contribution to basic anthropological faith (see REMARK C.1, p. 81).

A Tradition Composed of Witnesses

These four points should make it clear that it would be premature and confusing to call an anthropological faith "religious" simply because it contains transcendent data. My earlier arguments against Tracy's terminology hold true here also. Besides transcendent data, another element must be added to make faith "religious."

Faith is indispensable on the human level. Now as such a faith becomes adult, it runs against the *complexity* of existence (as well as ultimate limits). To that extent human beings are obliged not to go beyond faith on the human level (which is impossible to do) but to construct a synthesis of faith with the witness of different persons who have solved all sorts of different problems by appealing to a certain identicality of meaning-structure.

An example may help to make this clearer. In a particular meaning-structure, money—how to make it, save it, and spend it—can and must hold an important place. Many other values, however superior they may be, depend for their realization on the attitude which one has towards this means or subordinate value that occupies so much of the available time and energy in one's life. Now let us assume that a child's attention to his father is focused on the seriousness (combined of course with the satisfaction, without which no value appears as such) with which his father procures the money needed for family expenses. If the family happens to be middle-class, it is likely that a new problem will arise for the boy during adolescence, a period of unproductive expenses. He may well wonder whether the father's satisfaction in contributing money to the family really solves this new problem of seeming waste. What, after all, is the sense of spending money to satisfy people who cannot reimburse the sums used up on them over a long period of time?

At a later stage it is likely that his father's use of money will be examined from still another angle: i.e., that of providing for the future, when earning power will greatly diminish or cease altogether. In other words, saving will begin to be a relevant point in the faith the boy has placed in his father's values, at least in the particular aspect we are examining.

Now we could complicate the example in all sorts of ways. We could imagine that the boy easily appreciated the seriousness his father showed in earning, using, and saving money during a period of relative economic stability; but later the boy himself must do the same things in a period of economic recession. Will his *faith* disappear then?

In other words, the more a person grows in every sense, the more and more clearly he or she perceives that a given attitude towards some value never constitutes the best solution once and for all vis-à-vis the problem at hand. If his or her faith is to persist, it must increasingly be based on the *creative ability* to solve many problems, in line with the growing complexity of the reality with which he or she must deal. As reality and its unforeseeable twists and turns increasingly relativize every attempt to give ready-made, conclusive solutions to the problem of one's values,[16] one sees the growing importance of having faith in people who have *learned how to learn* as they lived their lives and moved from one problem to the next. Thus the ability to make a mistake, which destroys an infantile faith, becomes almost a prerequisite for continuing to have faith in someone when a person is going through a more mature stage in life. We put our human "faith" in people who have managed to maintain certain values, ones basically similar to ours, by learning how to achieve them despite change, uncertainty, and failure.

Moreover, at that stage in life it will normally no longer be possible for one single person to serve as the basis or trustee of our own "faith." We know that even the most perfect human being is limited, even if only by virtue of the circumstances in which he or she has to live. However rightly and creatively that person may have lived, he or she was forced to set aside problems that were alien to his or her own culture, age, and personal abilities.

Jesus was no exception to this rule. This helps to explain the clearly odd fact that the Christian community accepted the Old Testament as a revelation of *the very same God* who was revealed in the New Testament as God's own Word, according to the Gospel of John. The fact is that Jesus did not confront the problems and tasks of such figures as Moses, David, and Isaiah. And obviously he did not confront the problems and tasks facing a Christian today. Hence Jesus did not present himself as the *one solitary* revelation of God, his Father.

In reality Jesus identified himself with a "tradition," a specific history. It entailed a long series of referential witnesses to certain values, a process involving defeats, victories, and retreats.[17] Jesus made clear his continuity with a group of human beings who were deeply united in their anthropological "faith" and who found support in each other for the task of *learning how to learn*.

When Jesus proclaimed that the time was close at hand and the kingdom near, he felt he was giving a "reason" for the faith to which he was appealing. But his reason was not a demonstration. The reason would be seen only by those who already shared to some extent the values-structure in which the kingdom of God was associated with a piece of good news, a gospel. And it also presupposed that the listeners were capable of grasping those "transcendent data," thanks to their upbringing in the religious tradition of Israel.

It should also be noted that we are dealing here with a *tradition*, not with what is commonly called a "school" of thought. And here again we find that the defining factor is not the "divine" nature of what is being transmitted but rather the importance of the witnesses. In a school of thought it is the logic of the new arguments that is the defining factor. In a tradition the critical factor is to be found in the living experiences that teach people how to learn. A Kantian, for example, would accept Fichte or reject him on the basis of the cogency of Fichte's arguments; that is a clear sign that we are dealing with a school of thought. Christians, on the other hand, must somehow make their own the experience of Ecclesiastes and Deutero-Isaiah in order to be able to learn from the "revelation" made in Jesus Christ; that is a clear sign that we are dealing with a tradition. And what applies to the witnesses in the biblical past applies equally well to the witnesses of church tradition, of the new Israel that keeps on learning how to learn.

Here then we have the second element which, combined with *transcendent data*, transforms anthropological faith into authentic *religious* faith. The latter is a faith which defines values, not because those values are suddenly revealed to human beings who have been without them up to that point, but because this faith constitutes a system of learning-apprenticeship transmitted by historical witnesses which enables people to recognize and discern genuine transcendent data; and those data, in turn, become defining factors of people's meaning-structures (see REMARK C.2, p. 82).

The Role of Dogmas

The merit of the label "religion" is not the only issue that surfaces from the above discussion. Another issue is the importance of the specific *dogmas* that are associated with a religious tradition, as well as the whole matter of their history and development.

From the time when the Bible was written to our own day, dogmas represent the transcendent data recognized by that tradition. They are not mysterious things in which we must believe as a matter of course; nor are they fixed formulas which, rendered universal by a sudden act of the magisterium, resolve certain problems once and for all and thus do away with exploration into certain areas.[18]

Properly understood, dogmas are symbols of the world of values, of a world that is clearly in movement. They are symbols of a world engaged in a learning process, and hence they stand in opposition to any religion that is nothing but a set of instruments. Dogmas are intelligible only in the framework of values which pre-exist the religious realm, and dogmas, in turn, constitute data that are decisive for such values and their realization. They relativize the mere fact of something being "religious" or not. But they also are a far cry from any sort of metaphysics or from any organized body of concepts referring to objects which lie beyond any possible experience and which, therefore, would possess *cognitive consistency independent of the realm of values and immune from history*.

Here it will suffice to mention two examples of how dogmas evolve over time. Firstly, the importance of the truth revealed by God, and hence of belonging to the tradition which serves as its vehicle, gave rise to the famous expression: "No salvation outside the Church." How did this expression undergo development? In the same way that it arose in the first place: i.e., as an expression of values, not as the result of reasoning based on some fragmentary biblical passage. But consider what may happen if we look at the Christian message from the standpoint of the realm of values. If we do that, we may well see that the Christian message is living witness to the satisfaction one may find in joining the poorest, the most helpless, and the most oppressed. In that case the logic of *Christian* values may lead us to reject what we see to be a community of privileged beings. We may even go so far as to reject a God who seems to confer such privileges quite independently of the good will of the people involved. Simone Weil is a celebrated example of someone who took the first step,[19] and millions of other unknown people have carried that logic through the second step.

Thus the rectification of this apparent "datum," of this "dogma," is not due to the discovery of some new biblical or metaphysical argument unknown to our forefathers, to the work of some theological school. It is due to a "conversion." By virtue of such conversion believers cease to be dominated by the hardness of heart denounced by Jesus, and thus they are freer to immerse themselves more truly in the "tradition" to which they belong.

I shall only mention the second example. In the realm of dogma it was once claimed that the eternal misery of the damned in hell was compatible with the perfect happiness of the elect in heaven and even with the perfect happiness of God. In the realm of Christian values, on the other hand, insensitivity to the sufferings of others has been regarded, in principle, as a sin. In fact, Jesus himself traced it back to "religious" roots (see the parable of the good Samaritan and the wicked religious functionaries in Luke 10:29–37). Now thanks to a certain type of metaphysical ratiocination, people claimed to have arrived at the conclusion that at the very moment when human beings of good will received their definitive perfection, the latter would consist in the very thing which, during their whole earthly life, had constituted the antivalue *par excellence*: i.e., not loving others, not sharing their lives, not feeling and heeding their needs (see REMARK D, p. 83).

Summary

I hope that my comments in this and the previous chapter have brought out the suitability of the terminology adopted in Chapter I. Quite apart from the issue of terminology, I hope they have helped to specify and clarify the realities under discussion.

Insofar as terminology is concerned, I hope I have made clear the misunderstandings and inconveniences which can arise if such terms as "trust" or "religion" are used to replace my term "faith." I have been particularly concerned about the improper use of the term "religion" as a substitute. As we saw, in most cases our ordinary use of the term "religion," far from being identical with my anthropological "faith," refers to a realm of instruments. And there is the added problem that the sacral character of those particular instruments tends to close human beings off from the realm where questions of "faith" arise, and to induce "bad faith" in them when it comes to determining their values.

In certain instances, to be sure, anthropological "faith" can retain its proper character and still move on to become an authentically religious faith. In those instances no importance can be attached to giving assent to some purely divine testimony. The important thing is people's adherence to a specific tradition and the resultant acquisition of transcendent data that are decisive for the realization of certain values established by basic anthropological faith.

Only a religious faith of the latter type will be able to dialogue with ideologies.

Remarks

REMARK A.1 (see p. 60). We are still with the problem of possible substitute terms for my term "faith" as an anthropological dimension. In the last chapter I tried to show why Tracy's term "religion" was unsatisfactory. The first and most common use of the term refers to an "ideological" realm, a realm of instruments, rather than a realm of structured values held by a particular human being (which is what I mean by anthropological "faith"). But the term "religion" is also not satisfactory in the specific sense that Tracy uses it: i.e., as referring to the fact that every human being seeks values *as if* existence had no limits.

Insofar as "ideology" is concerned, I would like to remind my readers again of the distinction I made in Chapter I. "Faith" in referential witnesses to different satisfactions (related to different possible goals in life) gives structure to a realm of values *in themselves* in the life of each human being. "Ideology," on the other hand, refers to the objective realm of efficacy in the service of those values. In short, it is a realm of "hypothetical" value; its value is relative to that of the values which each human being seeks to realize.

This chapter will examine a second possible meaning of the term "religion," suggested by the attitude of Jesus himself. In this case, which is not the common one, religion designates an anthropological faith which becomes "religious" faith through revelation but which still continues to perform the basic function structuring a realm of values *in themselves* for every human life. And I have already indicated that in principle this possible meaning of the term "religion" also does not coincide with the meaning proposed by Tracy which we examined in Chapter II.

REMARK A.2 (see p. 62). The rest of this introductory section tries to support my contention that there can be an authentically "religious" faith which is in continuity with anthropological faith and has a defining impact on values. I try to show that the early Christian church, and even a portion of the church after it had been sociologically implanted in Western Christendom, was sensitively aware of Jesus' antireligious polemics without ceasing to be "religious," even as he was, in a particular sense. In this particular sense "religious" does refer to the realm of *meaning* rather than *efficacy*. That is the point we shall explore in this chapter.

REMARK B.1 (see p. 63). I begin with the *negative* side of the issue: what I do not mean by "religious" faith here. I try to show that people commonly establish a false relationship between religious faith (or religion) and anthropological faith. In particular, two misunderstandings seem to be at work here.

The *first misunderstanding* derives from language. There is no doubt that anthropological faith points to the absolute *for each and every human being*. By the same token, the God of the religion professed by a human being *is* the *Absolute*. If God were not the Absolute Being, the name "God" would not be applied to him.

Here we see that people equate as identical two things which are, strictly speaking, very distinct. The misunderstanding comes from confusing and identifying *absolute value* (i.e., a value that is unconditioned and above all others) with the *Absolute Being* (i.e., a perfect being who is independent of every other being by his very nature). The confusion is evident in the fact that people with very different absolute values can refer in their religious talk to the same Absolute Being (God) who is identified as creator, lawgiver, providence, and so forth.

It should be obvious, then, that a person's religion—even when it contains a definition or description of the Absolute Being—does not suffice to enable me to identify the absolute values which that particular person has set up for his or her life.

REMARK B.2 (see p. 65). The *second misunderstanding* derives from a theological presupposition. It is the assumption that anthropological faith becomes religious faith when it moves on from human witnesses to find its complete support in the witness and authority of God himself. I put forward three arguments to show that this conception of religious faith (as a determining influence on the realm of values) is totally unreal. Argument 1 is summarized in this section. Arguments 2 and 3 are given in the next two REMARKS (B.3 and B.4).

Argument 1 is based on the impossibility of arriving at any *purely* divine testimony that would spare us the task of basing our faith on the values of human referential witnesses. In the last chapter we saw that Jesus himself made authentic faith in him conditional on pre-existing human values and that those values could come only from the referential witnesses with whom one lived in history. The very fact that God has revealed himself to us is conveyed to us by human persons, whom we believe or don't believe on the basis of their values. Moreover, if a human witness to some event is to be able to identify that event in history as a "revelation from God," then he or she must bring his or her own values into play in order to be able to interpret what has taken place.

REMARK B.3 (see p. 68). *Argument 2* comes from the mental realm where problems about God are located, starting right with the problem of God's existence. Since this realm lies completely beyond any possibility of empirical verification, the lines of reasoning which guide us in that realm entail a great deal of uncertainty. This does not mean that they are invalid; it simply means that it is not logical necessity which leads us to follow them and accept their results. Thus the decisive factor in accepting or rejecting the validity of arguments about the existence of God will be the values represented by God. That is what experience tells us and what Jesus indirectly shows us in his polemics.

The interesting thing is that the Church itself implicitly admits this when it examines the case of atheism in *Gaudium et spes* (n. 19). Let me sum up the relevant points:

a. The conciliar document affirms the social character of our access to God. It says that human beings, by virtue of their way of living, are responsible for people's acceptance or rejection of God. If the arguments were sufficient in themselves, such a responsibility would not exist.

b. It affirms that a notion about God can be so falsified or obscured by the way of life of someone who acknowledges and invokes God that God ought to be denied. Why? Because despite the orthodoxy of the person who affirms God, the latter has in fact been turned into an idol.

c. This assumes that the question of God's existence must be decided by values which pre-exist rather than follow upon the acceptance of God.

d. Despite the three previous points, the conciliar text also assumes, as do the Gospels, that there ought to be some way in which faith in God (i.e., religious faith) not only confirms pre-existing values but somehow corrects or defines them as well. That is my guiding hypothesis here, which I examine in Section II of this chapter in more positive terms.

Here I would simply like to reiterate my point with regard to the negative side of the issue. Both the conciliar text and Jesus' polemics make it clear what does not constitute authentically religious faith. Faith does not become authentically religious because it refuses to "pass judgment" on God on the basis of some pre-established criterion of value and moves on to accept only those values and criteria which God has presumably revealed already as the proper ones.

REMARK B.4 (see p. 70). *Argument 3* against the direct appeal to God as the source of criteria for authentic religious faith derives from the course which David Tracy pursues in *Blessed Rage for Order*. Readers will recall that Tracy begins by using the word "religion" to designate an anthropological dimension that is present, at least implicitly, in every human being. It is obvious, however, that Tracy applies the name "religion" to this dimension in order to establish a bridge between it and existing religions in general.

Now when we examine existing religions, we find that not all of them are strictly capable of confirming, beyond the limits of concrete existence, a human being's confidence and trusting belief that existence, order, and value are indeed worthwhile. In the end that depends on what "god" one believes in, what sort of religion one holds. To orient us in this religious realm, Tracy then appeals to metaphysics (which, it so happens, created that false general notion of God in the first place).

But there is a further problem with Tracy's course. In the end, using arguments which would take us too far afield here, Tracy accepts only a metaphysics that is compatible with the Christian God. And he does so only on the condition that classical Christian theology would correct its most commonly taught notion about God and God's perfections. It seems to me that Tracy could have spared himself that long and self-contradictory trajectory if he had admitted at the very beginning that there was a value-criterion prior to, and determining for, the acceptance of God—or, more precisely, the acceptance of a specific God.

REMARK C.1 (see p. 74). We now come to the *positive* side of the issue. Through an exegesis of Jesus' own preaching, I try to show how a basic anthropological faith, while retaining its proper character, can become a *religious* faith and what happens then in the realm of meaning. In our exegesis we find *two elements* to be constitutive of such a faith: (1) the transmission of *transcendent data* which are decisive for the realm of values; and (2) *adherence to a tradition* of referential witnesses regarding the experiencing and acquisition of those data. Only when those *two* elements are present will we speak—with a certain precision—of "religious faith." In this REMARK I will consider the first element, leaving the second element for REMARK C.2.

Insofar as *the first element* is concerned, it is certain that Jesus appealed to pre-existing human values (the kingdom or reign of God, what is good for the human being, and so forth). But then, on the basis of such values, he called for "conversion"—which is to say, for a modification of one's values-structure. So here we simultaneously find continuity and discontinuity in the realm of values. How do we explain this?

Relying on an existential analysis, we find that a certain values-structure is open to being converted into a higher one along the same lines, provided that certain data are acquired. These data transcend any possible human experience (e.g., the victory of love over death, radical equality of possibilities for all human beings, and so forth). So "conversion" (i.e., discontinuity) does not negate the basic identity with already existing values (i.e., continuity).

The new values-structure does not replace or annul the earlier one.

Notice, however, that the presence of such *transcendent data*—be it explicit or implicit, witting or unwitting—is only *one* of the elements of religious faiths. By itself it would not suffice to qualify a faith as religious. In later chapters we will see that many transcendent data are to be found in expressions of value quite at variance with religious ones—e.g., in those of Karl Marx. What is more, every values-structure, however meager it may be, presupposes such data even though no account may be taken of them. So people can only create countless misunderstandings when they use the presence of such data to justify the application of such labels as "religion," "religious elements," or "religious faith." The transcendence to be found in any and every anthropological faith vis-à-vis the limits of human existence does not make such faith "religious."

REMARK C.2 (see p. 76). *The second element* of a truly religious faith is brought out clearly by Jesus' own approach. Paradoxically enough, Jesus grounds the transcendent data he is transmitting to his listeners on a tradition ("the time is close at hand") which did not possess the exact same data. Though profound differences exist between himself and Moses for example (compare Deut. 20 and Matt. 5:38–39.), Jesus tells his listeners: "If you believed Moses you would believe what I tell you" (John 5:46).

In fact, Jesus does not stick to some specific teaching of Moses. Instead he adheres to a tradition represented by him. Jesus adheres to a history of human beings who learned how to learn by looking to the experience of others for support. Amid real-life experiences that were different and often paradoxical or contradictory, they were wise enough to find transcendent data which define the same values-structure that leads to recognition of Jesus.

Neither in the tradition nor in Jesus himself does the "divine" show up as some "pure," extrinsic element. Instead it shows up as the very quality of the values in each witness and in the tradition as a whole. We have already pointed out that no one submits to this second-level learning (what some people call "deutero-learning")[20] without possessing pre-established values. But when people enter into the tradition, their whole world is set in motion. They find themselves retracing the experiences of other people that have been explored by a community and given suitable symbolization.

It should be noted that no isolated human experience, however profound or complete it may be, founds a religious "tradition." For that we must have a process of learning how to learn over a long history embracing many generations. Moreover, the tradition may not deal directly with any explication of the name of God. (People debate whether Buddhism and Shintoism, for example, are religions for that very reason.) The point is that the tradition is established by symbols which do the equivalent even though they may not name God directly. Finally, a "tradition" borne along by a chain of witnesses to certain values must not be confused with a "school" of thought. In the latter the chain is to be found in the logic of the proffered arguments, not in the quality of the people and their experiences.

REMARK D (see p. 77). At this point in my analysis I must point out that when I talk about the two elements which make up an authentic "religious faith," *I am not making an evaluation of religion in general.* Readers should not be led astray by the fact that I appeal to an exegesis of the gospel here. When I talk about *authentic* religious faith here, I mean one that is in continuity with anthropological faith, one that refuses to be turned into a system of sacred or magical instruments.

But one point does surface from this definition of authentic religious faith. It is that religion in itself does not constitute either a value or an antivalue. It does so by virtue of the *dogmas* (or, the symbols of values and transcendent data-items) that compose it. Here, as in the realm of anthropological faith, we confront a structure which can serve all sorts of values or antivalues— even though we may not be able to *prove*, in either realm, that one value, in and of itself, should be preferred to another. What is clear is that our definition is equally applicable to a religion that upholds love and to one that advocates egotism, to a religion whose dogmas stress the creative role of human beings and to one whose dogmas inculcate the most passive sort of resignation.

Finally, one further point deserves mention. Even though my definition claims to obviate certain misunderstandings, it can hardly change the fact that the boundaries are not always clear-cut in reality. Some values-systems, which claim to be lay or secular, have been infiltrated by elements proper to religious faith, whether their proponents realize it or not. We shall have occasion to study that whole phenomenon later on in this volume.

NOTES

1. "Pontiff" (Latin *pontifex*) means one who "builds a bridge" between the divine and the human world, thus permitting communication between the two. It was obviously a sacred or religious appellation.

2. A central theme in Galatians (see especially Gal. 3–5).

3. A central theme in the first four chapters of 1 Corinthians.

4. See 1 Cor. 6:12, 10:23, and *passim*. For an elaboration of this theme and its Pauline references see J. L. Segundo, *The Community Called Church*, Eng. trans. (Maryknoll, N.Y.: Orbis Books, 1973), Chapter 5, pp. 103–112.

5. See David Tracy, *Blessed Rage for Order* (New York: Seabury Press, 1975), p. 93.

6. This is the most common and likely interpretation of the following formulation by Vatican I: Faith is a "supernatural virtue whereby, thanks to God's inspiration and the help of his grace, we believe to be true what God has revealed, not by virtue of any intrinsic truth grasped by the light of natural reason, but *on account of the authority of the revealing God*, who can neither deceive nor be deceived" (Denz. 1789; Segundo italics).

Also see this statement by Thomas Aquinas: "In faith, the formal reason is the first Truth; that is to say, we adhere to the truths of faith *solely because they have been revealed by God*, who is the first Truth, and *to the extent that they have been revealed by God"* (idem); cited by A. Liégé in the anthology entitled *Initiation théologique* (Paris: Ed. du Cerf, 1952), vol. 3, pp. 490 and 518. Though his article does not sufficiently stress the point, the fact is that Liégé's article does already begin to point up the relationship between theological faith and preexisting human values grounded in human referential witnesses.

7. On this long journey towards the certitude of faith and its many human phases see J. L. Segundo, *The Liberation of Theology*, Eng. trans. (Maryknoll, N.Y.: Orbis Books, 1976), Chapter 6, Section 3: "Relative Factors Conditioning an Absolute Faith."

8. See J. L. Segundo, *Berdiaeff: Une réflexion chrétienne sur la personne* (Paris: Aubier, 1963), pp. 98f.

9. Vatican II, *Gaudium et spes*, n. 19; Eng. trans., Walter M. Abbott, ed., *The Documents of Vatican II* (New York: Guild-America-Association, 1966). I have already pointed up the danger of religion being distorted, and of referring to religion in the singular, in the previous chapter.

10. As we saw in the previous chapter, the ultimate charge that Jesus brought against the Jewish religious authorities when they asked for a sign from heaven was the charge of being "a wicked and adulterous generation" (Greek Matt. 16:4). This use of the term "adulterous" dovetails completely with that of the classical prophets of the Old Testament. Hosea, for example, accuses Israel, the bride of Yahweh, of adultery for running after false gods. Jesus does not hesitate to bring the same accusation against the most scrupulous and orthodox upholders of Yahwistic monotheism in his land.

11. Tracy, *Blessed Rage for Order*, p. 148.

12. Ibid., pp. 146f.

13. Ibid., p. 173.

14. Ibid., p. 189.

15. Camus provides an interesting case here. In *The Myth of Sisyphus,* Eng. trans. (New York: Knopf, 1969), he tells us that rejection of all transcendent data would render existence absurd, would deprive it of meaning. But for him that is a positive thing and absurdity is to be embraced. Camus writes: ". . . the absurdity springs from a comparison. . . . If I wish to limit myself to facts, I know what man wants, I know what the world offers him, and now I can say that I also know what links them. For me the sole datum is the absurd" (pp. 30–31).

Now if that is the "sole datum," it is the sole *immanent* datum, the sole datum inscribed in our concrete experience. According to Camus, it leads us to the absurd, to the destruction of any meaning-structure for human activity. But what about the possibility of *transcendent* data that could do away with this absurdity? Camus slips past that possibility:

> That *transcends*, as the saying goes, the human scale; therefore it must be superhuman. But this "therefore" is superfluous. There is no logical certainty here. There is no experimental probability either. All I can say is that, in fact, that transcends my scale. If I do not draw a negation from it, at least *I do not want* to found anything on the incomprehensible. I want to know whether I can live *with what I know* and with that alone. . . . I merely want to remain in this middle path where the intelligence can remain clear (p. 40; Segundo italics).

One final question comes to our minds: How can a person ground anything on the absurd? Camus replies: "It was previously a question of finding out whether or not life had to have a meaning to be lived. It now becomes clear, on the contrary, that *it will be lived all the better if it has no meaning*" (p. 53; Segundo italics).

But is that anything more than a brilliant piece of wordplay, belied by an analysis of any human life, including Camus's own life?

16. That is often what is regarded as a "dogma" in the vulgar sense. Here "dogma" means something different, and we may follow Karl Rahner to see what it entails ("Current Problems in Christology," *Theological Investigations* [Baltimore: Helicon, 1961], vol. 1). Rahner writes: "Yet while this [dogmatic] formula is an end, an acquistion and a victory, which allows us to enjoy clarity and security as well as ease in instruction, if this victory is to be a true one the end must also be a beginning" (p. 149).

Rahner immediately gives the reason for his statement: "It follows from the nature of human knowledge of truth and from the nature of divine truth itself, that any individual truth, above all one of God's truths, is beginning and emergence, not conclusion and end" (p. 149).

I doubt that this presentation of the argument, even if the argument itself is valid, will overcome the resistance posed by the classical conception of what dogmas are. Rahner comes much closer to my line of argument when he goes on to say: "Anyone who takes seriously the 'historicity' of human truth (in which God's truth too has become incarnate in Revelation) must see that neither the abandonment of a formula nor its preservation in a petrified form does justice to human understanding" (p. 150).

17. Consider the points when great breaks in the tradition took place: e.g., the exilic prophets, the Book of Job, and the deep skepticism of Ecclesiastes. On the prophets, for example, see Gerhard von Rad, *Old Testament Theology*, 2 vols., Eng. trans. (New York: Harper & Row, 1962), vol. 2, pp. 176–187: Part II, C, "The New Element in Eighth-Century Prophecy."

18. Though this may strike many people as strange, Chrisitianity does not possess any such universal solutions either. So we are told in one of the most extraordinary conciliar passages of Vatican II: "In fidelity to conscience, Christians are joined with the rest of humanity *in the search for truth*, and for the genuine solution to the numerous problems which arise in individual and societal life" (*Gaudium et spes*, n. 16; Segundo italics). Later, referring to the lay people who are directly confronted with such problems, the same document says: "Let lay people not imagine that their pastors are always such experts that, to every problem which arises, *however complicated*, they can *readily give them a concrete solution* . . ." (*Gaudium et spes*, n. 43; Segundo italics).

19. Consider Simone Weil's remark in *Attente de Dieu* (Waiting for God): "Christianity should contain all vocations without exception since it is catholic. In consequence the Church should also. But in my eyes Christianity is catholic by right but not in fact. So many things are outside it, so many things that I love and do not want to give up, so many things that God loves, otherwise they would not be in existence. All the immense stretches of past centuries, except the last twenty, are among them; all the countries inhabited by colored races; all secular life in the white peoples' countries; in the history of these countries, all the traditions banned as heretical, those of the Manicheans and Albigenses for instance; all those things resulting from the Renaissance, too often degraded but not quite without value. . . . There is an absolutely insur-

mountable obstacle to the Incarnation of Christianity. It is the use of the two little words *anathema sit*. It is not their existence, but the way they have been employed up till now. It is that also which prevents me from crossing the threshold of the Church. I remain beside all those things that cannot enter the Church, the universal repository, on account of those two little words. I remain beside them all the more because my own intelligence is numbered among them" (citation from the anthology edited by George A. Panichas, *The Simone Weil Reader* [New York: McKay, 1977], pp. 20 and 22).

　20. See J. L. Segundo, *The Liberation of Theology*, Eng. trans. (Maryknoll, N.Y.: Orbis Books, 1976), Chapter 4, Section IV, especially pp. 118–120.

CHAPTER IV

Ideology—Science—Reason

As we proceed with our inquiry, we come to the difficulties posed by the term I have opposed to faith: i.e., ideology. Back in the first chapter, I indicated why I chose to use that term in the way I did. I hope the sense of my choice will be even clearer when readers have completed the present chapter.

It should be obvious, however, that the difficulties do not stem from the term employed (ideology) so much as from its relationship to faith. It is a relationship of difference *and* complementarity. That is the thing which is hard for people to accept. In other words, it is not terminology that creates problems so much as it is the (anthropological) *dualism* underlying the terminology. Western human beings, particularly since the nineteenth century, have grown used to thinking that the meaning-structure of life is the prolongation or culmination of the efficacy-structure. And since the systematizing element in the latter is clearly reason or science, to either reason or science we must also attribute the values-system of each and every life. That has been the ideal, at least, although shortcomings in science or reasoning have often threatened both the efficacy and the meaningfulness of human life.

Unwillingness to use the word "ideology" is not really our first major obstacle. Our real obstacle is the fact that the term "ideology," as I use it here, suggests the existence of *another plane* besides that of science or technique (where rational principles reign). That is the first problem we will tackle in this chapter.

Our second problem, more directly noticeable, comes from the current connotations of the term "ideology." However equivocal the latter term may be, it certainly does not seem to coincide with the meaning that I have given it in this book. Is there an underlying problem here which goes far deeper than mere questions of terminology (see REMARK A.1, p 105)?

For two centuries it has been traditional to set up an opposition between faith and science, or, faith and reason. They are presented as opposed, not complementary, alternatives. So I shall begin with this opposition. Perhaps if we understand faith as I tried to define it in the first chapter, we will find that

87

the unalterable opposition fades into complementarity (see REMARK A.2, p. 106).

I. The Faith of Science and Reason

For my analysis here, I will use as an example a key Marxian notion that will crop up again in this book (see REMARK B.1, p. 106). According to official Marxism, if not exactly Marx himself, religion is supposed to disappear eventually, pushed out of the picture by science. Now can the same thing be said of "faith" in the sense which I use it here?

Machoveč: Marx's Scientific Program

From a Marxist perspective, the Czech professor of philosophy Milan Machoveč offers this interesting summary of what Marx was trying to do with his thought: "There can be no doubt that Marx wanted to organize all progressive people oriented towards the future, through a strict and objective scientific analysis of the central problems of his historical epoch. At the same time he wanted to lay down the foundations for a more human society, and hence for a more mature and free human individuality."[1]

If readers check the context of Machoveč's remark, they will find that it is not a careless, off-the-cuff statement. It comes in Chapter 1, the most critical and important chapter in his book. Machoveč is trying to spell out, as carefully as he can, how and why an atheistic Marxist can be interested in the life and teaching of Jesus of Nazareth while still remaining consistent with his own ideology.

Taking Machoveč's statement seriously, then, we find that it can be divided into two aspects. First he refers to an *intention*: "Marx wanted to. . . ." Then he refers to a *mediation*, a tool to be used: ". . . through a strict and objective scientific analysis. . . ." Note that Machoveč applies the adjective "scientific" only to the second aspect. He explicitly and deliberately leaves out of the scientific orbit the underlying desires or aims of Marx's thought. For Machoveč, then, the only *scientific* aspect is the *method* found by Marx to realize his desires and goals.

Moreover, Machoveč's statement indicates that Marx sought to *bring together as a group* "all progressive people oriented towards the future" who were looking "for a more human society, and hence for a more mature and free human individuality." He would offer them a scientific method of analysis that would make it possible for them to realize their ideals in history. But obviously those people with those ideals existed before Marx's science came along, and Marx's science did not determine the desires or ideals to be served.

The passage from Machoveč's work makes it clear that the scientific element operates in the realm of the relative or the conditional: "If you want that, this is the means to be used." Insofar as human beings engage in self-determination through the use of their freedom and the values which they choose, science belongs to the realm of the *hypothetical*, the realm that I have chosen to call ideology. It thus stands over against the realm of values, one of which at least always presents itself as *absolute*. Even when science tells me about experiential reality with absolute certainty, the absolute that really defines my existence still remains outside its competence. To phrase the matter in line with Machovec̆'s logic above, we can say that Marx's science was relevant and decisive only for those who were *already* united beforehand in a similar meaning-structure. To be sure, insofar as his science offered real-life possibilities to that meaning-structure, it did much to make it even more secure and firm. By declaring that utopia was a viable alternative, it canalized energies which may have lain dormant or gone no further than wishful thinking.

Machovec̆ also implies that Marx discovered his scientific method because he, in addition to his capabilities, had a value-grounded life which was oriented towards the new society and the new human individuality even before he developed his science. Indeed it is precisely on the basis of this preconditioning factor that Machovec̆ finds himself vitally interested in Jesus of Nazareth. He is looking for the meaning-structure without which the "mediation" of science would achieve nothing, whether before or after Marx (see REMARK B.2, p. 107).

Machovec̆ *believes* in Jesus, in anthropological if not religious terms, without ceasing to use the mediation of Marxist science. He writes: "An atheist . . . can readily admit that the moment when Peter discovered that Jesus was still victor, after Golgotha, was one of the greatest moments in history and human existence."[2]

Now this historical decisiveness, as attributed to the real-life, transmitted experience of a historical personage, can only be comprehended logically in terms of "faith" as I have been using that term here. It can only be comprehended in terms of a particular meaning-structure which, in principle, is in no way opposed to the use of science (see REMARK B.3, p. 107). Indeed Machovec̆ himself admits the same thing, at least implicitly, suggesting the great extent to which the meaning-structure not only confers value on, but also guides, the "scientific" analyses which serve as its necessary means or mediation. Here is what Machovec̆ writes: "Marx rightly foresaw that he was inaugurating a historically important movement that would win millions of adherents. But he did not take note of all the ambiguity and contradiction involved in the concepts of 'winning' and 'adhesion.' There are so many ways in which one can 'win over' the human heart!"[3]

This remark is particularly clear in bringing out the problem of transmitting afresh to each new generation, even in a socialist society, the values-structure to which Marx offered a scientific method that would make possible their realization in a new society. Even in such a society, where the political revolution leading towards the dictatorship of the proletariat has already taken place, there is no automatic way to form "progressive people oriented towards the future" who are seeking "to lay down the foundations for a more human society, and hence for a more mature and free human individuality."

Machoveč assumes, firstly, that people can "function" in a society based on those values without sharing deeply in them. They are the people who have scarcely been "won over" or converted. This does not mean that the victories achieved by changes in the sociopolitical structures are useless, of course, but it is clear to Machoveč that there is a real danger of human impoverishment.

Machoveč assumes, secondly, that adequate attention and adequate means must be given to the meaning-structure of each human being. If that is not done, if use is made too readily of government apparatus to solve problems, for example, then one is in effect teaching human beings to view their crises and failures solely in terms of efficacy. That, as we saw in Chapter I, mutilates human beings, reducing them to one-dimensional beings. Yet that is precisely the viewpoint or the criterion which has been introduced by science and technology and which has been accentuated to an almost inhuman degree by "scientism" or "technocracy." For the latter embody the human tendency to forget that the meaning-structure is prior and superior to any accumulation of data about experiential reality (see REMARK B.4, p. 107).

The one-dimensional nature of human beings who tackle crises solely in terms of efficacy is not exclusive to the socialist world, of course. But it is evident there too, according to Machoveč, for the reasons indicated. Machoveč makes the point bluntly: "Here the Christian reader is probably already aware of the fact that we are coming to the heart of the problem. If thousands and thousands of sincere socialists, Marxist intellectuals, and party-apparatus people can succumb to all that, then obviously they can no longer believe quasi-eschatologically in a 'totally new' life; they are obviously developing a greater appreciation for many situations which are described in the Bible, and which center around the figure of Jesus especially."[4]

Machoveč then proceeds to write in terms which will, I hope, remind my readers of my remarks about anthropological "faith" and its "referential witnesses": "The European Marxist of the twentieth century no longer finds in current Marxism clear models and indications for spiritual values in a consumption-oriented society, for a properly human death in an industrial world, for the painful moral conflicts already mentioned, or for a better understanding of other spiritual traditions and their approaches to humanness and happiness."[5] Prompt to acknowledge that age-old human egotism, pharisaism, and villany can reappear in new guises in a socialist society, Machoveč points up the potential value of the Judeo-Christian experience: "The Judeo-Christian tradition has already had much experience with these problems and has elaborated certain models for their solution. Even an atheist, for example, can find in the psalms a moving description of his or her personal situation in the twentieth century, a description that is extraordinarily 'up to the minute.' "[6]

In short, Machoveč has just been telling us that not enough attention has been paid to the complementarity between "faith" and "ideology" in Marxist thought when embodied in political reality. The only difference is that he uses the term "scientific method" where I use the term "ideology." The point is that some Marxists, who are more aware of the problems which remain to be solved even where Marx has, so to speak, been put into practice, are now realizing that those problems stem from overlooking or forgetting the nonscientific dimension. They are realizing that human beings are impoverished and mutilated when they confront crises, unless they are brought into the presence of referential witnesses to the various values-structures that have been explored by the great spiritual traditions.

Marxism has been accused of inconsistency, of harboring an unprofessed "religion." That point will be considered later. Here I simply want to call attention to the above citation from Machoveč and its import. Whether the other dimension should be called "science" or not depends on the terminological advantages or disadvantages involved, so long as the terms are correctly understood. I myself find disadvantages in such terms as "science" or "the scientific method." Quite apart from the difficulty of determining what is and what is not scientific in Marxist sociology or economics, there is a more serious problem here. The term is meant to refer to a basic anthropological dimension shared by all human beings in all ages. But "science," in the present-day sense of that term, seems to me to allude to a fact or datum that is very recent and hence limited. There have always been "techniques" and "methods" and "uses" employed by human beings to realize pre-established values, and they have been transmitted from one generation to the next. Indeed "religion" itself, as a corpus of instruments, was the "science" of bygone civilizations. So I prefer to use a term that can be applied equally well to the magic of an animist and to the measurements of a twentieth-century scientist in the West (see REMARK B.5, p. 107).

Bateson: Reason and Self-Validating Premises

Since I have been talking about scientists in the wider sense of that term, I will now choose an example from the area of the natural sciences and epistemology. It is an area that gave rise to another type of monist, the positivist. For more than a few decades, however, we have been witnessing a break away from the positivistic and scientistic dogmas that prevailed during much of the nineteenth century.

One of the most significant episodes in this changing picture may well have been the growing disappointment with which Bertrand Russsell viewed the development of his prodigy, Ludwig Wittgenstein. The latter was to have been the one destined to implant the positivist method once and for all in the totality of human discourse. But Wittgenstein, as his biographers tell us, never gave up his Kierkegaardian vision. Despite all appearances, he continued to believe that no question could be planted on solid intellectual foundations when it came to moral problems.[7]

Something similar could be said of the British scientist Gregory Bateson, who eventually settled in the United States. In his interesting book entitled *Steps to an Ecology of Mind*, which collects much of his work over the course of a half-century or more, he writes the following from a nontheistic stand-point: "The living man is thus bound within a net of epistemological and ontological premises which—regardless of ultimate truth or falsity—become partially self-validating for him."[8]

This is certainly not the place to show how Bateson arrives at that radical assertion. Instead let us see what the assertion itself contains.

Bateson talks about "epistemological and ontological premises." This ushers in the theme, not of science, but of *reason* and its relationship to human activity. The word "premise" alludes to the starting point of a rea-soning process, of a logical process in which everything else is either the me-chanics of the rational process itself (*consequentia*) or the outcome of the premises *plus* the rational process—i.e., the conclusion (*consequens*).

The point here is that it is precisely the premise that is removed from rea-son. It precedes reason. It is the thing on which reason works, just as raw material does not depend on the machine which turns it into a manufactured product. The premise is a-rational. Reason works on premises that are not created or verified by reason itself.

Now the most important and decisive use of reason is that of justifying or "validating" the conclusions that a human being draws from his or her "on-tological and epistemological" premises. What sort of premises are the latter exactly? Underlying the esoteric adjectives used by Bateson is a very simple human reality, precisely what I have been calling "meaning-structure" or "values-structure." One of the primary tasks of that structure is to measure or gauge reality, not in terms of what it is but in terms of what it ought to be: i.e., in terms of its value.

In order to begin reasoning about reality and my activity in it, I must see it as a potential complex of values, values which are structured rather than merely juxtaposed. Those are ontological premises. Epistemological prem-ises, as the term itself suggests, determine how exactly I am going to get to know concrete reality. Far from being a neutral photograph, cognition can present one and the same reality to me as either a triumph or a defeat—be it death, money, imprisonment, or whatever. It is not so much that I start right out evaluating them as such, but rather that I already *perceive* them in that way. They enter my cognitive field as data which, straight out of reality, either oblige me to revise my way of acting or confirm the latter as consistent with the data. Right here then, and even before I begin to reason, epistemo-logical premises decide what is going to penetrate into my cognitive field and how it is going to do it. And what *does* penetrate my cognition field will be shaped and synthesized into what I will call my experience.

The "circle" to which Bateson alludes in talking about "self-validating" premises embraces something much more basic than the difficulty of reason-ing clearly. He is talking about the most important things in life and the wide variety of ways in which people make decisions about them. And his point is that ratiocination seems to be able to do very little to "convert" human beings from one meaning-structure to another. According to Bateson, that is largely due to the fact that experience always seems to confirm what we hold.

As Bateson points out, what we call "experience" assumes that we detect in reality "sequences of events."[9] Because events recur in a more or less similar way, the person of experience is one who knows ahead of time what is going to happen.

There is a kind of "grammar" of reality. To recognize "sequences of events" is to "punctuate" what is taking place in something akin to phrases or sentences. Logically, then, our "experience" will depend on when and where we put the punctuation mark. It will depend on exactly when or where we think that one sequence has ended and a new one is beginning. To give a rough example, a "pessimist" is someone used to forming and recognizing sequences of events that end in sorrow, failure, or misfortune. He or she places the punctuation mark or period after the negative event has appeared. An "optimist," by contrast, is one who "punctuates" the series of events in such a way that it ends with a happy outcome. If failure follows, that is the start of a new sequence insofar as the optimist is concerned. The "premises" of the optimist and the pessimist are the different ways in which they "punctuate" the very same events. So what we call "experience" confirms, almost by definition, the "premises" of both. What I have been calling anthropological "faith" is intimately related to the method adopted to "punctuate" life's events. In most cases, therefore, it is shored up by experience.

It should now be clear to my readers that Bateson, in talking about ontological and epistemological "premises," is referring to the very same basic anthropological dimension that I have been calling "faith." I might add that when he comes to talk about how difficult it is for adults to change the "premises" of their life, he acknowledges the claim for religious "conversions" as one possible and rare example of such a change.[10] That is not of major importance here. The point is that his dimension of premises is synonymous with my dimension of faith because both stand as "self-validating" vis-à-vis *reason*.

When Bateson describes his "premises" as "self-validating," he is obviously withdrawing them from the control of reason and even more obviously from the control of science. There is no rational or scientific "proof" for them—or against them. At another point in his book Bateson even objects to the idea of labelling them "true" or "false," undoubtedly because such terms in his mind are bound up with the scientific possibility of verification or falsification.[11]

As I pointed out in Chapter I, human beings cannot travel to the boundaries of life to experience personally how satisfying their chosen meaning-structure will be. Their choice is basically made on *faith*. Viewed from a rational standpoint, that choice is a-rational and a-scientific, however human and necessary we may judge it. That is why we cannot assault the meaning-structure of anyone by waving a demonstrable "falsehood" in front of them. Suppose, for example, that we could demonstrate scientifically that a particular values-structure is *unrealizable* or unachievable—since reason and science *can* come into play here. Even that would not mean we were able to prove the underlying "faith" false, since that "faith" could put a high value on failure by claiming that reality is not what it ought to be. Practically all martyrs, religious or not, have preferred to maintain their meaning-structure even when confronted with the concrete unviability of their projects.

And the invulnerability of basic self-validating premises or basic faith is not restricted to the realm of the "sublime." A convinced criminal, too, has a meaning-structure which essentially invalidates any line of reasoning designed to prove to him or her that there is a respectable social order and that he or she would be "happier" by respecting it. In reality, the only thing one could prove to the criminal is that he or she would live more tranquilly, have greater freedom of movement, and be more integrated into the consumption-process of society. But how might one prove that *such a life* offers more happiness, when the criminal has associated the latter with another set of values and entrusted his or her happiness to very different experiences of value?

To be sure, Bateson attenuates the force of his statement (see p. 92) by including the word "partially" in it. He acknowledges the claim made for a "conversion," and he knows that every conversion follows certain paths and has its own mechanisms. But of course they are not based on any rational or scientific proof. As we shall see further on, one can "suggest" to another person that there is an inconsistency between his or her faith and his or her ideology; this might prompt the person to change his or her faith. That issue, however, will be treated later in the book (see REMARK B.6, p. 108).

Here I am not interested in a full-scale evaluation of Bateson's terminology as a substitute for my own terms. The point I want to make right now is that he is alluding to the very same simple fact which I have chosen to call "faith" as a universal dimension, even though his terminology may *seem* much more scientific.

Bateson also seems to imply that my term "ideology" might better be replaced with the word "reason," since he talks about "premises" underlying the use of reason when it comes to critical human issues. My problem with the term "reason" is that in the history of thought "reason" and "faith" have usually been presented as *opposed* rather than *complementary* elements. Bateson himself, however, talks about a complementarity between a-rational premises and the use of reason, just as I talk about a necessary complementarity between a faith that structures a world of meaning and a reason that studies real possibilities in order to implement one's values. If readers accept the arguments offered above and stop viewing faith and reason as necessarily opposed alternatives, they can perfectly well use Bateson's terms instead of mine without causing misunderstandings.

II. The Uses of Ideology

It is much more difficult to justify my use of the term "ideology" as the distinct but complementary counterpart of "faith." It cannot be denied that the two common meanings of the term "ideology" in our culture, the two meanings which have proved to be most fruitful and decisive, certainly do not seem to dovetail with my usage (see REMARK C.1, p. 109). Moreover, if we are to maintain the bipolarity I have been examining between meaning and praxis, it seems that the term "ideology" might better refer to their overall relationship and structure, with the emphasis falling on the pole of meaning, on the pole which I have chosen to call "faith." Indeed in ordinary usage the term "ideology" seems to refer to a *secular* or *lay* "faith."

The relevance of the term "ideology" for our culture is clearly due in large measure to the critical use of it by Karl Marx. As is frequently the case with writers who have left behind an enormous body of work, careful study of Marx's writings might well reveal that the term "ideology" could have a dozen or more different meanings in various contexts. At least that seems to be true in the case of the term "social class," which has been carefully studied by G. Gurvitch in the whole Marxian corpus.

Examining Two Current Usages

Since Marx, we find that the term "ideology" is used in two main senses which differ considerably, though that does not mean that the two senses are not mutually related. I would say that the first sense goes back to Marx himself, whereas the second sense is more derived from Marx than actually present in his own work. I would also say that the first sense of the term is *neutral* from the standpoint of value, and neutral in more than one respect; and that the second sense is obviously *negative* in its import.

Marx uses the term "ideology" to designate all the higher constructions of a culture, those which are due to thinking and *ideas*. Notice that by "higher" I do not mean higher or loftier in terms of truth. I simply mean higher on a speculative, cerebral, or, if you will, spiritual scale.

Notice this statement in *The German Ideology*: "Morality, religion, metaphysics, *all the rest of ideology* and their corresponding forms of consciousness, thus no longer retain the semblance of independence. They have no history, no development; but men, developing their material production and their material intercourse, alter, along with this their real existence, *their thinking and the products of their thinking*" (my italics).[12]

Marx frequently uses the term "consciousness" of a culture as a synonym for "ideology" or some ideological structure. Consider this passage: "The mode of production of material life conditions the general process of social, political, and intellectual life. It is not the *consciousness* of men that determines their existence, but their social existence that determines their *consciousness*. . . . The changes in the economic foundation lead sooner or later to the transformation of the whole immense superstructure. In studying such transformations it is always necessary to distinguish between the material transformation of the economic conditions of production, which can be determined with the precision of natural science, and the legal, political, religious, artistic, or philosophic—in short, *ideolog-*

ical forms in which men become *conscious* of this conflict and fight it out" (my italics).[13]

Here Marx applies the term "ideology" to the consciousness of a culture—the products of its thinking in such areas as law, politics, and religion. And he contrasts it with the determining economic reality, which takes in both the mode of production and the production or property relationships to which it gives rise. It would seem, then, that the term "ideology" is neutral from the standpoint of value. Depending on circumstances, in other words, laws, political structures, arts, and (?) religions might be good or bad, better or worse.

Today, however, there is something a bit anachronistic about interpreting Marx in the above way. We can now compare the various "ideologies" of capitalist countries and socialist countries. When Marx himself was writing, however, his term "ideology" referred to the "higher" forms of the *existing* culture: i.e., the capitalist culture. Since it referred to the conscious superstructure of a culture based on the division of labor and the right of private property, the term "ideology" had a negative value for Marx right from the outset. It was a false consciousness, an obstacle preventing people from adverting to the original, more fundamental and substantive reality. And the latter, in Marx's view, was bound up with the mode of material production.

Hence even in those passages where the term "ideology" seems to be more neutral, it still tends to have a negative connotation for Marx. At the very least it tends to allude to something artificial. This may be due to the fact that Marx never fully and clearly faced up to the issue of the function or eventual suppression of ideology *as such* in the future socialist society. In the passage from *The German Ideology* cited above (p. 95), for example, Marx notes that human beings also *alter* their thinking and its products when they alter their material production. However, he does not say that insofar as changes in the mode of production favor justice and the complete needs of all human beings, the thinking of human beings and its products will *cease to exist*. Marx does clearly say elsewhere that the state and religion will eventually disappear in the future socialist society. This raises the question: To what extent can we really talk about a *neutral* use of the term "ideology" by Marx? Some Marxists do find such a use; others deny it. Regarding Althusser, for example, one commentator writes: "In opposition to a scientistic and positivistic Marxism, Althusser accepts and acknowledges the consistency, function, and perdurance of ideology in any and every social formation, even including the communist one."[14]

Even if such a neutral use of the term "ideology" does exist in Marx's corpus, we must still note something that might seem to go against my purposes here. The fact is that ideology, as Marx sees it, denotes a human realm that lacks the precision of the natural sciences. Such precision can be found only when we study the economic changes in the area of material production.

That brings us to the *negative* sense of the term "ideology," which also stems from Marx. It should be noted that this negative use of the term has been a major landmark in the growth of the sociology of knowledge. Even non-Marxist thinkers and scholars (e.g., Karl Mannheim) have acknowledged that fact.

The ideological superstructure, after all, is situated in the lofty regions of thought and is easily dissociated from the realm of material production; indeed it tends to evade and hide the latter realm. So it is only logical to assume that ideology is not fortuitous but "interested." In other words, whether they believe in the ideology or not, those who profit from the existing mode of production are the authors and defenders of that ideology. An additional proof of this, though perhaps not readily noticeable at first glance, is the fact that other groups, even those which should be more interested in recognizing the nature and extent of the material exploitation to which they are subjected, share the ideologies which disguise, excuse, and even hallow that exploitation.

The senses tend to be fairly resistant to manipulation of any sort. Ideas, on the other hand, lend themselves to manipulation by virtue of their immateriality and their removal from real-life concreteness. And those who have an interest in manipulating ideas and keeping them apart from the real world are the people who benefit from this reality, whether they consciously realize this or not. That is why, said Marx, "the ruling ideas of each age have ever been the ideas of its ruling classes."[15]

Truth, then, insofar as that is possible for human beings, would lie not in having a "good " ideology but in having no ideology at all, in descending from something that can be manipulated and sticking to what is inseparable from reality. This explains why such terms as "ideology" and "ideological mechanisms" tend to designate something that is negative rather than neutral, something opposed to *real* knowledge or , to use a term now more frequently evident in "official" Marxism, *scientific* knowledge.

•••

To sum up, we have two meanings for the word "ideology." The more *neutral* sense refers to everything that lies outside the precision of the sciences, to the suprascientific or the superstructural realm. In that sense it is only logical to talk about a "Marxist ideology," even though one may recognize a "scientific" area in it, and we do hear such talk today. The second sense of the term is clearly *negative*. It refers to all the cognitive mechanisms which disguise, excuse, and even sacralize the existing mode of production, thus benefiting those who profit from that mode of production (see REMARK C.2, p. 110).

Relating Terminology to Our Theme

Neither of the two uses of the term "ideology" treated in the previous section seems to accord with the meaning which I gave the term in Chapter I. Both uses seem, at first glance, to refer more to what I have been calling "faith" and thus to inject further confusion into our discussion.

I would like to try to show, however, that this terminological challenge can help us to probe more deeply into the anthropological problem that I have posed. Without seeking to change current usage, we can benefit by deliberately departing from it in order to point up a serious lacuna in it. And this is all the more important insofar as the current usage tends to provoke, maintain, and accentuate commonplaces that are misleading or false.

Let us examine the process whereby people arrive at a false consciousness or, conversely, free themselves from it, according to Marx, later Marxists, and others who have examined the matter. Here I will again introduce the phenomenological analysis I offered in Chapter I and spelled out more clearly as I went along. I do so in the hope that it will help me to prove that the division between superstructure and structure, or between ideology and science, though basically sound, should leave room for much greater complexity and richness.

Take the case of those who benefit from the existing process of production. Marx could not, and did not, ignore the fact that this class of persons is divided into two groups. One group is composed of those people, such as Marx himself at the start of his career, who benefit from the production process because they live in a state of "false consciousness" with regard to the superstructure. This "false consciousness" prevents them from seeing what they are doing, or justifies the existing state of affairs since there does not seem to be any other way out. The other group is composed of people who, though freed from this ideological deception, will continue to take advantage of the existing mode of production since it is wholly and integrally consistent with the values-structure they have.

Clearly Marx's thinking begins to operate and pose problems only *after* this basic division. He is not interested in personal motives or existential analyses, even where that will decide the stance of people for or against the proletariat in the struggle. His own case and that of Engels interest him far less than the "collective" forces. This is in contrast with Lenin. Though the latter did not depart from the social dimension, he devoted particular attention to the fact that the founders of socialism had not been the exploited masses themselves but members of the exploitative bourgeoisie.[16]

So let us consider the case of Marx himself, his sensitivity to the liberation of the industrial proletariat and the commitment which soon developed from that. Obviously this meaning-structure or values-structure was decisive for his work and guided each stage of his development, analysis, and investigation. But it does not seem that we can include it in the content of the term "ideology."

First of all, it is quite obvious that it was not an "ideological" tendency in the negative sense of the term. It was, on the contrary, the decisive existential factor in setting in motion the whole "de-ideologizing" apparatus. It served as the springboard for his desire to open people's eyes to reality, however troublesome and compelling it might be.

Some readers might say that this is an example of "ideology" in the neutral sense, since the ethical and moral plane into which it translated is undeniably superstructural. But remember that Marx uses the term "ideology" in its most neutral sense to refer to such things as the "legal, political, religious, artistic, or philosophic . . . forms" of a given culture (see p. 95 above). Obviously, then, his basic values-structure does not make up any one of those collective "forms" which are part of what we call a "culture" in any given historical period. That basic values-structure is what I have been calling "faith."

Marx insists that "ideology," as the term itself indicates, is a construction made by ideas—i.e., an *instrument*. Suppose we asked him: an instrument or tool *of what*? He would reply that it is basically, though not necessarily always (as his own case shows), a tool of the *interests*, the values, of the class of people who manipulate it.

This explains the ultimately coercive character of the revolution once the exploited class takes cognizance of both its power and its interest. Once that point is reached, Marx ceases to worry about people's orientation towards love or egotism, solidarity or individualism. He assumes that this orientation depends more on the nature of the means to be used by people in the socialist or communist stage than on the meaning they give to their lives.

Thus we detect the *absence* or *lack* of something that would give meaning to the ideologies, the instruments used, in a socialist or communist society. We should not be surprised to find that this same lack has been noticed by Marxists themselves, even in periods of the most rigid Marxist orthodoxy.[17]

So we come to this conclusion: *the distinction between "ideology" and economic structure, valid and realistic though it be, leaves out a critical and decisive element that has to be given some name.* It seems clear that such fundamental attitudes as love, hatred, egotism, and solidarity should not be called "ideologies" in either of the two senses which Marx gave to the word (see REMARK C.3, p. 110). So in using the term "ideology," we must leave room above it for some anthropological "faith" that gives direction to the realm of ideology.

Which term in my use of terminology, then, should include "science" within it? Clearly it is the term "ideology," however much that clashes with current Marxist and positivistic usage of that term. For if the meaning-values of anthropological "faith" are to be implemented, science will obviously play an important role in that implementation.

Readers may object that an "ideological" use of science will open the way for a false science, that science as such, insofar as it remains faithful to itself, does not belong to the plane of ideology. Once again, however, things are not that simple. Anyone familiar with the literature on this subject, be it Marxist or anti-Marxist, is perfectly aware of the interminable debates as to what is or is not scientific in Marxism and whether Marxism is ideology, science, or theory (with a small *t* or a capital *T*).

Instead of getting into that whole debate, let us go back to the second Marxian text I cited on page 95. In it Marx contrasted the "ideological" forms of a culture with "the material transformation of the economic conditions of production, which *can be determined with the precision of natural science"* (my italics).[18]

Here we find a clear distinction being made between the domain of ideology and that of the natural sciences. But we can deduce very little from it concerning the possible use or precision of "scientific" knowledge regarding the ideological plane itself or concerning the potential infiltration of ideology into the "precisions" of the natural sciences. And the latter point is particularly true when we are dealing with the "natural" science of economics, as Marx is in this case.

Two points deserve to be brought out here.

1. It is clear that in Marx's view there exists some sort of scientific knowledge, properly so called, above and beyond the natural sciences. There is, for example, what is known as *historical materialism* in the Marxist vocabulary. Contrary to the many misunderstandings surrounding this term, it is not a "philosophy" or a theory of the origin or constitution of the universe. It is a scientific method, however limited its "precisions" may be. Mannheim rightly regarded it as a basic contribution to the *sociology* of knowledge: i.e., to any scientific explanation of the social factors conditioning the process of knowing.

In 1867, for example, Marx offered this description of what the "scientific" treatment of religious phenomena should entail: "Even a history of religion that is written in abstraction from this material basis is uncritical. It is, in reality, much easier to discover by analysis the earthly kernel of the misty creations of religion than to do the opposite, i.e., *to develop from the actual, given relations of life* the forms in which these have been apotheosized. The latter method is the only materialist, and therefore the only scientific, one" (my italics).[19]

From *The German Ideology* to *Capital*, then, it is clear in Marx's thought that the distinction between ideological superstructure and natural science does not rule out the possibility of *science* in the realm of ideology. Science is possible vis-à-vis ideology in the neutral sense because it has to do with an object that is not the material basis, that is not subject to analysis by the "exact" sciences. Science is also possible vis-à-vis ideology in the negative sense. In this case the *scientific* method is an ideological critique; it probes into ideologies which mystify authentic reality in order to unmask them. Marx fully realizes that we lose the precision of the natural sciences when we get to the human realm. But he also realizes that the attribute of *scientific* thinking is not lost altogether when it is applied to the ideological realm.

Of course there are problems involved in applying scientific methods to human thought, but they are not our concern here. The important point here is: *even in the earliest, most original vocabulary of Marxism one cannot simply invoke the word "science" to prove that one has left, or descended from, the realm of ideology* (see REMARK C.4, p. 111).

2. My terminology, which makes a distinction between faith and ideology, would not be criticized with leaving a sphere of purely objective science out-

side this classificatory scheme. Such science would be a part of "ideology" only to the extent that anything, depending on its own particular characteristics, can be *used* as an instrument by conscious beings endowed with will and the ability to plan things out. What would be "ideological" in such a case would be a particular "use" of science, based on values alien to science itself. The most objective meteorology, for example, could be used to commit an assassination. In other words, a science can be used for purposes whose values have nothing to do with the essence of the science in question.

So we might rest content with a simple observation: what Marx calls "natural science," with its objectivity and "precision," belongs to the realm of ideology only insofar as it can provide human beings with *technical* means to achieve their projects. But that way of solving the question is too simplistic, leaving a rich zone of human activity unexplored.

What exactly does Marx compare to the "precision" of the natural sciences? As we saw above: "the material transformation of the economic conditions of production." As he sees it, that can be determined with almost the same type of precision that is used to determine the nonhuman phenomena of nature, such as those found in chemistry, physics, and biology. This statement or assumption, it might be noted, is maintained in just about the same way by official Marxism and Western positivistic science (particularly in the United States). In this case both are indebted to a conception of science that was elaborated mainly in the nineteenth century.

Undoubtedly the "precision" of certain sciences, particularly when compared with the difficulties hindering progress in theoretical and philosophic thought, gave the practitioners of those sciences the impression that they were "touching the real." Indeed that argument obviously underlies the passage from Marx just cited. Ideological superstructures get lost in nebulous vagueness. Even such valuable instruments as Hegel's dialectics do not offer a solid basis for discovering new realities, unless their feet touch ground. They need some support-point in the concrete, the real, the scientific. According to Marx, on the human plane we reach such a level only when we get to "the material transformation of the economic conditions of production."

But let us examine this assertion a bit more closely. Exactly wherein lies this privilege of economic science? Whence comes the "precision" of economics? Marx would say it lies in the *concreteness* of economic facts as opposed to the *abstraction* of other cultural facts.[20] But if anything has become increasingly clear since Marx's day, it is that the exactness or precision of the sciences is in inverse, not direct, relationship to their concreteness. The course of the more exact sciences, such as mathematics and formal logic, shows clearly that their preciseness is in direct proportion to the *formal* character of the concepts they employ. And to say formal is to say abstract.

It can also be argued with some reason that scientific progress in precision has gone hand in hand with the development of instruments for observation and with the increased possibility—once never imagined—of recombining and manipulating a huge mass of data simultaneously and collectively. Scientific "memory," as embodied in computers, is growing today in a way qualitatively different from its growth in the past.

However, it can be readily seen and it is being acknowledged more and more openly in epistemology, that neither the formalism, exactitude, nor magnitude of the available information, in and of themselves, can account for the scientific advances in all areas.

Let me cite an example. Advances in chemistry are certainly related to our ability to "formalize" the elements under investigation without abandoning the field of *concrete observation*. The "definition" of water as H_2O, for example, enables us to formalize without abandoning our observation of the concrete behavior of water. Many things "seem" to be water at first glance, and it would be extremely difficult to observe the behavior of water unless the laboratory permitted us to verify at every point that the concrete element under observation was truly water. The "precision" of chemistry, in other words, lies in the possibility of isolating a variable (formalization) and then observing how it varies in its reactions to different "stimuli."

On the level of biology we already note a constant that will prove to be more and more decisive as we move on to the sciences which study human behavior. The more complex the reality under study becomes, the more "formality" and "observation" part ways. And if "formality" leads to some limit of tautological "precision," then "observation" leads to the accumulation of observations as exact as they are trivial. What has happened? The simple fact is that as the real becomes more complex, variables cannot be isolated from one another without falling into *formal* abstractions; they can only be observed when they are intermingled with the activity of other variables. This means that observation, however precise and abundant it may be, becomes *irrelevant* when it comes to extracting from it constants in which we might be able to trust.

Skipping a few steps, we come to economics. It seems obvious, to cite one example, that production will vary to some extent with the stimuli it receives. We can assume that a greater incentive will result in greater production. Now let us further assume, and this is far from being obvious, that we can calculate with some degree of precision what goes to make up greater or lesser "production." We are still left with the other variable. What is an "incentive"? Insofar as we formalize it, an incentive becomes the human factor that causes an increase in production. In this way the supposed *constant* turns into a hollow tautology. If we offer monetary rewards for an increase in production and we see that production does not increase, we will conclude that the monetary reward did not constitute an incentive.

If, on the other hand, we multiply our observations about the things we *agree* to call incentives (whether they effect an increase in production or not), if in other words we multiply our observations about hypothetical incentives, we will have to realize that there are an infinite number of variables, both psychosocial and even economic. As a result, a given monetary reward may not be appreciated as a reward in certain cases, and so it may not produce the desired effect. The multitude of precise data about the attitudes of human beings towards a given offer of money only leads us deeper into the woods as to what constitutes an incentive to production, to what extent, and why.

The fact is that Marx's claim to achieve the precision of the natural sciences when dealing with the concrete reality of material production is one of the myths of the nineteenth century. As Bateson points out, such categories as "economic" and "religious" are abstractions: "They are not phenomena present in culture, but are labels for various points of view which we adopt in our studies. In handling such abstractions we must be careful to avoid Whitehead's 'fallacy of misplaced concreteness,' a fallacy into which, for example, the Marxian historians fall when they maintain that economic 'phenomena' are 'primary.' "[21]

One need only read the single—and last—"scientific" work of Marx, Volume 1 of *Capital*, to meet with a surprise. In it we find formalizations and precise observations, to be sure, but the result is far from what we today would call a rigorous "scientific" result. Volume 1 of *Capital* is really a huge anti-ideological work, though Marx seldom uses that term. It does not offer constants which can be observed or applied in other situations or which permit us to foresee with precision what is bound to happen in England itself as the Industrial Revolution continues. What it does point up to readers is the difficulty of uprooting ideological prejudices from the human sciences, even when the latter focus on the mode of material production.

Marx's work on economics may well be the best example of Bateson's description of the real way that scientific discovery works. Bateson points out that the process is always a mix—or the alternate application—of broad knowledge and strict knowledge applied to a complex reality; indeed that should and must be the case when one is proposing to explain any human activity. And human activity in the realm of material production is certainly no simpler or more concrete than human activity in politics or the arts.

This does not mean that we have to give up the distinction between structure and superstructure. It simply means that the structure is not concrete just because it is *economic*. Equating the two may work as a merely formal postulate, and this is what has happened in official Marxism. But the result is a "scientific" inability to analyze the historical process in situations very different from that of England as it faced the Industrial Revolution, the situation of England being the only one that Marx himself "observed."

The case of Lenin is instructive, though I don't have time to analyze it in detail here. In the process of building socialism in Russia, Lenin had to confront and challenge the "economicists," i.e., those who were giving a purely "economistic" interpretation to Marx's thought. In *What Is To Be Done?* Lenin implicitly acknowledged that they stood for Marxist "orthodoxy." For in his refutation of them he stressed the fact that since Marx's time the "mass movement" had begun to play a major structural role.[22] Lenin sets up an opposition between the mass movement and economicist orthodoxy within the very structure of society. In so doing, he is admitting that economic variables cannot be isolated from other variables that are equally concrete and basic. In this particular case, the latter are variables having to do with the collective psyche. They help to explain something to Lenin which would otherwise remain inexplicable: i.e., the fact that the masses, even though they are greatly exploited, seem unable on their own to choose the revolution over "trade unionism" or reform-minded syndicalism.

From Marx's time on, not only the despised psychologists but, even more, the unsuspected anthropologists (including Marxists) have shown that the material structure of life, the basic and ultimate level of concreteness, is always constituted among human beings by variables which go far beyond what "economic" science can describe and explain. That does not mean one has to give up historical materialism. It *does* mean that people must give up a simplistic, nineteenth-century version of it (see REMARK C.5, p. 112).

In other words, nothing prevents us from maintaining that the dangers of superstructural forms, of ideology, increase as thought moves away from the material base to theorize *about* it. What should be kept clear is the fact that science does not protect us against that danger. Any science is obliged to theorize if it wishes to study such a complex and evasive form of concreteness. And once it begins to theorize, science itself enters the realm of *ideology* and must be analyzed from that standpoint; otherwise science will become dehumanized, serving as a pretext for new forms of disguised exploitation of real human beings and their labor. "Ideological" naiveté is always fatal, no matter how scientific it may be.

III. Conclusion to Part One

As we come to the end of these first four chapters on terminology, my readers may well get the feeling that we are right back where we started. That is true to a certain extent, but not wholly.

I have been considering faith and ideology as two basic anthropological dimensions. And the first problem to be faced in this matter was the connection between the two within human existence. In a field mined by prejudices and offbase commonplaces that are taken for granted, it was necessary to sharpen our terms, test their bite, and experiment with substitutes.

In these first four chapters I was not just discussing terminology. I was discussing anthropological problems bound up with terms that are used well or badly in everyday language. One set of terms included: faith or confidence, faith or dogma, faith or self-validating premises used to punctuate series of events in different ways in real-life experience. The other set included: e.g., ideology and reason, ideology and superstructural forms, ideology and human sciences. This was a long but necessary introduction to my discussion of the connection or lack of connection between faith and ideologies.

Let me reiterate a point made before. Once misunderstandings and misleading commonplaces have been overcome, it does not really matter whether readers agree to use my proposed terminology or not. What does matter is that people should make sure that their terminology, whatever it may be, does not hide basic anthropological problems, does not depict them as solved when in fact they are not.

And let me make one final observation. Readers familiar with the socio-political framing of issues may balk at any reference to "faith," even when used in a basic anthropological sense. They may also feel uncomfortable with my use of a phenomenological method of analysis and many elements in my discussion. They may regard my whole approach as too personalist, existential, and individualistic, feeling that in practice it comes down to denying the collective and social component of all authentic thinking. It should be obvious that I reject any such dichotomy. To ignore the social dimension of existential problems is to suffer a terrible impoverishment, in my view. By the same token, the collective standpoint, usually more closely related to ideologies, becomes incomprehensible if we forget that real human beings who engage in thinking and decision making are behind *all* social phenomena, even those social phenomena which are most defined by collective structures. We need only look at the phenomena occurring around us to recognize the real impoverishment produced in societies and individuals when we operate with mechanisms that are not grounded simultaneously in *both* dimensions.

Remarks

REMARK A.1 (see p. 87). *Starting out* in this chapter, I think it is well to stress that the strongest objections to my use of faith and ideologies for terminology derive from a tacit cultural evaluation which is conveyed through language. The very fact that the noun "faith" tends to be used only in the singular is significant, especially since "ideology" is not. If one mentions "ideology," people will tend to ask for specifics: *which* ideology. The assumption seems to be that the plural "ideologies" makes much more sense.

People are clearly adverse to the practice of labelling their own thinking as ideology. Rarely will a liberal talk about the liberal ideology, and even more rarely will a Marxist allude to the Marxist ideology.

If we trace this fact back to its roots,[23] we find that modern humanity is somewhere akin to where Kant was when he began his Critiques. Why do ideologies (like philosophies) oppose and succeed one another, whereas science grows and advances? In cultural language the term "ideology" is tacitly equated with mental constructions that do not progress. Today people are even talking about the "death of ideologies," which seem to be ineffectual when compared with the steady forward movement of technology. Ideologies are looked upon as vestiges of confused, irrational thinking as compared with the achievements of scientific methods and the rigorous use of reason (applied especially to science).

So my formulation of the whole issue comes as a bit of a surprise. I turn this accepted order upside down in dealing with what is commonly called "science" or "reason." I stress that these realities—even in the most scientific or rationalistic of individuals and groups and in societies that have developed both elements more fully—are subordinated to, and made problematic by, a realm of values which is alien and prior to them. I also stress that the term "ideologies" in the plural, which has a somewhat pejorative connotation, should be applied to the systematic attempts (always frustrated) to unify the existence of human beings and society around manipulations, explanations, and achievements of scientific rationality.

This little cultural "scandal" follows inevitably from my analysis in Chapter I, and it is the guiding thread of the considerations in this present chapter.

REMARK A.2 (see p. 88). In calling *one* of the two basic anthropological dimensions "ideology," I am going counter to the general tendency to view the universe, and humanity in it, as structured by one single dimension. Marcuse analyzed the cultural results of this tendency in *One Dimensional Man*.[24] In *The Secular City*[25] Harvey Cox sought to spell out the relationship between on the one hand, the modern human being, who is guided by pragmatism and technocratic criteria, and, on the other hand, religious faith. Indeed his discussion brought in anthropological faith as well.

But if one wants to follow this whole tendency from its roots in the Renaissance period onward, one should consult the fine historical treatment by W. T. Stace in *Religion and the Modern Mind*.[26] Stace points up the decreasing interest in final causes and efficient causes of physical happenings, due to the growing success in explaining the mechanisms of these happenings. Interest in the what and why gave way to interest in the *how*. The why and wherefore came to be regarded more and more as irrelevant. The meaning-efficacy dualism gave way to a monism which spread throughout our culture, and this monism was structured in terms of efficacy alone. Only in our own day do we see a reversal of this tendency. Wars, the threat of atomic destruction, ecological imbalances, and international economic crises have put the questions of why and wherefore back on the agenda. Once again we see this as a primary question. We want to know the *why and wherefore* of everything that operates and seems to have efficacy.

In Section I of this chapter I offer two examples of this newly dramatic logic, which is once again posing questions about basic anthropological faith and leaving room for talk about "ideologies" where once there was talk only about "science" or "reason."

REMARK B.1 (see p. 88). In Section I of this chapter we consider passages from two authors as *examples*. The two authors have different conceptions of the world, but those differing conceptions can be traced back to the same general tendency to picture human existence as something grounded on one single principle: science or reason.

I do not cite these authors as examples of *inconsistency*. My point is not to show that nonscientific or nonrational elements show up in their work despite themselves. I offer them as examples of *logical consistency*. My point is to show where every deep line of thought must lead more or less explicitly once it reflects on the limits to which science or reason can go in structuring human existence.

REMARK B.2 (see p. 89). For my *first* example I cite several significant passages from a Marxist thinker, Milan Machoveč. The passages are all the more significant when we consider the scientific and all-embracing claims made for and by Marxism. Analyzing the first citation from Machoveč's book, we can establish the following facts:

a. He makes a clearcut distinction between the realm of the *scientific*, restricted to some sort of *mediation* ("through"), and the mediated, nonscientific realm composed of pre-existing *values* and human intentions.

b. Thus the scientific realm can serve *differing meaning-structures*. The scientific clearly does not begin with, and is not limited to, the discovery of the methodology to be used for the construction of socialism.

c. The further implication is that the discovery of certain scientific methods rather than others was due to the orientation given to this quest by pre-existing values. Clearly Marx would not have founded the science for the construction of socialism if he had not been "progressive" and "oriented towards the future," etc.

REMARK B.3 (see p. 89). The second citation from Machoveč enables us to proceed further. We can now add two more points to our analysis:

d. Machoveč comments on Peter's "faith" in the resurrection of Jesus. For the moment I am leaving aside the question as to whether Machoveč is talking about anthropological faith or properly religious faith here. The point is that Machoveč's judgment establishes both the distinction between value judgments of this type and scientific judgments, and the superiority of such value judgments over the latter.

e. Machoveč's statements also affirm that this two-dimensioned reality with its corresponding two sets of structures is found in nonreligious human beings, in atheists. This proves that it must be regarded as a basic constituent of every human life.

REMARK B.4 (see p. 90). We come to the third passage cited from Machoveč's book. It adds another point to our analysis, which is connected with the preceding ones:

f. Efficacy (i.e., any scientific methodology), no matter how much it may be oriented towards some purpose, must be continually guided and checked by that purpose. The fact is that science (based on efficacy) is insensitive to the prices that must be paid for specific achievements or successes, and it also renders human beings insensitive to them. Machoveč cites the historical case of socialism. It can be constructed and maintained scientifically without people noticing that certain means employed in the process are radically undermining the humanist purpose for which socialism was conceived.

REMARK B.5 (see p. 91). The last three passages cited from Machoveč's book add further elements and points to those already noted. Two are particularly noteworthy here:

g. Use of the same scientific method, or similar ones, is not capable of conveying or transmitting the initial values of those from whom the method derives epistemologically to those whom it proposes to serve. Here we have another example of the difference and complementarity existing between our two basic anthropological dimensions.

h. The transmission of *meaning* (as opposed to that of efficacy) can be effected only through *models*: i.e., human witnesses to certain values in the face of problematic situations. Hence believers must "stay in contact" with those witnesses by cultivating two complementary attitudes. First, they must adopt a critical-minded spirit and willingly accept the problems posed to efficacy by values. Second, they must come in contact with the various spiritual traditions in which concrete human beings have struggled with such problems and encountered victory or defeat.

REMARK B.6 (see p. 94). This brings me to my *second* example. I consider several key passages in a book by Gregory Bateson, a thinker whose roots could well be classified as neopositivist.[27] The chief citation again enables me to extract various points which are most valuable for my present analysis. Here they are:

a. In using the term "premises" Bateson is alluding to a human structure which is supposedly rational, hence grounded on arguments that can be made explicit. Human beings must account for the why and wherefore of their actions. But the very meaning of the term "premises" indicates that at the basis of the ultimate argument lie facts and data which are not the results of logical argument, which are not provided by the reason that is arguing its case. These underlying facts are acquired in a different way—through intuition, perception, valuation, psychobiological mechanism, and so forth. Thus Bateson is already implicitly delimiting the field where reason, and science based on it, prevails in the structuring of human activity.

b. As Bateson sees it, the premises mentioned by him have to do with the fact that all human beings learn to orient themselves to events by imposing *an order on the mere flux of happenings*. It is not a totally arbitrary process since the flux itself presents repeated sequences of similar events—what Bateson calls "redundancy."[28] Human beings learn to perceive (epistemology) and value (ontology) events by placing them in sequences. Then, on the basis of these *premises*, they argue to prove that they are acting rationally. Bateson does not really concern himself with the origin of this fundamental learning, but from other data we can say that this origin is *social*: i.e., referential models or witnesses.[29]

c. Bateson also notes that these "premises" are *self-validating*. By this he means two things. (1) Experiential reality by itself can do little to alter them, since they determine what is perceived and how it is perceived. We might regard a certain event in another person's life as a failure. But that event might not lead the person to alter his or her premises because those premises preclude the event from being regarded as a failure by that person. Hence, says Bateson, we cannot really talk about the *truth* or *falsity* of such premises in any scientific sense. Why? Because here empirical reality cannot be the measure or criterion for deciding truth or falsity. Rather, the premises are the criterion for judging reality. (2) The value attributed to certain facts as opposed to others does not stem from anything that science or reason could decide. In itself a value is not true or false. It is a way of perceiving and evaluating reality, independent of the facticity of the latter.

d. A final point made by Bateson is also worth noting here. Linking this basic a-rationality with other elements of evolution, Bateson repeatedly points up its usefulness. It would be extremely dangerous, and contrary to the whole economy of energy, if these basic premises were at the mercy of variations introduced by trial-and-error experiences (homeostatic processes). Errors at that level would cost too high a price.[30]

REMARK C.1 (see p. 95). In Section II of this chapter I directly analyze the possibilities and the advantages of the term "ideology" when it comes to designating any system of objective efficacy as opposed to the values-structure that discovers and implements it.

An initial observation may be useful to my readers. Chapter I should have made clear the distinction between the realm (or structure) of *meaning* or values and the realm of *efficacy*. These two terms (meaning and efficacy) are concrete, so they provide an unmistakable guiding thread for what follows. Things change, however, when I use the words "faith" and "ideology" for those same two anthropological dimensions. When I say that the realm of meaning depends on anthropological faith in human referential witnesses, I am employing *concrete* language. Everyone knows what "faith" is in the most primary sense of the word and can verify this experience in the realm of his or her own values. But when I use the term "ideology" to refer to the realm of efficacy, I am using *abstract* and therefore much more arbitrary language. To give it content, I must go back to the concrete and connect ideology with efficacy. So why don't I use a term for the realm of efficacy that is as concrete as the term "faith" used for the realm of meaning? Simply because no such term exists. Let us say that the realm of values derives from something as concrete as the verb "believe." From what concrete verb might we derive the notion of being effective or efficacious? *Foreseeing* is certainly one of the factors in efficacy, but it is not the only one. *Knowing* or *know-how* may come close to what we are looking for. But since different values give rise to different systems of efficacy, we need a word to convey the plurality of know-hows involved. I rejected the word "science" because of its unitary pretensions. In the plural it refers to different branches of learning rather than pointing up the influence of different values. I also rejected the word "wisdom" because current language tends to associate that with the realm of ethics or values rather than with the realm of efficacy. Now despite its abstract character, the word "ideology" can designate any system of "ideas" about the connection between events when viewed as objective: i.e., independent as *facts* from the values on which they depend for their purpose or finality. So I take an abstract term and give it a fairly reasonable meaning-content, one which is not wholly arbitrary. Readers may not choose to adopt my terminology, but in order to understand what follows they should keep in mind the meaning which I give to my terms.

In the following pages I attempt to define my use of the term "ideology" and distinguish it from other common uses of the same term. I try to show that other uses entail real problems which go far deeper than a merely terminological argument.

REMARK C.2 (see p. 97). The *first step* is to note that in common usage the word "ideology" refers more to the cultural (sociological) level than to the individual (anthropological) level.

Marx's analysis was designed to change the (social) world, not explain it. He quickly focused on the different degrees of guarantee provided by the knowledge-data which a society had about itself: i.e., guarantees of realism and objectivity as opposed to potential distortions, more or less bound up with interests, resulting from subjective factors. It should be noted, however, that he was more concerned with subjective factors of a group nature rather than those associated with individuals.

From this basic standpoint, and even though various problems still remain (as we shall see), one thing seems obvious immediately. An area where one can make precise calculations (e.g., number of work hours, purchasing power of salaries, the cost of subsistence, the price of products) offers more guarantees than an area where one talks about the moral value of work, the nominal rights of the worker, his or her eternal reward, and so forth. This prompted the metaphor of verticality: the higher thought rises, the less its guarantees of realism. The upper level was named the *super*structure. By the same token, the more thought remains attached to the material *base* of existence, the more it offers guarantees of realism and preciseness. And since the material base of human life is *economic* activity, Marx talked about the economic (or material) structure or *infra*structure. By that he meant the means of production and human relations of production.

Now if we, like Marx, refer to the superstructural realm as "ideology," it would seem logical to assume that *in principle* this realm should be labelled *neutral*. For even though it dovetails with the interests of those who rule society in large measure, it is also the realm in which opposing lines of thought and symbols arise to challenge the existing order and its interests and to accompany a new order as it takes shape.

But when we look at the salient facts and the actual operation of the realm of ideology, we get a different picture. We find that it usually serves to hide and justify the harsh, disagreeable, and unjust realities of the material structure. Hence the term "ideology" quickly took on a *pejorative* sense, and that sense has taken priority over any neutral sense. To talk about ideology is to talk about a false social consciousness.

REMARK C.3 (see p. 99). Our *second step* is to examine both the *neutral* and the *pejorative* senses of the term "ideology." I begin with its neutral sense. Is the term "ideology" in its neutral sense opposed to what I have been calling "ideology" in this book? The answer would seem to be yes. After all, the realm of values—i.e., ethics, philosophy, and religion—is normally included in what Marx called the ideological superstructure; it is not something above that superstructure. But a closer and deeper analysis of what Marx called "ideological conflict" brings out several important elements:

a. If the notion of ideological conflict makes sense at all, it is because the material or economic structure does not fully produce on its own a clear consciousness of the interests at stake. If it did, then all ideological or political conflict, including Marxism, would be useless and contradictory. Or, at best, such conflicts would merely be "explanations" of reality rather than being forms of praxis designed to change it.

b. The social values-structure of a person—which set of class interests one chooses to side with—does not depend on belonging to that class in an objective or economic sense. Two major facts are related to this point. First, Marx's own thought arose within the context of bourgeois culture. Second, the vast majority of the proletariat possessed a false consciousness of their own situation, and Marx proposed to destroy that false consciousness.

c. "Ideology," even though defined in the last instance by the material base or structure and its forms, must necessarily leave room for a definition in the first instance of the meaning-structure. This defines a sphere prior to, and independent of, ideology. Marx did not dwell on this prior sphere, but it became a critical problem when his *ideology* found realization in socialist societies.

REMARK C.4 (see p. 100). That brings us to the *pejorative* use of the term "ideology." Here again we find that this use seems to be opposed to my use of the term. In my usage ideology takes in all the mechanisms of the objective world; thus it also takes in scientific knowledge. In Marx's thought, ideology in the pejorative sense stands opposed precisely to social knowledge that is *scientific* and objective. It is knowledge distorted by (subjective) interests. However, a more rigorous analysis along Marx's own lines reveals that this opposition is really superficial and misleading. Here two points are worth noting, and I will discuss the first one in this section.

The *first* point has to do with the distinction made between the (ideological) superstructure and the (material or economic) structure and with the realization that interests rooted in the structure distort superstructural knowledge. Once we get that far, why should we assume that the superstructure in line with the interests of the bourgeoisie is *ideological* (in the pejorative sense), whereas the superstructure in line with the interests of the proletariat is *scientific* (and objective)? Note the following observation by Adam Schaff:

> Such a subtle philosophical mind would have had to notice the problem immediately. If Marx did not pause over it, this was because he added another *premise* [my italics to point up the connection with Bateson's

term], . . . basically, the thesis about the differentiation of the interests of different social classes. By virtue of this differentiation, some classes have an interest in giving impetus to the evolution of society while others have an interest in maintaining the existing setup or blocking the transformations in progress. The point is that knowledge is distorted only when it is conditioned by the interests of the "descending" classes: i.e., those interested in maintaining the existing order and threatened by its disappearance. When knowledge or cognition is conditioned by the interests of the "ascending" revolutionary classes, who are in favor of the social transformations in progress, there is no cognitive distortion. At this point in his reflection Marx ceased to be interested in the problem of the social factors conditioning knowledge and the whole problem of cognitive distortion.[31]

Here, to use Bateson's terminology, we are dealing with an ontological and epistemological premise that is self-validating. It is a way of punctuating historical events which depends on implicit, pre-existing values. It is clear, therefore, that the difference between "ideological" (in the pejorative sense) and "scientific" does not depend on a difference in methodology, precision, or rigor. Instead it depends on taking a certain stance in the order of values. This is a confirmation of the passage from Machoveč which I cited near the beginning of this chapter: "Marx wanted to organize all *progressive* people *oriented towards the future*, through a strict and *objective scientific* analysis . . ."(my italics).

REMARK C.5 (see p. 104). The *second* point has to do with the fact that the pejorative sense of the term "ideology" seems to clearly distinguish ideology from "science" dealing with the material structure of human life in terms of the latter's greater guarantee of objectivity. As we noted already, "superstructure" and economic "structure" (or "infrastructure") were spatial terms designed to underline the greater guarantee of objectivity, scientificness, and truth in cognitive data relating to, or deriving from, the latter level. Wherein does this guarantee lie concretely, according to Marx's thought? It lies in the fact that science is more "precise" on the level of the structure or infrastructure.

This line of reasoning is subject to various observations that will be taken up again further on in this book. The common point underlying them all is the fact that even the most precise science is subject to ideological distortions. Hence it is impossible to establish a consistent boundary line between science and ideology. Notice the following two points:

a. Marx gives the label of scientific method to the method which he employs in *Capital* to combat ideologies. This means that ideologies are in a realm accessible to the sciences (the social sciences, to be specific). We find a distorting "ideology" in many ways of handling the *science* of humanity and society.[32]

b. The precision of the sciences does not derive from the fact that they have evaded ideology: i.e., from the concreteness of their object. It derives from an artificial simplicity in the variables isolated by means of abstraction. This abstraction enables the bourgeois science of economy, for example, to be just as precise as the Marxist one, without thereby having any more guarantees of objectivity. Here again we find that the real guarantees derive from the values held by the person who resorts to scientific preciseness, interprets it, and manipulates it technically. In short, it is not the mark of science as such to escape ideology or to work in a realm immune to ideology.

NOTES

1. Milan Machověc, *Jesús para ateos*, Spanish trans. (Salamanca: Sígueme, 1974), pp. 28–29; German edition, *Jesus für Atheisten*; English trans., *A Marxist Looks at Jesus* (Philadelphia: Fortress Press, 1976). Spanish edition used by Segundo is followed here, and pages refer to Spanish edition.

2. Ibid., p. 39. Machověc adds: "I am not saying that the majority of Marxists affirm this *explicitly*. I can only attest to the fact that hundreds of thousands of Marxists find themselves on the threshold of such an admission. Further steps in that direction will depend to some extent on Christians as well" (ibid., my italics).

3. Ibid., p. 33.

4. Ibid.

5. Ibid.

6. Ibid., pp. 33–34.

7. See Allan Janik and Stephen Toulmin, *Wittgenstein's Vienna* (New York: Touchstone Books, 1973), p. 31.

8. Gregory Bateson, *Steps to an Ecology of Mind* (New York: Ballantine Books, 1972), p. 314.

9. "We suggest that *what* is learned in Learning II is a way of *punctuating events*" (ibid., p. 300).

"In describing individual human beings, both the scientist and the layman commonly resort to adjectives descriptive of 'character.' It is said that Mr. Jones is dependent, hostile, fey, finicky, anxious, exhibitionistic, narcissistic, passive, competitive, energetic, bold, cowardly, fatalistic, humorous, playful, canny, optimistic, perfectionist, careless, careful, casual, etc. In the light of what has already been said, the reader will be able to assign all these adjectives to their appropriate logical type. All are descriptive of (possible) results of Learning II" (ibid., pp. 297–298).

For the moment I want to stay with Bateson's definition of Learning II as a "way of punctuating events." Further on in this book I will stress the difference between learning to do things (Learning I) and learning how to learn (Learning II). This will be a key point in developing the first part of chapter 5.

10. "The practitioner of magic does not unlearn his magical view of events when the magic does not work. In fact, the propositions which govern punctuation have the general characteristic of being self-validating. What we term "context" includes the subject's behavior as well as the external events. But this behavior is controlled by former Learning II and therefore it will be of such a kind as to mold the total context *to fit the expected punctuation*. In sum, this self-validating characteristic of the content of Learning II has the effect that such learning is almost ineradicable.

It follows that Learning II acquired in infancy is likely to persist through life" (ibid., p. 301; my italics).

Bateson also acknowledges the claim that there are examples of changing the way that external events are punctuated: "But it is claimed that something of the sort does from time to time occur in psychotherapy, religious conversion, and in other sequences in which there is profound reorganization of character" (ibid., p. 301).

11. "But a way of punctuating is not true or false. There is nothing contained in the propositions of this learning [i.e., Learning II] that can be tested against reality. It is like a picture seen in an inkblot; it has neither correctness nor incorrectness. It is only a way of seeing the inkblot.

"Consider the instrumental view of life. An organism with this view of life in a new situation will engage in trial-and-error behavior in order to make the situation provide a positive reinforcement. If he fails to get this reinforcement, *his purposive philosophy is not thereby negated*. His trial-and-error behavior will simply continue. *The premises of 'purpose' are simply not of the same logical type as the material facts of* life, and therefore cannot easily be contradicted by them" (ibid., pp. 300–301; my italics).

12. Karl Marx and Friedrich Engels, *The German Ideology*, Eng. trans. (New York: International Publishers, 1970), pp. 20–21.

13. K. Marx, "Preface" to *A Contribution to the Critique of Political Economy*, Eng. trans. (New York: International Publishers, 1970), pp. 20–21.

14. Summary by Jean Guichard in "Un procès à refaire," *Lettre* 201 (Paris, May 1975): 20.

15. Karl Marx and Friedrich Engels, *Manifesto of the Communist Party*, Eng. trans., in K. Marx, *The Revolutions of 1848: Political Writings I* (New York: Vintage Books, 1974), p. 85.

16. See V. I. Lenin, *What Is To Be Done?*, Eng. trans. (New York: International Publishers, 1929).

17. Leonid Leonov, *Doroga na Okean*. This novel has been translated into English as *Road to the Ocean* and *Toward the Ocean*. Note the following dialogue, written in the midst of the Stalinist period:

"The new man will create new human beings in his own image and likeness. In other words, he will be a god. He will be the soul of the gigantic machinery that will provide a plentiful supply of food, clothing, and pleasure."

"That is interesting," agreed Kormilitsin. "I have always enjoyed reading about the *miracles* of science and technology. But what about *the people* themselves?"

"They will have different associations. . . . For example, you might have an association of southern or northeastern linen producers. The only government organ would be the central office of planetary statistics that would make up annual comparative charts."

"And who would draw conclusions from these charts?"

"Well . . . Marx said nothing about that. But that is only a minor detail."

"Wait, I am talking about the man in whose hands all the threads of perfect knowledge will gather. Now don't get angry with me, but what if this man is an *egotist* like you, Protoklitov?"

"Such a man would be incapable of doing any damage. What is more, he will be superior. . . ."

"But can you recall any deity of the past who did not have defects?"
Protoklitov began to get angry. . . . He never liked provincial bumpkins.

18. Marx, "Preface," p. 21.

19. Marx, *Capital,* Book I, Part Four, Chapter 15, footnote 4; Eng. trans. (New York: Vintage Books, 1977), pp. 493–494.

The English word "develop" translates German *Entwicklung* here, and thus is ambiguous. My Spanish text gives "explain," which sounds too deterministic to me. I have seen an English version that offers "infer," and I would prefer some such word. The point, in any case, is that this passage and its whole context seem to underline the "relative autonomy" of the superstructure. For two interesting supportive commentaries by Engels on the latter point, see his letter to Joseph Bloch in Königsberg (September, 21–22, 1890) and his letter to Franz Mehring in Berlin (July 14, 1893). They are Letters 227 and 249 in Marx-Engels, *Selected Correspondence,* 2nd ed., Eng. trans. (Moscow: Progress Publishers, 1965).

20. However, Althusser rightly points out that the Marxist scientific method of dialectics for knowing reality (or, the concrete) starts out by going through three types of what he calls "Generalities" (Generality I, Generality II, Generality III). In other words, it goes through three different types of abstraction. See Chapter 6 in Louis Althusser, *For Marx*, Eng. trans. (London: Verso Editions, 1979), pp. 183f.

21. Bateson, *Steps,* p. 64.

22. Lenin, *What Is To Be Done?* New theoretical tasks are posed by the awakening of the masses:

That the mass movement is a most important phenomenon is a fact about which there can be no dispute [p. 46].

That is why the question of the relation between *consciousness and spontaneity* is of such enormous general interest [p. 31; my italics].

23. Clifford Geertz, "Ideology as a Cultural System," in David E. Apter, ed., *Ideology and Discontent* (New York: The Free Press of Glencoe, 1964), pp. 47–76.

24. Herbert Marcuse, *One Dimensional Man* (Boston: Beacon Press, 1964).

25. Harvey Cox, *The Secular City* (New York: Macmillan, 1965).

26. W. T. Stace, *Religion and the Modern Mind* (Philadelphia: Lippincott, 1929).

27. Bateson, *Steps,* pp. 264–266.

28. Ibid., pp. 406f.

29. Ibid., pp. 159f. and pp. 194f.

30. Ibid., pp. 406f.

31. Adam Schaff, "L'objectivité de la connaissance à la lumière de la sociologie de la connaissance et de l'analyse du langage," *Social Science Information* 7 (1968): 103–129. The Spanish text used here comes from the anthology edited by Eliseo Verón, *El proceso ideológico* (Buenos Aires: Tiempo Contemporáneo), 1973.

32. To be logical here, I probably should say "in all" of them rather than "in many." That is the uncomfortable conclusion which Mannheim was forced to reach, in what has come to be called Mannheim's paradox (akin to Zeno's paradox about Achilles and the tortoise): i.e., the fact that all ideologies are necessarily interested and mutually relativize each other. As Geertz puts it: "In Mannheim's case . . . the more he grappled with it the more deeply he became engulfed in its ambiguities until, driven

by the logic of his initial assumptions to submit even his own point of view to sociological analysis, he ended, as is well known, in an ethical and epistemological relativism that he himself found uncomfortable'' (Geertz, ''Ideology as a Cultural System,'' in Apter, ed., *Ideology and Discontent,* pp. 47–48).

Part Two

LINKING TERMS

CHAPTER V

Can Faith and Ideologies
Be Mutually Exclusive?

So far we have been scrutinizing terms and trying to clarify them in order to form a more realistic picture of the two complementary dimensions that must find a place in any coherent view of the human being. Once having done that, we would hardly seem to have any need to expatiate further on the necessary mutuality and interrelationship of faith and ideologies.

There is a widespread common assumption in our culture, however, that human beings divide into two basic groups. One group adheres to faith, the other group to different ideologies. In fact, there does exist a third group, the largest in terms of number but the smallest in terms of importance. It is made up of the "undecided," who adhere to no faith or known ideology. They live from day to day, adapting to every shifting wind of circumstances. Such is the common view.

Moreover, it is no accident that the word "faith" is used in the singular and that the word "ideologies" is used in the plural. People assume that the "religious" dimension, which is associated with "faith," is basically one. Those who are not religious, on the other hand, allegedly can be pigeonholed in the various ideologies unless they are weak, vacillating, and undecided. And it is also assumed that they can flit from one ideology to another with relative ease.

It is frequently assumed that "religious" differences are minor as compared with the crucial—and rather odd—fact of "having faith." But where faith is absent, ideologies divide human beings. In short, the realm of ideologies is ordinarily viewed as a "plural" realm, and the realm of faith is viewed as a singular world, in more than one sense.

It should also be noted that the realm of faith frequently seems to fear the realm of ideologies. When people detect a mix of both in an individual or a group, there is an undeniable tendency for them to start talking about "in-

119

filtration.'' It is as if some dangerous, alien element had been inserted on the sly into data which already sufficed to guide the existence of the given individual or group. People foresee ambiguities, shadings, and inconsistencies resulting from the adoption of opposing systems.

In our cultural life we also hear frequent admonitions, coming from both sides (faith and ideologies), to relativize the other side. The aim, it seems, is to make sure that the two planes are kept separate for the most part. This effort to keep the two planes separate impedes certain efforts. On the one hand it prevents people from admitting the obvious need to analyze "faith" from an "ideological" standpoint. On the other hand it prevents people from confronting ideologies with critical questions about the relationship between the means they employ and the values they seek to realize.

Finally, everyday language in our culture is also obscured by the "faiths" and "ideologies" which are openly explicated. It remains impervious to problems posed to both by the great majority of humans who do not seem to hold any recognized "faith" or "ideology," but who nevertheless are very consistent in their attitudes, formulations, values, and mediations as they go about their work. Such major present-day trends as technocracy, consumptionism, and bureaucracy do not constitute what are known as "ideologies," much less "religions," in the usual sense. Yet they do constitute coherent systems of values and mediations, of "faiths" and "ideologies" in my sense of the terms. They are realities to be dealt with.

In Part Two I shall begin to examine the possible relationship between the two human dimensions under discussion. I shall consider whether they can be mutually exclusive and show why the answer must be no. I shall also explore the relationships between them in terms of language. Then in Part Three I shall explore more deeply the complementarity between these two basic human dimensions.

I. Faith without Ideologies?

Back in 1976 the press reported certain statements attributed to Dom Helder Camara, statements which he made during a Eucharistic Congress in Philadelphia. The archbishop of Recife reportedly said: "One who has Jesus Christ does not need Marx."[1] Now we all know that the press is all too readily inclined to inject distortion into the statements of controversial personages and that the latter often nuance their remarks more fully than we learn from the press. So I was interested to see a very similar statement by Archbishop Camara in the monthly bulletin of CELAM, and this time there was more of a guarantee that it reflected his real thinking. In answer to a questionnaire he said: "With the gospel message, the social encyclicals, Vatican II and Medellín, we have no need to appeal to any ideology to inspire us in our sacred commitment to foster human betterment. . . ."[2]

I choose these remarks by Dom Helder Camara because no one could accuse him of representing or advocating that divorce between faith and life which Vatican II found so regrettable (*GS*:43). Dom Helder's words derive from a basic conception of faith which is the same as that of Vatican II. Insofar as the problems posed by history are concerned, "faith throws a new light on everything, manifests God's design for man's total vocation, and thus directs the mind to solutions which are fully human" (*GS*:11). It is because Dom Helder's words are framed within this basic conception of faith that they are relevant to my inquiry here.

So what do his words mean? Since we can assume that Dom Helder is referring to historical realities, "having Jesus Christ" must mean believing in him. It is most unlikely that Dom Helder is referring to possessing Jesus in paradise after death. His point, then, seems to be that having faith in Jesus exempts a person from dependence on Marx. What does "dependence" mean in that case? In what sense is Marx no longer needed? Again it is unlikely that Dom Helder sees Marx as someone proposing an approach, be it scientific or not, that is totally offbase. If that were the case, then no one would need Marx whether he or she believed in Jesus or not. So the most likely meaning of his statement is this: having faith in Jesus Christ, and specifically in the Jesus Christ who continues to live in the Catholic Church, exempts people from adhering to *ideologies*. That would also free them from dependence on Marx, the clearest example of an ideologist.

The Issue Raised

That brings us down to a basic question: the *why* and *wherefore* involved in such a statement. Why is it that ideologies are no longer necessary when one has the correct faith? The second statement by Dom Helder cited above offers an answer to the *wherefore*: "to inspire us in our sacred commitment to foster human betterment. . . ." So we have two clear alternative interpretations of his remarks. One interpretation would be that here Dom Helder is viewing ideologies as values-structures, as "faiths" in my sense of the word. In that case his statement is a tautology: one who already has a satisfactory faith does not need another. The other possible interpretation is that Dom Helder, in saying that no ideologies were needed any longer, was apparently forgetting that every "faith" (including the Christian faith, no matter how true it might be) structures certain values which then must find some way to concrete realization within the complexity of the real world. In short, every faith requires practical systems of implementation. Those systems evolve and change as reality does; all are not equally efficacious, much less neutral.

We could agree, then, that people who already possess a meaning-structure do not need an ideology *specifically for the purpose* of inspiring them to implement their values. But that hardly means that they *already* possess suitable methodologies for implementing those values in history.

Going back to Dom Helder's remarks above, we may now ask *why* the

Christian does not need Marx. Dom Helder seems to suggest that Christians do not need the elements provided by ideologies because they already are provided "with the gospel message, the social encyclicals, Vatican II, and Medellín." They do not need any (other?) ideology because they have sufficient criteria in those sources. To phrase the point in my terminology, the Christian "faith" has already produced its own "ideological" elements. And, according to Dom Helder, they are *consistent* with the Christian faith—perhaps the only criteria to be consistent with it—as well as adequate to the task of implementing it.

I have no doubt that this is what Dom Helder is trying to say here. This is true no matter what opinion one may hold about the partially "ideological" character of the first two sources cited by Dom Helder. I refer to the two more "dogmatic" texts, those of the Gospels and Vatican II. No matter where he may stand on them, Dom Helder must admit that at least the other two sources (the social encyclicals and the documents of Medellín) fall under the category I have labelled "ideology." Why? Because they are not solely and simply expressions of "faith"; as their authors indicate, they are "applications" of the faith to specific circumstances, areas, and regions.[3]

Here I am not interested in exploring the mechanism underlying the tendency to uphold the unity or oneness of the faith at all costs. In other works I have dealt with this whole tendency to reject ideologies which are regarded as alien and dangerous because they might undermine the basic oneness of the faith.[4] Nor am I greatly interested in pointing up the excessively high value placed on such obviously ideological elements as the social encyclicals, so long as they stem from the inner world of believers. It is another question that interests me right now: to what extent can more direct expressions of the Christian faith, such as the Gospels themselves, be considered free of ideologies?

I need hardly point out that the answer to that question cannot be derived from the terminology I have adopted. However, it is closely bound up with the *facts* which we have discovered and analyzed in the course of examining my use of terms. One central fact is that no "faith" can be expressed or transmitted except through concrete embodiments of it. It must find embodiment in deeds, which are the product of the envisioned ideals plus techniques employed to turn them into reality. While the ideals, in the abstract, may aspire to a certain ubiquity and nontemporality, every concrete realization of them and every technique used for this realization will bear the mark of the time and place in which they are to be realized.

Let me cite one example relating to Christianity. It was Vatican II that pointed out how anachronistic it would be for us today to give the same meaning and importance to almsgiving, as a technique for helping the needy, that Jesus gave it in the Gospels. That concrete means or technique and its efficacy bear the mark of Jesus' day. Today it would not convey the values of justice, love, and giving which it once did convey. In a situation of growing socialization and human interdependence, almsgiving would be associated with a typically individualistic attitude, and people would have every right to interpret it in those terms. Vatican II rightly pointed out that the payment of just taxes now holds the key place once occupied by almsgiving as an expression of realistic concern for those in need (*GS:*30).

Now isn't that the same as saying that almsgiving, as stressed in the Gospels, was an "ideological" element in my sense of the word: i.e., a specific technique for expressing the Christian faith, which was valid in equally specific historical circumstances? And if Christians refuse to change their ideological elements as change takes place in history, won't the attitudes that once conveyed and embodied certain Christian values turn into expressions of very different, even opposite values?

Faith and Works: Paul and James

I can go further and state that the earliest Christian communities were aware of the problem stemming from the necessary complementarity of faith and ideologies. Indeed the problem seems to have been associated with one of the few Christian topics which gave rise to open discussion and debate, if we consider the writings collected in the New Testament. I refer to the debate whether salvation came from faith alone or from faith with works.

On the one hand Paul writes: "For we hold that a man is justified by faith apart from works of law" (Rom. 3:28). On the other hand James reaches the following conclusion: "You see that a man is justified by works and not by faith alone" (James 2:24). My analysis in Part One of this book should help us to unravel this tangled web, showing that the two writers were arguing from different corners of the ring in the overall debate.

In his defense of faith alone as the means of salvation, for example, Paul was merely formulating in more abstract terms the very argument that Jesus had offered against those who sought to turn "religious" faith into a personal instrument for their own benefit. That should not surprise us, though at first glance we might not notice what Paul is doing. Paul himself rarely cited the words of Jesus, and we get the impression that he is trying to fashion a whole theology of his own. But in fact he was thoroughly loyal to Jesus' set of themes, though he expressed it in his own way.

Paul's great theme of faith shows clearly that he had grasped Jesus' polemic against turning religion into an "ideology" or set of sacred "instruments" instead of maintaining it as a "faith," a meaning-structure. When a canopy of sacredness and absoluteness is placed over so-called "faith," said Jesus, it is actually a cover for pragmatic interests and values that have nothing to do with love for neighbor or love for God.

Paul attacks the same problem at its existential roots. He points out that this mechanism is operative because, and insofar as, human beings feel insecure about their destiny. When religious instruments are labelled sacred and absolute, people feel tranquil about their ultimate fate. The root problem of human insecurity is the problem of being on the right side of God, the

Supreme Power, both in time and eternity. No one would ever dare to de-absolutize the religious realm, as Jesus demands, unless he or she entrusted personal destiny to something—or someone—that was not liable to fall prey to calculation or possessiveness. This trusting surrender is precisely what Paul calls "faith," faith alone. The "works" which Paul contrasts with faith are all those things which enable human beings, through the use of religion, to calculate what exactly their destiny is to be (see Rom. 3:19–20, 27; 4:1–2, 13–22; 9:30–32; etc.).

The context shows us clearly that Paul has created a new terminology of his own, so to speak. Not only does he use the term "faith" in his own distinctive way, as is commonly admitted; he also coins a new term, "works," for his whole discussion.

What Paul calls "faith" is neither anthropological faith, as I have been using the term in this book, nor religious faith. With good reason it has been equated with the term "trust." Paul is not talking about adopting a certain values-structure because one believes the testimony of another human or a divine source. Instead he is talking about entrusting the course of one's life to another. And for what purpose? Precisely so that one can stay free, can open one's heart—with or without religion—to a values-structure that will give direction to one's "works" from a center deep inside the individual person rather than from some alien center outside the person.

Paul's problem, in fact, had nothing to do with the question whether "believing" was to be preferred over "doing." His position was contrary to *both* Luther's interpretation *and* the traditional Catholic interpretation. *In Paul's view salvation does come from faith alone, but only because faith enables a person to act, to go to work, in a certain way.*

Thus two things stand out clearly in Paul's thinking. First, when Paul talks about "works" he is referring to what I would call a religious "ideology." Indeed when he wishes to express himself more clearly and pointedly, he talks about "works of the law" (Rom. 3:20, 28; 9:32; Gal. 2:16; 3:2, 5, 10). And by that he means things which pose as instruments endowed with the absolute power to save people. That is why even faith itself can be turned into a "work of the law," as Karl Barth perceived, insofar as it is conceived as a means. Instead of becoming a *liberation for*, it becomes a sacred, self-validating instrument for a religion of the lips instead of the heart.

The second thing follows logically from the first in Paul's thinking: i.e., that God continues to judge human beings *according to their works* (Rom. 2:6; 8:13; 13:12; 1 Cor. 3:13–15; 2 Cor. 11:15; Gal. 5:19; 6:4; Eph. 2:9–10; etc.). Even though Paul does not always make the point explicitly, we must make a clear distinction between "works of the law" and "works" in a good sense. The former refers to the manipulation of religion as a tool; the latter has to do with human action in history designed to flesh out values. For Paul, as for early Christianity in general, love remains the one and only commandment as well as the one and only criterion behind God's universal judgment (see Rom. 13:8–10; Matt. 25:31f.; John 13:34; 15:12, 17).

Perhaps it was the ambiguity or complexity of Paul's terminology that triggered the debate in the early Church to which I have been alluding. Clearly the writer of the Letter of James has a different definition of "faith" and "works" in mind, and one closer to everyday language, when he concludes: "You see then that a man is justified by works and not by faith alone" (James 2:24). What may not be so clear is the fact that James is arguing against a misunderstanding which stems from the ordinary usage of religious language. Here is his central argument:

> My brothers, what use is it for a man to say he has faith when he does nothing to show it? Can that faith save him? Suppose a brother or a sister is in rags with not enough food for the day, and one of you says, "Good luck to you, keep yourselves warm, and have plenty to eat," but does nothing to supply their bodily needs, what is the good of that? So with faith; if it does not lead to action, it is in itself a lifeless thing [James 2:14–17].

Here the writer is using "faith" in the sense which it has in ordinary usage: i.e., adherence to a religious creed. Unlike Paul, he is not thinking of the entrusting of one's personal destiny to the hands of the savior. This is clear from the passage cited and from two points made in the following verses. Pursuing his argument the author writes: "You have faith enough to believe in the one God. Excellent! The devils have faith like that, and it makes them tremble" (James 2:19). Here we have a clear instance of what the author means by "faith alone." He means faith without works. The demons have such faith. They accept an "orthodox" religious truth, but that acceptance doesn't save them.

The second point is that James, like Paul, cites the case of Abraham in support of his position. Both Paul and James, in fact, allude explicitly to Genesis 15:6. James writes: "Abraham put his faith in God and that faith was counted to him as righteousness" (James 2:23). Paul suggests that these words refer to Abraham's pure and complete trust in God's promise that he would have progeny. That is why Abraham's "believing" is mentioned much earlier (Gen. 15:6) than his supremely "righteous work": i.e., his willingness to sacrifice Isaac (Gen. 22). James views the matter from a different angle. As he sees it, Abraham's faith in God's promise of progeny found no expression until God demanded the sacrifice of his promised son, Isaac. Only then did he merit the divine judgment in which his faith, now carried into deed, was counted to him as righteousness. As the Letter of James puts it:

> Was it not by his action, *in offering his son Isaac* upon the altar, that our father Abraham was justified? Surely you can see that *faith was at work in his actions*, and that by these actions the integrity of his faith was fully proved. Here was *the fulfillment* of the words of Scripture: "Abraham put his faith in God, and that faith was counted to him as righteousness" [James 2:21–23].

Paul would certainly agree that Abraham's faith found its complete fulfillment in the sacrifice of Isaac. But he rightly points out that such a sacrifice
could be performed as a "work" and conceal a lack of "faith," though that
did not happen in Abraham's case. It could be an absolutized manipulation
of religion to stay in good with God and win God's blessing without really
opening one's heart to God.

James, on the other hand, would certainly agree that accepting the datum
of a promise made and having subjective certainty about its fulfillment is
faith in the ordinary sense of the word. But he points out that it is meaningful
as faith only insofar as it is converted into a different way of acting. God
desires faith so that human beings will effectively adhere to certain values and
carry them into practice. The "orthodoxy" of the demons has nothing to do
with real, living faith. Indeed nothing can really be called faith unless it is
reflected in a consistent pattern of action, in deeds designed to flesh out specific values in history. Believing that God is one or that Christ is the savior is
worthless, says James, if one's fellow humans lack daily necessities, if faith is
not transformed into a meaning-structure and effective action in history.

Thus we find continuity between the thinking of Paul, James, and Vatican
II. "Faith" (in Paul's sense) is needed to free human beings from their obsession with their own safety and security. With such "faith" they are freed
from "religious" inhibitions as they immerse themselves in a relative and
changing history and go to "work" (in James's sense) in accordance with the
values-structure implied by their faith and demanded by reality.

Let me paraphrase the thinking of James in my terminology, while still
remaining true to his thrust: *a faith without ideologies is, in fact, dead.*

The Issue Resolved

Now then, what am I to think of the two statements by Dom Helder Camara which were cited earlier? I would say that they represent a typical current example of what both Paul and James meant by lack of *faith*. From a
Pauline point of view, what sound basis is there for such a smug and self-
satisfied assertion of ideological sufficiency? Remember that "faith" in the
Pauline sense frees people from a paralyzing concern for their own destiny
and from obsession with religious techniques for ensuring the right outcome.
Human beings are set free so that their creative powers can be turned into
concrete, effective love. To human beings who have such "faith" what
would it matter whether the methods used to implement and practice love
came from within the circle of believers or from outside?

Human beings truly liberated by faith (in Paul's sense) would not give a
hoot about the brand name of their instruments. Their primary criterion
would be whether those instruments were effective or not. To be sure, their
evaluation of efficacy would not be purely pragmatic; it would be based on
those values which were consistent with their "faith." *Yet it is precisely that
criterion of efficacy which is nowhere evident in the remarks attributed to
Dom Helder Camara.*

Moreover, any specialist in economics, sociology, or political science can tell you that there is no society where, for example, the social encyclicals have been put into practice in structural terms. All we can say is that isolated individuals have let some of their moral options be guided by those principles.

Speaking from Paul's standpoint, I must conclude that Dom Helder's statement propounds and exemplifies the primacy of "works" over "faith." It exemplifies the fear that anything which does not derive from the realm of religion and orthodoxy, whether the latter is effective or not, will have a pernicious result. For what? Certainly not for the solution of human problems, which are left completely unsolved, but for the only logical goal left: i.e., salvation.

Speaking from the standpoint of the Letter of James, I must conclude that Dom Helder's words are an example of a lack of faith. For James makes clear that faith without works is dead. Something that has to be there is missing. Forgive me for the following little paraphrase of his text in modern terms:

My brothers, what use is it for man to say he has faith or the social encyclicals of the church when he does nothing to show it? Can his faith or his social encyclicals save him? Suppose a brother or a sister is in rags with not enough food for the day, and one of you says to them, "Good luck to you, keep yourselves warm and have plenty to eat, thanks to the social encyclicals," but does nothing to supply their bodily needs, what is the good of that?

Irreverent as my paraphrase might seem, it is actually in line with the biblical writer's thinking. And one can substitute other words for "the social encyclicals": e.g., gospel message, Vatican II, or Medellín. The biblical writer is, in fact, denying the value and worthwhileness of any meaning-structure which does not structure anything outside the person, anything in the real world, that dovetails with the values associated with faith.

So, to stick with the social encyclicals as my example, we come to the critical question: Why is it that the social encyclicals have not become clothing and daily food for the millions of people living in so-called "Christian" countries? Why have they not been translated into new societal structures for better human coexistence?

Only two possible answers can be given to the question, and both are essentially related. One could argue that it is up to Christians to apply the social encyclicals and that as yet they have not done so. Or one could say that something is missing in the social encyclicals themselves because they do not provide the mediations needed to implement their imperatives.

Let me briefly analyze the two alternative arguments. First, let us assume that the social encyclicals are complete and perfect. Unlike the case with other ideologies, however, Christians have failed to make the necessary commitments and sacrifices needed to implement the social encyclicals. Now if that is the case, isn't it rather odd that Christians should have such a monopoly on ineffectiveness? After all, we see many, many social changes—some of them certainly beneficial and many of them difficult, risky, and calling for sacrifices—being carried out by other ideologies. We would have to say that in this case Christians offer a perfect example of what James called dead faith. What justification, then, is there for any smug sense of self-sufficiency, such as we find in Dom Helder Camara's statement?

Here some people might object that all those changes effected by other ideologies were useless or harmful because effectiveness was purchased at the price of violence or even worse evils than the ones people sought to correct. In that case Christians are eternally doomed to being right and going unheard. They can only tell the needy: "I wish you well. I can't do anything for you with my faith." Once again a smug sense of self-sufficiency seems out of place. No Christian seems entitled to state flatly that he or she needs no ideology to inspire them in their work for human betterment.

Now let us look at the second alternative answer, which formulates the issue in more radical, and probably more realistic, terms. Its underlying hypothesis is that the inefficacy of the social encyclicals, their lack of historical realization, is due at bottom to the fact that Christians put their trust in a faith which will be without works, as they themselves dimly suspect. They work up a model of social duty, of what ought to be, without simultaneously working out an effective methodology for implementing it. Without admitting it to themselves, Christians are really trying to find some way to combine their faith with the reigning evil because the latter is so hard to uproot. So they end up with a sort of compromise. On the one hand the real situation is unjust and should not be that way. The Christian today admits that, just as James's Christian encourages the needy to get proper food and clothing because he or she knows that their present situation is not right. But on the other hand it is very difficult to effect any radical change in the social structures responsible for this injustice. So Christian faith is reduced to merely individual acts or to the proclamation of unrealized and unrealizable values. Thus the needy go on being needy, as they were in the Letter of James. The faith of the Christian is a dead faith.

Two comments by Karl Mannheim may help to make the underlying mechanism clearer to my readers. In the first Mannheim explains how an established order—this would be capitalism, in the case of the social encyclicals—can coexist peacefully with a "faith" advocating contrary values:

> One can orient himself to objects that are alien to reality and which transcend actual existence—and nevertheless still be effective in the realization and the maintenance of the existing order of things. . . . Consequently representatives of a given order have not in all cases taken a hostile attitude towards orientations transcending the existing order.[5]

Mannheim then proceeds to explain how this works in practice. One form of peaceful coexistence between transcendent ideals and an existing order involves the distortion of the former when they are put into practice. The following remark might well be applied to the social encyclicals, though we should remember that they advocate broad social demands rather than merely individual moral dictates:

Ideologies are the situationally transcendent ideas which never succeed *de facto* in the realization of their projected contents. Though they often become the good-intentioned motives for the subjective conduct of the individual, when they are actually embodied in practice their meanings are most frequently distorted. The idea of Christian brotherly love, for instance, in a society founded on serfdom remains an unrealizable and, in this sense, ideological idea, even when the intended meaning is, in good faith, a motive for the conduct of the individual.[6]

Here, then, we have a classic instance of "bad faith," of wanting and not wanting something at the same time. And that is precisely what the Letter of James is discussing when it talks about "dead" faith.

So we arrive at the conclusion that a faith without ideologies is a dead faith, a faithlessness. If an absolute is unwilling to immerse itself in the relative, it ceases to be absolute; indeed it fails to attain even the value of that which is "relatively" alive and operative. It is inferior to a "live" ideology.

The Realization of Values

Now I would like to make the same point in more general terms. As I suggested in Part One, the word "value" leaves room for many misunderstandings because it is rather abstract. It has its uses when we are talking in fairly general terms. But when we want to observe or express a concrete value, we soon realize that we are talking about some sort of satisfying experience achieved through certain specific procedures. A value recognized as such in the concrete is a value realized, a value put into effect. And it depends on the technique or method employed to realize it.

Suppose, for example, I get satisfaction from driving a car. I would have to be crazy to think that the same "value" is involved whether I bought the car or stole it. To give another example, we do not picture or talk about lovemaking in the abstract, as if it were the same thing no matter what form the sexual relationship took. We see it differently, depending on whether it was the result of mutual consent, resignation, deceit, or physical violence.

In short, we cannot really reach any understanding about values or talk about a specific anthropological "faith" unless the *means* of achieving them are somehow included in our picture of them, which means that there is no anthropological faith, and hence no religious faith, without ideologies. Suppose, for example, that people are trying to define what "Christian" love is: i.e., love that supposedly dovetails with faith in Christ. Almost at once they will begin to use adjectives which point to ideologies: e.g., "disinterested," "unselfish," or "nonviolent."

But it is not just when we want to express the concrete embodiment of a value that we have to introduce ideological elements. It is not just when we want to identify certain values and distinguish them from other values. Even though ideological elements are controlled in a general way by the meaning-structure of faith, they also have their impact on the latter and prevent it from lapsing into evasion. The following statement by Clifford Geertz makes a point which is central to my discussion here. I add my own remarks in brackets to show how it relates to my terminology and general position:

> The social function of science [ideology] vis-à-vis ideologies [values-structures] is first to understand them [in terms of the concrete embodiments towards which they point] . . . and second to criticize them, to *force them to come to terms with* (but not necessarily to surrender to) *reality* [my italics].[7]

One further question that might be raised here is whether a given ideology—nonviolence, for example—becomes part of the absolute of faith when it is clearly united with a specific value—or, if you prefer, a specific referential witness—that is declared essential in Christian revelation.[8] In this connection I would remind my readers of one of the points I made about religious faith in Chapter I. There we saw that faith, particularly as it grows more adult, comes to realize that a value can never be inextricably associated with one specific technique for its implementation and realization. Problems and their formulations change with history. A given value must search out its effective realization in the face of new data, obstacles, and possibilities. Insofar as Christianity is concerned, we saw that not even Jesus himself, viewed as the Word of God, dispensed his believers from "faith" in the Old Testament. And in the Old Testament we find countless instances where love for God and human beings was translated into terms of violence and exclusivity.

In short, I noted that revelation, the object of faith, did not teach us prefabricated things, recipes, or modes of conduct: i.e., ideologies. Instead it taught us how to learn, how to create ideologies or accept ideologies created by others insofar as they forced values "to come to terms with" historical reality.

Every single effort to separate faith from ideologies in order to preserve the former is bound to stifle and kill faith—the very thing one is seeking to preserve.

II. Ideologies without Faith?

Now let us look at the other side of the coin, which is real too. We do have ideologies, or systems of thought that are called such, which boast that they exclude any and all *faith*.

Of course such a boast may be due to differences in the use of terminology, and we should not start off assuming that those systems of thought are saying the opposite of what I am trying to say here. But if we do find someone really claiming to build an ideology which is responsible only to reason or science for the values it proposes to realize, then we are obviously confronted with something more serious than a mere question of terminology.

Can an ideology turn against its grounding faith, and against *all* faith, as it seeks to project the latter into the complex, "economic"[9] reality of all concrete existence? Whatever the theoretical answer to that question may be, it does seem that some claim to offer a "yes" answer to it in practice. Both Marxism and scientific positivism, for example, pose as ideologies *and* as methodologies which can reject any and all faith on rational, scientific grounds. Let us see if such a claim can be substantiated.

Machoveč: The Impossibility of Believing in a Savior

In the book which we have already cited in Chapter IV, Milan Machoveč starts right out with a basic assumption: "The Marxist cannot 'believe' in a savior because he or she is obliged by methodology to ask how the idea of a 'savior' arose and won acceptance in history."[10] He is clearly saying that his methodology, centered around exploring how the idea of a savior arose in history, makes it *impossible*—i.e., illogical and contradictory—to believe that someone like Jesus is the savior of human beings. He is also saying that this methodology is intrinsic to a well-known ideology, Marxism, so that it constitutes a "methodological" obligation for Marxists.

What are we to make of such statements? Machoveč's statement above is open to two main interpretations. Putting it briefly, we can say that one interpretation would stress the difficulty or impossibility of "believing," whereas the other would stress the difficulty or impossibility of believing specifically in a "savior." Note that both words are set off in Machoveč's text. Let us explore both aspects a bit and see where they lead us.

The *first* interpretation, which focuses on "believing," suggests that "beliefs," as opposed to scientific data and theories no doubt, necessarily lose their value when we explore their historical origins; and this is especially true when we find that they are conditioned by the different forms of (economic) life specific to different historical periods. In this case Marxists would be methodologically and necessarily constrained to be people who do not "believe." Why? Because science would show them the inanity of any and every belief: i.e., its earthly or self-interested kernel.

The *second* interpretation in no way contradicts the first one above, but it emphasizes the impossibility of believing in a "savior." Here the difficulty would lie in the magical connotations associated with the very idea of "salvation." As we saw in the previous chapter, Machoveč acknowledges the importance of Jesus as a "model" of "spiritual values." But he does not feel this obliges one to be a "believer" in Jesus and certainly not a believer in Jesus as "savior." Perhaps what we would have to do here is make a distinction between two things. One would be the scientifically discernible *effects* of considering Jesus as a model and of his spiritual values. The other would be the belief that Jesus enjoyed "supernatural powers" enabling him to transform history or the life of a human person.[11]

Now obviously any "critical" ideology can pose objections of this sort. It can challenge faith in general as an anthropological dimension, and it can challenge any faith which is specifically religious. Let us examine these critical challenges a bit more carefully.

Machovec's methodological claim against "believing" in someone might seem obvious to many readers. But I would contend that it represents almost a word-for-word contradiction of Marx's comment in *Capital* which I cited in Chapter IV. Here is the passage again:

> Even a history of religion that is written in abstraction from this material basis is uncritical. It is, in reality, much easier to discover by analysis the *earthly kernel* of the misty creations of religion than to do the opposite, i.e., to develop from the actual, given relations of life the forms in which these have been apotheosized. The latter method is the only *materialist*, and therefore the only *scientific* one [my italics].[12]

But notice what Machovec is saying. He is saying that when someone uses the Marxist method and hence uncovers the "earthly kernel" of all human creations, that person will be methodologically bound to rule out any and all belief. Such a stance runs directly counter to Marx's statement above. For in the latter Marx seems to be saying that any approach which involves a systematic ruling out, such as Machovec suggests, does not deserve to be called "materialist" or "scientific."

Some readers might try to defend Machovec here by saying that he is not claiming to disqualify Jesus by using the historico-critical method, that he is only claiming to rule out "faith" in Jesus. Only the first tack, it might be argued, is declared unscientific by Marx. But it is worth looking closely at Marx's statement. Note how it seems to propose a "certain relativization" of any overall rejection or disqualification, whether the latter has to do with valuation or some faith (in my basic anthropological sense). Though he is not always consistent, Marx seems much more interested in *integrating* ideological phenomena into the cognitive-operational whole than in discarding certain zones of such phenomena as being "human, all too human." It is the first approach, the one of integration, that he would call the only materialist one. This confirms an impression one gets from reading the whole Marxian corpus: i.e., that his use of the adjective "materialist" is much more akin to the "realist" method than to any "materialist" approach evident in other metaphysical systems which were around in his day.

Now does Machovec's statement seem to be talking about a similarly "realist" method? I don't think so. We have seen that "faith" seems to be a basic and inescapable dimension of human experience. If Machovec's method of historical materialism rules out any and all such faith, and such faith is needed to structure a scale of values and provide the basis for ideologies (including the approach of historical criticism), how can it be considered sound or realistic?

As we noted in Part One, even the most scientific and objective methodology is grounded on an existential structure. Even the most abstract science is possible and real only on the basis of some nonscientific *wherefore* which is imbedded in an anthropological "faith." There must be a belief in something; otherwise the scientific and critical nature of the methodology isn't worth anything. Its importance derives from some absolute sought by human beings, from something that becomes our "savior" once it is attained even though it does not cease to be human. That something is the absolute criterion of what is good for us.

I have just offered one way of refuting the first possible interpretation of Machoveč's statement. My refutation might seem to be awfully sketchy and brief. I think it is, even though I also think it is basically sound. For there is a deeper and more interesting problem buried here. It has to do with the relationship between faith and ideology, and we cannot do justice to it simply by talking about contradictions.

It is true, I think, that no methodology can decide *a priori* about the validity of faith as a basic human dimension. But something else is equally true and worth noting here. Historical materialism and any other critical reading of history, when they are practiced systematically, will somehow tend to undermine and corrupt the faith held by a person before he or she began to use that critical method. In Chapter I, for example, we noted how a small child's faith in its parents is undermined as it gets older and examines the *real-life* history of its parents. The important point here is that if my line of argument is correct, the child's "relativization" of its parents' wisdom, due to history, cannot become an end in itself.

Let us consider an extreme, and indeed impossible, case. Suppose the child's relativization of its faith in its parents did not proceed by stages. Suppose it became absolute in one fell swoop. That, I think, would only prompt the child to look elsewhere for another object of faith. (Indeed I would do better to say another "subject" of faith.) For we run into a contradiction if we try to carry the work of historical criticism into infinity, demolishing one faith after another. Indeed the wisdom of nature seems to stop us before we reach that point. The fact seems to be that the process of relativizing faith cannot be generalized even if we wanted to do that. Instead of becoming universal, such a process would undermine faith and cause operational paralysis in the human being. The basic anthropological dimension involved is stronger and deeper than any relativizing methodology; it would revolt against the latter and its ultimately fatal consequences if carried too far.

What really happens is one of two things. The sounder result is that the relativizing process itself ends up being relativized. The more paradoxical result is that the relativizing process itself is absolutized and deified, thus rendered immune from any and all criticism. We can see this latter distortion around us all the time. While Machoveč's thinking is free of it for the most part, the sentence we have been examining in his work bears witness to the tendency.

And so we come to a central point. It is a dialectical point, as we shall see in later chapters, particularly in Part Three. *It is sound and necessary to relativize a certain kind of infantile faith, evident even in adulthood. But when this method or process gets out of hand, when it evades the control of some higher balancing instance, it not only loses its positive value but actually becomes counterproductive and contradictory.*

This point could be proven even from the Marxist standpoint if that were my aim here. In the very same place where Machoveč talks about the method-ological impossibility of belief, he also talks about Marx's offering of a scien-tific method to those who were seeking to realize in history a certain creed: i.e., their option against injustice and in favor of the oppressed. Now clearly the existential premises of that option must also lie within the realm affected by the relativization due to the historical method. For example, we could ask Machoveč such questions as the following: To what extent is Marx's anti-bourgeois option to be explained in terms of the conflict between his Jewish background and his Protestant upbringing? To what extent, then, is his op-tion to be relativized on that basis?

Bateson: The Need for Digital and Iconic Languages

Let us set aside such *ad hominem* arguments and probe this fascinating problem more deeply. What is the higher—or decisive—instance which keeps within positive limits the relativization of beliefs as a result of exploring their historical origins?

Once again Bateson can come to our aid here, at least indirectly. His help, in my opinion, derives from the fact that he comprehends and appreciates the "economic" mechanism of evolution. By that I mean that there is a certain economy of energy at work in evolution which sets limits on the appearance of new, higher qualities. And it acts wisely in setting such limits, in my opinion. From the standpoint of real, "economic" evolution, all that glitters with newness is not gold. Bateson discusses static genetic qualities as opposed to homeostatic, trial-and-error mechanisms, but that discussion is more rele-vant to a later chapter. Here his discussion of the relationship between *digital* and *iconic* languages is more relevant.

An example of digital language could be any word in the dictionary or in accepted social use. Let me use a measuring word here: "five." The typical characteristic of instruments in the digital code is that variations do not affect their meaning. Whether I whisper or shout the word "five," whether I say it fast or slow, its meaning remains the same.

In iconic language, however, the instruments of meaning and the meaning itself are so closely bound up with each other that they are interdependent. If

I want to signify the equivalent of the word "fight," I will have to start fighting in reality. Why? Because a real fight, even if it be only the beginning, is the *image*—the icon—of what I want to signify. Iconic language, in other words, obliges me to demonstrate in reality what I am trying to signify. And as the signifying instrument grows, so grows the signified—which does not happen in the case of digital words or digital language. If I can signify "fight" only by fighting, then, as the instrument of language grows, so grows the real-life fight and its extralinguistic consequences.

This brings us to the points made by Bateson which are relevant to my whole discussion here. First, iconic language is the mode of communication for almost all, if not all, animals. Digital language, by contrast, presupposes a higher degree of evolution and permits abstraction. If it is not exclusive to human beings, it is certainly typical of them. It is part of that second nature which we call human culture.

Second, there is a danger underlined by Bateson. It is the danger of thinking that what is "better" or "superior," what is more advanced on the typical evolutionary scale, can simply replace what seems to be "inferior." Not so, points out Bateson:

> If, therefore, [digital] verbal language were in any sense an evolutionary replacement of communication by means of kinesics and [iconic] paralanguage, we would expect the old, preponderantly iconic systems to have undergone conspicuous decay. Clearly they have not. Rather, the kinesics of men have become richer and more complex, and paralanguage has blossomed side by side with the evolution of verbal language. Both kinesics and paralanguage have been elaborated into complex forms of art, music, ballet, poetry, and the like, and, even in everyday life, the intricacies of human kinesic communication, facial expression, and vocal intonation far exceed anything that any other animal is known to produce.[13]

What is the explanation of this evolutionary "economy"? Bateson proceeds to present it in clearly finalistic, purposive terms. This runs counter to the practice of scientists, of course, who are frequently opposed to the notion of purposiveness even when they talk about evolution. What interests us here is precisely a law which becomes purposive on the human level at least. For on that level it affects the realm where human beings must make decisions, establishing a goal and the means to achieve it. Here is Bateson's explanation of this evolutionary economy:

> It seems that the discourse of nonverbal communication is precisely concerned with matters of relationship—love, hate, respect, fear, dependency, etc.—between self and vis-à-vis or between self and environment and that the nature of human society is such that *falsification*[14] *of*

this discourse rapidly becomes pathogenic. From an adaptive point of view, it is therefore important that this discourse be carried on by techniques which are relatively unconscious and only imperfectly subject to voluntary control [my italics].[15]

Stripped of scientific jargon, this passage makes clear how a feature that is clearly superior in the evolutionary process would prove fatal if it were to become generalized at the expense of the proper economy of energy. Hence no "idealism" should prompt us to forget that digital language is not a methodology designed to systematically replace every possible form of iconic language. It is equally erroneous to think that historical criticism can replace every manifestation of "faith" in the basic human sense. If that were to happen, then the economy of energy in which human beings are inserted would cause the latter to go backward instead of forward. The seemingly superior quality would become "pathogenic" and cause illness. Interestingly enough, Machoveč himself bravely and frankly bears witness to such social illness in the Marxist camp insofar as anthropological faith is concerned. For he talks about the lack of value-models and the impoverishment of meaning-structures for human living.

Readers should not be surprised at this point if I seem to talk about faith as if it were a huge fund of energy-savings at our disposal for use. That should have been clear from the very beginning of my treatment. At the very start I noted the great problem facing human beings. They do not enjoy the (energy) possibility of traveling to the end of their lives and then knowingly choosing the values they wish to realize. So "faith" serves as their necessary "short-cut," as the fund of saved energy on which all human planning is based. The relativization of faith, which must necessarily come to some extent from historical criticism, is not an alternative option or approach. Why? Because the energy for such relativization comes precisely from the energy-savings represented by faith.

Transcendent Data: Machoveč

That brings us to the second possible interpretation of Machoveč's statement, the one which would focus precisely on the impossibility of believing *in a savior*. The argument would be that historical criticism is irreconcilably hostile to any properly *religious* faith.

Now in Part One we saw how religious "faith" might erroneously be interpreted as faith in a certain set of instruments. In such a case faith would really be an ideology covered with a "sacred canopy," to borrow Peter Berger's expression. Obviously any method of historical criticism would lead people to reject "magical" use of tools. If by "savior" one is referring to the possessor and provider of such a false tool kit, then Machoveč's statement is perfectly acceptable. For it does not refer to what I am calling *religious faith* here.

That would be an easy way to settle accounts with Machoveč. One could even say that was what he had in mind, though this is doubtful in my opinion. We are still left with the more radical question, however. Can a critical methodology prevail *against* all religious faith and wipe out the latter entirely, even when it is religious faith in the sense I mean here? In other words, can it prevail completely against a faith which somehow determines a person's meaning-structure through recourse to a tradition which involves revealed data that transcend any and every possibility of experiential verification?

It seems obvious to me that this is the position taken by Machoveč in the citation we are discussing, and it is well worth examining by way of example. Note that Machoveč does not just assert the impossibility of believing in Jesus as savior. From the very outset he also makes it clear that he is an "atheist" and that his perspective on Jesus is an atheistic one. To rephrase it in my terminology: his anthropological "faith" in Jesus is that of an atheist.

Now let us go back and examine the immediate context surrounding the sentence in which Machoveč spells out how Jesus had an impact on the meaning-structure of his life as an atheist. Here again is the sentence: "An atheist who takes seriously 'unto death' his life and work for the movement he loves, and who does so without cynicism or opportunistic reservations, can readily admit that the moment when Peter discovered that Jesus was still victor, after Golgotha, was one of the greatest moments in history and human existence." Before he gets to the end of the paragraph, however, Machoveč adds the following comment in parenthesis:

Even though there was no external apocalyptic miracle on Golgotha, even though there was no *deus ex machina* there, and even though there was nothing but a desolating and concrete death by crucifixion.[16]

Obviously this reservation would not be acceptable to St. Paul: "If Christ was not raised, your faith has nothing in it. . . . Then it follows also that those who died within Christ's fellowship are utterly lost. If it is for this life only that Christ has given us hope, we of all men are most to be pitied" (1 Cor. 15:17–19). Paul here is stressing the crucial importance of the transcendent datum—real resurrection or not—in determining values relating to the absolute value of happiness.

At first glance there is real plausibility in Machoveč's reservation. He could say that Jesus' voluntary acceptance of his passion and death, combined with the rest of his life, offers sufficient witness to a satisfactory lifestyle. In other words, there is no need to go further and explore his fate after death.

However, I find reasons to doubt that the transcendent "datum" has not had an influence on Machoveč's "faith," whether he realizes it or not, wishes it or not.

Here is the *first* reason. Machoveč is acquainted with Jesus because of a (gospel) account in which this transcendent datum (the resurrection) colors the whole life of Jesus. We can summarize this influence in the words which

John puts on Jesus' lips: "For this reason the Father loves me, because I lay down my life, that I may take it again. No one takes it from me, but I lay it down of my own accord. I have power to lay it down, and I have power to take it again . . ." (John 10:17–18).

Being a good exegete, Machoveč is well aware that such a summary can be interpreted in two different ways. Either it accurately expresses the pre-paschal thinking of Jesus himself or else it is a postpaschal view of Jesus which his disciples arrived at after they came to believe in the resurrected Jesus. One can offer reasons for either interpretation, so let us see how the two possible interpretations square with Machoveč's reservation.

According to the first interpretation, the love which led Jesus to lay down his life freely had value for Jesus because he himself associated it with transcendent data: i.e., the value which the Father (God) attributes to self-giving and the possibility of again taking up a life laid down out of love for others. Now if that was Jesus' own meaning-structure, his own valuation of his love, Machoveč can hardly claim that he is adopting Jesus' values-structure. For Jesus' satisfaction in self-giving is inextricably bound up with the transcendent data about love which are part of his consciousness (see Luke 22:15–16). That is undoubtedly what Paul thought when he offered the argument cited above.

According to the second interpretation, Jesus had no paschal anticipation as he practiced his historical love. He simply lived his death as an unrecompensed failure. He preferred that "failure," however, to one which he supposedly regarded as even worse: i.e., changing his scale of values and adapting it to the real world and its laws of efficacy. That, it would seem, was the "victory" lived by Jesus in Gethsemane and comprehended by Peter at the empty tomb.

Two possible objections crop up here, however, for anyone who adopts this second interpretation, and that is what Machoveč seems to do throughout his book. First of all, one is forced to rework his or her image of the real Jesus, clearly distinguishing it from that presented by the Gospels. And we must ask ourselves whether there really is a sufficient foundation for (anthropological) faith in the life of Jesus so conceived. For it is then a life which is devoid of some decisive transcendent data and which grows more and more anxiety-ridden as Jesus is confronted with the futility and failure of his work: "My God, my God, why hast thou forsaken me?" (Matt. 27:46).

That brings us to the *second* reason suggesting that Machoveč has not in fact managed to weed out the transcendent data in the faith he espouses. In another passage of his book, Machoveč spells out a very important point about the critical impact of the historical method on spiritual and religious traditions. We must examine it here:

This modern Marxism understands the method of historical materialism in more or less the following terms. It is completely proper and even necessary to track down the socio-economic roots of every spiritual idea; but that does not mean that the task is completed with that search. Once the "roots" have been uncovered, the more important task remains. One has to ask which of those ideas offer true and positive cognitive data about the being and existence of humanity. In other words, one must ask whether those ideals provide us with the moral ideas, models, and values in the absence of which even the best organized, most affluent, and most technically advanced society must remain sunk in barbarism. Those values have to be supported, worked out, and spread by everyone—even by the materialist who expects no help from on high![17]

Let me note a few interesting points about this passage. First, we can hear in the final phrase an echo of Machoveč's refusal to believe in a savior. Second, as I indicated above with regard to the first possible interpretation of his thought, it is clear that the application of historical criticism does not, in Machoveč's mind, rule out the faith which I have labelled anthropological.

Now what about specifically religious faith? It must be said that the criterion which Machoveč offers in the above passage for accepting or rejecting the values of spiritual traditions remains pretty vague: "which of those ideas offer *true and positive cognitive data* about the being and existence of humanity." To make it a bit more clear, let us go to a specific case where Machoveč does find that sort of cognitive data—the Psalms:

Even an atheist, for example, can find in the Psalms a moving description of his or her personal situation in the twentieth century, a description that is extraordinarily "up to the minute."[18]

Machoveč seems to be telling us that the Psalmist's description of human situations offers us not only true but also positive cognitive data. The Psalmist does not merely console us in our difficulties. He offers us "clear models and indications for spiritual values."

But one thing should be perfectly obvious to any biblical exegete and indeed to any reader of the Psalms: the only possible thing that can differentiate the Psalms from other literary elegies or laments about human ills is the Psalmist's "belief" in *transcendent data*. They include such convictions as the following: that God is going to change the course of events; that evil will always end up in its own snares; and that righteousness will eventually triumph on earth.[19] Take away those data and the Psalms become nothing more than reflections of the myriad forms of human suffering.

Are we not forced to conclude that Machoveč only "believes" he can derive true and positive cognitive data from the Psalms without accepting the transcendent data that are crucial to their meaning-structure and that this "belief" of his derives from one of the most tenacious misconceptions of nineteenth-century Western culture? I refer to the notion that investigators, using scientific and critical methods, can adequately and fruitfully approximate the value-experiences of others without participating at all in the act of "faith" in transcendent data which is implicit in such experiences, whether one uses the word "religion" or not, and whether one adheres to a spiritual tradition invoking God or not.

Transcendent Data: Marx and Camus

Here I do not propose to consider whether transcendent data are inextricably bound up with *every* experience of values. My point is simply that such data are unconsciously intermingled in any "methodology" far more than people think. They are frequently to be found in any ideology, as I use that term, and that is all to the good.

Two examples, one positive and one negative, will suffice for my point here. The first comes from Karl Marx:

> Mankind thus inevitably sets itself only such tasks as it is able to solve, since closer examination will always show that the problem itself arises only when the material conditions for its solution are already present or at least in the course of formation.[20]

I am not concerned here to discuss the premises on which Marx's above conclusion is based. My point is that such a conclusion lies beyond any possibility of empirical verification. In short, strange and scandalous as it may seem, we are confronted with a *transcendent datum* in a thinker who calls himself a materialist. If Marx had said that only certain problem-posings are possible in specific material conditions, his statement would not go beyond the empirical level. But Marx says much more: i.e., that such conditions indicate not only the presence of certain problem-posings but also the mediate or immediate presence of the corresponding *solutions* for those problems. To use a present-day example, Marx is not simply saying that when certain material conditions are given, humanity will pose the whole issue of whether or not the planet is to be destroyed by atomic bombs. He is also saying that when such material conditions are present, human beings will also have at their disposal all the elements they need to solve that problem, to confront that new task.

What can we say about such a claim? Several things should be noted. First, the history of human societies, or even of biological species, could have taught Marx that the presence of problem-posings—be they conditioned or not—does not likewise imply the *real* possibility of finding solutions for them. That is why we know of the fall of civilizations and the extinction of species. Why couldn't the same thing happen in the future?

Second, suppose we grant that Marx's equation (material conditions—the posing of tasks—and the real possibility of solving them) had been demonstrated in the past. Nothing but "faith" (no pejorative connotation implied here) would permit us to infer that the same thing would necessarily happen in the future.

Third, this datum, which obviously transcends the empirical level, is not peripheral but rather crucially important to the "scientific" planning of society that Marx is working out. We find this "faith" in his view of the internal conflicts of capitalism, in his vision of the intermediate socialist state and its duration, and in his final image of communist society.[21] It is not an accidental appendage. It plays a central role in forming and arranging Marx's hierarchy of values as well as the criteria to be used in judging their realization in history.[22]

That this "transcendent datum" is not "religious" is obvious, unless we want to indulge in word-play. What is far from obvious, on the other hand, is that this datum is qualitatively different from one that is religious insofar as materialist criticism is concerned. Indeed it would not be difficult to trace the "spiritual" trajectory which led Marx, amid the ideological panorama of the nineteenth century, to place such confidence in the destiny of humanity.

By that I do not mean to discredit Marx or his thought. I am simply trying to bring within proper bounds the claims of any critique which poses as an all-encompassing methodology. Here, in the light of Marx's statement, we might well reiterate Machovec̆'s observation, but modifying its thrust just a bit: "Once the 'roots' have been uncovered, the more important task remains. One has to ask which of those ideas offer true and positive cognitive data about the being and existence of humanity. . . ." Suppose one accepts that much. Where else is he or she to go to find the value-criterion for deciding the latter question except to "faith," which is inextricably bound up with such "transcendent data"?

A second example, this time negative, is worth noting here because it considers an extreme possibility: i.e., that of having an anthropological "faith" without any datum which transcends the empirical plane. And to its credit, this example alludes explicitly to the price which must be paid for rejecting every transcendent datum: absurdity. In the *Myth of Sisyphus* Camus writes:

> . . . the absurdity springs from a comparison. . . . If I wish to limit myself to facts, I know what man wants, I know what the world offers him, and now I can say that I also know what links them. For me the sole datum is the absurd.[23]

The rule of method alluded to above appears here. If I judge that a thing is true, I must preserve it. If I attempt to solve a problem, at least I must not by that very solution conjure away one of the terms of the problem. For me the sole datum is the absurd.[24]

How does one conjure away the second term of the problem posed? According to Camus, one does so by introducing something extra into what the world offers the human being. Specifically, one introduces something that does not derive from experience: a "transcendent datum" in my use of terms. Writes Camus:

That transcends, as the saying goes, the human scale; therefore it must be superhuman. But this "therefore" is superfluous. There is no logical certainty here. There is no experimental probability either. All I can say is that, in fact, that transcends my scale. If I do not draw a negation from it, at least I do not want to found anything on the incomprehensible. I want to know whether I can live with what I know and with that alone. . . . I merely want to remain in this middle path where the intelligence can remain clear.[25]

This formulation is all too clear and precise. The only thing we might question is the exaggerated nature of some adjectives: e.g., "incomprehensible." And we might like to ask whether such a formulation isn't something like the case of the serpent eating its own tail. What exactly is the *logic* which leads Camus to accept the *absurd*? It is a lot easier to talk about leading an "absurd" life than to do it in actual experience without cheating. A bit further on Camus writes:

It was previously a question of finding out whether or not life had to have a meaning to be lived. It now becomes clear, on the contrary, that it will be all the better if it has no meaning.[26]

On the surface we seem to be confronting the most lucid logic and a more than Copernican revolution. But if we look beneath the surface, we might ask: Where do you get your "all the *better*"? What *value* can there be where there is no *meaning*? Isn't it meaning, by very definition, which tells us what is better or worse? And what about the loyalty to experiential data which forms the explicit basis of Camus's position? What is that if not a value, a meaning?

•

After all that has been said in this chapter, perhaps none of my readers will feel that they are being conned when they feel obliged to conclude that faith is never faith without ideologies and that an ideology without faith is never an ideology.

NOTES

1. *El País* (Montevideo), August 6, 1976, p. 11.
2. *CELAM* (monthly bulletin of the Latin American Episcopal Conference), n. 107, July 1976. The next sentence, which may be important in shedding light on the correct interpretation, reads: "We have *everything* to be in the service of the second continental independence" (my italics).
3. This is expressed repeatedly in different ways in the *Conclusions* of the Medellín

Conference (Eng. trans., *The Church in the Present-Day Transformation of Latin America in the Light of the Council* [Washington, D.C.: Latin America Division of the United States Catholic Conference, 1970], Volume 2). We find it in the *Introduction to the Final Documents*: "The goal of our reflection was to search for a new and more dynamic presence of the Church *in the present transformation of Latin America in the light of the Second Vatican Council*" (2, 50; my italics).

Obviously its truth does not depend solely on a sound understanding of Vatican II, but also on its (historical and sociological) interpretation of the "present transformation of Latin America." Indeed one can say that the latter is more important because it conditions the former. As the *Message to the Peoples of Latin America* puts it: "We interpret the aspirations and clamors of Latin America as signs that reveal the direction of the divine plan . . ." (2, 38). The inherent limitations of the first social encyclicals, insofar as they referred exclusively to countries already affected by the Industrial Revolution, are equally obvious.

4. For example, see Chapter 5 of my book, *The Liberation of Theology*, Eng. trans. (Maryknoll, N.Y.: Orbis Books, 1976), pp. 125–153.

5. Karl Mannheim, *Ideology and Utopia: An Introduction to the Sociology of Knowledge*, Eng. trans. (New York: Harcourt Brace Jovanovich/Harvest Book, 1936), pp. 192–193.

6. Ibid., pp. 194–195.

7. Clifford Geertz, "Ideology as a Cultural System," in David E. Apter, ed., *Ideology and Discontent* (New York: The Free Press of Glencoe, 1964), p. 72.

8. See the basic biblical and theological grounding for this in Chapter 5 of my book, *The Liberation of Theology*.

9. By "economic" here I mean something complementary rather than opposed to the term's meaning in historical materialism. I mean the fact that all human activity is carried out against the backdrop of a limited supply of energy. This means we must always calculate the cost of anything to be achieved, the areas of life which this displacement of energy will leave unstressed and unprotected. Only in that way can we decide whether this particular energy-structure is the one which will best help us to realize our values. New functions and new efficacies are never "created" *ex nihilo*. We must transfer energy from some functions to others. Hence what we call "freedom" is more akin to a form of economic planning than to a mental deliberation followed by an exercise of free will. In its *concrete* forms this energy-calculus shows up more clearly and urgently as we draw closer to material production, its modes, and the social relations engendered by it.

10. Milan Machoveč, *Jesús para ateos*, Spanish trans. (Salamanca: Sígueme, 1974), p. 28; German edition, *Jesus für Atheisten*; Eng. trans., *A Marxist Looks at Jesus* (Philadelphia: Fortress Press, 1976).

11. In terms of Marxist thought, the first formulation of the issue would be more connected with what has been called "historical materialism," while the second formulation would be more connected with "dialectical materialism." I shall examine this relationship in later chapters. Right now I simply want to present one of the commonplaces accepted by our culture: i.e., the two-pronged claim of a critical-minded ideology, be it Marxist or positivist, to attack and undermine faith in both of the two senses which I presented in Part One of this book.

12. Karl Marx, *Capital*, Book I, Part Four, Chapter 15, footnote 4; Eng. trans. (New York: Vintage Books, 1977), pp. 493–494.

13. Gregory Bateson, *Steps to an Ecology of Mind* (New York: Ballantine Books, 1972), p. 412.

14. Here "falsify" is used in the ordinary sense of the term rather than in any scientific or logical sense. It simply means to "deceive."

15. Bateson, *Steps*, pp. 412–413.

16. Machoveč, *Jesús para ateos*, p. 39.

17. Ibid., p. 40.

18. Ibid., pp. 33–34.

19. See, for example, Psalms 71 (Vulgate 70), 73 (V 72), 84 (V 83).

20. Karl Marx, "Preface" to *A Contribution to the Critique of Political Economy*, Eng. trans. (New York: International Publishers, 1970), p. 21.

21. "The goal of total revolution and of communism shows up as a limit-concept or a transcendental idea in the sense of Kant's 'thing-in-itself.' . . . My principal thesis is this: the limit-concept is a special problem of feasibility, and the realization of the limit-concept goes beyond the human condition itself; it constitutes what might be called a barrier of feasibility which is fundamental and metahistorical rather than historical. All present-day ideologies try to avoid a rational confrontation with this transcendental concept in the social sciences. On this point we see agreement between Soviet ideology, Marxist structuralism, all forms of positivism, and the critical thinking of Bloch, Sartre, and Marcuse" (Franz Hinkelammert, *Ideologías del desarrollo y dialéctica de la historia* [Buenos Aires: Ed. Nueva Universidad—Paidós, 1970], pp. 78–79).

22. See ibid., Chapter III, section 3, "El concepto finalista: La sociedad comunista," especially pp. 62–67.

23. Albert Camus, *The Myth of Sisyphus and Other Essays*, Eng. trans. (New York: Knopf, 1969), pp. 30–31.

24. Ibid., p. 31. Referring to Kierkegaard further on, Camus writes: "He makes of the absurd the criterion of the other world, whereas it is simply a residue of the experience of this world" (ibid., p. 38).

25. Ibid., p. 40.

26. Ibid., p. 53. Admitting the absurd means renouncing any quest for happiness and accepting "desperation." Then Camus offers this unconvincing aside: "Everything considered, a determined soul will always manage" (ibid., p. 41).

CHAPTER VI

How Are Values Expressed in Language?

Earlier in this book[1] I noted that human beings encountered great difficulty when they tried to express in words their values-structure, their meaning-world. That is often not a big problem in practice, however, or it is not viewed as such. In most cases the structure in question functions without any need for it to be spelled out, and it is perceived fairly clearly by others. So we do not have to make big speeches about how we picture our values-world.

Things change, however, when we change culture. Even within the same culture we cannot minimize the phenomenon known as *noncommunication* or *lack of communication.* The term has a specifically *personal* sense insofar as we are concerned. Human beings can live in a world crisscrossed by millions of communications per second and still be *incommunicados.* Despite all the general communication going on around them, they do not manage to make themselves heard and understood *as persons,* to express their personal world. That personal world, as we saw, is constituted by the meaning-structure of the individual.

When we talk about lack of "communication" between husband and wife, for example, we mean that each party frequently and even systematically is mistaken about the *meaning* of the other party's actions. The so-called "generation gap" is another example of this sort of noncommunication. Parents do not comprehend the import of what their children are doing or want to do.

All this suggests that the problem of a language expressive of our meaning-world or value-world should not be sidestepped. Many of us are all too ready to do that, trusting in our inner mechanism to clearly convey our *ends* through our *means.*

By way of summarizing all that has been said so far, then, I propose to analyze a linguistic passage which seeks to establish that sort of "communication.'' I will then try to draw the proper conclusions which flow from my analysis.[2]

I. Analysis of a Poem

It is no accident that romantic poetry should particularly suit my purpose here since such poetry characteristically seeks to express the ego of the poet. So I have chosen a *Rima* by Gustavo Adolfo Bécquer, perhaps his most famous one. Here is the text:

Volverán las obscuras golondrinas
en tu balcón sus nidos a colgar
y otra vez, como ayer, a tus cristales
    jugando llamarán.
Pero aquellas que el vuelo refrenaban
tu hermosura y mi dicha a contemplar,
aquellas que aprendieron nuestros
    nombres,
ésas, no volverán.

They will return, the dark swallows,
to hang their nests on your balcony,
and again, as yesterday, to knock on
    your windowpanes as they play.
But those who checked their flight
to contemplate your beauty and my good
    fortune,
those who learned our names,
they . . . will not return.

Volverán las tupidas madreselvas
de tu jardín las tapias a escalar
y otra vez, a la tarde, aún más hermosas,
    sus flores se abrirán.
Pero aquellas cuajadas de rocío,
cuyas gotas mirábamos temblar
y caer como lágrimas del día,
    ésas, no volverán.

They will return, the thick honeysuckles,
to scale your garden walls
and again, in the evening, to open
    their flowers, even more beautiful.
But those that were curded with dew,
whose drops we saw tremble
and fall, like the tears of day,
    they . . . will not return.

Volverán del amor en tus oídos
las palabras ardientes a sonar;
tu corazón de su profundo sueño
    tal vez despertará.
Pero mudo, y absorto, y de
    rodillas,
como se adora a Dios ante su altar,
como yo te he querido, desengáñate,
    así no te querrán.[3]

They will return, the ardent words
of love sounding in your ears;
your heart from its deep slumber
    will wake, perhaps.
But mute, absorbed, and on bended
    knees,
as one adores God before the altar,
as I have loved you—make no mistake:
    they will not love you *so.*

Its General Structure and Theme

The general scheme of this *Rima* is extremely simple. Three paired stanzas present three comparisons. Each comparison first describes—in positive terms—things that time repeats, either in nature or in the world of human relationships. The first word of the three stanzas is *volverán*. The second part of each stanza, by contrast, begins with the word *pero*. It seeks to show that despite some similarities certain things do not come to be repeated—hence their value.

Among the things which return with time the poet mentions two which are part of the world of nature. The swallows will return to build their nests on the balcony and to hit the windowpanes in their play. The honeysuckle will return to scale the garden walls and to display their flowers drenched with dew. In the area of human relationships—which is where the poet is trying to get through nature—there can be a repetition of love-declarations by other men in other circumstances.

But (*pero*) there is that which has a unique value precisely because time is incapable of repeating it. What is it? In fact, it is the same repeatable things *insofar as* they are related to concrete persons. Thus the swallows and the honeysuckle flowers of next year will look the same, but they will not be those which accompanied a lived experience of love. The same holds true for the realm of persons as depicted in the third stanza. Future declarations of love may seem similar to those which she has already heard, but they will never be the same ones. The latter are unique.

Let us dip a bit into the world of values which is expressed here. At first glance we seem to have one of those accustomed laments of humanity in the face of the fleeting nature of time: sadness for everything that does not return, that time, like the wind, carries away forever. But here we find something different. What does not return has more value than what is repeatable. What has lived once is worth more than what could be lived tomorrow just as today.

It is not easy to ground this statement. Indeed it has little relation to the fleeting nature of time. Interestingly enough, in the second stanza the poet admits that the new honeysuckle flowers could be "even more beautiful."[4] Why suffer, then, over the disappearance of the first set of flowers, which might even be inferior to the next batch?

Moreover, there is a certain incongruence in the third stanza where the poet tries to describe his love as unique and unrepeatable: "as I have loved you— make no mistake: / *they* will not love you *so*." After all, what is so radically unrepeatable about the poet's love? The poet describes it in these terms: "mute, absorbed, and on bended knees, / as one adores God before the altar." However exaggerated they may be, none of these gestures are unrepeatable in themselves. The logic here, as in the case of the honeysuckle flowers, is that an "even more beautiful" love is, or could be, perfectly possible for his lady love.

Now this little incongruence is very rich in meaning, in my opinion. Things are unique, I said above, only in relation to persons because each person is unique. The value of personal "uniqueness," not of fleeting time, is the real theme of our poet. Through his comparisons he wants to awaken his beloved from her "deep slumber." And since love seems to exist and flourish between them, or to have done so in the recent past, the deep slumber attributed to his beloved can only allude to her unawareness of what is unrepeatably personal. That is why the poet twice invites her to experiences of unrepeatability in the realm of nature. That is why he admonishes her that his present love for her exceeds the results of those experiences since *"they* will not love you *so"* ever.

And here we come to the root of the incongruence mentioned above. However much the poet may be persuaded of the eminence of values established by unique and personal relationships, he cannot verbally describe his own love in *unique* terms. That is the tremendous human paradox. As soon as we use words, we are in what is general and hence repeatable. Words are like swallows and honeysuckle flowers; they all seem the same. They are universal, and hence the uniqueness of the personal necessarily escapes them.

Hence the persuasive power that can be exercised by the experiences of unrepeatable value which the poet proposes to his beloved in the first two stanzas. Can we talk of "persuasion" in the case of this type of poetry? Yes we can because the poem seeks to convince someone of something. It is not by chance that it ends up trying to disabuse someone of an error: "Make no mistake: / *they* will not love you *so.*"

At this point one might be tempted to say that we have covered everything analyzable in the poem. To say that, however, is to forget that all we have said so far is *prose.* When a poet seeks to persuade, he or she uses different elements even when it is our language being used. Poets use rhyme and rhythm in their choice of words, taking the first step towards music. It is not surprising that many musicians carry on from there and turn poems into songs. That is not the case with this poem. What we have in this case is a personal attitude which is conveyed in nondigital terms and which accompanies the monologue. It is a special tone of voice, akin to a gesture, which mutely invites the reader not to resist the suggestive implications of the poem.

Besides all that, we might note the beauty and tenderness of certain images: the swallows knocking on the windows and listening curiously to the sounds of the two lovers; the dew drops falling like the tears of day; and so forth. Obviously no analysis like the one given above can replace direct reading of the poem itself insofar as the process of real persuasion is concerned.

Its Expression of Values

Even if we had no other specimen of poetry by this poet or from the school of romantic poetry to which he belonged, the stanzas of the poem cited above would bear eloquent testimony to a world of meaning and a values-structure. As we read the poem and reflect upon it, we clearly glimpse what exactly is appreciated and valued by the poet. We also realize some of the things that he does not value.

Right away the scheme of persuasion used by the poet allows us to assume that the beloved and the poet appreciate different things so long as she does not repudiate her "mistake." It seems that she values what time brings back again and again, that she is insensitive to the personal differences which distinguish each one of those things or experiences insofar as they are related to a concrete person. The fact is that only that concrete person makes them unrepeatable. By contrast, to value what is repeatable is to value the generic qualities of things and experiences.

That is precisely what the poet rejects: a world of values depending on universal qualities. For him each person is a center of value that relativizes the rest, unless in the rest he finds another person, another center. If the latter case is verified, then a new personal attitude is generated: devotion, desperation, or whatever. As a result of these premises, the poet must prefer anything that deepens interpersonal relationships to any universal quality to be found in things or events. Certain flowers may be less beautiful from some general standpoint of beautifulness. But they are worth more than others if they help to establish or heighten the unique relationship of one center to another center, of one person to another person. It is this relationship that makes them unique, that transposes them out of the realm of the commonplace, however much we may recognize the intrinsic virtues and qualities of the latter.

This basic, initial preference displayed by the poet leaves us in the dark about many things, to be sure. But it also gives us some idea of his meaning-world and of that of his beloved. The latter, too, is another way of understanding the poet.

Besides her preference for the objective, the poet's beloved also seems to have even more concrete preferences. If we look at the poem closely, we can glimpse some of them. In particular, she seems to appreciate or value the beauty of nature and the occasions for play which nature affords. Nothing permits us to assume that she values money, for example. But the poem suggests she is somewhat insensitive to the personal realm. Such insensitivity could very well go hand in hand with a trace of voluntary or involuntary cruelty, and her appreciation of beauty and play could very well be compatible with a quest for the money and the power needed to enjoy those things. Remember that the poet's beloved does possess a garden with walls and a balcony.

If we focus on the preferences of the poet, it seems that we can say little except that he values unrepeatable experiences which are conveyed in and through deep personal relationships. Without more data we do not know whether he is capable of bringing more persons besides his beloved into such unrepeatable experiences. We don't know his social outlook, for example, though we might suspect that the experiences he describes and idealizes in the poem are not too compatible with a profound appreciation of the social realm.

We do know something else about him, however. In his eyes the unrepeatable is bound up with a total personal commitment. That is how he sees his love in any case. His love is absorbed: i.e., impervious to all other sensations or considerations. He loves as one adores God; all other considerations and values are relativized in the face of this one personal absolute.

Finally, there is one more datum we have which might well seem contradictory. The poet's chosen preference for the unrepeatable quality of each personal life so loved renders him *mute*. I have already alluded to the probable cause of this muteness and even its limits: i.e., the universal cast of every spoken human language and its inability to grasp and convey the unique, personal element in a relationship. But the poet is far from being mute! He speaks—much too much, we might say, for a mute. The reason seems clear. When he speaks as he does in this poem, he obviously has the impression that he is breaking through the general nature of language in some way and to some extent. He feels that he is speaking in a personal idiom and communicating his inner self, even though he sometimes must struggle against the inevitable conditionings of language and even succumb to them. Perhaps he would tell us that it is only on such sad occasions that he has the sensation of talking at all. For he is a poet, and the words filled with rhythm and music that he utters now seem more like gestures and caresses than words.

II. Language Analysis

I now want to pursue this analysis of language further. In so doing, I would like to use another author as the backdrop for my remarks. I cannot dialogue fully with his book here, but some points of difference and disagreement are discussed in the Notes of this chapter. I am referring to John Macquarrie and his book entitled *God-Talk*. In it he deals with the possibilities and limitations surrounding language dealing with God. His effort to re-examine and reformulate the whole problem of religious language prompts him to make a detour by way of poetic language, which is the route I took in Section I of this chapter.[5]

Denotation, Connotation, and Verifiability

In the early stages of Anglo-Saxon logical positivism—exemplified, so it was thought then, by the *Tractatus Logico-Philosophicus* of Ludwig Wittgenstein—every effort was made to strip away from human discussions all those things based on a confused, improper use of language.[6] What was the criterion for distinguishing proper and precise usage from improper and imprecise usage? A common answer was that the former *denoted* things or facts susceptible of objective verification through experience. The latter, though superficially seeming to be the same, merely *connoted* (i.e., expressed acceptance or rejection through) subjective impressions which could not possibly be verified. Perhaps they could be verified by the subject who was speaking, but they certainly could not be verified by others to whom that person was speaking.[7]

It was felt, for example, that things would get better if people got in the habit of using different forms of language to denote that, on the one hand, the cat is on the doormat and to *connote* that, on the other hand, they don't like the cat. Alas, that is not the case. So when one hastens to correct a person and point out that the cat is on the windowsill rather than on the doormat, he or she might be told: "I don't give a damn where the cat is. My point is that I have had enough of that cat!"

There are obvious connotations in the poet's statement: "They will return, the dark swallows . . . But those who checked their flight / to contemplate your beauty . . . will not return." The poet is expressing nostalgia for the latter, who were present to witness his love affair. The problem is that such obvious connotations are expressed in a language which any zoologist could take for denotation. For it seems to state a fact that can be verified empirically. Isn't the case the same when people make affirmative or negative statements such as "God exists" or "God does not exist"?

If that is the case, then the only concern or question we could put to *connotative* language, insofar as we cannot do without it altogether, would be this: does my interlocutor really *feel* what he or she is saying, though the language seems to denote facts or describe events? The question is all the more crucial insofar as logical positivism would include under connotative language the whole of poetry, ethics, metaphysics, and religion.

Now the two-part analysis of Bécquer's poem above gives rise to a different interest or question. And why should I not go all the way and say that it is a *superior* interest? The question is: is the poet *right* in his argument with his beloved? For whether his use of language is good or bad, the poet is not purporting merely to *connote* the pleasant or disagreeable sensations aroused by the events he describes or *denotes;* he is purporting to offer a certain type of *reasoning* in which there are premises and conclusions.

In its earliest, most reductionist phase, positivism consistently maintained that the criterion for differentiating good or bad use of language was the possibility of *verifying* or *falsifying* empirically what was conveyed by language. One had to be able to show the truth or falsity of statements. What sense would there be in something spoken if no one could know whether it was true or false? Why not say exactly the opposite?

Now another point is worth noting, and even logical positivism had to open up a bit to it. It is not just what language *denotes* that can be verified or falsified. What language *connotes,* too, is able to be subjected to a similar criterion, even though the demonstrations are less direct and precise. For example, language can connote that a speaker is sad; yet other gestures or words of the speaker may show that in reality he or she is happy. We find abundant examples of this in ordinary life. But even poetic or literary language sometimes alludes to the difficulty and necessity of verifying or falsifying connotations.

In one of his poems, for example, the Colombian José Asunción Silva (1865–1896) pictures a poet addressing anguished questions to the earth. One senses that anguish is the connotation of the poem. But in the last stanza we suddenly realize that the core connotation of the whole poem is irony. We are brought up short by the lines:

La Tierra, como siempre silenciosa y callada,
al gran poeta lírico no le contestó nada.

The Earth, silent and hushed as always,
Answered nothing to the great lyric poet.

Another, more famous example would be *Don Quijote*. Perhaps the best thing about the work, as some have rightly noted, is that the very events narrated in it force us to pass judgment on the initial *connotation* we get, that we are dealing with the ridiculous behavior of a madman.

All this is moving us towards an approach which is far more open than logical positivism. Indeed it is moving us in the same direction that Wittgenstein was pointing in his later work when he suggested that every type of language has its own logic.

To begin with, we find that the logic of poetic language is seeking to inform us about something which is at least as important as the denotation of facts or objective things: i.e., the affective *connotations* of our interlocutors. (I use that term since we must have some way to name what a person *feels*.) And the *first type of verifiability* associated with poetic language is rooted in precisely that.[8]

By now my readers may well have realized what I am talking about here. I am talking about *access, through the medium of language, to the vast, structured realm of meaning and values*. I need not have used the word "connote" at all, since it has pejorative overtones. Indeed in the jargon of positivism it suggests the second-rate quality of such linguistic information as compared with purely objective information. But from our analysis so far it is obvious that poetic language connotes much, much more than mere sensations of pleasure or displeasure. Even the small poetic sample we analyzed above gave clear, though indirect, expression to an emotional *complexity*.

To put it another way, we are confronted with values, thanks to which some things are sad and others pleasant. And we are confronted with a diversity of values, the *structure* of which permits us to establish what things would be pleasant if the existence of higher values did not give them a negative qualification. Thus the "more beautiful" flowers in the poem must cede to ones which are perhaps less beautiful but which had dewdrops that were seen and admired by the two lovers together. Thus the poetic expression analyzed above enables us to *assume* what the consistent valuation of other things (e.g., money) would be. The data obtained in and through this type of language, insofar as they reach as far as the valuational structure, provoke discernment and commitment.[9]

Here we have a *second type of verifiability* associated with the poetic language we have been examining. It is a kind of ethical—or if you prefer, existential—criterion. In other words, a language has sense and meaning if my whole way of acting or living is different because of it or what it says, if that difference *depends* on the latter.

Here I might introduce a well-known parable which was originally designed to attack poetic language of the type I have been discussing.[10] Two explorers in the jungle suddenly come upon a clearing that has the features of a garden. To one explorer it means that a gardener shows up now and then to cultivate the spot. But every effort by the two explorers to prove the presence of any such gardener is in vain. As the process proceeds, the explorer who maintains the existence of a gardener is forced to use negatives to describe the "objective" qualities of the alleged gardener. The gardener must be *in*visible, odor*less*, *im*mune to electricity, *in*corporeal, and so forth. Each test only adds a further "not" to the definition of the gardener. Finally his companion asks him how his affirmation of the gardener's existence, reduced to such negatives, differs really from the sheer and simple nonexistence of the gardener. How does his definition of the gardener make the latter different from a nongardener? The point is that his affirmation of the existence of a gardener seems to be the same as a negation of that existence. The explorer favoring the existence of a gardener is using language which is devoid of any possibility of verification, claims his companion.

But remember what we have noted above. In saying "a gardener exists," the one explorer may not so much be denoting an objective gardener as connoting a sensation of his own. He may be indicating that he feels himself "accompanied" by someone besides his fellow explorer, that he feels "more or better accompanied" than he did before. If that is what the explorer means, then in principle his language is not liable to the reproaches made by the other explorer. His real, new joy would be the first verification, not of the existence of a gardener, but of his own feeling of really being more or better accompanied. We could say that the other explorer was not alert to the logic peculiar to the language of his companion and that the latter got caught up in the confused intermingling of two different types of language.

But there is more here. Feeling accompanied in a new and fuller way need not be merely a personal sensation. It might also be turned into a premise or principle of one's actions. In other words, while the two explorers are in that clearing, or even in the jungle, the explorer who affirms the existence of a gardener may do everything very differently because he will act *as if* the clearing were inhabited and cultivated.

Here we have a second type of verifiability.[11] Just as iron acts *as if* the magnet attracts it, so one explorer will act *as if* the clearing is inhabited. Hence his behavior will differ, objectively and profoundly, from that of his companion. And the logical congruence associated with that difference will verify or falsify his language. How can his companion claim that his language has no meaning when that language offers the former nothing less than the key to understanding, for a certain time at least, the whole attitude and behavior of the companion with whom he has to share everything?

Language and Transcendent Data

But we must go even one step further. As I indicated in the analysis of Bécquer's poem, the poet seems to be pushing for an even higher or further type of verifiability. He does not just announce what the basic premise of his own conduct is going to be. He also maintains that his beloved, too, can and should verify his premise. She should put it to the test and see if she too should not accept it and act upon it as the norm for her own conduct.

Here we come upon something that might well seem ridiculous and senseless if we had not already encountered it in our analysis of human life and its meaning-structures in Part One of this book. So let me now relate my earlier analysis to our present discussion about language.

I noted earlier that when we are looking for the explanation of some physical phenomenon (in the broadest sense of the term), we try different *as ifs* (commonly called "hypotheses") until we find the key, until experiment and experience show us that *this* is really the way things go. We try different premises, in other words, until we find the one which experience forces upon us as the most "economical" explanation of phenomena.

But how does it work in the realm of values, meaning, and signification? There, too, we have premises which order and structure the complex web of the ought-to-be. They are very much like the hypotheses I mentioned in the previous paragraph, though at first glance they do not seem to be. For hypotheses are *subjected to* reality ("placed under" reality as the Greek word *hypo-thesis* suggests), while these value-related premises are *imposed on* reality. In that sense they are self-validating, as Bateson points out, and they do not provide verification or falsification. Take our poet, for example. There certainly is something capricious about his insistence that his beloved center her whole values-system around a preference for the unrepeatable. Indeed he doesn't so much "demonstrate" this to her as ask her to have "faith" in that particular value.

But remember that Bateson said such premises were only *partially* self-validating. And so they are. Any analysis of human life will reveal that when human beings request or demand "faith" in certain values, they do so in the name of "reality" and not just for the sake of mere whim. They are convinced that reality is on their side. They are saying that in the *ultimate instance* one will see that *this* way of acting rather than some other will prove to be satisfying. They are appealing to an experience that could well be called "eschatological"—taken here in a human sense, not a religious sense. The judge will be some *ultimate instance* of reality.[12]

To some extent, then, every values-structure is necessarily grounded on the *ultimate* satisfaction one expects to get from the conjunction of reality with the practice of some value or set of values.

The judgment which serves as the basis for this "faith" thus transcends everything which can presently be verified empirically.[13] It presupposes a provisional way of acting *as if*. Reality, so dealt with, will presumably confirm that way of acting in the ultimate instance. In every anthropological "faith," then, we find a curious mixture of what *ought to be* and of what presumably *is*. But the "is" is a wager, you might say, since it cannot be experienced here and now.

Now what "is" is always expressed as a *datum*. To use the linguistic terminology of this chapter, I could say that language "denotes" it rather than "connoting" it. This is where the possibility of confusion arises, however, for in this particular case the basic *datum* differs from immanent data. Why? Because no present empirical process, prior to the total realization of the value in question, can or ever will be able to verify it empirically. That is why I call it a *transcendent datum*.

That is why our poet's claim differs from a mere whim. His *ought-to-be* is not merely personal caprice. It supposedly is confirmed by a certain disposition of reality itself. He cannot yet verify it. He can only glimpse it in and through fragmentary experiences. Hence he proclaims it as an *ought-to-be,* not equating it with the reality he can grasp and verify right here and now. But he *also* announces the disposition of reality as a *datum which transcends* any present possibility of verification. In so doing he is not departing from what is reasonable and falling into confusion. He is simply making the wager that every human being is forced to make, whether he or she knows it or not, in order to give structure to the meaning of his or her life.

Appealing to this kind of transcendent data is not equivalent to postulating a "heaven," a future life beyond death, the immortality of the soul, or what have you. One may simply be talking about the possibility of some satisfaction open to human beings if the present state of the world changes or if they change it by utilizing their possibilities. Both revolutionary messianisms and conservative views include transcendent data.

So our poet has given us a hint of a general framework underlying every human life. To repeat briefly, it goes like this: *Given this datum, which I take as true even though I cannot verify it empirically right now, in the end it will be seen that it was better to act thus and so.* The fact is that every human being of sound mind and spirit, even the most rabid logical positivist, guides his or her action by a similar calculus. It is not language that introduces it because it is intrinsic to the human being. Language merely expresses it. What are we to make of brave efforts to rub out the expression as inconvenient while still leaving intact, as one must, the content![14]

III. Language and Culture

Since we began this chapter by analyzing the elaborate language of an accomplished poet, we might raise the question: are only those who have refined the art of such language capable of expressing what is a basic dimension of the life of every human being? Or, since we are dealing with the dimension of ethics,[15] one might ask: is it only the poets who express themselves ethically?

The basic answer is no, of course, though with certain reservations which I will consider later in this chapter. The possibilities of poetic language are largely shared by all *iconic* languages (as opposed to *digital* language).[16] It was logical positivism, in its most narrow and reductive form, which tried to turn all language into digital language and then give the latter a secure and certain logic.

Values and Iconic Language

Why does the realm of values or signification require an iconic language? Because things or facts are not values by virtue of their mere presence, but rather because of the various types of satisfaction they produce. Only in relation to that satisfaction can they be said to have meaning for human beings.

But how is satisfaction or the lack of it communicated? The only "realistic" and effective way, undoubtedly, is to present the thing or fact with signs associated with satisfaction, to evoke satisfaction with regard to the things or events. There are many such signs or images available to iconic language. (Remember that icon means "image.") Some are more closely bound up with the fact or thing; others are more general, such as verbal rhythm, music, movements, and tone of voice.

So now we see how human beings learn values, how they come to recognize them in others and practice them for themselves. They learn values through *images* of other people's concrete satisfactions. Of course the latter can be transmitted in abstract terms. For example, in describing a thing or narrating a fact, a person may add some word such as "satisfaction" or "value." But you know that such words merely *indicate* satisfaction; they do not *provoke* it. And it is precisely by *feeling* satisfaction that we associate it with certain things or facts. That explains the necessity of presenting concrete images and, in the last analysis, witnesses to values.

Moreover, human beings tend to live out many values, not just one. They have to structure that complex realm of values so that the realization of certain values will not inadvertently eliminate others that are equally or even more desirable.

So we must establish some logic in the realm of values. That is why every human being, as Bateson points out, seems to be organized or structured by certain premises in this area. Their ontological and epistemological premises cause them to see and value things in a certain way. These premises are what I have chosen to call "transcendent data," and they give a certain direction to one's whole values-structure.

Now it should be obvious that these premises or data become transparent in the concrete valuations which flow logically and consistently from them. Insofar as some line of conduct is *consistent*, it becomes to some extent the *image* (iconic language) of the meaning-structure one has given to one's life. Other people comprehend the other person's premises that have been so revealed, and sometimes they may even translate them into their own languages.

But we must be careful not to underestimate an important fact. The realm of values is complex, and the process of imposing them on reality is a slow one. As people go through this process, the consistency of their meaning-world often falters. When a human being reflects on his or her own activity, he or she often does not grasp the import or sense of it (Rom. 7:15f.). How much less sense it makes to other human beings!

Add to this the whole problem of culture.[17] Every more or less complex society bombards us with varied or even contradictory transcendent data. We get them through individuals whose activity is the silent language testifying to very different meaning-premises. But we also get them through various explicit languages which in this case are always iconic, always poetic to some degree.

It could be said, and indeed it has been said without using my specific terminology, that for centuries ancient Greece lived off the "transcendent data" conveyed pedagogically by Homeric poetry.[18] The Latin Americans of our Río de la Plata area can trace the ethical influence they have received from the poetry of the Gauchos and its transcendent data: i.e., its opinions as to what human beings could or could not expect from the total human reality, as to what premises should structure their values and their lives.

The Intermingling of Digital and Iconic Languages

At this point I want to go a bit further and bring in another example closer to present-day life in Latin America. The tango is a poetic form, a language in which various elements are added to give expression and force to the digital part: e.g., music, the voice, and dancing. Consider the little Spanish verse on the left below. If it were in ordinary prose, we might well disregard it completely. But when it dons all the trappings of a tango, it can quickly make a deep cultural impact:

Aunque te quiebre la vida,	Though life may break you,
aunque te muerda un dolor,	or a sorrow bite you,
no esperes nunca una ayuda,	*don't ever expect any help,*
ni una mano, ni un favor.[19]	*or a hand, or a favor.*

Let me offer several observations that have much to do with our whole discussion here. The *first* observation about this little verse is that here again we are confronted with a transcendent datum, a premise that structures a whole realm of meaning or values. Many values-systems would still be possible and meaningful if that datum, unverifiable right now, is affirmed as true and certain. But there are certainly many other values-systems that would not be compatible with that vision of reality.

I need not point out again that repeated experience of a different reality does not suffice, in most cases, to make us change the system. Such premises are not only ontological but also epistemological. They affect the very way we see reality. On the basis of the underlined premise in the tango, a proffered friendship or helping hand would be viewed as ephemeral or treacherous.

The *second* observation is more closely connected with our consideration of the relationship between poetic language and culture. Notice how iconic language greatly helps the transcendent datum of the verse to exert real cultural influence.[20] The New Testament, for example, offers a transcendent datum directly opposed to that of the tango: "We ourselves have known and put our faith in God's love towards ourselves" (1 John 4:16).[21] The greater cultural prestige of the tango datum over the latter is certainly not due to the intrinsic value of the tango's message. Indeed, since Bateson points out that such premises cannot properly be called true or false, we might do better not to talk about the *intrinsic* value of transcendent data at all.

In any case the value or strength of the tango formulation, insofar as its impact on popular culture is concerned, clearly lies in what we could call its *iconic harmonies*: the rhythm of the verse, which is not that of ordinary prose; the tango music, which leads directly to the heart, or at least to a certain realm of sensibility; and behind all that, the image of a singer as the exalted living symbol of the struggles, successes, and tragedies of an era. All those harmonies or resonances are of great importance in making the datum *convincing* to people, in opening them up to the possibility of living on that hypothesis. Yet they have nothing to do with the *digital* language which apparently enunciates a fact: "Don't expect any help." Just as if it were saying: "Don't expect the train to get here before 11:30."

Now the contrary datum cited above, "We know and believe the love, . . ." seems culturally weak and doomed to failure by comparison. Why? Because we are reading it in its digital version. But suppose we give it poetic expression, suppose we relate it to the figure of Jesus and the ritual gestures of Christianity. Then all those iconic elements will reinforce and increase its cultural possibilities, its plausibility, and its attraction.

The *third* observation takes us back to the question raised earlier: do we need to be poets to express those transcendent data? Remember I answered no, with certain reservations. Now it is time to talk about those reservations or limitations—which happen to be cultural ones.

The fact is that the human being is the only living being who can put transcendent data, the underlying premises of its actions, in *express*, explicit language. For that very reason the human being is the only *cultural* being. And this possibility of explicitly expressing transcendent data derives from the fact that it is possible for the human being to mingle the two types of language, *to mix digital and iconic language*. Without iconic language, digital language would not communicate with the realm of values. Such is the case with mathematics, for example. Without digital language, iconic language would not communicate explicitly about the conception of reality on which the realm of meaning is built. Such is the case at the other extreme of the language spectrum: i.e., music.[22]

This possibility of language-mixing not only allows the human being to reflect on his or her own acts on the individual level; it also generates culture on the social level. For culture is not an artificial world of things where there is merely music or merely mathematics. Culture, as distinct from civilization, is a human society endowed with certain signs which can transmit to its members meaning-structures.

For that task poetry is somehow essential. Perhaps it need not be acquired in any professional sense. But there must at least be the poetry that arises in every human being from its ability to mix digital and iconic language in a real, effective way. It is said that there is a little of the poet, the healer, and the fool in all of us. It is that "little" which makes us, or keeps us, cultural beings.

When I talk about poetry here, of course, I am not talking about the ability to speak *in verse*. Prose can be poetic. Verse is one of many iconic elements. Theatrical productions are another. Prose may even try to imitate the iconic elements of music, as more than one novelist has suggested.

Taking the word in that broad sense, we can affirm the importance of poetic expression for society and culture. If the capacity for poetic expression is not cultivated among all the members of a society, then that society will lack cultural depth and perhaps even culture itself.[23]

Moreover, transcendent data cannot be eliminated by logical arguments. They can only summon adepts through the free poetic expression and existential fulfilment of values. And this is the strongest argument for proving the intimate relationship that exists between democracy and culture.

IV. Language and Religion

Now if that is the specific logic, the ballgame, of poetic language, we do well to ask ourselves what the logic of religious language is or might be. It would be unwise to assume such a logic without proof.

To make sure I am understood in this delicate area, I am tempted once again to introduce a distinction I made much earlier. Remember that I made a distinction between religion as the mere instrumental use of supernatural forces and religion as an authentic extension of basic anthropological faith. Having said that much, I will let my discussion speak for itself, and we can hope to verify the distinction.

Examples from the Old Testament

It seems fair to assume that in the Bible we will find a genuine religious language for our analysis. This is not to say that such language is to be found only there, but it should be there, too, if it exists at all. In this section I focus on the Old Testament.

It is really very easy to see that in the more poetic writings of the Old Testament, in what is called the sapiential literature, we find examples which are exactly parallel to those already analyzed in this chapter. Here I will consider two examples which are quite characteristic. One is the deuterocanonical Wisdom of Solomon (or, Book of Wisdom), and the other is the Book of Ecclesiastes.

In the first five chapters of Wisdom, human life is depicted as a kind of bet or *wager*. To one group "justice is immortal" (Wis. 1:15); it is stronger than death. To the other group it seems that righteousness or justice will not survive death: "Our life is short and full of trouble, and when a man comes to his end there is no remedy" (Wis. 2:1).

It is a wager because neither set of data can be verified right now; both are transcendent. Yet a whole values-structure will depend on which set of data is chosen, as readers of the chapters in Wisdom can readily see. People will live differently, depending on whether or not they accept the datum that justice is immortal.[24]

Now if the result of the wager were deprived of all possibility of ever arriving at human verification, there would not be much sense at all in studying the respective logic of the two positions. By the same token, there is a real risk involved since the wager does structure everything. But it is one thing to say that we cannot for the time being eliminate the risk, and something else again to say that it is illogical to talk about it.

The Book of Wisdom assumes that *in the end* (see Wisdom 5, in particular) those who bet on righteousness are going to win. There is not going to be reward or punishment, according to Wisdom. Instead each will get what they chose in their wager. Those who chose to act *as if* nothing survived death will see the logical result of that attitude. Drained by death, they will disappear after an instant of verification. Those who chose to act *as if* righteousness were stronger than death, will find, beyond death, the righteousness they accumulated and practiced.

Now it is interesting to compare those first five chapters of Wisdom with the earlier Book of Ecclesiastes. In the latter we see that the writer has not yet found the solution which balances and justifies the stance taken by the righteous in the Book of Wisdom.

The author of Ecclesiastes clearly does not believe that righteousness is immortal. Nothing points him in that direction: "For man is a creature of chance and the beasts are the creatures of chance, and one mischance awaits them all: death comes to both alike. They all draw the same breath. Men have no advantage over beasts. . . . Who knows whether the spirit of man goes upward and the spirit of the beast goes downward to the earth?" (Eccl. 3:19–21).

If it were not anachronistic, we could say that in a way the author of Ecclesiastes seems to be paying tribute to the logic of the Book of Wisdom and drawing his own conclusion: it is vanity, folly, to seek after righteousness. "Moreover I saw here under the sun that, where justice ought to be, there was wickedness, and where righteousness ought to be, there was wickedness" (Eccl. 3:16).[25]

Nevertheless the author of Ecclesiastes does not go down the road of the wicked as it is described later in the Book of Wisdom. The ethical consequence of the *datum* for him, and he repeats it incessantly, is a disillusioned indifference in which some commentators see the influence of Stoicism: "I know that there is nothing good for man except to be happy and live the best life he can while he is alive. Moreover, that a man should eat and drink and enjoy himself in return for all his labours is a gift from God" (Eccl. 3:12–13). The same basic sentiment can be found in many other passages of Ecclesiastes (e.g., 2:24; 3:22; 5:17–18; 8:15). And there is the picturesque comment on the whole situation: "This alone I have found, that God, when he made man, made him straightforward, but man invents endless subtleties of his own" (Eccl. 7:29).[26]

The Book of Ecclesiastes also presents another point of the utmost interest. In an indirect but suggestive way it underlines the quality of *transcendence* which is part of the *data* on which its counsels are based. Although the work was written much later, the author of Ecclesiastes presents it as deriving from the experience of Solomon. He wants to give weight and authority to his central assertions, to the "premises" from which his ethical conclusions follow. To do this, he imagines Solomon doing something akin to what Caligula does in the play by Camus. He imagines Solomon taking advantage of his status as king to explore *all the ultimate possibilities of the human being*. This lack of verisimilitude is the first thing that shocks us as we read the book. Solomon dedicates himself to total wisdom (Eccl. 7:19) and to total folly (Eccl 1:17). He explores the possibilities of total pleasure (Eccl. 2:1) and wealth (Eccl 5:9). Nowhere is there an indication that such exploration is really impossible or contradictory, that one route excludes the other, that in the last analysis the premises of the author are not drawn from "experience" any more than those of any other human being.

One might say, as I have already insinuated, that this interpretation of religious language in the Bible is particularly clear in those parts of the Bible that really are poems. In those parts, one might add, the *mythical* elements are reduced to a minimum of expression and can easily be translated poetically into transcendent data, data of the kind that every human being wittingly or unwittingly includes in his or her meaning-structure.

So let us move on to passages of a more obviously mythical cast. All that seems to be "history" in the Bible—from God's intervention in creation, the flood, the Sinai experience, the conquest of the promised land, and the development of the monarchy to God's intervention in the life, death, and resurrection of Jesus—belongs to the genre of *myth*. Whatever descriptive definition we may give to that word, those kinds of events or their narratives must be included in that category.[27]

Let us consider one of the most typical of these narratives, that of *the flood*. As we know, we have two versions of the flood in the Bible, in Genesis to be specific. The two redactions are separated by perhaps five centuries, and they belong to very different cultures. The first redaction comes from the pen of one of the oldest biblical redactors, who is known as the Yahwist. The other belongs to a much later account known as the Priestly account, which was written during the exile or a little later.

The two versions, as we shall see with a few examples, present opposed data. Even at this point it is interesting to note that the final redactors of the

Bible, who had great freedom to suppress discordant versions or choose one over the other, let stand two such versions of the same events.[28] The point is important because it reveals that the authors "believe" in the mythical events they are narrating, but in a very particular way that is far from naive.

Let me move on to another fact that is perhaps even more indicative. It has always seemed fairly obvious that the myth of a "flood"—of a flood that covered the whole visible earth, to be more precise—was hardly likely to have arisen in the rough landscape of Palestine. Its more likely place of origin was the Mesopotamian plain, which was periodically inundated by the waters of the Tigris and the Euphrates. Later discoveries confirmed this hypothesis, showing that myths of a flood sent by the gods existed in Mesopotamia long before they were found in Israel. Indeed the arrival of the myth in Israel was to be explained by migrations, wars, and commercial contacts between neighboring peoples.

Now that explains the arrival of the myth in Israel. But what about its acceptance? In what sense and to what extent can we presume that Israelites, perfectly aware of the myth's foreign and "heterodox" origin, believed in it? And by "believed" here I mean "believed in the *facts or events* narrated in the myth."[29]

Setting aside the central theme of a universal flood, we see at once that the "facts" of the Mesopotamian myths have been radically altered and, what is more, altered in different ways, by the two biblical redactions. In one of the primitive Mesopotamian myths, the flood is provoked by the anger of the gods with the noise made by human beings on earth. In the more primitive biblical version (Gen. 6:2), that of the Yahwist, it is provoked by the marriage of angels (the sons of Elohim) with female humans (the daughters of men). In the later Priestly account, the cause of the flood is the pervasive wickedness of the human heart (Gen. 6:5) and the human exploitation of fellow human beings—what the Bible calls "violence" (Gen. 6:11).

I cannot delve into all the details of the two biblical versions and compare them with their various mythical prototypes here.[30] What should be obvious to my readers is the complete disinterest of the biblical redactors in establishing what we moderns would call the "historical data" about the flood. Where, then, is their interest centered?

Gustave Lambert has analyzed this question in an excellent article.[31] His title suggests the answer to the question: "Never again shall there be a flood." In short, we are confronting a transcendent datum on which there is broad agreement between the Yahwist tradition (Gen. 8:21) and the Priestly tradition (Gen. 9:11, 15).

Neither biblical tradition was interested in the Mesopotamian myth as an alleged historical phenomenon which they could establish by consulting documents or by tracking down some actual historical flood that had served as the nucleus for later legends. The myth of the flood, originating in other cultures, interested them as poetic material through which they could convey a very different transcendent datum which dovetailed with other data of their own faith: human beings should not handle or cultivate the earth as if the latter depended on the gods and were sacred; when the Israelites are cultivating the land, they should feel that they are on their own profane land, since Yahweh gave it to them forever. This desacralization of the earth, so contrary to the content of the Mesopotamian myth, will have an enormous impact on the further development of a faith which is essentially turned towards historical interpretation and opposed to the worship of nature.

It is clear, however, that just as the biblical writers on this occasion chose a *mythical* [32] account to convey a transcendent datum, so on other occasions they did something similar with facts or events which were more or less *historical.* [33] Even in this case we assume that no one would or could demand the same sort of documentary proofs that today would elevate an event to the category of a scientifically historical fact. When you have nothing more than oral traditions, both myths and true history pass through those traditions indistinctly. Sometimes the remote nature of the events, insofar as the writer is concerned, lead us to wonder whether that writer was or was not equipped to differentiate the mythical from the historical. Such is the case, for example, with the crossing of the Red Sea by the Israelites or by certain Israelite tribes. In other cases the sources, though oral, deserve the good opinion of the present-day historian because they are close to the events and serious in their purpose. Such is the case, for example, with the magnificent literary piece which narrates, shortly after the events themselves, the details of Solomon's ascent to the royal throne of David, his father (2 Sam. 5–1 Kings 1).[34]

Let us take that piece and examine it for a moment. It is obvious to any reader of the Bible that the author of that piece was not interested in "historiography," in writing scientific history. It is equally obvious that he would not succeed in conveying what he wanted to convey through his narrative if he distorted or falsified a history that was quite familiar to his contemporaries. Thus only the tiniest indications here and there will enable us to perceive that even in this account the biblical author is trying to communicate to us what I call *transcendent data,* and what others might call *mythical* data (in the broad sense of divine interventions in human history). Thus, in the midst of facts and events which seem to be motivated by chance or by very human interests and actors, the author inserts only three passages (2 Sam. 11:27; 12:24; 17:14) where he communicates to us something that transcends any possibility of human experiencing. For example, he tells us: "It was the Lord's purpose to frustrate Ahithophel's good advice and so bring evil upon Absalom" (2 Sam. 17:14). In other words, the writer is offering us a datum which justifies the rest of the narrative and gives it sense: "It is no blind play of chance that the writer is depicting, but the fulfillment of destinies in the strict sense of the word. . . . God himself acts upon the sinner through the *jus talionis.* . . ."[35]

But watch out: *don't try to say that the writer's whole account comes down to saying that!* Throughout my analysis of language in this chapter I have been stressing that *iconic* language is never *reducible* to its *digital* summary. Who would say that the narrator of the marvelous story of David was a fool?

Imagine him expending his energy in a prolonged literary effort simply because he did not realize, primitive that he was, that he could have said the same thing more advantageously in a single sentence![36]

The Resurrection Accounts in the New Testament

We find a similar problem about ten centuries later in the New Testament when we confront the Gospel accounts—and especially those dealing with the resurrection of Jesus.[37] For a long period of time people read the latter accounts exactly as they read the rest of the Gospel narratives. They read them, in other words, with all the doubts and uncertainties prompted by a "history" reconstructed from memory by believers, not historians, a few decades after the events; but they also read them in the basic certainty that the accounts echoed facts gathered from an *experience* which covered time both prior to, and after, Jesus' death. To that extent the accounts of the resurrection were regarded as an *experiential* proof of the divinity—or at least the messiahship—of Jesus of Nazareth.

So we confront a rather odd situation. The resurrection of Jesus seemed to verify his teaching, yet that teaching was precisely that people should not look for that sort of verification! The very Jesus who, according to the Gospel accounts, refused to give a sign from heaven, to appeal to some prior communion of values, apparently ended up succumbing to the hypocritical desire of those who wanted to know first whether God was talking, so that they might then consult God as to what values they should cultivate![38]

Some time ago, however, exegetes noticed that there was a big difference between the narratives of events prior to Jesus' death and the narratives of the events following his death and relating to his resurrection. To be more specific, I should say the narratives dealing with his appearances to his disciples.

It is rather suggestive, after all, that no similar experiential, irrefutable "proof" was offered to those who refused to believe, or to everybody at large, if faith is supposed to *follow from* that event. Whatever one may think of Jesus' post-resurrection appearances, it seems that they were restricted to those who *already had* faith,[39] to those who already shared the same values as the crucified Jesus.

Let me move on directly to the accounts themselves. Three characteristic features differentiate them from the other Gospel narratives, and I should like to dwell on those features now.

1. The most intimate friends of Jesus, his full-time companions (Mark 3:14; Acts 1:21–22), were not able to recognize him easily when he appeared to them after his resurrection; and they make that fact clear (Matt. 28:17; Luke 24:16, 31, 37–38; John 20:16). On the other hand the Gospel narratives leave no doubt that the resurrected Lazarus was really Lazarus returned to normal life. So why should Jesus' friends doubt that Jesus was the resur-

rected one, unless they realized that they were confronting *a different type of reality* which Jesus was bringing with him from some "beyond"?

2. When it seems that "believing" should finally give way to "knowing" (based on such experiential proof) or even to "seeing," we find that instead it is the necessity and exigency of "believing" that is underlined by the events and by Jesus himself. "Believing" or "not believing" are the expressions which abound in the accounts of Jesus' appearances, and they are applied to the witnesses themselves (Mark 16:11, 13-14; Luke 24:41; John 20:25, 27-28).

Two indications from Luke will help us to put in its proper place this curious alternative of believing or not believing in the face of the resurrected Jesus. The first is a reason discussed by the two travelers to Emmaus for recognizing Jesus in their mysterious traveling companion: "Did we not feel our hearts on fire as he talked with us on the road? . . " (Luke 24:32). The second seems to be a contrary reason: "They were still unconvinced, still wondering, for it seemed too good to be true" (Luke 24:41).

Under point one I noted that the resurrected Jesus brought with him a new type of reality. We now perceive what sort of reality it was: a reality *in accord with the values* in which his disciples believe. This is the odd quality of a reality which prolongs and justifies the vital maintenance of faith: the resurrected Jesus provides a *transcendent datum,* not any empirical proof, about those values. Enthusiasm over this datum can help faith; but unbounded enthusiasm, recognized as such, can also put obstacles in the way of faith. One can say: it is too beautiful to be true.

3. Also surprising is the kind of teachings that come from the resurrected Jesus. In his earlier preaching we find transcendent data mixed with empirical observations and ordinary acts or gestures. Now his teachings are transcendent data *exclusively:* the forgiveness of sins, salvation for his disciples and the baptized, the fullness of power and authority, and his continuing presence with them until the end of time (Mark 16:15-18; Matt. 28:18-20; Luke 24:44-49; John 20:23).

Does that mean that we are dealing with a specifically poetic language and that the resurrected Jesus, even without speaking, is the living image of the fact that the hoped-for realities have been fulfilled? The answer is yes, of course. But does that mean that the resurrection is not a historical datum? No, it *is* historical, but in the way that a transcendent datum can be "historical." Its verification is not the ordinary empirical verification. Its verification is eschatological, hence an object of faith *up to the very end.* Like all the examples studied above, the narrative is framed in a basic scheme which could be expressed as follows: *Given the resurrection of Jesus, which I as a believer assume to be true (or historical), in the end it will be seen that it was better to act as Jesus acted and taught.*

That is how Paul interpreted Jesus' resurrection. He summed up his view in the following passage, and I take the liberty of adding in brackets a few phrases that will relate his remarks to what I have been saying:

If Christ was not raised [historically], your faith has nothing in it. . . .
If it is for this life only [without a datum that transcends it] that Christ
has given us hope, we of all men are most to be pitied. . . . If the dead
are never raised to life [consequently], "Let us eat and drink, for tomorrow we die" [1 Cor. 15:17, 19, 32].

Now if all the above is right, our analysis of this language,[40] the very language of "revelation," forces us to confront one final question. Besides providing us with transcendent data for our actions, what can this language tell
us concerning *who or what God is* in himself?

Let's start from one certain point: for such a communication God does not
possess any special *divine* language—in the sense of a nonhuman language.
The Letter to the Hebrews sums up this divine communication with humanity
as follows: "In former times God spoke to our forefathers *through the
prophets*. But in this final age he has spoken to us *in the Son*" (Heb. 1:1; my
italics). And, for that purpose, we know that the divine *Word* "became flesh;
and he came to dwell among us" (John 1:14).[41]

In that sense *all the data* which God's communication can provide us with
are transcendent data regarding us, our actions, our meaning-world, and our
values. So whether we picture God as a being or as Being itself, we cannot
apply to God a language ruled by the mechanisms which are used to establish
empirical reality and which cause us to talk about a reality *in itself*. It does
indeed make sense to talk about a reality *in itself* when the latter, through
instruments of empirical verification, controls (i.e., verifies and falsifies) our
bits of knowledge about it. That, as we know, is not the case with the transcendent data conveyed by poetic language; yet we cannot say that such data
are the object of our fantasies.

Here again we find a tenacious misunderstanding which I attacked in Part
One of this book. Perhaps it will show up even more clearly at precisely this
point in my analysis. Whether we will it or not, transcendent data are operative in all structured human conduct. Whether they show up explicitly in our
language will depend on our ability to handle iconic and digital language
simultaneously. But those data are not transcendent because the language is
divine in its origin or because it speaks about God or some "beyond." One
can be frankly and consistently atheistic, yet one will be forced of necessity to
establish as valid certain data that cannot be verified empirically.

The misunderstanding noted above is the very common one of thinking
that transcendent data appear in language only when God is talking to us
(revelation) or when we are talking about God.[42]

Eliminating this misunderstanding would have important consequences
for ideologies (in the usual sense of the term) which, because they are secular
or atheistic, think that they are excused from considering and transmitting
transcendent data or the cultural problem posed by such data.

It would also have important consequences for authentic religious faith,
for that faith which prolongs and deepens anthropological faith, and for its

more intellectual language of theology. Iconic language conveys attitudes: i.e., behavioral relationships with other beings who act with or upon us and who also have attitudes that affect us. When digital language is introduced into iconic language, it broadens rather than changes this function of individual beings "relating" to each other.

Now the transcendent data under discussion here are also data about reality, but not about just any sort of reality. They inform us as to what *relational* reality can offer us in the final analysis. They tell us about the reality that runs between persons, that we share with other beings like ourselves. Readers need only recall each and every one of the examples I have given in this chapter, from Bécquer's poem to the biblical accounts.

Perhaps my readers will now realize that the sum total of those data does not furnish us with a metaphysics or an ontology but rather with the image of *interlocutors,* be it one person or groups of persons. Thus the basic scheme for transcendent data given earlier (p. 165) could be filled out as follows: *Given that this person or these persons are thus and so, in the end it will be seen that it was better to act in this way.*

Note the implications. Through the transcendent data which speak of God, God *necessarily* appears on a personal level and with personal characteristics. We talk about biblical "anthropomorphisms," which depict Yahweh or the three persons of the Christian Trinity as subject to "attitudes" comparable to those of human beings. But those "anthropomorphisms" are not a sign of primitivism, irrationality, or critical weakness. It is talking about God as a being or Being itself that bears the mark of primitivism, lack of critical-mindedness, and the absence of any rational analysis of language.[43]

Thanks to the transcendent data of the tradition which constitutes our faith, we are learning, in the only way possible to human language, *who* the God is to whom we are relating and on whom is grounded and structured our meaning-world. Instead of "God," atheists will use abstract terms to fix their transcendent data in language. But a perceptive analysis will always discover under those terms, not God to be sure, but indeed various types of personal relationship with one or more interlocutors who are more or less anonymous.

And I would add one final warning. It is all the more hazardous for us to try at all cost to discover God under those anonymous interlocutors insofar as we have very good reasons for erasing the name of God where it is put by many religious persons (*GS* 19).

NOTES

1. See Chapter I, section on "The Problem of Values," pp. 16ff.

2. It is not just that language is a product of human beings. Human beings, in turn, are the product of language. Hence in a real sense this chapter on language recapitulates the existential analysis I offered in Part One of this book. On the circularity between the human being and language see Adam Schaff, "La objetividad del

conocimiento a la luz de la sociología del conocimiento y del análisis del lenguage,"
Spanish version in the anthology edited by Eliseo Verón, *El proceso ideológico*
(Buenos Aires: Ed. Tiempo Contemporáneo), 1973.

3. Gustavo Adolfo Bécquer, *Rimas* (Buenos Aires: Ed. Sopena, 1976). This is
"Rima LIII," pp. 94-95.

Bécquer (1836-1870) is regarded as one of the major starting points for modern
poetry in Spain, even though he produced only this one collection of poems. He is
considered by some as the best Spanish poet of the nineteenth century.

4. Here "even more beautiful" could refer to the flowers of evening as opposed to
those of the morning. Since the latter are not mentioned, however, that would be mere
padding that added nothing to the poem. I choose to see a more profound and original
intention here. Bécquer is saying that in the repetitiousness of time there can be things
that are "more beautiful" in themselves, yet even the latter cannot match the value
associated with persons.

5. John Macquarrie, *God-Talk: An Examination of the Language and Logic of
Theology* (New York: Harper & Row, 1967).

Unfortunately I think his detour is very inadequate. One difference between his
formulation of the issue and mine appears slight at first glance, but it grows in importance as his analysis proceeds. It is the fact that Macquarrie begins directly with religious language, and indeed with theological language. And he adds: "Thus 'God' is
the key-word in the theological vocabulary" (*God-Talk,* p. 99). The problem with
such a starting point is that the author lacks a solid anthropological foundation which
might shed light on God-language through ordinary usages of language.

Macquarrie's move toward poetic language is positive in thrust (*God-Talk*, pp.
204-205), but it remains superficial and peripheral. When he does focus on it more
directly in Chapter 7, for example, he does not discuss the poetic medium as such;
instead he follows Heidegger's ontological interpretation of poetics.

The fact is that Macquarrie begins with the mistaken notion that the aim of poetics
is aesthetic (see *God-Talk*, p. 173 and, in particular, pp. 194-195). So for him poetry
leaves the serious realm of life and becomes a display of virtuosity by *homo ludens*.
This vague and ambiguous use of the term "aesthetic" in contemporary Western
culture, along with its resultant misunderstandings, has done much harm to anthropology. It has often distracted Westerners from close study of poetics. So we often
read that societies move from a mythical stage to a rational stage. The mythical stage
is not poetic because myths are assumed to be works of the unconscious. Neither is the
rational stage poetic. It is guided by reason (says the positivism of Comte) or by
science (says Anglo-Saxon positivism). The absence of poetics as a factor can also be
seen in the work of Freud.

6. On the development of logical empiricism see Macquarrie, *God-Talk*, Chapter 5.

7. Ibid., pp. 94f.

8. As I noted on pages 135-36 above, the merely abstract formulation of this
connotation—in such terms as "hatred" or "friendship," for example—is less trustworthy than some less "digital" language. Hence it is also less possible to choose to
express the connotation digitally.

9. Macquarrie, *God-Talk*, p. 118. Nevertheless Macquarrie seems to assume that
such discernment and commitment are peculiar to religious language, but not to
poetic language. His understanding of the "aesthetic" clashes with his view of the
"ethical," precisely where discernment and commitment occur. Referring to a line

from Matthew Arnold he writes: "This is a vivid metaphor that presents a situation to us in a sensitive and dramatic way *and perhaps even involves us in this situation*; but it involves us *aesthetically* rather than personally or *morally*" (*God-Talk*, p. 195, my italics).

10. As presented by Anthony Flew and Alasdair MacIntyre (*New Essays in Philosophical Theology* [New York: Macmillan, 1964]), the parable serves the aims of logical positivism. Macquarrie points out that its original version by John Wisdom is much less reductionist (*God-Talk*, p. 115).

11. Macquarrie seems to be alluding to this when he writes: "In other words, the study of these parables seems to indicate an acknowledgement on the part of analytic philosophers that there is a language (let us call it 'symbolic' language) that is not merely emotive but has the power of opening up and illuminating *levels of experience* in a way that cannot be done through the use of propositions having a straightforward empirical reference. This by no means rules out the possibility that even our most oblique 'symbolic' language has some relation to *our everyday experience*, and perhaps the 'justification' for such language would consist in *showing how it is in fact ultimately anchored in our everyday existing*" (*God-Talk*, pp. 116–117, my italics).

12. This "final verifiability" is also recognized in principle by Macquarrie at one point, where he lists the empirical elements which he (not I) feels do persist in theological language despite appearances. Here is his fifth point on that matter (*God-Talk*, p. 237):

> Finally, there are arguments that appeal to the concrete results of faith in human experience. If such faith does indeed conduce to the fuller being of the individual and to an authentic community, then by these very facts it is establishing a claim to validity . . . and to this extent it might be compared to a scientific hypothesis. A successful scientific hypothesis is one that is able to account for a great many scattered facts, and the more it does so, the more it establishes its claim. If in following out a faith, one finds that the interpretative power of this faith is an expanding one and that it makes sense of more and more of the events of life, then this faith is empirically establishing itself. I believe myself that the Christian faith does establish itself in this way.

13. I agree with Macquarrie that religious language—and I would add, a great deal of all human language—is inextricably bound up with what he calls "limit-situations" (*God-Talk*, pp. 80f.). When I refer to "transcendent data," I am talking about something which is relevant for human beings precisely because the latter are operating continually in a "limit-situation." In other words, they get beyond the limits surrounding them through a wager.

I also agree with Macquarrie's rebuttal of those who appeal to Bonhoeffer in order to discredit "limit-situations" (*God-Talk*, pp. 80–81). It is not a matter of swooping down on people who find themselves in a desperate, self-degrading situation. It is a question of responding to human beings who notice the real-life limits of their existence even in the full exercise of their powers. However, I think that the transmission of transcendent data for these "limit-situations" goes far beyond strictly religious language.

14. The inner logic here could be put as follows: "Given the fact that I take it to be true that the language which leads to natural discoveries is always the most useful (a nonprovable datum), then in the last analysis it would be better to eliminate every

other type of language." Precisely the language-formula one wanted to eliminate! And without there being any possible escape-hatch.

15. Insofar as it has to do with acting in accordance with some meaning or sense. That is why Adam Schaff talks interchangeably about "ethical" questions or questions dealing with "the meaning of life" (see Note 5 of Chapter I in this volume, p. 29). "Ethical" language was precisely one of the ones ruled out as hopelessly vague by empiricist reductionism.

16. Recall the descriptive definition of these two languages which I took from Bateson earlier (see Chapter V, pp. 134ff.).

Macquarrie seems to be totally unaware of the profound difference and relationship between *iconic* language and *digital* language. He simply talks about "language." He seems to view poetic discourse as a digital language to which are added, for "aesthetic" reasons, *metaphors* or *symbols*. In this way poetic discourse is turned into "indirect" language (*God-Talk*, pp. 97–98; also see Chapter 9 of *God-Talk*). Thus, in my opinion, Macquarrie closes off one of the most important approaches to the understanding of language and its anthropological function. At the same time he opens other dead-end approaches. For example, he asks whether *things themselves* provide some analogical basis for (theological) symbolism. What he is doing is posing questions to iconic language that properly relate to digital language.

17. Macquarrie makes one comment about the "myths" of primitive societies which he later extends to the "secularized" myths of modern societies: "Nevertheless, a myth properly so-called has its social or communal dimension. It serves not only as a cohesive force in the community—perhaps by telling a story of its origin such as will give it standing and significance—but also as a kind of basic ideology, in relation to which the various events that happen in the community's history can be referred and explained" (*God-Talk*, p. 178).

I shall deal with specifically religious myths further on in this chapter (see p. 161).

18. See Werner Jaeger, *Paideia: The Ideals of Greek Culture*, 3 vols., Eng. trans. (New York: Oxford University Press, 1945).

This is how Jaeger describes the basis of this privileged relationship between culture and poetry:

> Art has a limitless power of converting the human soul—a power which the Greeks called *psychagogia*. For art alone possesses the two essentials of educational influence—universal significance and immediate appeal. By uniting these two methods of influencing the mind, it surpasses both philosophical thought and actual life. Life has immediate appeal, but the events of life lack universal significance: they have too many accidental accompaniments to create a truly deep and lasting impression on the soul. Philosophy and abstract thought do attain to universal significance: they deal with the essence of things; yet they affect none but the man who can use his own experience to inspire them with the vividness and intensity of personal life. Thus, poetry has the advantage over both the universal teachings of abstract reason and the accidental events of individual experience. It is more philosophical than life . . . but it is also, because of its concentrated spriritual actuality, more lifelike than philosophy (*Paideia*, I, 36–37).

19. Enrique S. Discépolo, "Gira, Gira," in *Tangos*, selected and introduced by Idea Vilariño (Montevideo: Ed. Arca, 1967), p. 65.

20. Sociologists could track down this cultural influence with better instruments. Undoubtedly they would find that in the outlook of many people, and particularly in certain social strata, that transcendent datum is an integral part of the meaning of life, finding reflection in many different ways in specific patterns of ethical behavior.

21. I leave for Section IV of this chapter my examination of the specifically religious tint of this formula. Its full formulation, as we find it in the New Testament, might be put thus: "We have seen the love which God has for us, and we have believed in it." Even though the New Testament witnesses say "we have seen" or "know from experience," they are not talking about an immanent datum. This is clear from the fact that the very witnesses who possess this knowledge also must "believe." The point is that in this realm, no matter what one may "see," one must generalize this witness to *all* reality in order to order and arrange values. In short, one must convert it into a *transcendent* datum.

22. All the procedures of poetic language combine both languages in differing degrees. Neglect of this fact has given rise to senseless polemics, such as that about the legitimacy of allegory. The latter has often been regarded, not as poetic language but as "disguised" speculative language. On this "false" problem I shall merely cite a relevant passage by Jorge Luis Borges:

As far as I know, the best refutation of allegory is that of Croce, and the best defense is that of Chesterton. Croce accuses allegory of being a tiresome pleonasm, a game of idle repetition. . . . To give an example, first we are shown Dante guided by Vergil and Beatrice. Then we are given to understand that Dante is the soul, Vergil is philosophy, or reason, or natural enlightenment, and Beatrice is theology or grace. Croce would argue (though the example of Dante is not his) that Dante supposedly first had this thought: "Reason and faith effect the salvation of souls." Or else: "Philosophy and theology guide us to heaven." Then he replaced *reason* or *philosophy* with Vergil, and *theology* or *faith* with *Beatrice*. In short, a kind of mascarade. . . .

Croce offered this refutation in 1907. Back in 1904, Chesterton had already rebutted it unwittingly. . . . Chesterton admits that Watts has written allegories, but he sees nothing wrong with the genre. He reasons that reality is interminably rich, and that human language does not exhaust its intoxicating wealth. Chesterton points out that human beings know full well that the soul has far more tints and shades, unnamed and disconcerting, than the forest in autumn. Yet he feels they can be represented accurately . . . by an arbitrary mechanism of grunts and groans. . . . Chesterton infers that there can be different languages which somehow correspond to intangible reality. The languages of allegory and fable would be among them.

See Jorge Luis Borges, "Otras inquisiciones," in *Obras completas* (Buenos Aires: Ed. Emecé, 1974), p. 672. Note that Chesterton alluded to iconic language and how it intermingles with digital language to enrich the latter.

23. In particular, it would lack something essential for any human cultural group: the ability to educate, i.e., to transmit culture from the past to the future. That cannot be underestimated, as it all too often is. Purporting to be totally rationalist and scientific, many familiar ideologies in our culture present their case in "prose" and think they are prescinding completely from *poetry* and *transcendent data*. Yet that is obviously not true. Take Marx, for example. If he had written only *Capital*, he would

have survived only as an object of abstruse scholarly study. But he also wrote the *Manifesto of the Communist Party*, which begins by evoking a "spectre" and which is replete with *transcendent data* of hope.

24. I leave it to my readers to verify this for themselves. They will find that the Wisdom of Solomon (also known as the Book of Wisdom) identifies "ungodliness" with a wager on the victory of death. It leads logically to a frantic pursuit of pleasure and to the exploitation of the weak and the scrupulous (who draw back because they believe in the triumph of justice over death). By contrast, the Book of Ecclesiastes would deny that a wager on the victory of death leads necessarily to ungodliness. In other words, it would reject the logic which the Wisdom of Solomon uses to draw ethical conclusions from the transcendent data which it offers.

25. Admittedly the writer adds: "God will judge the just man and the wicked equally" (Eccl. 3:17). But two points should be noted : (1) this will happen only after death; (2) it will not alter the earthly situation of the two.

26. The data of the Book of Ecclesiastes cannot help but scandalize many who are looking to the Bible for transcendent data that are uniform, universal, and valid once and for all. Indeed some exegetes claim that the scandal was so ancient that a pious scribe mollified some of the more sceptical statements in the book, sacrificing its logic in the process. Be that as it may, I have already pointed out that the Bible does not provide that sort of transcendent data. It is a process of second-level learning (or, deutero-learning) that is involved here: i.e., learning how to learn. Therein lies the importance of the Book of Ecclesiastes. Without the profound human crisis embodied in it (i.e., taking seriously the human condition as being-for-death), the postmortem solution of the Wisdom of Solomon would be facile escapism. Indeed that is what it became for Christians when they failed to go through the whole process involved.

27. In effect, we are dealing with divine interventions in human history. But we would have to reject any definition which went beyond classification to a value-judgment: e.g., "illusory" or "mistaken."

28. According to the *Jerusalem Bible* these narratives reveal the influence of various traditions as follows: the Yahwist tradition in Genesis 6:5-8; 7:1-5, 7-10 (retouched), 12, 16b, 17, 22-23; 8:2b-3a, 6-12, 13b, 20-22; the Priestly tradition in Genesis 6:9-22; 7:6-11, 13-16a, 18-21, 24; 8:1-2a, 3b-5, 13a, 14-19; 9:1-17.

29. Failing to make a serious analysis of poetic language, Macquarrie (and others) assumes that a myth "has come out of the unconscious depths" (*God-Talk*, p. 131). The data we are examining here proves that this generalization is excessive. In this case, at the very least, we can borrow Macquarrie's own statement that "the symbols are recognized as symbols" (*God-Talk*, p. 132).

30. It is precisely here, as Macquarrie points out (*God-Talk*, pp. 180-181), that we encounter a perhaps inevitable weakness of myth as compared to other poetic forms. Much more than sapiential poetry, for example, myth depends on the cultural suppositions of an age. For people removed from those suppositions, the content of myth must come through the *weak* channel of speculative exegesis. Of course it could also be reworked in another poetic manner, but the reworking could no longer be equated with the culture's original myth.

31. See Gustave Lambert, "Il n'y aura plus jamais de déluge (Gn IX, 11)," *Nouvelle Revue Théologique* (1955): 581-601 and 693-724.

32. In the strictest sense: a fabulous account of original events.

33. On this transition in religious language from the mythical to something that is somehow historical see Macquarrie, *God-Talk*, pp. 179f.

34. See Gerhard von Rad, *Old Testament Theology*, Vol. 1: *The Theology of Israel's Historical Traditions*, Eng. trans. (New York: Harper & Row, 1962); specifically the section on "Israel's Anointed," pp. 306–354.

35. Ibid., p. 314.

36. There is equally a danger in trying to suppress these observations regarding transcendent data as being irrelevant to the narrative. Von Rad himself cites a passage from E. Meyer (*Geschichte des Altertums*, II, 285) which seems to go in that direction: "All religious colouring and all thought of supernatural guidance are utterly excluded; the course of the world and the nemesis which is consummated in the concatenation of the events through one's own guilt are pictured with complete objectivity, just as they appear to the spectator" (cited in Von Rad, *Old Testament Theology*, I, 314, footnote 11).

The temptation in this case is obviously just the opposite of the one that ensnares frankly "mythical" language. Here the elements of *digital* language can prompt us to forget that we are confronting a *poetics*, not a *history*; that what is involved is a world of values, not a faithful reconstruction of the past.

37. Of course divine interventions in the history of Jesus are not limited to the accounts of his resurrection. Those who follow Bultmann in applying the term "myth" to any account of divine intervention in the world would find myths scattered throughout the four Gospels. All that, however, can be interpreted by taking due account of cultural changes and literary genres. That is what Paul did, in fact. He stripped his (written) theology of all anecdotal allusions to Jesus before Easter—with the exception of the eucharistic meal. But there is a limit, and it is the resurrection. As we shall see, Paul cannot get away from the question whether the transcendent datum of Jesus' resurrection is true or not (as a datum). It is not enough that it be "significant." And this problem continues to be crucial in the criticism directed against Bultmann's type of demythologization.

38. See pp. 16-19 and 48ff. in this volume.

39. At least faith in the anthropological sense: i.e., sharing the values of Jesus himself. If that faith is particularly weak and vacillating at the moment of the resurrection, the reason is that it is confronted with what it assumes to be a *transcendent datum*: i.e., the definitive failure of Jesus.

40. Macquarrie extends this analysis to strictly theological language by offering an exegesis of various passages from the *De Incarnatione* of St. Athanasius. See *God-Talk*, Chapter 6, pp. 126f.

41. Commenting on the Prologue of John's Gospel, St. Augustine correctly offers this observation about one of the loftiest transmitters of a "divine" language: "Perhaps not even John spoke the reality as it was, but as he could; for he, a human being, was speaking of God. He was inspired by God, of course, but in the last analysis he was a human being. Because he was inspired by God, he could say something. . . ."

42. Macquarrie is strangely anxious to distinguish between "symbols" and "analogues" in religious language (*God-Talk*, pp. 194f.), and to give priority to the latter. This is one more indication of his ignorance concerning the essence and function of poetic language. Analogues interest him because that would imply that in empirical reality there are things "analogous" to the divine realm. That would establish a *bridge* between one realm and the other, over which language would cross. So he writes:

Just how wide a gulf can this symbolism bridge? One can see that an analogy, for instance, may very well be illuminative for another situation *of the same order*—for instance, one legal situation may help toward understanding another analogous one. But how could any *everyday* situation be illuminative for another one *of a quite different order*—or, to make the point quite concrete, how could things we can say about kings, portraits, or the sun be illuminating for something *so remote* from these relatively intelligible matters as the incarnation? [*God-Talk*, p. 134; my italics].

Thus Macquarrie, like Tracy, feels it necessary to go by way of metaphysics or ontology in order to provide the bridge that is the real "analogy" between beings and Being. Unlike Tracy, however, once Macquarrie has made that trip, he talks to us about a God that has little or nothing to do with the God of the Christian Trinity (see *God-Talk*, pp. 221–230).

43. Strictly speaking, this is not a theological work. Thus my preceding remarks are not intended to formulate the whole scope and range of theological language. Fragments of such a formulation can be found in other works of mine. My task here is to dispel as much as possible misunderstandings which stem from commonplaces. One of those misunderstandings is the effort to separate theological language from poetic language and illegitimately assert its resemblance to the language of the sciences. Indeed the relevance of poetic language for the ethical plane is a central point in my analysis of the interrelationship between faith and ideologies.

Part Three

EXPLORING
THE COMPLEMENTARITY
OF TERMS

A. Problematic Aspects
of Marxist Thought

CHAPTER VII

Faith and Historical Criticism: The Role of Historical Materialism

Chapter V introduced us to the whole question of the coherence between faith and ideology, two different but complementary dimensions that are equally necessary for human beings. My approach in Chapter V was merely negative, however. Through two important examples, I tried to point out the contradictory consequences resulting from any effort to assert the self-sufficiency of either dimensions alone and to reject the complementary dimension. A values-structure which ignores the complex problem of its effective realization will end up serving different values. An efficacy-structure which forgets the values it is serving and gets carried away by its presumed autonomy will lose the achievement-oriented efficacy it exhibited at the start.

I. Marx's Historical Critique

It was no accident that we found our example of the first possibility in the realm of Christianity and our example of the second possibility in the realm of Marxism. To be sure, Christianity is not the only faith and Marxism is not the only ideology. In the cultural panorama of Western history Christian faith has clashed with many ideologies. Liberalism, positivism, and Nazism have opposed Christianity and its faith more or less directly, and they have also confronted each other as one faith confronts another. Taking faith in a broader anthropological sense, we also know that Marxism has engaged in polemics against psychoanalytic thought and existentialist thought. And Marxism, in this case upholding the postulates of what I call anthropological faith and denying the possibility of a values-free science, has also engaged in polemics against behaviorist sociology and its claims to be a values-free science.

Marxism versus Christianity

All those polemics and conflicts clearly relate to the problem which I posed in Part One of this book. But it is equally obvious that in none of them has the antinomy between faith and ideology been explicated so clearly by both sides as in the conflict between Christianity and Marxism.

In most other cases the parties ended up by disdainfully keeping their opponent at arm's length. Each side staked out its ground and a no man's land was created between them. Such has not been the case in the conflict between Christianity and Marxism. Here we have a faith and an ideology that anathematize each other as a whole. The authorities on both sides bring all their power into play in order to defend their respective orthodoxies and to oppose the other side.

Such anathemas come all the more easily in a world divided into two major power blocs, one bearing the official label of Marxism and the other vaguely representing "Christian" culture, since modes of coexistence are sought out beyond the realm of basic principles. As scientific, technical, and even political forms of opposition give ground in the face of inevitable expansion, official Marxism openly continues its fight against religion while the West expects the Church to act as a mental curb on Marxist ideology. And the Church accepts that role in one way or another. In an earlier day the Catholic Church declared Marxism to be "intrinsically perverse";[1] today it declares that "atheism continues to be an essential element of Marxism."[2]

Some years ago Roger Garaudy, then a recognized Marxist spokesman but declared heterodox later, wrote something which bears the unmistakable imprint of historical realism. "It is inevitable," he said, "that any militant thought, particularly in times of extreme historical tension and polarization of forces, should feel obliged by the necessity for vigilance and battle to adopt a certain rigidity in its openness to thoughts coming from other sources. But, even granting all the guessing and mistakes, I don't think any Marxist would deny that Marxism itself cannot survive and grow except by taking in and going beyond what is truly vibrant and alive in contemporary philosophy. Marxism would not be Marxism if it decided to reply to Sartre with the replies that Marx himself hurled at Stirner, to Husserl with Lenin's response to the theories of Ernst Mach, or to Desroches and Teilhard de Chardin with the arguments of Ludwig Feuerbach."[3]

Garaudy also noted that dialogue must have a similar effect on Christianity and that it has had such an effect in the past: "Catholic doctrine enjoys the old age of a long tradition. But it has had to confront new exigencies and respond to new problems. All that is most vital in Catholic thought today arose as a response to those exigencies."[4]

Now if all that is true, we face a historical task that cannot be postponed any longer. We must liberate both the ideology and the faith from their one-sided, superficial, and self-sufficient aspects. Such liberation will go hand in hand with the relativization of both. But to relativize them does not mean to reduce their importance; it means to extract from both the worthwhile, durable, human, and dialogical nucleus they contain. We will thus rescue them from a tradition which, for various reasons indicated, has transmitted them in corrupted ways. Specifically they have been corrupted by routinism in pragmatic thought, by authoritarian exigencies in aggressive orthodoxy, and by the general fear that all relativization and dialogue will quietly turn into weakness and defeatism.

Here some readers might interject that in the end time will take care of this matter, as it has taken care of many problems in the past: e.g., ecclesiastical anathemas against the French Revolution. One might say that current anathemas, like past ones, will eventually be seen as obsolete and incomprehensible.[5]

But there are two reasons for not counting on that. The first is that the problems associated with the complementarity of faith and ideology are our problems here and now today, and they are inescapable. Only their solution can save us from passivity, desperation, and disintegration. The second reason is that the slow decanting of time is not a good judge. All too often the "peaceful coexistence" which follows outright antagonism is nothing but a symptom of fatigue. The most important thing is no longer an object of conflict, or of dialogue.

So let us begin our task right now by trying to salvage the imperishable nucleus of the Marxist ideology insofar as it does relate precisely to faith. Readers should remember that I am using Marxism as merely the most salient example of an ideology, that what I say here will hold true, almost always *a fortiori*, for other ideologies.

The Core and Limits of Marx's Methodology

As we saw in Section II of Chapter V, Machoveč faced a real problem in trying to reconcile his interest in Jesus as a model of relevant values with the method of historical materialism, which he sees bound up with his "atheism."

So here we have our first problem. Is atheism, as a negation of all religious faith, included in the system of thought called *historical materialism*? If the answer is yes, then we face two possible hypotheses. One is that this inclusion is decided as soon as one talks about *materialism*. The other is that this inclusion occurs only when materialism is *combined* with *historical criticism*. Leaving the first hypotheses and a fuller discussion of Marx's materialism for Chapter IX, I will focus here on the second hypothesis.

My readers will not be surprised if I begin my discussion of the issue with a quote from Gregory Bateson: "The living man is thus bound within a net of epistemological and ontological premises which . . . become partially self-validating for him."[6] Here Bateson makes a distinction between premises that are validated by experimental reality—i.e., scientific premises, and those which are self-validating—i.e., those which are freely chosen for themselves, which are not directly at the mercy of a confrontation with reality, and which thus constitute an ought-to-be.

Applying this distinction to our question here, it is easy to see that Marx's own historical materialism clearly aims to be a scientific premise. It is not an ought-to-be, a self-validating premise. It is meant to be an understanding of what is, validated by actual experience of reality. So whatever may be our opinion about the validity of this "method," as Marx and Machoveč call it, we must remember that it claims to be *scientific*, with all the prestige and cost entailed by that designation.

Now let us bring in once again the *descriptive* definition of historical materialism, applied specifically to any history of religions, which the mature Marx offered in *Capital*. Instead of discrediting ideological forms by pointing up their human kernel, Marx says that any such history becomes *materialist* (i.e., *scientific*) by elaborating or inferring what ideologies correspond to a given period of production.[7]

Examining Marx's description more closely,we find it posits three elements. Without these three elements, it would have no sense or coherence at all. Let us consider these three elements.

1. There is a certain necessary and determining (i.e., causal) relationship between the mode of production and the particular ideology in question. The fact is that all elaboration or inference would be impossible or pretentious if there existed no kind of determinism linking each period of material production with a parallel period of ideological production. Of course there still remains the task of establishing exactly what sort of determinism is involved and how it works. But it is clear from the outset that the historical materialism so described does not come down to saying merely that one plane exerts some sort of "influence" on the other.

Moreover, there is another point that is often disregarded. The term "mode of production" is much less *materialist* than is often assumed by both its advocates and its opponents. As Marx repeatedly stresses, the mode of production—or, the concrete economic structure—does not just take in the organization of the means of production: i.e., its more quantitative and hence "materialist" aspect. It also takes in the "human relations" generated by the type of production in question and by the appropriation of the means of production. And in these relations between human beings, effected in and through work, are included many elements which we could rightly call "spiritual" and which are not nebulous idealizations. The concrete is complex. It is material and spiritual, even for historical materialism—or at least for the historical materialism of Marxism's founders.

It is a false cliché, generated perhaps in the struggle, to situate the spirit on the plane of ideology. Only the human mind or spirit, to be sure, is capable of evading the concrete with abstractions and nebulous idealizations. But that spirit, too, is concrete. And consciousness, its organ or product *par excellence*, must return to the concrete in order to construct its practical projects on that basis.

Theoretical praxis which seeks to transform the world is precisely the activity of the spirit geared towards the creation of a new world. Hence "materialism" cannot be an alternative to the spirit and its functions. Rather it is the orientation which seeks to restore creative efficacy to the spirit by getting the latter to start off from the concrete.

The two other elements we will examine here with regard to the descriptive definition of historical materialism confirm and bolster this important datum.

2. This necessary and determining relationship is not immediate. It is operative in the last instance or ultimately, and hence it is open to a relative autonomy. If the determinism linking ideology with the mode of production of each historical period were direct and immediate, then it would also be general or generalized. The only things that might possibly escape it would be more or less fortuitous or insignificant details of the ideological superstructure.

As I have indicated before, there is no doubt that in designating this necessary relationship Marx frequently uses verbs which seem designed to suggest a causality that is practically all-embracing and total. Thus he uses such words as "determine" and "produce," and he denies that the superstructure has a history "of its own." But besides explicitly affirming that such determinism holds only "in the last instance," Marx often subtly nuances such expressions with adverbial phrases which can only be regarded as allusions to the last-instance nature of the determination. Thus we find such phrases as "sooner or later," "in general," and "finally."

It is worth pointing up a curious paradox in this connection. Within the Marxist camp those most impatient for revolutionary transformations are often the very same people who stress unreservedly the most deterministic sort of relationships between the economic structure and the ideological superstructure. They are the very same people who are inclined to deprive the ideological superstructure of any and all autonomy, be it relative or not.[8]

What is accomplished by that tack? Does it hasten the process? It certainly does not, and by very definition. In fact, it cleaves the *praxic* bridge between impatience and deeds. It is as if one sought to give greater efficacy to a hammer by trying to strip away all autonomy from the arm that wields it and claiming that the arm is determined in the first instance by the very instrument it is using. A further step along these lines would be to posit another possible point of rupture: i.e., with the mental commands to the arm muscles to use the hammer somehow or not to use it at all. If one impatiently seeks the result by suppressing autonomy here, then all one gets is the total passivity of a spectator pretending to be a decisive actor. That approach does not increase the force or power of the transformer. It is as if one expected a hammer, on its own dynamism and without any outside intervention, to go into motion with the direction, rapidity, and force inscribed in its own internal makeup.

The youthful Marx declared that the aim of his thinking was not to *explain* the world but to *change* it.[9] Any immediately deterministic conception of the relationship between structure and superstructure, however, logically ends up as an "explanation" of what must necessarily take place. For in such a conception the material base deterministically produces everything essential on the plane of consciousness. But since only the plane of consciousness could, voluntarily and initially, introduce changes in the economic process itself (i.e., in the mode of production), it follows from the above conception that all meaningful change must remain alien to human will and praxis. Such things as the class struggle, the consciousness-raising work of the Socialist parties, and both national and international politics would have no strategic importance whatsoever. Ideological deviationism would have no consequences, and repression would be unnecessary.

Now I am not suggesting that this enables us to decide in positive terms what makes up that "determination in the last instance." I am simply pointing out that we can say something about what it is *not*. If one attaches no importance to Marx's adverbial qualifications and reservations, then one disqualifies Marxism itself as a source and structure of human praxis. Ideology is turned into a metaphysics. Indeed it is turned into the most conservative type of metaphysics, one which undermines the very foundation for any historical efficacy dependent on human beings.

3. This necessary and determining relationship does not permit us to value, in the first instance, any ideological element without further ado. An obvious problem is posed, for example, by the very rise and formation of Marxist thought itself, with its powerful ideological critique on the level of the superstructure where the ideas of the ruling classes prevail.

Of course there may be no problem for those who acknowledge a determinism in the first instance. They can always assume that when a given mode of production enters a crisis, sooner or later there will somewhere arise the superstructure that corresponds to the new mode of production in the works.

Here I will leave aside two matters connected with such a position. First, Marxists of that persuasion would have to admit that in all likelihood they would not have been Marxists if they had lived in Marx's own time; indeed that they would probably have been in the ranks of those who opposed him.[10] Second, as I hope I have demonstrated above, such a determinist hypothesis is basically inconsistent with the fundamental postulates of Marxism.

That still leaves us with another problem. How is one to discover and judge what are called "deviationist" phenomena within societies where socialism has been established? Must one not assume, on the basis of such a position, that such phenomena are to be attributed to new modes of production that are opening up within those very societies? Or must one wait to see who wins before one can know whether we are facing deviationism or the new and *necessary* superstructure? In that case it is useless to combat it. *Mutatis mutandis*, one could have said of the "Prague Spring" what Gamaliel counselled regarding the early Christians. To quote and paraphrase his remarks:

Keep clear of these men, I tell you; leave them alone. For if this idea of theirs or its execution is of human origin [i.e., a caprice against historical or economic determinism], it will collapse; but if it is from God [i.e., in accordance with historical or economic determinism], you will never be able to put them down, and you risk finding yourselves at war with God [i.e., opposing necessity] [Acts 5:38-39].

Althusser himself suggests that the existence of such a tendency is proved by the attribution of phenomena in the Stalinist era to psychological causes,[11] as if their very insignificance in detail fell outside the kind of analysis proper to historical materialism.

But suppose we assume, as Marx points out, that the latter was not conceived to discredit equally everything that is part of the ideological superstructure. Suppose that even after we have tracked down the origin of each and every product of thought, we must still decide whether we are dealing with something Machoveč calls "true or positive." What will be the criterion that decides about this value?

If all thought is conditioned *in the last instance* by the interest arising out of the mode of production, then so was Marx's thought. If that does not discredit his thought, why is that so? What is *the first instance* which complements, with a decisive value-judgment, what the last instance alone cannot provide? Schaff is in line with this formulation of the issue when he writes that it is interesting to note that Marx, the founder of the sociology of knowledge, encountered no difficulty on this point. But such a subtle philosophical mind would have had to notice the problem immediately. If Marx did not pause over it, this was because he added *another premise* to the reasoning process. I tried to reconstruct above—basically, the thesis about the differentiation of the interests of different social classes. By virtue of this differentiation, some classes have an interest in giving impetus to the evolution of society while others have an interest in maintaining the existing setup or blocking the transformations in progress. The point is that knowledge is distorted only when it is conditioned by the interests of the "descending" classes: i.e., those interested in maintaining the existing order and threatened by its disappearance. When knowledge or cognition is conditioned by the interests of the "ascending" revolutionary classes, who are in favor of the social transformations in progress, there is no cognitive distortion. At this point in his reflection Marx ceased to be interested in the problem of the social factors conditioning knowledge and the whole problem of cognitive distortion [my italics].[12]

While Schaff's formulation does justice to the issue raised, I don't think his solution does justice to Marx's humanism even though he, unlike Althusser, does acknowledge the profound unity between young Marx and the mature Marx. The fact is that Schaff's solution smacks of opportunism. It suggests that it is a matter of betting on the horse that is going to win. Take John Stuart Mill and Marx, for example. The only difference between the two men, both conditioned by the same economic structure, would be that Marx had made the better wager. The whole effort of young Marx to define an integral human being as the orienting thread for the construction of a society would thus vanish as mere futility.

It is interesting to note that it was Karl Mannheim who drew the most scientific (i.e., most impartial and generalizing) consequences of historical materialism. He proposed to turn it into a real *sociology of knowledge* and, in my opinion, he succeeded. But in so doing, he found himself obliged to generalize the influence of interests in the production of thought instead of stopping at the point where Marx's theoretical interest stopped, according to Schaff.

If the ideological superstructure depends in the last instance on interests stemming from the mode of economic production, then that must hold true for *all* products of thought, including those placed in the service of the proletariat and the "ascending" classes. In short, it holds true for Marxism.

This generalized relativization, which is known as Mannheim's Paradox and which Schaff attempts to answer in the passage cited above,[13] leads logically to another question: how and from where can there arise an *absolute* that will put order into all that relativity in a praxis? As we have already seen, action cannot be structured without something unconditioned that subjects everything else to unity. That unconditioned need not be God or a metaphysical entity, but it has to be a value. And science ignores values, or else it sneaks them in the back door in disguise.

The latter is precisely what Schaff did with his "ascending" and "descending" classes.[14] And that is precisely what Mannheim ended up doing when he disguised a value-judgment under his famous distinction between *ideology* and *utopia* as two chief types of ideas that transcend the situation:

> Ideologies are the situationally transcendent ideas which never succeed *de facto* in the realization of their projected contents.
>
> Only those orientations transcending reality will be referred to by us as utopian which, when they pass over into conduct, tend to shatter, either partially or wholly, the order of things prevailing at the time [my italics].[15]

I think readers can readily see how little help that distinction offers people in choosing or valuing one idea over another in the face of an uncertain future. They would have to let history go by to know whether a given thought was realized *de facto* or not.

I feel that Marx's thought deserves better understanding than that. But that can only mean that we must take seriously an anthropological faith to be found in him: i.e., his humanism. It was this humanism which, even though depending in the last instance on the mode of production of his age, enabled him in the first instance to place himself in the service of the more human cause while so many others were adapting themselves to the existing ideological structure.

II. Three Levels and Their Interrelationship

In the previous section I dealt with the negative side of an issue. I tried to set down the guidelines and boundaries we would need to pinpoint the nature of the ideological superstructure's dependence on the economic, material structure. We thus saw the reefs of incoherence which menace historical materialism if it attempts to move off in any direction beyond the point where its truth and its fertility converge.

We are still left with a very important issue. Within those logical limits, how and in what way does one plane depend upon the other? What exactly is the relative autonomy involved? What exactly are the first and last instance of that determinism?

Lest my investigation become too abstract and tiresome at this point, I would like to place it against the backdrop of an exaggerated description or caricature of our object. In *The Glass Bead Game*, a novel set in the future, we find an allusion to historical materialism. The author, Herman Hesse, depicts the future decline of a sect, pedagogical rather than religious, which from the Marxist viewpoint could be described as the trustee of the idealist tradition of culture. The protagonist, Knecht, takes a critical part in this decline. That is not the case with several eminent members of the sect. One of the latter is Tegularius, who at one point says:

> It reminds me of a sect fairly widespread in the nineteenth or the twentieth century whose members seriously believed that the sacrifices, the gods, the temples and myths of ancient peoples, as well as all other pleasant things, were the consequences of a calculable shortage or surplus of food and work, the results of a tension measurable in terms of wages and the price of bread. In other words, the arts and religions were regarded as mere façades, so-called ideologies erected above a human race concerned solely with hunger and feeding.

At this point Knecht steps in and raises the issue we are raising here:

> Knecht, who had listened with good humor to this outburst, asked casually: "Doesn't the history of thought, of culture and the arts, have some kind of connection with the rest of history?"

That brings us to the most serious part of the response—even though it is even more of a caricature:

> "Absolutely not," his friend exclaimed. "That is exactly what I am denying. World history is a race with time, a scramble for profit, for power, for treasures. What counts is who has the strength, luck, or vulgarity not to miss his opportunity. The achievements of thought, of

culture, of art are just the opposite. They are always an escape from the serfdom of time, man crawling out of the muck of his instincts and out of his sluggishness and climbing to a higher plane, to timelessness, liberation from time, divinity. They are utterly unhistorical and antihistorical."[16]

Granting the initial caricature, we notice that the latter part of Hesse's text introduces a point which ought to make us stop and ponder. Can historical materialism reject or discard as mere deceitful façades the human ideals embodied in the realm of the superstructure—beginning right with those of Marx himself, and with young Marx specifically?

This point is all the more interesting insofar as efforts have been made to correct or complement historical materialism, otherwise known as the "interest theory." Clifford Geertz writes:

> If interest theory has not now the hegemony it once had, it is not so much because it has been proved wrong as because its theoretical apparatus turned out to be too rudimentary to cope with the complexity of the interaction among social, psychological, and cultural factors it itself uncovered.[17]

Geertz describes the two theories and then highlights the "strain theory" that seeks to displace or complement the (class-) interest theory:

> There are currently two main approaches to the study of the social determinants of ideology: the interest theory and the strain theory. For the first, ideology is a mask and a weapon; for the second, a symptom and a remedy. In the interest theory, ideological pronouncements are seen against the background of a universal struggle for advantage; in the strain theory, against the background of a chronic effort to correct sociopsychological disequilibrium. In the one, men pursue power; in the other, they flee anxiety. As they may, of course, do both at the same time—and even one by means of the other—*the two theories are not necessarily contradictory;* but the strain theory (which arose in response to the empirical difficulties encountered by the interest theory), being less simplistic, is more penetrating, less concrete, more comprehensive [my italics].[18]

So understood, *strain* is much like the dissatisfaction of human beings who, in the face of historical reality, feel that their values-structure is nothing more than an unrealized ought-to-be. And such dissatisfaction, according to Tegularius in Hesse's novel, would be the origin of the ideological superstructure. Now wouldn't that contradict historical materialism?

In this context we should not forget that Marx himself endorsed the strain concept to some extent when he made the following remark about religious feeling as one of the forms of the ideological superstructure: *"Religious* suffering is at one and the same time the *expression* of real suffering and a protest against real suffering."[19] Marx certainly went on to attack sharply the inefficacy and escapism of that particular expression and protest. The point here is that his phrasing here suggests at least an initial acceptance of the strain theory rather than the interest theory.

All this may serve as a basic framework for my following attempt to spell out more positively the exact nature of the determination played by the structural mode of production on the ideological superstructure; and to extract from that relationship the most scientific and trustworthy methodology possible. To do this task properly within the boundaries defined in Section I of this chapter, we have to distinguish three planes or levels, and that is what I shall do now. I shall discuss in turn the level of the materials, the level of the last instance, and the level of the first instance.

The Level of the Materials

The ideological superstructure is fashioned wholly out of materials coming from the concrete world. However much they may later be brought to high degrees of abstraction or distortion, the means of production of an epoch and the human relations generated therein by the concrete division of labor forge both the "material" and the spiritual materials with which ideological abstraction works. Even when such abstraction camouflages its origin and turns into an inverted reflection of the material base,[20] it cannot work with elements other than those coming from that base.[21]

The social creation of language, for example, in every epoch conveys very clearcut data about the type of society—understood in an economic, material sense here—around which words and syntax formed or changed.[22] And all the structural forms, the majority of which were forged by language to begin with, present similar unmistakable signs of the mode of production belonging to the period in which they arose. They do so through the materials with which they were constructed.

Whether one accepts the interest theory, the strain theory, or both together, one must agree that the form and the relations of concrete human labor provide what the ancients called the *material cause* of any culture, even of the most sophisticated one. In other words, they provide the *framework* or limit, outside of which ideological creations cannot have any contemporary validity, whether they are good or bad, right or wrong.

Here some readers might say that this is obvious and well known and that historical materialism goes much further. That may well be, as we shall see later. But in my opinion neither those favoring Marxism nor those opposed to it usually draw all the conclusions that flow from this first level of structure-superstructure relations.

I think two examples will bring out the scope of these consequences much better than abstract reflections might. When the Soviet "thaw" set in after

Stalin's death, the Chinese Communist Party and the Russian Communist Party began to argue about the proper interpretation of Marxism. One issue raised was the possible use of the atomic bomb to establish socialism in the world. The Chinese party saw nuclear war as a secondary or negligible question since it had not been raised, much less resolved, in the writings of Marxism's founders. Here is what the Soviet leaders wrote in response to Mao Tse-tung's twenty-five points: "According to them, the main thing is to put an end to idealism in the shortest time possible. To them, knowing how to do that and at what price is a secondary question. But for whom is it a secondary question? For the hundreds of millions of people who are bound to be annihilated in the event of nuclear war?"[23]

Two elements in this Soviet reply deserve attention. The first and most obvious is that in order to resolve the issue the Soviets have recourse to what Schaff would call the level of "ethics" or "the meaning of life." It seems clear to them that the "ideology" which enlists violence in the service of socialist efficacy must, in turn, be enlisted in the service of values. And the values in question are obviously those which established socialism purports to serve. At bottom this is an appeal to Marx's humanism, to what he would have thought about a particular type of "efficacy" in achieving the goals he sought.

Clearly there is no little element of interest in the fact that the Soviets are appealing to what I would call the level of anthropological faith. But there is an even more interesting point in connection with our topic here. It is the fact that the Soviets, confronted with a literal interpretation of Marx, clearly see that the material base of human society, from the time of Marx to our own day, has caused substantial change in the meaning of such words as "war" and "violence." Hence they must reformulate Marx today in order to be strictly loyal to him, and it was for that very reason that they had to go back to his faith, his system of values, his basic humanism.

Such reformulation, then, is postulated by the Soviet Marxists for this first level of historical materialism. That is not done for other levels, however: the level of religion, for example. Now Marx did not just refer to the concrete religion with which he was familiar. In his works he often alluded to religion in general, to what we might call the essence of religion. But Marx did that without even being able to suspect that some day the word "religion" could evoke something very different—just as the word "war" could some day evoke the destruction of hundreds of millions of human beings.

Now if we accept this first level of historical materialism, we cannot say that Marx knew in advance all the historical meanings and connotations that the word "religion" might take on with the change in the mode of production and production relationships entailed in the coexistence of socialist and capitalist countries.

Perhaps Marx believed that he had resolved once and for all the problems relating to this sector of the superstructure. But if he had really done that, then he would have had to arrive at the conclusion that historical materialism is not what Althusser calls "the science of the evolution of social formations,"[24] but rather a metaphysics of essences—just another idealism. It cannot be both at once, especially when we realize that each grounds different and even opposed policies with historical consequences that may well be decisive.[25]

The acceptance of this first and primary level of dependence on the material base is also of the utmost importance for any faith, be it anthropological or religious.

As should be obvious, and as Marx makes clear in the comment on religious history in *Capital* which I have quoted several times, faith is not invalidated but *situated* by historical criticism. Such criticism points up the base which makes faith possible by providing it with materials for expression and realization, and thus it also points up the limitations of faith.

The fact is that no values-structure can remain identical with itself as it goes through different historical periods. Just take the simple fact that we recognize it through some concrete expression which is limited by the resources and materials of its age. How could we recognize it as a living thing in another age, except through a process of re-creation, using the new materials resulting from new modes of production, labor, and society? Clearly Christ, even though he be the revelation of God, is subject to this same type of limitation by virtue of his incarnation.

The challenge which confronts us here must be clearly recognized. It is not that we should deny, contrary to the facts, that there is an absolute which is realized historically (in line with each given values-structure). It is that we must recognize that every absolute must be pondered and realized anew over and over again amid the relativity of history. If we do not do that, if we give in to convenience, routine, or conservatism, then the absolute in which we say we believe will imperceptibly turn into an idol. It may preserve its earlier label, but it will not be the reality it was before.

The Level of the Last Instance

Marx had a rich, scientific, basic intuition when he discovered that the ruling ideas (or ideologies) of every age in history were always the ideas of the ruling classes. Even in societies without clearly defined class-phenomena, the same statement would hold true for the ruling groups. But this basic intuition lacked a more precise scientific framework.

To begin with, what does "ruling" mean? Suppose it refers to those who manipulate the mechanisms of culture because they have access to them. In that case Marx is enunciating nothing more than a truism. Suppose, on the other hand, "ruling" refers to the proportionate power possessed by the different social classes in a given epoch. In that case it is not clear why the ideas of the vast majority of the population, in a more or less democratic system, for example, would not represent the interests of that same majority. In other words, one would have to explain why those who are dominated economically are not decisive in the formation of a culture.

Secondly, Marx would have to make clear how these mechanisms work.

How exactly are the ruling ideas of a culture shaped to suit the truly ruling classes? What does an artist do, for example, to create an art that serves the interests of his or her own class? Does he or she just set out to do that baldly? Or does the artist just end up there, whether he or she wanted to? And if so, what exactly is the mechanism that acts in despite of his or her intention?

If we assume that interest *consciously* manipulates ideology, then we have two annoying problems. First, the most rigorous and scientific information about the "conscious" life of the best artists would tend to bring us, at least at first glance, much closer to the conception of Tegularius in the *Glass Bead Game*: at the moment of creation, the artist's intention was far removed from any quest for power or advantage of a personal or group nature. The *strain* theory, the notion of a tension between the ugliness and vulgarity of the world on the one hand, and the loftiest values on the other, would be a much better explanation of such cultural phenomena as *La Gioconda* and *Don Quixote*.

There is a second annoying problem. It is hardly credible to attribute such conscious intentions to a ruling minority without proceeding to explain in a convincing way how or why the vast majority accepts the ideological products, wholly unaware that these are tools expressly created against their own interests. Take Lenin, for example. In *What Is to Be Done?* he begins with the hypothesis that what precludes this awareness in the proletarian masses is lack of information about a very complex issue. But he ends his analysis by attributing this lack of awareness to a simplism and immediatism that are common to human beings of all social classes, hence to the human beings of the ruling classes who supposedly turn culture into an element serving their interests!

On this level, then, I am convinced we must resort to a scientific element that is definitely missing in Marx. And by "missing" I mean that it is absent and yet logically postulated by the system itself.

What we are looking for is an equivalent or analogy in culture to the *entropy* that governs thermodynamics in the field of physics. I am talking about the irreversible tendency of energy towards degradation.

The existence of this phenomenon, of this radical imbalance between originality and vulgarity, creation and imitation, disinterest and interest, has been noted and expressed in countless ways by cultural writers of all sorts. It is evident in Hesse's character, Tegularius, for example. He sees culture as a qualitative effort to escape the quasi-principle that has gotten all sorts of suggestive, metaphorical names: "line of least resistance" (Lenin), "inertia" (Ortega y Gasset), and "gravity" (Simon Weil).

What thermodynamics adds to this basic perception is the first steps towards a possible explanation, an explanation based on an analogy between this human tendency and a basic law of matter already visible at the level of physics and chemistry. Starting from the logical premise that the supply of energy remains constant, we find that the richest and most complex syntheses of energy attempted by nature—those which translate into more profound, decisive, and transformative phenomena—are those which pay the highest price in energy. Thus they are also the most fragile and hazardous syntheses as well, and they are minority phenomena at every level. This is true in physical nature, in society as a whole, and in each individual no matter what his or her social class may be.[26]

From this I would draw three conclusions which, in my opinion, help to explain and clarify the last-instance determinism exercised by the structure on the ideological superstructure.

1. The first has to do with the phenomena of *large numbers* or multitudes which can be computed at the end of long processes. They are statistically predominant and hence are predictable after a good number of efforts.[27] The large numbers *always* yield expressions of degraded, easy, cheap energy. They embody syntheses of an undemanding nature, accumulations of similar elements, and mechanisms of a repetitive and routine sort.

Sociocultural syntheses follow the same road. Simplism and immediatism, which Lenin saw as characteristic features of mass conduct, are nothing else but the result of this tendency toward degradation—a tendency that is computable and predictable in the long run. For that very reason the pursuit of class interests in the elaboration of cultural syntheses is carried out in a largely unconscious way.

Geniuses and minorities may qualitatively overcome this tendency to simplism in certain areas or works that constitute exceptions. But even they, in the rest of their lives, are victims of the same mass mechanisms. No one has sufficient energy to be a minority on every level. The energy displaced into a difficult synthesis is necessarily drawn from the cheap energy with which one fulfills other sociocultural functions and roles. Take Cervantes, for example. In much of his literary work he pays tribute to the routine and lack of criticism in his art.

When it comes to culture, perhaps the most important point to note is that the exceptional work is exceptional when it comes into being, but it becomes part of culture only insofar as it exerts general influence. *Don Quixote* is cultural because it has been read by generation after generation. The phenomenon is reproduced with much more universal characteristics. For one original reading there are a thousand accustomed readings. And the accustomed ones are conservative by very definition, even when the works in question are revolutionary. In the long run, in other words, the "system" or culture *retrieves* something which was originally a negation and criticism of it from a qualitative standpoint. If we add to this the much larger number of cultural forms which were not negative and critical, even at the start when they were created, we will have a much more realistic picture of the formation of a culture.

Marx himself did not escape this iron law. Incorporated into the sociological and economic programs of the capitalist countries and scrutinized, copied, and cited as the official ideology in socialist countries, he loses his critical and revolutionary value. Entropy translates him into a degraded cultural form: i.e., part of the information needed to fullfill social roles in the existing system.

Thus historical materialism does not demonstrate or prove any law to the effect that a small group consciously manipulates culture in order to impose the group's ideas on it and thus make the culture serve its group interests. The ruling class, the class which has more room to maneuver in the domain of culture, interprets and uses the latter without being conscious of the fact. Insofar as the ruled are concerned, the easiest synthesis and the cheapest energy in surviving morally and physically is to accept the culture with its corresponding mode of production. That is done, as we saw, by "degradation": i.e., without taking cognizance of the fact or making any effort to do so. It is what Lenin called the "line of least resistance." That is why in the long run the ruling ideas of an age are always those of the ruling social groups.

2. The second conclusion or consequence is this: in the domain of the superstructure, as at every other level of universal evolution, we must acknowledge and accept phenomena which go by the name of *neg-entropy*. Throughout the evolutionary process we find that, here and there, random individuals and groups of a critical or genial nature overcome the tendency to degradation and effect rich and costly syntheses.

I will dwell more on these exceptional cases when I deal with the next level. What I want to do here is to point up the less "political" interpretation or translation of Marx's comment on the ruling ideas of an age. It might be put as follows: "Every culture is necessarily conservative." In other words, it is truly culture *only* when it is conservative.

Culture is not *one* masterpiece, *one* poem, *one* legal constitution, *one* philosophical work, *one* religious dogma. All those things become culture when they are transmitted cumulatively—i.e., with cheap energy; when they are turned into the general way of seeing, judging, and facing the world; when the qualitative becomes quantitative. It is precisely here that *entropy* enters victoriously with its determinism "in the last instance"—by very definition.

Thus Clifford Geertz commits two errors when he sets up an opposition between the strain theory and the interest theory. First, insofar as the level of cultural creation is concerned, he puts on the same level two explanations which operate on different levels: the level of the first instance and the level of the last instance. Second, he oversimplifies the functioning of "interest."

Geertz confuses and equates the economic *factor* (i.e., the desire or intention to have more, to make a profit, to win advantages and power) with the economic *structure*.[28] The existing mode of production causes a superstructure consistent with it to appear as the easiest, most immediately gratifying, and hence the most "natural" and acceptable.[29] Now obviously this superstructure will *also* be in accord with the *objective* interests of those who profit from this conservatism. But it is silly and nonsensical to attribute the rise of those cultural forms directly to those interests.[30]

3. There is a third important consequence to be considered. On the level we are examining here, the level of the last instance, it is impossible for us to determine the "qualitative" results of any specific cultural form (including religion). In other words, there is something that escapes us and that is an essential element for any historical critique: i.e., the *specific* influence of particular superstructural elements.

Adopting the very standpoint of historical materialism, Sartre offers the following criticism of any analysis that stops at determining the "interest" of a creative ideological agent, a writer like Valéry for example: "Valéry is undoubtedly a petit-bourgeois intellectual. But not every petit-bourgeois intellectual is a Valéry. The euristic inadequacy of contemporary [official] Marxism lies in those two sentences. What Marxism lacks is a hierarchy of mediations to grasp the process which produces the person and his product within a given class or society at a certain historical moment."[31] What is lacking, in other words, is everything connected with the instances which are not specifically the last instance. And if they are lacking, or have been lacking, it is because people have failed to draw the logical consequences deriving from the basic intuition of historical materialism.

The Level of the First Instance

In his protest against his own caricature of historical materialism, Tegularius did not take note of the level of the last instance at all. He focused simply on the level of the first instance. On that level he was right. On that level the strain theory is also right, but only on that level. If it were true on the level of the last instance, if interest and strain vied for primacy there in determining the cultural superstructure, then historical materialism could simply be discarded without further ado. Indeed so could any theory which said that class interest was the mechanism that intentionally brought about the rise of a particular cultural form, or that allowed us to evaluate as positive or negative, large or small, the form's influence on the rest of the superstructure and on the objective possibility of changing the existing mode of production.

As I noted before, it is not just a matter of *explaining* the world of the ideological superstructure; it is a matter of changing it. An explanation still remains just an explanation if it simply affirms "*the relative autonomy of the superstructures and their specific effectivity.*"[32] Without discarding the level of the last instance, we must realize that if this specific efficacy of superstructures is important on their own level, then the *praxis* of *ideological* struggle is going to demand a critical, situated evaluation of each and every cultural form—of religion as well as of Marxist thought. What values does it serve here and now today? What are its concrete possibilities of influencing the course of the history of thought in the desired way, and hence of influencing the course of the mode of production and its attendant human relations?

Having come this far, we have every right to conclude that "last instance" does not signify an influence which shows up as decisive at some moment we might call the *last* moment. Nothing of the sort is the case. Studying the level of the last instance, we saw that the determination of the ideological super-structure by the economic structure shows up as something *constant* and *on-going*, though visible only in long-term accumulations.

Well, so it is with the level I am analyzing here. The influences that are decisive in the first instance work continually. They are not interrupted by some "last instance" that steps on the stage and manipulates the course of the plot:

> The economic dialectic is never active *in the pure state*. In History, these instances, the superstructures, etc.—are never seen to step respectfully aside when their work is done or, when the Time comes, as his pure phenomena, to scatter before His Majesty the Economy as he strides along the royal road of the Dialectic. From the first moment to the last, the lonely hour of the "last instance" never comes.[33]

That does not mean we should proceed *as if* the last (determining) instance did not exist. On the contrary, we shall see that the resistance of entropy on this second level means that the study and evaluation of human super-structural projects has to take a dialectical path. *Historical* materialism and *dialectical* materialism do not meet by chance. Correctly understood, they cry out for each other.

III. The Need for Marxian Suspicion

Before I move on to the next chapter and a consideration of Marxian dialectic, I would like to rein in and rest on the issue which served as my focus in this chapter.

It should be clear that historical materialism cannot be a metaphysics, without betraying itself. It cannot propound general, atemporal statements about God or atheism, or even about basic, human anthropological faith. It was, it is, it will always be, a critical tool of any such faith.

What historical materialism does, to the extent that it avoids relapsing into coarse determinism by ignoring the level of the first instance, is establish in a richer and more realistic way the often unnoticed relationship between the values one professes and the realizations one accepts. If Marx has been called one of the great "masters of suspicion," it is precisely because he showed that human beings committed to certain values allow themselves to be convinced that existing cultural forms do in fact represent those values; that they spend their days in the face of realities which belie those values without even notic-ing it; that their own experience of sustaining values is infiltrated by the dis-torting influence of their adaptation to a reality whose forms are totally op-posed to their values.

Nothing would seem more obvious than the fact that Christians need that sort of *suspicion*, if Christianity is concerned about reality rather than fiction. But it is not at all obvious or logically clear that the systematic exercise of such suspicion will do away with Christianity itself, not just with some of its manifestations. At the very least I would say that it is not clear why this should happen to Christianity and not to Marxism itself, or to any other type of anthropological faith.

NOTES

1. See Pius XI, *Divini Redemptoris*: "Communism is intrinsically perverse. In no area can collaboration with it be allowed for those who wish to save Christian civilization." The context makes clear that the pope is not talking about any and every sort of communism, but specifically about Marxist communism.

2. The phrase itself is a logical misstep, but a significant one. If atheism is an "essential" element of Marxism, then it makes no sense to say that it "continues to be" that. If, on the other hand, the point is that atheism has been *considered* important or essential up to now, then the Spanish text in question here should have used the verb *estar* rather than the verb *ser*; the latter indicates a permanent quality of an essential nature. See the working draft of the Permanent Commission of the Chilean Episcopate entitled "Evangelio y Paz," dated September 5, 1975, in *Mensaje*, no. 243 (October 1975), p. 468.

3. Roger Garaudy, *Perspectives de l'homme* (Paris: PUF, 1960), p. 10. At that point in time the "live" interlocutors for Garaudy were Marxism, Christianity, and existentialism. Though the explicit relevance of existentialism would not be accorded the same recognition today, even by Garaudy himself, his arguments retain their force.

4. Ibid., pp. 7–8.

5. See, for example, Leo XIII, *Graves de communi*: "It is not licit, however, to relate the term 'Christian democracy' to politics. . . . In the present matter it should be understood to mean beneficent activity on behalf of the people, setting aside any and every concept of politics. . . . In no way should there be a tendency to desire or to try to introduce one social regime in preference to another."

What would the Chilean episcopate make of this papal condemnation? They have bet the Church's chances on its strategic union with Christian Democracy as a concrete political party. Also worth noting is the fact that in saying no to any option for socialism, they use the very same argument which was used by Leo XIII in the last century to forbid the application of the term "Christian democracy" to politics.

6. Gregory Bateson, *Steps to an Ecology of Mind* (New York: Ballantine Books, 1972), p. 314.

7. See Chapter V in this volume, p. 132.

8. Note this quote from Gramsci, cited by Louis Althusser in *For Marx*, Eng. trans. (London: Verso Edition, 1979), p. 105, n. 23:

The determinist, fatalist element has been an immediate ideological "aroma" of the philosophy of praxis, a form of religion and a stimulant (but like a drug) necessitated and historically justified by the "subordinate" character of certain social strata. When one does not have the initiative in the struggle and the struggle itself is ultimately identified with a series of defeats, mechanical determinism becomes a formidable power of moral resistance, of cohesion and of patient and obstinate perseverance. "I am defeated for the moment but the nature of things is on my side in the long run," etc. Real will is disguised as an act of faith, a sure rationality of history, a primitive and empirical form of impassioned finalism which appear as a substitute for the predestination, providence etc., of the confessional religions. We must insist on the fact that even in such cases there exists in reality a strong active will. . . . We must stress the fact that fatalism has only been a cover by the weak for an active and real will. This is why it is always necessary to show the futility of mechanical determinism, which, explicable as a naive philosophy of the masses, becomes a cause of passivity, of imbecile self-sufficiency, when it is made into a reflective and coherent philosophy on the part of the intellectuals. . . .

9. The point is not confined to Marx's famous thesis on Feuerbach. The Marx of the *Communist Manifesto* must be viewed in the same terms. It is true that *Capital* might be construed in different terms, particularly where the dialectic seems to go to extremes of fatalism. Thus, for example, Marx writes as follows in Book I, Part Eight, Chapter 32 (Eng. trans. [New York: Vintage Books, 1977], p. 929):

The capitalist mode of appropriation, which springs from the capitalist mode of production, produces capitalist private property. This is the first negation of individual private property, as founded on the labour of its proprietor. But capitalist production begets, *with the inexorability of a natural process*, its own negation. This is the negation of the negation. It does not re-establish private property, but it does indeed establish individual property on the basis of the achievements of the capitalist era: namely co-operation and the possession in common of the land and the means of production produced by labour itself [my italics].

Now if this passage assumes the uselessness of ideological struggle, the automatization of the class struggle (without the need for any appeal to proletarian unity), and the irrelevance of economic analysis itself for a process that will take its course anyway, then we do indeed have two Marxes. But even in that hypothetical case, the dividing line would come much later than Althusser assumes.

10. If some determinism replaces affinity of values as the cause for people's adhesion to a new line of thought that is emerging, then there is no reason to think that admiration for Marx *today* would have *then* overcome the overwhelming probability of thinking like the vast majority, the path which determinism travels.

11. Even though they be attributed to a kind of "social psychology" (see Althusser, *For Marx*, p. 116). Also see the section entitled "Marxism and Humanism" in the same volume, pp. 221–47.

12. Adam Schaff, "La objetividad del conocimiento a la luz de la sociología del conocimiento y del análisis del lenguaje," Spanish text in the anthology edited by Eliseo Verón, *El proceso ideológico* (Buenos Aires: Ed. Tiempo Contemporáneo, 1973), p. 52. For a French text see Note 31 of Chapter IV in this volume.

13. In reality, Schaff's response to Mannheim's Paradox goes a step further (ibid., pp. 54–55):

An analysis carried out thus enables us to see that Mannheim's sociology of knowledge is grounded on certain important epistemological premises that are implicit. After all, how does this author, who judges that knowledge is socially conditioned, move on to a judgment that denies knowledge the value of objective truth—except with the aid of a supplementary premise to the effect that a judgment is true only when it is so *in an absolute way*? If he has not assumed that premise, nothing would have prevented him from asserting that a particular specific judgment, though partial, does possess an objective truth even though it be a relative truth. . . . The only legitimate conclusion to be inferred from Mannheim's sociology of knowledge would then be that knowledge of social phenomena is always socially conditioned and hence never wholly impartial. Mannheim's attempt to radicalize that theses, which ended up denying any objective truth to knowledge of social phenomena, is bound up with a tacit premise which equates objective truth with absolute truth. Hence his attempt is a failure.

But no structure functions unless something in it is unconditioned—and that by very definition. And the unconditioned in Marx is his conception of the human being. To be sure it is not a conception of the *eternal nature* of the human being, which is what Althusser understands by "humanism" and hence denies as a part of the mature Marx.

14. The terms "ascending" and "descending" can only signify a mathematical calculus, an historical forecast, or a value. A simple mathematical calculus would show, for example, that revisionism is on the rise in the Soviet Union. Must we then declare it an "ascending" group? A historical forecast brings us to Mannheim's distinction between ideologies and utopias, which is discussed next. So we are left with a value and the problem of determining what it is.

15. Karl Mannheim, *Ideology and Utopia*, Eng. trans. (New York: Harcourt Brace Jovanovich/Harvest Book, 1936), pp. 192–94. Note that his definition of "ideology" does not correspond to any definitions studied in this volume and that it has not been accepted in ordinary usage either.

16. Herman Hesse, *The Glass Bead Game* (*Magister Ludi*), Eng. trans. (New York: Holt, Rinehart & Winston, 1969), p. 278.

17. Clifford Geertz, "Ideology as a Cultural System," in David Apter, ed., *Ideology and Discontent* (New York: The Free Press of Glencoe, 1964), p. 53.

18. Ibid., p. 52.

19. Marx, "A Contribution to the Critique of Hegel's Philosophy of Right: Introduction," in *Early Writings*, Eng. trans. (New York: Vintage Books, 1975), p. 244.

20. "This state and this society produce religion, which is an *inverted consciousness of the world*, because they are an *inverted world* " (ibid.).

21. To this level the mature Marx devotes various important pages. See, for example, his "Introduction" to the *Grundrisse*, Eng. trans. (New York: Vintage Books, 1973), pp. 83–111. Note his comments on the arts, pp. 110–11.

22. See Schaff, "La objetividad del conocimiento."

23. This is a translation of the version published in the French press at the time: "Reply of the Communist Party of the U.S.S.R. to the Twenty-Five Points of Mao Tse-tung."

24. Althusser, *For Marx*, p. 184.

25. See, for example, the proposals made to Christians from the Marxist camp by G. Marchais, Secretary General of the French Communist Party, in an interview given to the Catholic paper *La Croix* (November 19, 1970). Discussing the difference between the "scientific" construction of socialism and the "ultimate philosophical foundations" of that construction, Marchais said: "This in no way prevents Christians from adhering fully to scientific socialism—i.e., to a particular analysis of society and its development, to a definition of the objectives capable of ensuring the liberation of the workers, to a method of collective struggle—without having to adopt as their own the ultimate philosophical foundations of scientific socialism."

What exactly is this philosophy that is distinct from Marxist science? That problem is not made clear. It is an area which is not opened up to dialogue. Regarding the political implications of that reserve, see the sound critique of Christian Grenier, from whom I took the above quote: "La stratégie du P.C.F. par rapport aux masses chrétiennes," in *Lettre*, nos. 202–203 (June-July 1975), pp. 13–17.

26. See Charles Péguy, *Clio* (Paris: Gallimard, 1932), p. 24:

So we have a perpetual fluctuation, a temporally eternal oscillation, a perfecting that is never perfect, an imperfection which alone can indeed become complete and perfect, because this is the temporal order and that is its law and its very mechanism. In this order and this common act, in this common operation of reader and read, of author and reader, of text and reader, the perfectings, the crowning completions, the increases and increments are never assured or established eternally and irrevocably. On the other hand, the degradations, losses, and involutions *can* become eternally assured, temporally eternal, and irrevocable. Here we have the law, the game, the way the temporal mechanism works. Positive values cannot be heaped up imperturbably, indefinitely, perpetually, surely and irrevocably. But negative values *can.* . . . The values of increase, growth, and crowning perfection are never securely crowned. The values of involution, diminution, and de-crowning *can* be. . . .

27. On this point see Teilhard de Chardin. In Book One of *The Phenomenon of Man* he works out the elemental laws of matter in terms of an analogy with phenomena perceptible at the human level. See *The Phenomenon of Man*, Eng. trans. (New York: Harper & Row, Torchbook, 1961), pp. 37–74.

28. See Karel Kosík, *Dialéctica de lo concreto*, Spanish trans. (Mexico City: Grijalbo, 1967), pp. 125–35. In that book Kosík attributes the rise of this confusion to Labriola and Plekhanov. He writes (ibid., pp. 130–31):

The distinction between economic structure (Marxism) and economic factor (sociologism) constitutes the premise needed to demonstrate and verify scientifically the primacy of the economy in social life. The theory of factors, which maintains that one privileged factor—the economic one—determines all the rest (state, law, art, politics, and morality), bypasses the problem of how the social whole (i.e., society as an economic formation) arises and takes shape. It presupposes the existence of that formation as a given, as an exterior form, or as the sphere in which a privileged factor determines everything else. By contrast, the materialist theory starts from the notion that *the social whole (the socio-economic formation) is shaped and constituted by the economic structure*

. . . i.e., by the whole network of social relations which human beings contract in *production* and their relationship with the *means of production*. . . .

29. Even for those who suffer under it. There is a fatalism which makes them see the culture as "natural," even though it mirrors the historically existing mode of production. Moreover, one need only offer a small token of hope to the exploited (a salary increase of a kopeck per ruble, noted Lenin) in order to ensure that in terms of energy the conservative synthesis will appear simpler and easier to them than a new revolutionary synthesis.

30. Did Marx himself succumb to that inconsistency? Up to now I have been trying to spell out the negative arguments. But there is no lack of evidence that he did in fact succumb to it. First, Marx seems to think that the growing pauperization of the proletariat will necessarily lead the latter to estimate the revolutionary change as cheaper than acceptance of the existing order, however gilded the trappings of the latter may appear in the superstructure. But that did not happen in that way.

Second, Marx seems to assume that after a brief period of necessary coercion (after the revolution), an association of free producers on a universal scale will end up in the dictatorship of the proletariat and will be able, even without state pressure, to establish a new mode of production. Here again reality gave the lie to that assumption. The fact is that in every socialist country it has been a minority that violently won power, and that there has been an accentuation of the role of the party and of government repression, which Marx could not have foreseen. That does not go so far as to disqualify historical materialism, but it does point up how important it is for historical materialism to study the factor of *entropy*. For entropy is closely bound up with human motivations and with the corresponding distribution of quality and quantity in the social whole.

31. Jean-Paul Sartre, *Critique de la raison dialectique: Question de methode* (Paris: Gallimard, 1960), I, 44. Sartre's work on Flaubert (like that on Valéry) arose out of a debate with Roger Garaudy, then an orthodox communist, about the practical possibility of an analysis that would add such a "hierarchy of mediations" to a simple characterization of "class interest" and thus get down to the singular historical phenomenon. See Simone de Beauvoir, *La force des choses* (Paris: Gallimard, 1969), II, 98.

32. L. Althusser, *For Marx*, p. 111.

33. Ibid., p. 113.

CHAPTER VIII

Dialectical Orthodoxy:
The Role of Dialectical Materialism

The remarks of the last chapter might well apply to any ideology which attempted to set itself up as a critique of its own faith. But here it is obvious that we are broaching the whole question of the relationship between a specific ideology (Marxism) and a specific faith (the Christian faith). The difficulty of any possible complementarity between faith and ideology clearly centers today around the two terms, Christianity and Marxism. Our culture commonly tends to oppose materialism to faith. Some may admit that materialism, particularly historical materialism, needs elements of anthropological faith that cannot derive from science. But it seems obvious to everyone that *dialectical materialism* signifies atheism.

A close look should make clear that the militant atheism of almost all the countries whose societal life finds its inspiration in Marx's thought is a relic of the nineteenth century. Both atheism and theism exceed what can be proved or verified empirically or scientifically. Nevertheless an *agnostic* denial of God might well be essential to any method which calls itself *materialist and dialectical*.

Whether Marxism is a faith, an ideology, or both combined, the issue of what is *essential* in Marxism is critical, both for those who approach it from other standpoints of certitude and for those who seek higher certainties within the Marxist camp.

Let us assume that Marxism disqualifies certain modes of thinking. We must know, to begin with, whether that disqualification is accidental—e.g., because it was Marx's opinion at some point—or whether that negative view is so intimately bound up with the system that we are faced with choosing between two, and only two, logical alternatives: giving up our old certainty or turning our back on Marxism.

The issue is not a vague, hypothetical one. First of all, there are in fact as many Marxisms as there are Marxists, particularly outside the socialist countries. That in itself would seem to rule out reference to *one* Marxism as the authentic thing, as the version which contains all the essentials of the system and nothing else but those essentials.

Secondly, there are hundreds of millions of people who claim to believe in God, however much the mental content of their assertion may differ. They have a right to wonder whether and to what extent a society organized by Marxism will grant them freedom to practice their belief in God. They also have a right to know to what extent they can rightfully call themselves Marxists, fully realizing that Marx himself was an atheist who established a relationship between his atheism and the rest of his system. Is that relationship systemically *essential*? Does it extend to all belief in God—past, present, and future?

Thirdly, we have already noted the close relationship between an authentic faith in God and the faith which structures the praxic values of every human being. So we may ask: what is the relationship between Marxism and faith as a basic anthropological dimension?

In other words, our question is: where or how do we establish Marxist "orthodoxy"? On some other level it might well be much more relevant to know what Marxists and their doctrinal or political authorities think today, since historical movements do not always follow strict logic. Nevertheless the issue of "orthodoxy" must be posed in Marxism and given some sort of answer if that movement is to perdure through the course of historical changes.

I. The Centrality of the Dialectical Method

To talk about "orthodoxy" is to talk about preserving that without which Marxism would no longer be Marxism, no matter how many citations from Marx one might put together. Here I cannot overlook a thinker of the stature of George Lukács, though I must point out that I am not interested in how many other thinkers he represents or what authority he holds in terms of official power. Lukács writes:

> [Marxist] orthodoxy refers exclusively to *method*. It is the scientific conviction that dialectical materialism is the road to truth and that its methods can be developed, expanded, and deepened only along the lines laid down by its founders. It is the conviction, moreover, that all attempts to surpass or "improve" it have led and must lead to oversimplification, triviality, and eclecticism.[1]

In the above passage it is clearly the adjective "dialectical" which chiefly characterizes the method and distinguishes it from any other method claiming to be "Marxist."

Now let us grant that a dialectical method need not aim at the transformation of history. Lukács, like everyone else, writes about Hegel's dialectical method, for example. But we must still ask: what characteristic must a cognitive method have in order to be considered "dialectical"? That is the basic question we are asking, even though we admit that one would have to explore further to see which existing dialectic was the true one or the only one that might deserve that appellation.

We find ourselves in a thicket of conceptual misunderstandings. Various terms are used without the slightest assurance that they are being used univocally: e.g., contradiction, dialectic, reality, realism, idealism, and materialism. Indeed it could be said that the more one of these terms is used as obvious, the more we confront crucial ambiguities and end up in a dialogue of the deaf.

Here I am going to try to move into this thicket, making sure of each step before I take the next one. And I begin with the term which, according to Lukács, is the key to Marxist orthodoxy, the essential element in its methodology: i.e., dialectic.

Lukács: The Meaning of Marx's Dialectic

We find constant allusions to dialectic, both in thinking derived from Hegel and thinking derived from Marx. Hegel offers a more theoretical explication of the dialectical method, not in a particular passage but in the course of his whole opus. At least we see him constantly applying it in the various parts of his philosophy. Without offering so many explications, Marx applies it to experience and to social experience in particular. That is a common assumption at least,[2] and I shall operate with it here since it is basic to the above assertion by Lukács. And I would simply add that the experience to which Marx applies the dialectic is not only social but practical.

Reversing the chronological order here, I prefer to begin with the Marxist use of the dialectical method. My guide will be the chapter in which Lukács focuses on that method as the criterion of any "orthodox" Marxism.

Since this matter is so elementary and crucial, some readers might feel it would be better to begin with a clear definition, or with a clearcut, unmistakable example of the application of the method. But I must confess that I have found neither in the vast literature which makes explicit use of that methodology, or at least of that dialectical terminology.[3]

What is more, I have a suspicion that the term "dialectical" is applied to almost any thing or any problem where two opposed elements have to be kept in mind at the same time. And the fact is that two opposed elements can be found in anything, however unimaginative one may be. A specific temperature can be viewed as the precise state at a given moment of the struggle between heat and cold. Everything visible can be measured, and measure can be applied analogously even to things of the spirit. A specific measure can be viewed as the present state of the struggle between more and less, and thus we get two opposites in conflict. Any specific thing can be viewed as the result of the struggle between two opposites: the general and the particular. And so one can proceed *ad infinitum*.

Sometimes, however, the opposites seem to indicate something which pertains more to the essence of our theme. Note what G. Mury, a Marxist, has to say about Pascal in the following passage: "The author of the *Pensées* was clear on this point. One would have to know the parts to comprehend the whole, and to comprehend the whole in order to know the parts. Here we have a *real reclamation of dialectic*."[4]

The first impression we get from such a remark is that the author is seeking to give a strange, esoteric name to a type of cognition which common sense has been using since *homo* became *homo*. There would be no watchmakers without "dialectic," for example. Faced with a repair problem, they must understand the whole mechanism in order to know which parts are not working, and they must concretely know the parts in order to understand what the overall functioning or nonfunctioning of the watch is based on. And if one is going to talk about a watchmaker, then why not talk about a conservative government, for example?

Either the term "dialectic" is a pedantic reference to the well-worn pathways of universal common sense or it is an allusion to something which goes deeper than what is explicitly stated. Let's go back to my example of a conservative government. Suppose it wants to maintain the established order and is willing, to that end, to pay a high price in "reform." In such a case it is clear that the rulers must have "dialectical" knowledge of their functions, and I mean "dialectical" in the explicit sense already indicated. It is equally certain, however, that they are not going to reveal publicly this organic relationship between the parts and the whole of the sociopolitical order. In the idea or ideology they publicize, they will tend to separate the elements or parts which compose it and also to offer an isolated, eternal (nondialectical) definition of the individual parts. They will proffer them as if they were not part of something. Each part will be presented as if it were a whole with fixed rules flowing from its very essence, as if it were intelligible in and of itself. The question of the "why" of each piece will be dissociated from the purpose or "wherefore" of the whole. In short, the rulers will conceal the *finality* of the social whole.[5] Thus, no matter how dialectical they may be in their practice of government, those rulers will publicize and inculcate a nondialectical conception of society as a whole.

Once we have taken this first step, one thing at least should be clear. The dialectical method of cognition, as simply described above, may well be very simple and natural. But its critical and threatening nature is evident as soon as it becomes awareness vis-à-vis a totality which is shaped by a *human project* and in which the parts are, or involve, other human subjects or projects. That such an assertion is on target is confirmed by Lukács when he writes:

If such methods seem plausible at first, this is because capitalism tends to produce a social structure that in great measure encourages such views. But for that very reason we need the dialectical method to puncture the social illusion so produced and help us to glimpse the reality underlying it. The "pure" facts of the natural sciences arise when a phenomenon of the real world is placed (in thought or in reality) into an environment where its laws can be inspected without outside interference. This process is reinforced by reducing the phenomena to their purely quantitative essence, to their expression in numbers and numerical relations. . . . In this way arise the "isolated" facts, "isolated" complexes of facts, separate, specialist disciplines (economics, law, etc.) whose very appearance seems to have done much to pave the way for such scientific methods.[6]

Here let us sidestep the question as to what sense there is in applying a dialectical cognitive mechanism to the "natural"[7] sciences *par excellence*: e.g., mathematics, physics, and chemistry. At first glance it does seem difficult to determine what exactly is the whole and what are the parts in a merely natural process. The two do become recognizable once physics becomes *technology*, no matter how material or "physical" the process may seem to be: e.g., in making or repairing a watch. In this case the clarity derives from the fact that we are dealing with an *artifact*: i.e., a physical process made total by a purpose, by a human project.

So by very definition the realm of dialectic is the realm of *history*, where human projects succeed and relate to one another. Lukács tells us as much:

The opposition between the description of an aspect of history and the description of history as a unified process is not just a problem of scope, as in the distinction between particular and universal history. It is rather a conflict of method, of approach. Whatever the epoch or special topic of study, the question of a unified approach to the process of history is inescapable. It is here that the crucial importance of the *dialectical view* of totality reveals itself. For it is perfectly possible for someone to describe the essentials of an historical event and yet be in the dark about the real nature of that event and of its function in the historical totality, i.e., without understanding it as part of a unified *historical process* [my italics].[8]

It is equally obvious, then, that dialectical cognition is eminently practical. It is not just a knowledge of history. It is part of history, giving direction to the latter and hence making it. Thus the dialectical process is to be viewed as "the whole unity of history and thought."[9]

And there is another point worth noting here. Some people make a distinction between *historical* materialism and *dialectical* materialism, even if they go no further than regarding them as two different steps in the same direction. What "materialism" means in this case I will leave for the next chapter.[10] The important point to note is that Lukács, in the process of stressing what is essential in the dialectical method, totally equates the two terms. Indeed he even goes so far as to use one term where we would expect precisely the other term.[11]

But this initial characterization of dialectic, the axis of Marxist "orthodoxy" according to Lukács, leaves me unsatisfied. Granted that in his chapter on "orthodox" Marxism Lukács repeatedly stresses that the interrelated study of the whole and the parts—of the process and its moments, if you prefer a more historical thrust—is a method which is simultaneously cognitive and practical. Granted that he points out that this method was employed continually by Marx throughout his life and that his use of it protected him from obvious deviations such as opportunism and bourgeois scientism. (Opportunism entails detaching the moment from the process and subjecting it to intuition. Bourgeois scientism entails detaching the moment from the process and establishing nontemporal laws for it.)[12] Still, unless I misunderstand Lukács, he does not convince me that this method is so revolutionary and so fundamental that it defines the "orthodoxy" of Marxism.

I say this for two reasons. First, I don't see why a conservative or reformist system might not make use of the very same method—though it might not publicize it. Indeed the very evolution of capitalism, which has differed greatly from Marx's material forecasts, seems to prove that dialectic in that sense has been precisely the method whereby it prevented its surfacing and inherent contradictions from leading it to disaster.

Second, while Lukács acknowledges that there are important differences between Hegelian idealism and Marxist materialism, he also stresses their similarity on this point: "We would draw the attention of readers with a greater interest in questions of methodology to the fact that in Hegel's logic, too, the relation of the parts to the whole forms the dialectical transition from existence to reality."[13] Now something common to both cannot, in and of itself, constitute the key to the Marxist method. Moreover, the Hegelian dialectic does not limit itself to postulating the interrelationship between the whole and its parts, the process and its moments. Even in its most popularized forms—e.g., the well-worn triad of thesis, antithesis, synthesis—Hegel's dialectic goes further than what has been said above. Are we then to incorporate those elements into the dialectical method which was used and, to some extent according to Lukács, *founded* by Marx? Or is it in precisely those elements that we find the difference between the two?

Only once in the chapter under discussion here does Lukács allude to one of the most characteristic features of what is commonly called *dialectic*, a feature which gives further specificity to the interrelationship we are considering. Going back to the fonts of Marxism, Lukács reminds us of Engel's arguments in *Anti-Dühring*:

> He contrasts the ways in which concepts are formed in dialectics as opposed to "metaphysics"; he stresses the fact that in dialectics the definite contours of concepts (and the objects they represent) are dissolved. Dialectics, he argues, is a continuous process of transition from one definition into the other. In consequence a one-sided and rigid causality must be replaced by *interaction*.[14]

Thus a dialectical approach to knowledge does not consist in the mere fact of viewing parts as moments of a whole in process. It consists in the fact that the moments mutually interact and change. When something happens in that way then everyone, Marxist or not, agrees in using the term "dialectic." For a curious reason, which I shall try to pinpoint later, Lukács bypasses this whole point in his treatment of Marxist orthodoxy. Here I shall try to point up what it means in the concrete. That will be our second step in this chapter.

II. Nature and Dialectics

In the previous section I recorded my surprise at the fact that the only system which expressly includes the appellation "dialectical" in its name (Marxism) usually does not offer a clearcut definition of this key word. It uses the term freely and frequently, to be sure. Readers cannot help but wonder if its users are talking about a real, specific methodology or simply using "dialectical" as a wild card which can mean anything they want it to mean for certain lines of argument or conclusions.

Now here one might object that there is no great need to define the term "dialectical" because it was not invented by Marx. He simply borrowed it from the cognitive method used by Hegel from one end of his work to the other. But then we are in for another big surprise! Hegel, you see, is noted for never defining anything anywhere. That was an essential part of his whole methodology. So Hegel never gives us even a concrete glimpse into what his dialectic consists of! Take Lalande's dictionary of philosophical terms, for example, which takes pains to offer clear definitions of terms. When it comes to Hegel's dialectic, that work makes a few vague comments that leave us more in the dark than we were before.[15]

If we choose to read and study Hegel for ourselves, we come up with the basic notion that his thought always centers around processes, not around unvarying essences. Moreover, in talking about those processes, Hegel uses the term "negation" with abandon. Each "moment" is negated by some other moment, which is then negated in turn. The latter does not go back and become the first original moment; it, too, is negated, and so the process continues.

In the work of Hegel, and even more in that of his followers, one gets the impression that one is not dealing with a set method. They use as many "negations" as are necessary to get where they want to go and prove what they want to prove. If they used one further negation, then the conclusion could and would have been very different. In any case, everyone agrees that Hegel's dialectic is very important though no one seems to be able to say concretely what it consists of.

Engels: Three Dialectical Laws

To take a second step in my investigation, I think we would do well to turn to Friedrich Engels. In his work entitled *Dialectics of Nature*, a very polemical work, Engels indicates that for him the Hegelian dialectic contains three laws, which he himself adopts:

The law of the transformation of quantity into quality and *vice versa*;
The law of the interpenetration of opposites;
The law of the negation of the negation.[16]

In his "Outline for the Plan of the Whole Work" Engels spells out these three elements of the dialectic and adds a fourth:

Dialectics as the science of universal connection. Principal laws: conversion of quantity into quality, reciprocal penetration of the polar opposites and conversion of one into the other when they are carried to the extreme, development by contradiction or negation of the negation, spiral form of development.[17]

As I indicated above, the application of dialectics to the natural sciences, a road taken by Engels but not by Marx, is debatable. The theme, however, serves Engels in defining *objective* and *subjective* dialectical knowledge, the former being what I would call the dialectic of history itself:

Dialectics, so-called *objective* dialectics, prevails throughout nature, and so-called subjective dialectics, dialectical thought, is only the reflex of the movement in opposites which asserts itself everywhere in nature, and which by the continual conflict of the opposites and their final merging into one another, or into higher forms, determines the life of nature.[18]

If we look at these three definitions or descriptions of dialectics by Engels, we can immediately reduce the elements. In the first passage cited, we note three elements or laws. In the second, the fourth element added is really nothing more than the consequence of the other three: spiral form of development. It is Engels's imaginative translation of the Hegelian term *Aufhebung*. Let us set aside that fourth element and focus on the other three.

In the third passage cited, we find the three elements reduced to one which is the key to the others. Readers will recall that it is precisely the element which Lukács mentioned in his reference to Engel's dialectic: reciprocal interaction and change of the elements in the process. In the third passage Engels tells us that in opposing each other the contrary elements condition, at the very least, history by their "continual conflict . . . and their final merging into one another, or into higher forms." (Whether they also condition nature is an issue we shall set aside here.) And in the second passage cited above Engels adds that this conversion of one into the other takes place "when they are carried to the extreme."

There is every indication, then, that this second element in the first two definitions is central and decisive for the dialectical method, and that the first and third elements are suppositions or explications of this second element.

Let us get into some concrete examples that will clarify and refine all these concepts and assertions. All too often the latter are reiterated in abstract terms without much footing in the real world.[19]

To begin with, the supposition of mutual interaction or change between the opposites must be the passage of quantity into quality, or what is also called the "qualitative leap": i.e., the first element of the dialectic noted by Engels. It is something that seems simple, numerous examples of which can be found even in physical nature. The most obvious and well known is the example of water. As its temperature gradually mounts, water remains practically the same kind of liquid. After passing a quantitative threshold, however, everything changes. Water changes into steam, and the qualities of the latter, like those of gases, are fundamentally different from those of liquids. The same quantity of water (chemically speaking) which was inert before, now, at a certain *quantitative* degree of temperature, has the *quality* of moving a locomotive or a ship. A dropping in the temperature of the water would likewise lead us to the qualitative leap in which the liquid turns into a solid: i.e., ice.

Speaking of this law, of which we could offer countless natural examples, Engels refers to it as "the law of the transformation of quantity into quality and *vice versa*." I have three observations to make about his formulation in those terms.

The *first* observation has to do with his use of "vice versa," which here would mean the transformation of quality into quantity. It is debatable that there really is any such thing as a "quantitative leap" distinct from a qualitative one. As far as I know, the Hegelian dialectic knows no such thing. One might object that we do have examples of such a leap. When a living being dies, it would seem that what was essentially vital *quality* before becomes a mere process of disintegration dominated by diminishing quantitative processes. But it is not clear why we should not talk about a qualitative change here too. If one does not, is it because the quality of the dead body is considered to be merely *negative*? If that is the case, what is the sign of the conversion of water into steam or ice? Perhaps what we can and should say at the level of natural beings is this: we see that they remain apparently stable during a long process of quantitative increases or decreases, then at some particular threshold they rapidly acquire qualities very different from the ones they had before. But in that case Engels would have done better to talk about ascending or descending "qualitative leaps" and not bother to add "vice versa."

The *second* observation is this: these qualitative leaps—what Engels calls transformations of quantity into quality—do not seem to have "antagonists" in nature. When water is transformed into steam or ice, by quantitative increases or decreases in temperature, we nowhere see "the opposite." Steam and ice are not *opposed* or *contrary* to water. Neither can cold and heat be opposed in a dialectical sense, i.e., in the sense of mutual interaction and change.[20] Indeed one cannot even say that quantity and quality are opposed or opposites, at least in the examples given. The "qualitative leap" does not consist of the passage of a substance ruled only by quantity (water) into another ruled exclusively by quality (steam). What we see is that in certain bodies or objects a minute quantitative variation suddenly produces qualitative changes that are "disproportionate" to the transformation taking place on the quantitative level.

We also find an interesting linguistic problem here. If we talk about quantity and quality, this assumes some "substantial" unity, or whatever term one might use for "substantial." To put it linguistically, one assumes the unity or oneness of the substantive or noun, of which quantity and quality are predicated. In the above examples, quantity and quality refer to water or, in the case of a living or dead animal, to the animal in question. So we see Hegel talking about the adventures of a given concept, which assumes the unity or oneness of the concept throughout its transformations.

Language tells us that water, through a gradual change in temperature, passes from the state of liquid to the state of gas. But if we wanted to use more precise language, we would have to remind ourselves that steam continues to be water only from the standpoint of chemistry. The noun *steam* belongs to the genus of gases, not to the genus of liquids. One might object here that the chemical formula of water remains the same. But we must remember that language does not use substantives or nouns in accordance with chemical formulas, or not solely in that way at least. Thus, for example, it is permissible to apply the terms "oxygenated water" or "heavy water" to bodies that do not have the same chemical formula as water.

Take a dead dog. Is it a dog or not? Or, for how long is it a dog? So long as certain "qualities" or "quantities" last—mostly external and superficial ones?

Let us drop the question here. It might well seem to be an irrelevant side-issue, a vestige of hoary nominalism. But remember what we are doing here. Through all this broad and confusing usage we are investigating the possible meaning of the word "dialectic," and we cannot take too many precautions in trying to avoid the clichés which have given rise to numerous misunderstandings.

The point here is to realize what it means when we drop the question here. It means that when we talk about some "qualitative leap" or, even more, when we talk about "the transformation of quantity into quality" and then go further and add "vice versa," then we are employing a highly imprecise way of speaking, at least with regard to natural phenomena. Further on I shall consider whether historical processes permit us greater accuracy and precision for the terms "dialectic" and, at the same time, similar or parallel experiences.

The *third* observation is merely a consequence of the second. Since there are no "opposites" or "antagonists" in the above examples drawn from nature, there is no reciprocal change or interaction and hence no "negation of the negation" (the third dialectical law cited by Engels).

One can play with words, to be sure. We have talked about "qualitative leaps" in cases where we don't even know whether we are dealing with the same object (water, dog) or a different object (steam, carcass). Obviously we can, with a certain measure of linguistic goodwill, equate something becoming something *else* with the *negation* of the former, whether we are talking about an object, a property, or a moment. Steam can be called the "negation" of water, and water the "negation" of steam. But since the chemical substance remains the same, as we saw, then any given physical property would be the negation of any other physical property. A given difference would be the "negation" of all others, and we would populate the world with conflicts as useless as they are nonexistent.

This manner of speech, which Hegel certainly uses *ad nauseam*, ends up being extraordinarily confusing in the long run. For if we want to understand the real world, a key datum is the "indifference" of things and events. Unlike a small child, an adult human being knows that a chair is not really the negation of a table, ever. Nor is the canine carcass the negation of the dog, to go back to one of our examples. Later on we shall see why Hegelian idealism found itself obliged to use that sort of peculiar language. But certainly in the present case, where there is no human *purpose*, project, or intention, mere differences are not negations. The latter term should not be employed even metaphorically. *Only if I want to sit down*, and deliberate where to sit down, *can* the chair become metaphorically the "negation" of the table, and vice versa.

•

My readers may feel that in this second stage I have made a long and needless journey to reach a conclusion which I hinted at near the start: i.e., nature is not dialectical,[21] but history—the succession and intercrossing of human projects—is, and it is in the latter that we must try to find and spell out the laws which Engels uses in reference to nature.

Let me briefly explain and defend the journey I have taken, before dropping the point. I began this chapter by exploring the exact nature of Marxist "orthodoxy." Following Lukács, we found that the final and sufficient criterion of Marxist orthodoxy was the dialectical method. To see where it was operative, we examined the laws of dialectic. In our second step we saw that the first law might possibly be viewed as operative in natural things and events, though there are reasons to doubt even that. But the other two laws, which are much more central and basic, certainly are not operative there.

Now one thing that has continued to hover on our horizon as we pursued our investigation of Marxism was the question of the relationship of atheism to Marxist "orthodoxy." Our findings here in Section II of this chapter clearly suggest that both atheism and theism can be discussed only insofar as they are *human projects*, if we are viewing them from the standpoint of Marxist "orthodoxy." In other words, affirming or denying the existence of God as one might *natural* events or data is not part of the dialectical method and cannot be treated from that point of view.

From what we have seen so far about dialectic, the key to Marxist orthodoxy, God can be judged only as an integral element of historical projects or
processes, as qualifying them in one way or another. God cannot be judged as
a metaphysical issue. While some might say that is clearly what Marx does, I
don't think the matter is that clear at all. In any case, the point is that the
atheist position must be reserved for the historical processes concretely studied by Marx. It is impossible to generalize or universalize that stance, in the
name of dialectic at least.

III. Human History and Dialectics: Four Observations

Let us move on to the realm of human projects, the realm of history, and
see how dialectic is operative there. Let us also see the application of Engels's
three laws to this area, particularly his crucial second law.

From the very start we notice that in this realm all talk about the "dialectical" method takes on much greater realism and precision, though that does
not rule out misconceptions completely, to be sure.

Let us begin with the recognition that every human project runs into obstacles. Wherever human will is set in motion, we find antagonisms. We can
identify the latter. We find either opposing human wills or else some existing
tendency that opposes a human will and seeks to overcome it (and vice versa).

Now we all know that in struggling to achieve our goals we often run into
"counterproductive" or "self-defeating" effort. A seemingly simple decision to pursue the same effort or to carry a victory beyond certain limits ends
up in defeat. There is a critical point beyond which further pushing in a certain direction produces unexpected contrary effects.

Examples of this abound. In the marketplace the interests and aims of
buyers and sellers can be said to be antagonistic. Buyers want the lowest
possible prices; sellers want the highest possible prices. Here the metaphor of
a "negation" sinks its teeth more solidly into the real. Now let us suppose
that the prices of some product are rising "quantitatively" and thus benefiting the interest of the seller. There will come a critical moment when our
hypothetical buyer will no longer purchase the product since it is too costly to
serve his or her interest. What has happened? A simple quantitative change,
an increase in price which could be considered infinitely small, produces a
qualitative leap: the buyer no longer buys.

A more complex example, but still illustrative, is the one offered by Hegel
in his *Phenomenology of Spirit*.[22] I shall simply describe the outline of what
happens since I do not want to follow Hegel's whole treatment in faithful
detail. To do the latter I would have to plunge into Hegel's whole conception
of dialectic, which is different from the conception of Engels that I am examining here. Hegel basically depicts a total, primitive struggle between two
human beings. He suggests that the winner in the clash is often the one who
does not fear death; the party subject to the fear of death capitulates. Thus
the person who is freer from fears becomes the lord, and the one more dependent on fears becomes the bondsman. The latter stays alive, but he also gives

up and offers his services in exchange for his life. But what happens once the struggle between them ends? The lord uses the bondsman to do things which he did for himself before or which he did not do at all because of the economy of energy. So the party that was more independent at the start (the winning lord) gradually becomes more and more dependent on the party that was more dependent at the start (the losing bondsman). Through an imperceptible process—let us call it a quantitative process—the qualities of dependence and independence finally are inverted. In place of the original struggle we gradually get a division of labor that gives rise to culture, culture in the more general sense of an opposition to merely individual impulses or projects.

Various observations arise out of these two examples, to which we could add many more examples since analogous processes can be found at every level of human life.[23] I want to focus on four observations here.

The Locus of Authentic Opposition

The *first* observation is that the real opposition, the only authentic "yes" or "no," cannot be placed in things, or even in persons in a general way; it can only be located in intentions, impulses, or projects. Thus the buyer and the seller are not opposed *persons*. What is truly opposed and antagonistic are the intentions they bring to the market. Hence the very same situation of antagonism (with its possible dialectics) is to be found inside one and the same person.

In the dialectic of lord and bondsman, language itself would be the cause of confusion and error if it led us to assume that the two persons in question were antagonistic. The antagonism lies in the will of each party to dominate the other or, as Hegel puts it, to win recognition from the other. To call them "lord" and "bondsman" is to unduly totalize—from the standpoint of linguistic preciseness—the specific quality which generates the antagonism or results from it.

This observation is important. If we do not take note of it, then we reduce "lord" and "bondsman" to cogs in a mechanism. We fix their destiny for them, if you will. We overlook the fact that, if we assume liberty, the relationship between the two initial adversaries can have very different turns or results: ranging from the death of both to the waste of the bondsman.[24]

Fessard, a theologian who is a follower of Hegel, draws our attention to one kind of dialectic to which St. Paul alludes often in his letters, and especially in his Letter to the Romans. The Jew, seemingly destined for faith, follows his or her own way in the face of the crisis that Christ ought to represent and ends up an unbeliever. On the other hand the pagan, seemingly destined for unbelief, enters into crisis and is converted to the faith in large numbers.[25] Now it is certainly very interesting and instructive to follow the steps of this Jew-pagan dialectic, which is very similar to Hegel's lord-bondsman dialectic. The problem is that such an approach takes flesh-and-blood human beings and hypostatizes them "dialectically." In reality those human beings are more total and complete than their specific role as dialectical moments. So Fessard loses sight of the fact that the more important historical phenomenon lies in the very people overlooked by this dialectic, in the very people where this dialectic does not operate. It is the minority fact, which would prove decisive for the world, that an extraordinary group of Jews did make the creative journey to (Christian) faith.

Antagonism Alone Not Enough

My *second* observation is closely related to the first. For there to be a dialectic, there must be an antagonism: two terms opposed to each other as a "yes" and a "no." But antagonism *does not suffice* to ensure the existence of a dialectic.[26] Here the passages of Engels cited above are very clear. That is not true of Marxist thought in general, as we shall soon see.

Recall the second quote from Engels cited above (see p. 207). There Engels talks about a second (and central) dialectical law: "reciprocal penetration of the polar opposites and conversion of one into the other *when they are carried to the extreme*" (my italics).[27] Now remember that the German word in question *(wenn)* can be translated "when" or "if," depending on what the context demands. So the subordinate clause in our quote from Engels could be translated: "*if* they are carried to the extreme." This would bring out the unforeseeable nature of the process, as we shall see. Engels's point is clear, in any case. One term is not converted into the other *before* it is carried to the extreme: i.e., to the critical point where an intention, the more it is realized, turns "counterproductive."

In the third text cited above (see p. 207), Engels is even more explicit about the vicissitudes of any "antagonism." He talks about the movement in opposites which "by the *continual* conflict of the opposites and their *final* merging into one another, *or into higher forms,* determines the life of nature."[28] Here Engels affirms that the opposition remains constant so long as the contrary impulses are not carried to their *end* or *extreme.* But he also asserts that once they reach that point, there are two possibilities. One possibility is the conversion of one into the other: buyer into seller, lord into bondsman. The other possibility is their conversion into a higher synthesis, which is obviously not the same as the first possibility. To go back to Fessard's example, that would be the case of the Jews who made a synthesis of their religious tradition and the Christian faith.

In line with Engels's remarks, then, we can say that there is an open-ended spectrum of possibilities where we find a process of antagonism between two opposed intentions or tendencies. And our daily experience confirms this.

Now it is precisely this fact which makes dialectic, not the *contemplation* of the mechanical and necessary succession of historical events,[29] but rather an orientation towards *praxis,* towards changing the world. A new synthesis, for example, would require: (1) that the conflict be carried to the critical or extreme point where the antagonism ceases to be the continual struggle between the protagonists; and (2) that we avoid the mere conversion of the antagonists into their respective opposites, so as to make room for a higher synthesis of both.

Ambiguities in the Term "Contradictions"

A *third* observation follows immediately from the previous one. I mentioned earlier that the texts of Engels clearly do not seem to conceive dialectic as a mechanism which, once set in motion, enables us to see right away where its inner necessity will lead it. I also suggested that other texts, of Marxism and Marx himself, do seem to be much more ambiguous on this point.

I am thinking especially, though not exclusively, of those passages which talk about "contradictions." It is in them that one gets the strong suspicion that Marx, despite his protestations, never freed himself sufficiently from the idealist dialectic, the dialectic of Hegel.

The word "contradiction" is highly ambiguous. In its most common usage it signifies a lack of logic in reasoning. In Hegel's work it is used to designate two things: (1) the tensions and antagonisms existing in any given system; and (2) the "counterproductive" aspect, the outcome of the critical moment where a tendency *turns into its opposite*. What permits Hegel and his followers to use the word "contradiction" in both senses, each pointing to different moments of the process? It is the fact that in Hegel's idealism dialectic is the mechanism of all reality. The first moment leads necessarily to the second, so one and the same word can cover both. The protagonist of the whole process of "negations" and "contradictions" is one and the same Absolute Spirit.

By contrast, as we have just seen, the remarks of Engels are much more realist than idealist. They point to different ways of resolving the contrary tendencies or tensions.

At first glance, and without my having made an exhaustive study of the matter, it seems that Marx employed the term "contradiction" as a synonym for strain or tension: i.e., for the clash between opposites. In the *Manifesto of the Communist Party,* for example, he writes: "Our epoch, the epoch of the bourgeoisie, possesses . . . this distinctive feature: it has simplified the class antagonisms ['contradictions'—Marx]. Society as a whole is more and more splitting up into two great hostile camps, into two great classes directly facing each other: bourgeoisie and proletariat."[30]

Here we see that "contradiction" has always accompanied the existence of classes created by the division of labor. It is a synonym for tension. The existence of one class does not render impossible (for the moment) the existence of the other, so that rules out the other meaning that the term "contradiction" might have. The clash between the contraries is called a "contradiction" even before it has reached the critical point where the ruling class, carrying its domination to the extreme, gives rise to the qualitative leap that will prove to be its destruction.

In other words, if we had only this passage from Marx, we would not be correct in saying that the existence of "contradictions" indicates a necessary end, much less a close end, to any given social system harassed by inner tensions. This obviously runs counter to the widespread use of the term "contradiction" in Marxism, where it is applied to capitalism to prove its imminent end. The word "contradiction," in other words, is used to *predict* inevitable events, and this usage, if I am correct in my analysis, does not dovetail with the dialectical laws as described by Engels.

I said that Marx himself does not seem to use the term "contradiction" in that way. Nevertheless it is clear that he sometimes turns dialectic into a tool for predicting inevitable events: e.g., the eventual end, sooner or later, of the capitalist system and the destruction of the bourgeoisie, by virtue of the very forces that constitute them.

Again in the *Manifesto* Marx writes: "Hitherto, every form of society has been based . . . on the antagonism of oppressing and oppressed classes."[31] This initial sentence in the passage is significant in terms of our discussion. It tells us something different about the antagonisms which Marx called "contradictions" in the previous passage (see p. 214). We know that those antagonisms or contradictions, far from indicating the terminus, refer instead to the basis or duration of certain social systems, not to say all social systems. But Marx goes on to say:

> But in order to oppress a class, certain conditions must be assured to it under which it can, at least, continue its slavish existence. The serf, in the period of serfdom, raised himself to membership in the commune, just as the petty bourgeois, under the yoke of feudal absolutism, managed to develop into a bourgeois. The modern labourer, on the contrary, instead of rising with the progress of industry, sinks deeper and deeper below the conditions of existence of his own class. He becomes a pauper, and pauperism develops more rapidly than population and wealth. And here it becomes evident that the bourgeoisie is unfit any longer to be the ruling class in society, and to impose its conditions of existence upon society as an overriding law. . . . Society can no longer live under this bourgeoisie, in other words, its existence is *no longer compatible* with society. . . . Its fall and the victory of the proletariat are equally *inevitable* [my italics].[32]

This long quote tells readers that Marx seems sure that the class antagonisms, which always existed, are inexorably reaching that critical point or qualitative leap where the relationship between ruler and ruled is going to be inverted (before disappearing).

In effect, this destroys the range of possibilities which Engels saw open to dialectical knowledge. Whence comes the "contradiction" in the stricter or stronger sense of the word, i.e., the necessity of the opposite tendencies being carried to their extremes and the result necessarily being the victory of the proletariat? Let us disregard for the moment the underlying gnoseological problem and note a highly significant historical fact. J. K. Galbraith has noted ironically that the mistake of Marxism lies in underestimating the inventive ability of the bourgeoisie and capitalism to survive.[33] The fact is, and it is important, that the dialectic can be used by the opposite side. There is no doubt that Marx's "forecasts" served as an alarm bell, helping to ensure that the class antagonism was not in fact carried to its critical extreme. This accounts for the actual situation today in the countries for which Marx made forecasts. They avoided the growth of pauperism and successfully used the old tactic of offering the dominated class the possibility of climbing up a little bit (from proletariat to petty bourgeoisie). Hence the capitalist system simply went on "based . . . on the antagonism of oppressing and oppressed classes." The inevitable did not take place.

To put it in Engels's terms, the opposites were braked in their tendency to reach the extreme. Hence the terms of the antagonism were not inverted (oppressed becoming oppressor), nor was a higher synthesis achieved (a classless society)—unless one wishes to regard current neocapitalism as such.[34]

Once again Engels was right in proposing dialectic as an open-ended system of possibilities in which human inventiveness and freedom remain decisive.[35] It is of no importance to our theme here that Engels did not always remain faithful to that conception of dialectic.

Ambiguities in the "Negation of the Negation"

My third observation, stemming from the above examples and from the passages of Engels, is that the so-called law of the "negation of the negation" entails a terrible ambiguity.

It is obvious to any reader of Hegelian or Marxist texts that the "negation of the negation" is not synonymous with antagonism. If we take two opposed tendencies, A and B for example, we could apply that term to their interaction. We could say that A is the negation of B, and B the negation of A. Hence either one could be called the negation of the negation, insofar as it exists and fights by negating the negation of itself which the other tendency represents.

That is not the way that "negation of the negation" is generally understood, however. Usually the term refers to the ultimate stage—the *outcome,* if you prefer—of the dialectical conflict. And it is here that the expression becomes highly ambiguous and misleading, causing infinite misunderstandings and obscurities.

In Book I, Chapter 32 of *Capital,* Marx writes something which is very closely connected to the last cited passage of the *Manifesto* (see p. 215). In *Capital,* however, he expresses the point in the Hegelian terms of negation:

The capitalist mode of appropriation, which springs from the capitalist mode of production, produces capitalist private property. This is the *first negation* of individual private property, as founded on the labour of its proprietor. But capitalist production begets, *with the inexorability of a natural process,* its own negation. *This is the negation of the negation.* It does not re-establish private property, but it does indeed establish individual property on the basis of the achievements of the capitalist era: namely co-operation and the possession in common of the land and the means of production produced by labour itself [my italics].[36]

We notice at once that the passage bears the imprint of a determinism, of a mechanical process due to the dialectic. Marx describes it as "the inexorability of a natural process." I have already suggested that the use of dialectic as a predictive tool indicates a failure to cut the ties with idealist Hegelianism. As if to confirm that suggestion, Marx here uses the Hegelian term, "negation of the negation," to describe the process. But it is also clear that Marx does not feel completely comfortable with the use of that term since he goes against its most obvious meaning. Capitalist property deprives the proletarian individuals of property. It is the negation of the latter. Logically, then, the negation of the negation would be "the restoration of the private property of the proletariat." In other words, it would be the self-limiting of the first tendency and hence the cessation or attenuation of the antagonism which began with the first negation.

Since this is not the outcome foreseen by Marx, however, the inexorability of the process has to lead to a new type of property and ownership, which is to occur in socialism first, and communism later; and that is what Marx proceeds to describe.

Why is it that Marx tries to prove the inexorability of the advent of his third term by using a procedure whose obvious outcome would be a return to the first term or at most, if you will, the whole range of possibilities mentioned by Engels?

I think the most likely answer to that question goes something like this. When Marx uses dialectic to point up inexorable processes, processes which logically are independent of the problems and orientations of praxis, he is really being nothing more than a post-Hegelian. He is overlooking or forgetting the process by which he seeks to put the dialectic of Hegel back on its feet.[37] In short, he is forgetting the central role of praxis.

One of the typical artifices of Hegelian idealism is to obscure *who* is negating the negation. If someone negates the negation, it is the first term, the thing negated in the first instance by the second thing. Thus, as Marx's passage above makes clear, the logical thing would be to assume that the negation of the negation *restores* the first term with its qualities and properties.

If it does not happen that way *in Hegel's dialectic,* if the negation of the negation does not have an active subject and the phenomenon is usually expressed in the passive voice, it is because the subject *par excellence* of the process as a whole is the Absolute Spirit. The latter *makes use of* (hence the "cunning of reason") the two opposed terms to negate certain aspects of the first and then the second. So the outcome of the negation of the negation is a *new* term, a third element: in the case cited by Marx it is socialist individual property.

Marx, however, does not grant any such abstract, ideal, impersonal *subject.* For his materialism—or realism, if you will—dialectic is a concrete struggle between real protagonists who negate each other reciprocally, but they do so in terms of partial and variable aspects. Such would be capitalist and proletarian, for example. Experience teaches us that the outcome of the process will vary, depending on the distinctions made in this mutual negation. If the negation of the interests of the proletariat by the capitalist does not go so far as to deny to many members of the proletariat basic survival or even access to the next highest social class, then the negation of the negation by the proletariat, as Lenin indicated,[38] might not go beyond certain salary demands or claims for legal and vacation benefits. That in fact is what happened in the developed capitalist countries.

I am not saying that is good. I am simply pointing out that when the subject of mutual "negations" are real entities, individuals, or human groups, no historical process has "the inexorability of a natural process." The dialectic needs praxis, and praxis needs the dialectic.

IV. Marx's Dialectic versus Dogmatic Marxism

Having come this far, I think we would do well to sum up some points that seem quite justifiable. They certainly seem justifiable to me, at least.

Experience proves that when two concrete human projects oppose each other openly or tacitly, dialectic teaches us to relate each moment of the antagonistic process to a whole with manifold possibilities, and hence to conduct those moments, in praxis, to that possibility which constitutes the best outcome.

This presupposes something which is of the greatest importance. Neither the judgment about the (hypothetical) outcome that is to take place nor the judgment about its valuation is provided *by the dialectic itself.* But those judgments can and should be conveyed in a dialectical praxis.

I also feel that a close reading of the above citations from Engels about the essence of the dialectical method moves us far away from certain historical certitudes and valuational dogmas proffered by vulgar Marxism. Vulgar Marxism claims to extract them from the dialectic, and it does so by using and abusing its esoteric vocabulary. When that happens, and it happens in certain passages of Marx as well, my hypothesis is that dialectic has fallen back into Hegelian idealism once again after having been put back on its feet by Marx.

There remains to be studied where precisely, and to what extent, the dialectic under examination here differs from the Hegelian dialectic. Here too, of course, we find the most varied opinions.[39] I intend to avoid intricate school quarrels and focus on the simplest and most obvious facts. That will be our subject in the next chapter.

NOTES

1. George Lukács, *History and Class Consciousness: Studies in Marxist Dialectics*, Eng. trans. (Cambridge: MIT Press, 1971), p. 1.

The title of Chapter I, which is under consideration here, is: "What Is Orthodox Marxism?" The study dates back to 1919. In his "Preface to the New Edition (1967)" Lukács repeats verbatim a passage from his 1919 version: "Let us assume that recent research had proved once and for all that every one of Marx's individual theses was false. Even if this were to be proved, every serious 'orthodox' Marxist would still be able to accept all such modern conclusions without reservation and hence dismiss every single one of Marx's theses—without being compelled for a single minute to renounce his orthodoxy. Orthodox Marxism . . . does not imply the uncritical acceptance of the results of Marx's investigations. It is not the 'belief' in this or that thesis, not the exegesis of a 'sacred' book" (ibid., pp. xxv–xxvi).

2. Here we come across our first surprise, and a big one. Althusser, like other Marxist thinkers of his stature, examines a critical issue for contemporary Marxism: i.e., the fact that neither the founders of Marxism nor Lenin wrote a Logic, explained what they meant by *dialectics*, or pointed out how theirs differed from that of Hegel. Althusser goes on to say (*For Marx*, Eng. trans. [London: Verso Editions, 1979], p.182):

> I said that Marx left us no *Dialectics*. That is not quite accurate. He did leave us one first-rate methodological text, unfortunately without finishing it: the *Introduction to the Critique of Political Economy*, 1859. This text does not mention the "inversion" by name, but it does discuss its reality: the validating conditions for the scientific use of the concepts of Political Economy. A reflection on this use is enough to draw from it the basic elements of a dialectics, since this use is nothing more nor less than the dialectics in a practical state.
>
> I said that Lenin left us no *Dialectics* that would be the theoretical expression of the dialectic in action in his own political practice; more generally, that the theoretical labour of expressing the dialectic in action in the Marxist practice of the class struggle had still to be performed. This is not quite accurate. In his *Notebooks* Lenin did leave us some passages which are the sketch for a *Dialectics*.

Now, even supposing that everything is true in that passage, it is curious that Althusser seems to assume that the ongoing thought of Marx and Lenin was not dialectical enough for people to extract clearly from it the procedure they were using. To what extent then, contrary to popular thinking, did Marx and Lenin think in terms of dialectical materialism? If their method does not clearly mirror the dialectic employed, is it licit to make the *dialectical method* the criterion of Marxist orthodoxy?

3. Entire books devoted to the subject of dialectics never bother to define the term or to offer a concrete example of its functioning. Such is the case with the work on dialectical materialism by Henri Lefebvre, entitled *What Is Dialectics?* Other Marxist works on dialectics focus exclusively on Hegelian examples.

4. Gilbert Mury, *Cristianismo primitivo y mundo moderno*, Spanish trans. (Barcelona: Ed. Península, 1968), p. 92.

5. This example suggests two important things which will be examined further on. First, since dialectics is a law of reality, it is *used* as much by conservatives and re-

formists as by revolutionaries, though the former may not explicate the fact. Second, the dialectical relationship between whole and parts is given by the *purpose* or finality involved; hence that relationship disappears to the extent that the idea of finality fades.

6. Lukács, *History and Class Consciousness*, pp. 5–6.

7. See ibid., pp. 10–11: "From this angle we see that the conflict between the dialectical method and that of 'criticism' (or vulgar materialism, Machism, etc.) is a social problem. When the ideal of scientific knowledge is applied to nature it simply furthers the progress of science. But when it is applied to society it turns out to be an ideological weapon of the bourgeoisie. For the latter it is a matter of life and death to understand its own system of production in terms of eternally valid categories: it must think of capitalism as being predestined to eternal survival by the eternal laws of nature and reason. Conversely, contradictions that cannot be ignored must be shown to be purely surface phenomena, unrelated to this mode of production."

8. Ibid., p. 12. Further on Lukács deals even more specifically with this point: "A situation in which the 'facts' speak out unmistakably for or against a definite course of action has never existed, and neither can nor will exist. The more conscientiously the facts are explored—in their isolation, i.e., in their unmediated relations—the less compellingly will they point in any one direction. It is self-evident that a merely subjective decision will be shattered by the pressure of uncomprehended facts acting automatically 'according to laws.' Thus dialectical materialism is seen to offer the only approach to reality which can give action a *direction*. The self-knowledge, both subjective and objective, of the proletariat at a given point in its evolution is at the same time knowledge of the stage of development achieved by the whole society. The facts no longer appear strange when they are comprehended in their coherent reality, in the relation of all partial aspects to their inherent, but hitherto unelucidated roots in the whole: we then perceive the tendencies which strive towards the centre of reality, to what we are wont to call the ultimate goal. This ultimate goal is not an abstract ideal opposed to the process, but an aspect of truth and reality. It is the concrete meaning of each stage reached and an integral part of the concrete moment. Because of this, to comprehend it is to recognize the direction taken (unconsciously) by events and tendencies towards the totality. It is to know the direction that determines concretely the correct course of action at any given moment—in terms of the interest of the total process, viz., the emancipation of the proletariat" (ibid., p. 23).

9. Ibid., p. 28. This phrase comes from the essay entitled "The Marxism of Rosa Luxemburg." In the same essay Lukács offers the same argument from the other side of the coin: "The destruction of a totalising point of view disrupts *the unity of theory and practice*" (ibid., p. 39).

10. See Chapter IX below.

11. Lukács does this, for example, when he writes that the starting point for *dialectical* materialism is Marx's proposition: "It is not men's consciousness that determines their existence, but on the contrary, their social existence that determines their consciousness" (*History and Class Consciousness*, p. 18). Most Marxist thinkers see in this proposition, and others like it, the starting point for *historical* materialism. See Chapter VII above.

12. See ibid., p. 13 and p. 25 n. 20.

13. See ibid., p. 25 n. 14.

14. Ibid., p. 3. As we shall see, however, one must be careful not to identify the *overcoming* of the contrapositions with their *mutual interaction and change*: i.e., with the conversion of one into its opposite.

15. "Dialectics consists essentially in recognizing the inseparability of the contra-
dictories and in discovering the principle of this union in a higher category. Thus
[Hegel] gives the label 'dialectical moment' to the contradiction itself and to the shift,
in this contradiction, from one term to the other" (André Lalande, *Vocabulaire technique et critique de la philosophie* [Paris: Alcan, 1938], p. 162). Contrast the poverty,
obscurity, and ambiguity of that definition with the long and careful reflections on
other terms that are to be found in his book.

16. Friedrich Engels, *Dialectics of Nature*, Eng. trans. (New York: International
Publishers, 1940), p. 26.

17. Translator's note: this citation and outline come from the French edition of
Dialectics of Nature used by Segundo: Engels, *Dialectique de la nature*, French trans.
(Paris: Ed. Sociales, 1952), p. 25.

18. Engels, *Dialectics of Nature*, pp. 206–7.

19. In his interesting essay *On Contradiction*, Mao Tse-tung follows Engels's
thinking in its least defensible aspect, its application to nature. He thus falls into this
kind of imaginative abstractionism: "As a matter of fact, even mechanical motion
under external force occurs through the internal contradictoriness of things. Simple
growth in plants and animals, their quantitative development, is likewise chiefly the
result of their internal contradictions" (*Selected Works of Mao Tse-tung*, Eng. trans.
[New York: Pergamon Press, 1965], I: 313).

Further on Mao Tse-tung cites a similar passage from Lenin: "Lenin defined the
law of the unity of opposites as 'the recognition (discovery) of the contradictory,
mutually exclusive, opposite tendencies in *all* phenomena and processes of nature
(*including* mind and society)' " (ibid., p. 316).

20. The fact is that, far from competing in a parallel development and exchanging
characteristics, one simply diminishes "quantitatively" while the other increases, and
this goes on independently of any "qualitative leap."

21. Even in Hegel, despite his panlogism, it is difficult to accept the idea of a dialectic of nature. Note this comment by Alexandre Kojève, one of the finest commentators on Hegel: "In the *Encyclopaedia* Hegel says that *every* entity can 'overcome'
itself and consequently is dialectical. But in the *Phenomenology* he asserts that only
the *human* reality is dialectical, while Nature is determined by Identity alone. . . .
Personally I share the point of view of the *Phenomenology* and do not accept the
dialectic of natural Being, of *Sein*" (Kojève, *Introduction to the Reading of Hegel*,
Eng. trans. [New York: Basic Books, 1969], p. 199 n. 10; see also pp. 217–18).
It seems to me that Marxism, in its opposition to idealism, should follow the critical
position of Kojève with regard to Hegel.

22. Part B, IV, A: "Independence and Dependence of Self-Consciousness: Lord-
ship and Bondage." See G. W. F. Hegel, *Phenomenology of Spirit*, Eng. trans. (New
York: Oxford University Press/Galaxy Book, 1977), pp. 111–19 nn. 178–96.

23. Hegel does not offer the dialectic of lord and bondsman as a *mere* example. For
him, lord and bondsman constitute *necessary* moments of human self-consciousness.
This fact proves that in Hegel's thinking dialectic is not just a cognitive process (identity, negativity, totality). Instead, or in addition at least, it is for him the representation of something that occurs in reality. My further remarks on dialectic assume this,
and this seems to be the use which Marxism ordinarily makes of the Hegelian dialectic.

24. It is also interesting and significant to see that various historical contradictions,
according to Mao Tse-tung, are resolved in very different ways. In his essay *On Contradiction* he writes: "Qualitatively different contradictions can only be resolved by
qualitatively different methods. For instance, the contradiction between the proletar-

iat and the bourgeoisie is resolved by the method of *socialist revolution*; the contradiction between the great masses of the people and the feudal system is resolved by the method of *democratic revolution*; the contradiction between the colonies and imperialism is resolved by the method of *national revolutionary war*; the contradiction between the working class and the peasant class in socialist society is resolved by the method of collectivization and mechanization in agriculture; contradiction within the Communist Party is resolved by the method of *criticism* and *self-criticism*; the contradiction between society and nature is resolved by the method of developing the productive forces" [my italics] (*Selected Works of Mao Tse-tung*, I, 321–22).

We have every right to ask: is this difference a postulate of the dialectic itself or is it merely an ascertainment of fact? In speaking of qualitative differences Mao seems to be inclining to the first alternative. But in my opinion he offers no convincing argument to prove that this alternative is compelling.

25. On this dialectic of his own invention Gaston Fessard writes extensively in the two volumes of his work entitled *De l'actualité historique* (Paris: Desclée, 1959).

26. Lukács, *History and Class Consciousness*, p. 11.

27. See Note 17 of this chapter.

28. Engels, *Dialectics of Nature*, pp. 206–7.

29. To maintain this, Althusser is obliged to add to the dialectic a (new) element of unpredictableness: *which* contradiction or antagonism is going to be *overdetermined* (i.e., decisive) in any given situation. But that only raises a new formulation of the issue for him: does this overdetermination depend on the dialectic itself? If the answer is no, then a practical Marxist such as Lenin becomes nothing more than a genial "opportunist," someone who intuited the great opportunity in the overdetermined contradiction which was *de facto* present in the Russia of his day. If the answer is yes, then one ends up back with mechanicism, only one of a more complex sort. And one faces the further difficulty of having to explain how or why the dialectic overdetermines now this particular antagonism and now that one. See Althusser, *For Marx*, pp. 206–18.

30. K. Marx and F. Engels, *Manifesto of the Communist Party*, Eng. trans., in Marx, *The Revolutions of 1848: Political Writings I* (New York: Vintage Books, 1974), p. 68.

31. Ibid., p. 78.

32. Ibid., pp. 78–79.

33. "The Marxian capitalist has infinite shrewdness or cunning on everything except matters pertaining to his own survival" (J. K. Galbraith, *The Affluent Society*, 2nd ed. [Boston: Houghton Mifflin, 1969], p. 66).

34. Following Rosa Luxemburg, Lukács seems to assume that even though the critical point may not have been reached as simply as was assumed, it cannot fail to occur: "In Rosa Luxemburg's hands the doubts about the possibility of [capitalist] accumulation shed their absolute form. The problem becomes the *historical* one of the *conditions* of accumulation and thus it becomes certain that unlimited accumulation is not possible. *Placed into its total social context* [my italics], accumulation becomes dialectical. It then swells into the dialectics of the whole capitalist system. As Rosa Luxemburg puts it: 'The moment the Marxian scheme of expanded reproduction corresponds to reality it points to the end, the historical limits of the movement of accumulation and therewith to the end of capitalist production. If accumulation is impossible, then further growth in the forces of production is impossible too. And this means that *the destruction of capitalism becomes an objective historical necessity* [my

italics]. From this there follow the contradictory movements of the last, imperialist phase, which is the terminal phase in the historical career of capital,' '' (Lukács, *History and Class Consciousness*, pp. 36–37).

35. Otherwise, to repeat myself, one of the fundamental elements of dialectic in Marxism, according to Lukács, would be missing. *Praxis* would be reduced to nothing, to a mere appendix of details or to a synonym for the intelligent contemplation of history. Recall Gramsci's text cited in Chapter VII, Note 8, pp. 195–96.

36. Marx, *Capital*, Book I, Part Eight, Chapter 32, Eng. trans. (New York: Vintage Books, 1976), p. 929.

37. In short, Marx forgets to strip the Hegelian dialectic of its essentially idealist element—namely, the assumption about an Absolute Spirit which, through dialectics and the cunning of reason, leads human projects to the ends it proposes, thus generating a necessity which goes above and beyond those human projects.

38. See Lenin, *What Is to Be Done?* Eng. trans. (New York: International Publishers, 1929).

39. See Althusser, *For Marx*, especially Chapter VI, pp. 161–218: "On the Materialist Dialectic." Throughout my Chapter VIII I have tried to stay out of the whole polemic as much as possible. My aim has simply been to ascertain and set forth the *minimal* content that this inversion of the Hegelian dialectic must have if one wants to maintain that it is consistent with the principles of Marxism.

CHAPTER IX

Materialism and Transcendence: The Role of Philosophical Realism

In the two preceding chapters I pointed up two *scientific* facets deriving from the thought of Marx. I say "scientific," even granting all the impreciseness surrounding the various sciences that deal with human beings. I have tried to establish that both *historical* materialism and *dialectical* materialism do enable us, within certain limits of inner coherence, to better discover existing reality and then transform it, through praxis, into what we feel it should be.

By the same token a coherent (anthropological) faith does not fall under the imperative jurisdiction of either historical or dialectical materialism. Their data are *hypothetical* with respect to praxis, as I suggested in Part One of this book: *if* you want a society with these particular features, then you must consider the efficacy of this or that set of mediations.

So can an ideological critique "checkmate" a faith? Yes it can, to the extent that faith is inconsistent or incoherent; it can unmask "bad faith." Human beings do sometimes claim to have a certain system of values and to be guided by that system in their actions, but the mediations used by them indicate clearly to close observers that wittingly, unwittingly, or half wittingly they are acting in *bad faith* and seeking a very different set of values.

Take Jesus' criticism of the religious ideology of the Pharisees, for example. Jesus points out that the Pharisees, through their use of the religious realm, are actually worshipping a different God, not Yahweh. They are actually seeking values very different from those to which they appeal in terms of Yahwist orthodoxy.

Note, however, that Jesus' line of argument does not prove that the religion of the Pharisees is bad or *evil*. Instead it points up the exact nature of the faith or the system of values underlying their religious interpretations (i.e., their ideology).

In the same way, and with more highly developed mediations, both historical and dialectical materialism can criticize any vaunted faith, be it merely anthropological or religious, showing us where the mediations used by it actually lead. They can show up the real faith which lies wittingly or unwittingly behind an ideologically defined praxis.

By the same token, however, and precisely to the extent that they are confirmed (validated) by reality, neither historical materialism nor dialectical materialism can claim to determine the value (the "ought-to-be") possessed in and of themselves by premises which are, by definition, *self-validating*— i.e., which belong to the realm of meaning.

This means that both methods, precisely by virtue of their scientific status, are confined to the area of experience and experimental proof. They cannot pass judgment on something which, also by its very nature, lies outside their boundaries: i.e., the realm of *faith*, which decides what "ought-to-be."

Here we come up against a question. No science calls itself "materialist." The adjective belongs in the realm of *philosophy*. Does that mean that Marxism, besides being a science, is also a *philosophy*? Is it in that capacity that it prevents Machoveč, for example, from believing in Jesus *qua* savior?

On the one hand we find a tendency in Marxism that goes back to Lenin at least. One example of that tendency is given by G. Marchais. In proposing political collaboration between Marxists and Christians, he makes a distinction between "scientific socialism" and the "ultimate philosophical foundations" of Marxism. Christians could presumably adopt the former, the ideology informing the practical realization of a socialist society, but they could never accept the latter philosophical foundations.[1]

On the other hand, and paradoxically enough, we find the young Marx saying something rather different in his *Economic and Philosophical Manuscripts (1844)*. In describing Feuerbach's improvements over Hegel, Marx says that one of Feuerbach's achievements is "to have shown that philosophy is nothing more than religion brought into thought and developed in thought, and that it is equally to be condemned as another form and mode of existence of the estrangement of man's nature."[2] Now the fact is that from that period on Marx oriented his studies around the "methods" of the human sciences which we know as historical and dialectical materialism, and then around economic "science." So we have every reason to conclude that his comment on philosophy was not a casual or precipitate one.

So we must consider several questions here. In what sense, consistent with the rest of its makeup, can Marxism be called *philosophy*? And if it can be called a philosophy at all, in what sense can it call itself a *materialist* philosophy?

I. Philosophy and Transcendent Data

My readers may have noticed that in this study I have not specified the role or place of the type of knowledge which our culture calls "philosophy." I have talked about faith and ideology, and I have described them as two complementary and *sufficient* dimensions of every human life. Scientific knowledge, which is validated by experimental reality, clearly belongs to the realm of ideology. As far as the realm of meaning and meaningfulness is concerned, we have seen that it proceeds from faith. Hence it is an ought-to-be or, to use Bateson's term, a "self-validating premise."

The Nature of Philosophical Cognition

Where, then, are we to situate philosophical cognition? The first thing we ought to note here is how recent it has been that this type of cognition attained an autonomous status. We often forget that the formation of philosophical knowledge, particularly its conception of humanity and the universe, was closely bound up with, and conveyed by, types of knowledge belonging to the religious or poetic realms. That held true for a long time. Until very recently the philosopher was the "wise man," and "wisdom" meant living prudently and rightly in accordance with the prevailing religious conceptions. The "sapiential" (Latin *sapientia* means "wisdom") literature of the Bible is the best example of a "philosophy" that is intrinsically bound up with religious reflections.

Even today, as philosophy assumes the role of an independent discipline, we cannot possibly write its history without considering how the tradition of Greek thought, even in its most "philosophical" areas, was heavily influenced at different times by religious thought: Hebrew religious thought, Indian religious thought, and the influence of Latin Christianity exerted through such religious thinkers as Augustine and Aquinas.

Let us set aside for now those fringes and ambiguous areas. Let us consider what is most independent and typical in philosophy as a type of knowledge. It may seem to be an impossible task to find a common denominator in philosophical thought, which stretches over so many centuries and has such varied, profound content. Yet it does seem clear that from the time of the first Greeks regarded as "philosophers" to our own day, philosophy has had two more or less explicitly related functions: (1) to unify scientific data into a coherent picture of the objective universe; (2) to examine what exactly the meaning-structure of life ought to be for the human being. Its task, in other words, has been to introduce systematization and the rational method into the two anthropological dimensions I have been discussing: ideology and faith.

Examples of the first function would be: the theory of the four elements; the battle against the dialectic method of the sophists; Aristotelian logic; the Cartesian and Kantian grounding for scientific knowledge; formal logic; and Teilhard de Chardin's theory of evolution. Examples of the second function would be: the summons to "know thyself"; ethical Platonism and Neo-Platonism; stoicism and epicureanism; medieval and Renaissance theories about the moral virtues; the Kantian imperative; and existentialism.

Some readers might object that various "ontologies," philosophical treatments of *being* in general, are not covered by my dichotomy. But that only seems to be the case. For one thing, all existing ontologies are a generalizing extrapolation from scientific knowledge-data. For another they wittingly or unwittingly claim to offer the "first" or "primary" *realist* justification (following the self-validating premise) for the values-systems that the human being possesses.[3]

If we view ontologies as the summit of philosophical thinking, then we must agree with a philosopher of the spirit such as Berdyaev when he writes: "Philosophy is anthropological, or it does not exist. If it knows being, it does so in and for the human being. And the whole problem resides in *elevating the quality* of that anthropologism to the point where it brings out what I would call the *transcendental human being*" [my italics].[4]

K. Kosík writes much the same from a parallel orientation, though his is materialist: "In that sense *all* philosophy is 'philosophy of the human being,' and it becomes superfluous to underline the human character of philosophy with some specific designation. But 'philosophy of the human being' also has another meaning: *every* problem-complex of philosophy is essentially an anthropological problem-complex, since the human being anthropomorphizes *everything* with which he or she comes into contact theoretically or practically."[5]

The Verifiability of Philosophical Cognition

Now if all that is true, and there is no doubt about that, then we must still examine the *verifiability* of this sort of "philosophical" knowledge-data. By that I mean the guarantee of being true which they afford, the criterion of truth which we might coherently apply to them.

We can say with no fear of error that wherever philosophy sought for direct verifiability, wherever it sought to be guaranteed as true by some experimental or experiential proof, it has sooner or later been replaced by a parallel *science*. Thus various branches of philosophy came to be sciences, with the dose of precision appropriate to their respective fields. A good part of psychology, logic, the sociology of knowledge, etc., gradually slipped over into the scientific domain.

To say that is to say that philosophy continues to be validly autonomous knowledge insofar as it aspires to a *different kind* of verifiability. We can readily see what it is exactly if we consider the two poles of philosophical thought mentioned above: i.e., the rational systematization of experimental (or scientific) knowledge-data and the rational systematization of the realm of meaning or values. In both cases this rational systematization is characterized by the introduction of *transcendent data*.[6] That is the sort of data which enters, by way of hypothesis, to simplify the areas of scientific knowledge and meaning. And it has value to the extent that it fulfills this function.

To take an example in the area of scientific knowledge, the theory of the four elements worked out by the earliest Greek philosophers has been neither *verified* nor *falsified*. Strictly speaking, it could not be, since it is philosophical, not scientific. It has simply been cast aside because it has not proved fruitful in the overall orientation of the physical and chemical sciences towards empirical discoveries.

In a somewhat similar manner, on the plane of meaning, the Kantian moral imperative could hardly be *verified* or *falsified* by experience, since it belongs to the realm of ought-to-be, not to the realm of *it-is*. If it has been rejected, it is because it did not fulfill the function assigned to it: i.e., simplifying the realm of moral knowledge. The fact is that the rule of erecting into a moral norm only something which can be universalized in the realm of natural reality clashes (as a nondialectical contradiction) with another principle which is even more intimately bound up with Kant's moral system. The latter is the principle that the human person ought never be used as an instrument.

Here we see, among other things, the price that must be paid by any scientist who wishes to remain a "scientist" rather than turning into a "philosopher." He or she must not use transcendent data. The only other possibility, which I shall examine in the next section, is that there might be a philosophy which consists specifically in rejecting all transcendent data. Leaving aside that highly unlikely possibility, the scientist would have to stay within the bounds of his or her science. He or she could not generalize the scientific knowledge-data, nor use them to build an overall vision of the universe— even though he or she, as a human being, needs such a vision.

The fact is that every science uses its own concepts and instruments for measurement and experimentation, and they are valid for that science alone. We might even go so far as to say that a science comes into being only when its concepts and instruments have been created. Uniting the knowledge-data of one science with another can only be done through some end or finality (applied science, technology) or by means of "analogies" between the concepts and instruments of the two. And the basis for such "analogies" does not lie in experience. It is universal rationality, God, or some other transcendent datum.

And notice that it is transcendent because it always has to do with some limit-concept. Even though we might arrive at empirically verifiable discoveries by pursuing such analogies, neither God nor the ultimate rationality of the universe would be "proved" thereby.

The Affinity between Philosophy and Religion

This points up the affinity between philosophy and religion, which Marx noted. Or, if one prefers, one might call it the affinity between philosophy and religious faith as I defined it in Chapter III. From our standpoint here we can say that the affinity justifies Marx's comment that "philosophy is nothing more than religion brought into thought." I would add the adjective "rational" before the word "thought," thus introducing a noticeable difference between the transcendent data of religion and that of philosophy. Both do have transcendent data. But the transcendent data of religion rests upon a *tradition of referential witnesses*, whereas rational philosophical thought begins its journey to transcendent data anew with every philosopher, starting from ground-zero insofar as systematization is concerned. Religious tradition, by contrast, has a principle of systematization imbedded in its very process. It presupposes that the "witnesses" are not located in history in a sheerly accidental or fortuitous way. Their *rationality* lies in their location. That is the only thing that differentiates religion from philosophy.

These specifications may well be important, but what I want to stress here is something else. Notice all that must be admitted by anyone who claims that Marxism—or historical materialism and/or dialectical materialism—is a *philosophy*. And that this philosophy, and it alone, deserves the label "materialist."

It is not surprising that Althusser, for example, hesitates before the word "philosophy" and chooses to escape the problem—tangentially, in my opinion—by talking about Theory with a capital *T*. That supposedly enables him to differentiate it from a simple science on the one hand and a philosophy on the other, the latter being nothing more than "religion brought into thought," according to Marx himself.[7] But since Althusser cannot coherently provide any status for his Theory, the science-philosophy alternative persists.[8]

That brings us to crucial commonplaces in our culture, and so we must examine the two possible alternatives, however briefly and inadequately. One is that Marx, despite everything, did have a philosophy of his own, and that it was a materialist one in some sense which remains to be defined. The other alternative is that Marx confined himself to laying the foundation for two related sciences—the sociology of knowledge and his dialectic—which were designed to bring to reality some humanism that Marx refused to establish in a strictly philosophical manner.

II. Marxism: A Materialist Philosophy?

If we start with the first alternative, then obviously we must try to define the adjective "materialist" that qualifies Marx's philosophy. This is all the more true because when we read Marxist literature, and even the writing of Marx himself to some extent, we get the definite impression that the language is deliberately forced. In the history of philosophic ideas certain classic opposites have been canonized, so to speak: *realism versus idealism* on the one hand, *materialism versus spiritualism* on the other. I need hardly point out that the two sets of oppositions do not designate the same thing.[9] One gets the impression that a Marxist writer is inclined to shock us by using the term "materialism" where the ordinary writer would use the term "realism." He or she tries to convey the impression of being anti-*spiritualist*, when in fact he or she is merely anti-*idealist*. So if we do not want to fall into a trap, we must stay clear about the distinction between the labels "realism" and "materialism" in philosophy.

The distinction does not mean that a philosophy can't be both at the same time, of course. There is no doubt that many Marxists, and official Marxism as well, not only believe themselves to be but actually are both realists and materialists. Nor can we reasonably doubt that Marx himself was both, even though he was much more critical than his later followers about what happened to be called "materialism" in his own day.

We should not assume uncritically at the start that we are faced with a real, concrete association of realism and materialism. But even when we are, and when there is solid coherence in the association, we must still ask ourselves whether the two concepts are equally a logical consequence of the basic principles of the thought in question. Take Marx's thought, for example. It is clear that in some passages of his work Marx assumes that religion will disappear as *science* (not philosophy) progresses. But we still have a right to ask whether that forecast is consistent with the rest of his system. Moreover, even if we find consistency in that respect, we might still ask whether other, more central elements in his thought do not justify the conclusion that such a prediction is *only* valid for a religion which arose as a means to fill the gaps in scientific knowledge.

Newton, for example, resorted to the hypothesis of angels to explain why certain small differences he observed between his calculations and the real functioning of the planetary system underwent correction instead of accumulation.[10] Obviously "angels" would be shunted aside insofar as those kinds of problems were solved scientifically. But even though they might be deprived of that specific function, one may still ask whether that is their only function, or their principal one.

Remember our search for the "essential" core of Marxism and Lukács's response about the proper criterion of "orthodoxy":

> Let us assume for the sake of argument that recent research had disproved once and for all every one of Marx's individual theses. Even if this were to be proved, every serious "orthodox" Marxist would still be able to accept all such modern findings without reservation and hence dismiss all of Marx's theses *in toto*—without having to renounce his orthodoxy for a single moment. Orthodox Marxism, therefore, does not imply the uncritical acceptance of the results of Marx's investigations. It is not the "belief" in this or that thesis, nor the exegesis of a "sacred" book. On the contrary, orthodoxy refers exclusively to *method*.[11]

We also have seen that Lukács identifies this essential method as "materialist dialectic."[12] Let us go along with him. Marxist "orthodoxy" does not consist in routinely accepting each and every one of Marx's concrete assertions in his day. It consists in being loyal to the creative core of his thought, his method. If that is the case, then it becomes more urgent with every passing moment to separate that creative core from all the specific ideas of Marx's day, even though "separate" may not necessarily mean that we "discard" the latter. It should be obvious to everyone that if we tie Marx down to ideas which are stuck with the past, then we are only making it increasingly difficult for people to obtain access to him and hence to realize his goals.

Realism and Idealism

Let's start with what might seem to be a very minor point. It is curious that Lukács does not employ the more current term: *dialectical materialism*. Instead he talks about the "materialist dialectic."[13] We have every right to assume that the noun is the first thing to be understood, and that it is further qualified by the adjective, which only then takes on precise meaning. That poses an interesting hypothesis, and in fact the whole essay by Lukács examines the *dialectical* method. The adjective "materialist" is left hanging and is not treated explicitly. Even if only by way of omission, Lukács thus brings out the dependence of the concept on Hegel. Only now and then does he make clear that the dialectic under examination is that of Marx, not that of Hegel, and to characterize it more concretely, he uses not only the adjective "materialist" but also such adjectives as "realist," "practical," and "revolutionary."

We have already seen the reason for such adjectives, for the first three at least. We also know, not only from Lukács but from Marx himself, that all those adjectives are opposed to one adjective. Specifically, they are opposed to the adjective which designates the dialectic of Hegel: "idealist." There is no hesitation or ambiguity in the use of the latter term.

Here, then, we have a promising starting point for exploring our questions. Why is the Hegelian dialectic idealist, even though it is a real dialectic? What new perspectives appear when that characteristic is dropped?

There is no doubt that Hegel is an *idealist*. Nevertheless it is not easy to determine all the specific features of his dialectic which flow from his idealism, and which had to be rejected or overcome by Marx in the process of standing the dialectic on its feet on solid, concrete *material* ground.

Let us begin by adopting a historical approach. In the history of philosophy the terms "realism" and "idealism" have a meaning that is all the clearer insofar as they refer to the *greater or lesser* intervention of the subject in the formation of knowledge-items. That clarity disappears, however, when an opposition is set up between "idealism" and "materialism."

When the opposition between realism and idealism is posed in the history of philosophy, what is at stake is the problem of *truth*. But for truth to constitute a problem for us, it is necessary that we conceive knowledge as a copy, image, or reflection of reality. Only then are we confronted with the question of the copy's *fidelity* to the "original" and with the painful consequences of that question. Here language is decisive. We call fidelity "truth" and infidelity "error," and both truth and error are basic experiences of human life.

There is an additional problem here, however. When we make copies with instruments or artifacts, we measure their fidelity by comparing them with the original, which is transmitted by our direct experience and is "original" only in that sense. When it comes to cognition, however, we cannot do the same thing. For our cognition, by very definition, is the first and only access we have to things themselves. There exists no "original" with which our cognition might be compared.

For example, it makes no sense to ask ourselves whether things in themselves have *color*, whether the pen I am using now *is* blue or I only *see* it as blue. Since I have no other sense or instrument to provide a distinct, credible proof about colors, I must rest content with the fact that I *always* see the pen as blue and that other people concur with that judgment. In trying to verify whether things have colors, it is of little help to me that physics tells me that different frequencies of vibrations emitted by objects under light affect my nervous system differently, and that *I call* those registered differences "colors."

The problem of verification quite logically begins *only* with the painful experience of *error*. For example, after reaching agreement with other people about colors through language, I may see green where other people see red. Or I may discover that something has a color different from the one it usually had in the past, without there being any known cause for the difference. In short, it would never enter my head to talk about an "original" and a "copy" with regard to cognition if "reality" did not often present me with disagreeable surprises and if new items of knowledge did not often remedy these mischances in some fashion.

For example, experience can show me that "the cat scratches." I can also read the word "cat" in a book and think that the *written* "cat" also scratches—though one who knows how to read would probably not fall into that trap. Experience of that error would lead me to make a distinction between a *real* cat (actually an image perceived by my senses) and its *copy* in words. To put it another way, I would have to notice that there was a "reflection" relationship between the two "cats."

This indicates that no philosophy can ever renounce the conception of knowledge as a "reflection" and of truth as a "faithful" reflection. Total, absolute realism is a contradiction in terms in that sense, as is total, absolute idealism. Both suppress the notion of "reflection" and run counter to the basic human experience of *error*, the very motor of human cognition.

The fact is that no philosophical theory has viewed itself as total, absolute realism. If the copy were identical with the original, one could not speak properly of a reflection; knowledge would become reality. The "image" of a house would have all the qualities of a house: three dimensions, same price, place of shelter, and so forth. One would only have to think of a house to be able to step inside it.

On the other hand there is the fact that we do find philosophical claims to total, absolute idealism. Hegel would be the clearest and most famous example of this current, which goes back to Fichte—certainly *not* to Kant. But if we assume that knowledge creates its object completely, why speak of "knowledge" at all? Why not call it simply "reality"? In that case what would be the difference between such idealism and a parallel realism?

Thus the simplest refutation of absolute idealism was offered by Sartre in existential terms: "The reality of that cup is that it is there and that it is not me. We shall interpret this by saying that *the series of its appearances is bound by a principle which does not depend on my whim*" (my italics).[14] Total idealism does not even possess the merit of offering an alternative to realism. For if it were indeed true that knowledge creates its object completely, then it creates a problematic and painful reality, a reality as fraught with problems as those which must be faced by realism.

My will, then, encounters appearances of things which prove to be painful for it. It then tries to increase and improve its cognitive approximations in the hope that new cognitive data might lead to more satisfactory approximations. Here we have the whole history of human cognition, all of which is based necessarily on the hypothesis of knowledge as a reflection or copy of reality.

We find, then, that there are differing orientations which are *more or less* realist or idealist. We distinguish them on the basis of their reaction to error. If I experience an error with regard to colors, for example, I might be more inclined to seek out disturbances affecting the light waves reaching my sight; that would be the "realist" orientation. Or I might be more inclined to look for some possible defect in my own vision; that would be the "idealist" orientation.

So we arrive at the significant fact that the sciences, the whole realm of what is experimentally demonstrable, can operate in an idealist system just as well as in a realist system.[15] In fact it combines the two. Or, to be more precise, it uses methods emphasized by one or the other.

Wherein lies the appreciable difference between realism and idealism insofar as our topic here is concerned? If we examine the history of thought, we will see that realism, insofar as it associates error with the complexity of the object known, generally tends to view reality as variable and malleable—as an object of *practical* transformations. I am not suggesting that a realist cannot succumb to a deterministic vision of the world. I am simply saying that nothing specific to realism would lead a person to that view. On the other hand idealism, insofar as it reacts to error by trying to understand our cognitive mechanisms better, tends to emphasize necessity—whether the latter is devoid of purpose or not.

To get back to dialectic specifically, we have already seen that it was affected by Hegel's idealism to some minimal extent at least. For Hegel knowledge is necessary and purposive. There is an Absolute Spirit who functions and unfolds within the process of knowing. The "cunning of reason" runs the route to perfect knowledge: i.e., perfect self-consciousness. Thus it situates every human being, every group, and every society within the necessary process whereby the aims of Absolute Spirit are realized, whether the former realize this or not. And the linchpin of this movement, the thing that keeps reason from stopping or stagnating, is the opposition of the contraries—call it contradiction, antagonism, conflict, tension, or what you will. Cognition is dialectical because it is in process, because it does not terminate in painful opposition, and it is in process because it is dialectical, because the painfulness of the tension keeps it moving.

Now if we move from idealism to realism, dialectic changes profoundly. First of all, there is no one and no thing *behind* it. Its terms are real beings. No "cunning of reason" uses it as a tool. Opposition and further development of the dialectic will depend on the terms themselves, the latter being human projects in history. Hence the determinism of the dialectic gives way to the various possible outcomes of the opposition: cessation or maintenance of the opposition, qualitative leap or quantitative increase, negation of the negation or transition to a higher synthesis.

What is more important for my analysis here, however, is the fact that Hegel's dialectic, since it is idealist, will be characterized by a valuational indifference on the part of the philosopher (and the dialectic itself) as he or she deals with the opposites in a given situation of conflict. Take the term "negation of the negation," which we have already seen to be very ambiguous. That term itself clearly suggests that Hegel (and his dialectic) does not make either one of the opposed terms his own. Neither the lord nor the bondsman, the skeptic or the stoic, incarnate a value or get any preference. If there is any value in Hegel's dialectic, it is to be located in the opposition itself, not in either one of the antagonists. Values are conveyed by the process of opposition only.[16]

In the previous chapter I alluded to Marx's famous and debated assertion that he had stood Hegel's dialectic back on its feet. And while people might debate endlessly about the *maximum* scope of that assertion, I think its *minimum* import is obvious enough. Marx was saying that he had brought dialectic back down to realism, to "real human beings."

His image itself makes the point clear: dialectic is an engine for moving forward. In the idealist system of Hegel it moved in a vacuum. Thanks to the realism of Marx, the machine now touches real ground. There is real movement and real changing of the world. What cognition now finds before it is a realist hypothesis: the world is the way it is because a real someone is interested in it being that way. And once philosophy (or cognition) is applied to the praxis of changing that objective world, dialectic shows us how that *practical* process is set in motion.

Something else should be obvious here. This realist relocation of the dialectic likewise and inevitably entails the accentuation of some *predialectical* "faith," in the sense I have been using the term "faith." So dialectic can hardly attack the basis of such faith. It is not the dialectic that leads Marx to place himself on the side of the proletariat and his system to entrust the proletariat with the destiny of humanity once the division of labor has occurred. Marx's position is not one of opportunism abetted by predictions which the dialectic makes possible. It is not a matter of climbing aboard the winning horse. By the same token there are no winners in a pure, idealist dialectic; on that point Hegel, Marx, and Engels agree. When Marx joins the struggle on the side of the proletariat, he is not paying homage to necessity willy-nilly. His option is an effort to change the world by establishing values.

Marx's Reworking of Hegel's Dialectic

To confirm the point just made, let us go back to Lukács to find the two chief characteristics implied in Marx's *realist* reworking of Hegel's dialectic and his abandonment of Hegelian idealism.

First, and this is fully in accord with what we have been saying, dialectic ceases to be the law of all happenings in general. It now becomes the cognitive and practical weapon of *only one* of the antagonists:

> *For the proletariat* the truth is a weapon that brings victory; and the more ruthless, the greater the victory. This makes more comprehensible the desperate fury with which bourgeois *science* assails historical [*dialectical*] materialism: for as soon as the bourgeoisie is forced to take up its stand on this terrain, it is *lost*. And, at the same time, this explains why the proletariat and *only* the proletariat can discern *in the correct understanding* [my italics] of the nature of society a power-factor of the first, and perhaps *decisive* [my italics], importance.[17]

The italics, I hope, bring out the thread of dialectic as conceived by Marx and rejected by Hegelian idealism. Lukács indicates that only the proletariat can use the dialectic as its own crucial weapon against the ideological "science" of its dialectical adversary, the bourgeoisie. This is brought out even more clearly in another passage where Lukács is talking about the *historical task* of the bourgeoisie. Logically enough, that task is to preserve the existing order and offer an "apologia for the existing order of things or at least the proof of their immutability." It is a contradictory task because it is "historical" and yet leads to the denial of history. Lukács cites Marx: "Thus there has been history, but there is no longer any." Then he adds that this is:

> . . . a dictum which applies with equal force to all attempts by bourgeois thinkers to understand the process of history. *(It has often been pointed out that this is also one of the defects of Hegel's philosophy of history.)* As a result, while bourgeois thought is indeed able to conceive of history as a problem, it remains an *intractable* problem. Either it is forced to abolish the process of history and regard the institutions of the present as eternal laws of nature which for "mysterious" reasons and in a manner wholly at odds with the principles of a rational science were held to have failed to establish themselves firmly, or indeed at all, in the past. . . . Or else, *everything meaningful or purposive is banished from history* [my italics]. It then becomes impossible to advance beyond the mere "individuality" of the various epochs and their social

and human representatives. History must then insist with Ranke that every age is "equally close to God," i.e., has attained an equal degree of perfection and that—for quite different reasons—*there is no such thing as historical development* [my italics].[18]

The passage is quite clear, so I have quoted it at length and italicized sections freely. Contrary to what might seem to be the case, (Hegelian) idealism cannot logically view history in a dialectical way. Lukács's description of its option is a negative way of bringing out the qualities of dialectical thinking which we have already examined. Secondly, Marx's realist dialectic does not *explain* the world. Instead it seeks to change the world, to develop it in accordance with a purpose, with a particular conception of meaning and value. Thirdly, only those who share this meaning and values-structure can use Marx's method of cognition and action in a logical, effective way. That group is the proletariat, according to both Marx and Lukács.

That brings us to the *second* major characteristic of dialectic as reworked by Marx and stood back on its feet. Dialectic is no longer the principle or motor of cognition, as it was in Hegelian idealism. Now it is the tool or weapon of a certain kind of knowledge aiming towards a *goal*, a goal which logically precedes it. Hegelian idealism, says Lukács, necessarily is devoid of all concrete meaning and purpose. For it, there is none embodied in the dialectical protagonists. Hence Hegelian idealism is doomed to be a-dialectical, even though Hegel talks about an *abstract* goal upheld by an ideal being, Absolute Spirit.

Establishing a goal, a value, a concrete meaning-structure, is, logically speaking, *prior* to any dialectic and hence to any Marxist "orthodoxy." This may seem strange to those who have heard the familiar strains of vulgar or official Marxism. But the point was obvious in Marx's own writings, as far back as his eleventh *Thesis on Feuerbach*. Lukács confirms it here, and he goes on to confirm it clearly but indirectly elsewhere.

If finalism or purposiveness does not proceed or result *from* the dialectic, if the exact opposite is true, then how exactly are the dialectic and its results related to the value in question? In the course of his essay Lukács reiterates three times that the outcome of the dialectic is knowledge of *the objective possibility* of taking concrete, effective steps to *achieve* that value or finality:

> The relation with concrete totality[19] and the *dialectical determinants* arising from it transcend pure description and yield *the category of objective possibility*. By relating consciousness to the whole of society it becomes possible to infer the thoughts and feelings which men *would have* in a particular situation *if they were able to assess* [*fully*] both it and the interests arising from it in their impact on immediate action and on the whole structure of society. That is to say, it would be possible to infer the thoughts and feelings appropriate to their objective situation [my italics].[20]

It should be clear by now that these significant changes wrought by Marx in Hegel's idealist dialectic derive from the fact that Marx exchanged Hegel's idealist perspective for a *realist* one. One need only be a realist in philosophy to introduce those radical variations in the conception and use of dialectic. Why, then, did Marx call himself a "materialist," as if to suggest that the adjective "realist" were not enough to bring one to stand the Hegelian dialectic on its feet?

From the historical standpoint we have adopted here, the explanation might well be that use of the term "realism" might have suggested that Marx was *going back* to positions which antedated the flowering of idealism and which were now regarded as naive.[21] Marx did not want to equate his critique of Hegel with a return to preidealist formulations. In Marx's day only *certain forms of realism* in philosophy seemed bold, modern, and revolutionary: i.e., *materialist* forms of realism.

Historically speaking, we know that the materialism familiar to Marx had not in fact been greatly affected by the philosophical problem of realism versus idealism. The only exception, a very ambiguous one, might be the "materialism" of Feuerbach.[22] The origin of materialism as a philosophy in Marx's day was to be traced to the scientific developments of the time. Moreover, that scientism expressed itself in realist terms insofar as the problem of knowledge was concerned.

The materialism of the eighteenth and nineteenth centuries arose from the discovery that the mechanical processes governing inert matter continued to operate in the loftier realms attributed to mind or spirit. It was therefore tempting to hypothesize that those processes not only applied to the human spirit but also *explained* it. By the same token materialism, in its ontology or general conception of being, entailed a principle which negated or denied philosophy completely. Its reductive ontology simply tended to generalize scientific explanations. Rejecting nonexperiential explanations for spiritual phenomena, materialism was perhaps the first attempt by "philosophy" to reduce itself to science, to eliminate all data *transcending* experience in its systematization of knowledge as a whole.

Now anyone can see that there is much of this in Marx from youth to maturity, whether it is logical or not. His anti-idealism was materialist in that sense, and it is quite obvious in the mature Marx. Note the equation which he sets up in *Capital* between the "materialist" method and the "only scientific one" when it comes to studying the history of religions.[23] Here he was being faithful to the equation he had set up in the *Economic and Philosophic Manuscripts of 1844* between "genuine materialism" and "positive science." It is the explicit project espoused in *The German Ideology*:

> The premises from which we begin are not arbitrary ones, not dogmas, but *real* premises from which abstraction can only be made in the imagination. They are the *real* individuals, their activity and the material conditions under which they live, both those which they find already

existing and those produced by their activity. These premises can thus be verified in a *purely empirical* way [my italics].[24]

I might also add that this reduction of the ideological form, philosophy, to a type of knowledge supposedly immune to ideological influence because it is scientific is highly regarded by many Marxists. Indeed, writes Althusser, it is "that most precious of all the things Marx gave us—the possibility of scientific knowledge."[25]

Be that as it may, we are still left with important and unanswered questions. To what extent is the course taken by Marx on this matter the logical one? To what extent does it form part of the "orthodoxy" in Marx's method? Or is it merely historical fact, which can be explained by the context of his time and place?

First of all, we saw that what was essential to the critical functioning of dialectic was its detachment from idealism. Thus the functioning of the dialectic is not affected at all by the question whether so-called "spiritual" phenomena are or are not reducible to explanations derived from the structure of matter. But we must go further and say something more about the dialectic. If (material) nature is not dialectical, if dialectic really begins with history, then we have proof that dialectic is irreducible to ontological materialism.

Secondly, and we have already seen this point too, a materialist dialectic in the sense under discussion here would be deterministic and hence would not constitute the theory of historical praxis. Insofar as we are talking about a dialectic oriented to praxis, both idealism and ontological materialism lead us by different paths to the same dead end.

Thirdly, it is difficult to attribute a materialist ontology to Marx because he always criticized materialism, the materialism of Feuerbach included, for reducing praxis to the merely cognitive activity of the senses (just as he rejected idealism's reduction of praxis to the cognitive activity of reason). In *Thesis I on Feuerbach* Marx wrote:

The chief defect of all hitherto existing materialism (that of Feuerbach included) is that the thing, reality, sensuousness, is conceived only in the form of the *object of contemplation*, but not as *sensuous human activity, practice,* not subjectively.[26]

I think the final word is crucial for understanding Marx's standpoint against ontological materialism. Since the latter reduces being to the processes of matter, it cannot be a philosophy of the human being, particularly of the human being who struggles and fulfills itself in history.

We can now draw two conclusions, I think. The first is that Marx, as time went on, drew further and further away from that "secular" form of religion known as philosophy, even materialist philosophy, and moved towards science, which was now recruited to help build socialism. The second conclusion is that it is not advisable to regard Marx's withdrawal from philosophy as a new materialist philosophy. Such a view runs counter to essential points in his thought, for any such approach would confront him with two inescapable alternatives.

Either that philosophy is a practical realism, materialist only in its concern for the proper starting point[27] so that it may avoid mistaken abstractions (in that case "materialism" would merely signify a tendency towards abstractionism—materialism versus formalism) or else Marx's philosophy is philosophical materialism in the strict sense. In that case we again have two possibilities. His philosophical materialism comes down to abandoning philosophy for science, in which case it must renounce itself by refusing to make assertions about data that do not fall under its domain. Or else his philosophical materialism is an explicit ontological rejection of the human spirit and its functions, one which allows only for mechanical explanations such as those which apply to physico-chemical matter.[28] In that case Marx would have to renounce any dialectical materialism which proposed to transform history through praxis.

III. Materialism and Marx's Humanism

One important point remains to be cleared up. Is there any relationship between materialism and what has come to be called Marx's "humanism"?

It might be argued that not everyone agrees that Marx espoused any humanism. It might also be argued that the impasse described above applies to any humanism which sought to call itself Marxist and materialist at the same time.

There is a real advantage, however, in dealing explicitly with the theme of Marx's humanism, particularly after what we have seen above. It will enable us to frame more clearly the whole issue of *values* and *faith* in Marx's thought.

Even in its most scientific aspects, Marx's thought is a curious type of science. As Erich Fromm writes: "It must be noted that labor and capital were not at all for Marx only economic categories; they were *anthropological* categories, imbued with a *value judgment* which is rooted in his humanistic position" (my italics).[29] I don't think there can be any doubt about that fact. It is the most obvious impression one gets when one reads Marx's writings, be they the writings of his youth or his mature years. Moreover, everyone agrees that young Marx had what is called a humanism or a philosophy of the human being up to *The German Ideology*, even if they put a dividing line before or after that work. They agree, in other words, that Marx found in the very concept of human being what human beings ought eventually to be.

The Debate about Marx's Humanism

It is here that debate begins. Did Marx break with his earlier humanism somewhere around the time of *The German Ideology*, and particularly in his later writings on economics? Those who answer yes may go so far as to talk about Marx's "antihumanism,"[30] by which they mean his opposition to any general, abstract idea as to what the human being ought to be.

Whence comes this attempt to strip Marxism of its more appealing and "ecumenical" statements about an ideal future where humanity will have found itself once again in a new society? My readers may have already noticed that such an approach is closely bound up with one conception of materialism described above, specifically the one which negates philosophy and seeks to reduce thought to science. As this view would have it, the thought of the mature Marx ceased to be philosophical, hence subject to *ideological* criticism, and came to constitute a verifiable science.[31]

I do not propose to follow the twists and turns of this whole polemic, which really has to do with a contingent historical fact in the last analysis. Moreover, the pervasive internal unity of Marx's thought over the course of his whole life leaves little room for doubt.[32] What I want to do here is to point up the consequences of the two positions because they touch upon the very principles of Marx's thinking and they will confirm and clarify what I said in the preceding section.

As I indicated, those who uphold Marx's fidelity to his youthful humanism have no difficulty in proving this by appealing to Marxian texts. It is obvious that young Marx brought to all his writings an *ideal* concept of the human being.[33] It was partially derived from Hegel, particularly in its vocabulary and forms of expression, but it was also radically different in some respects. Marx is looking for a certain kind of society because "the society that is fully developed produces man *in all the richness of his being*" (my italics).[34]

I won't go into details about the very specific content which Marx saw in that concept of the human being, a human being who could not exist in capitalist society. Marx talks about "real human needs" as opposed to "imaginary" ones, about the "self-estrangement" of human beings who are deprived of the direct fruit of their creative labor as opposed to the "appropriation of the human essence" by human beings who are "complete," "independent," and "free."[35]

The point here is that with such talk about what the human being *ought to be* we find ourselves right in the middle of philosophy. The essence of the human being, as a criterion for ideal human fulfillment and satisfaction, is a *transcendent datum* par excellence. It is as far removed from empirical verification as is the existence of God. Marx derives it by abstraction and reasoning based on his study of the things which concretely make human beings unhappy here and now.[36] And that is no more "scientific" or "objective" than lines of reasoning about the existence of God. And, I might add, Marx's humanism in that respect is full of "ideals" as opposed to the "materialism" of capitalist humanism.

One thing is certain. The humanism under discussion here is not "scientific." Its premises rest on an alleged "essence" which looks an awful lot like one of Bateson's "self-validating premises." And it certainly cannot be reduced to a verifiable datum. That is why those who prefer to see the mature

Marx devoted to science exclusively have to assume that he broke with his earlier expressions of humanism.

The break would be based on the fact that Marx gradually came to realize the full import of his sixth *Thesis on Feuerbach*: "The human essence is no abstraction inherent in each single individual. In its reality it is the ensemble of the social relations."[37] Thus nowhere do we find anything like a "human essence" which might serve as a scientific premise. What we find are different human beings, the product of different societies.[38] Quite apart, then, from the fact that the mature Marx of *Capital* continues to talk about "human nature" in normative terms,[39] we must also note here that in renouncing any *ideal* of the human being as such, one also renounces any and every value-judgment that might orient the practice and theory of Marxist scientific thought, not to mention concrete politics.

It is highly significant that Althusser, the great advocate of Marx's scientific "antihumanism," calmly ends his essay on "Marxism and Humanism" without discussing any values which might serve as replacements for those values which Marx defended in his youth. He seems to feel no need to do that.

I say that is significant for two reasons. First, Althusser tacitly leads his readers to believe that science itself provides those values, right after he has rejected philosophical humanism precisely because it introduces value-judgments into science. Second, in that way Althusser can make use of all the ideals *implicit* in Marx's works (including *Capital*), without having to explain *where* those values *come from* and what sort of role (major or minor) they play in the formation and control of "scientific" data and their application to history.[40]

Marx's Materialism Unrelated to Atheism

As we come to the end of this chapter, we find ourselves verifying once again the point made at the start of this book. The relationship between *faith* and *ideology* is not one of identity or mutual exclusion; it is one of complementarity. There is a necessary complementarity between the realm of meaning and values on the one hand and (scientific) systems of efficacy on the other.

Logically speaking, in Marx's work materialism can be a tendency towards concreteness and scientificness, but it cannot be an ontology loaded with the transcendent datum that transcendent data do not exist at all. It can combat religion for the same motives and reasons that Jesus himself combatted and corrected the religion of his contemporaries. It can, in short, combat religion in one of its historical forms.

There is no more of a relationship between atheism and a materialism consistent with the thought of Marx (be there one Marx or two) than there is between atheism and historical materialism, or atheism and dialectical materialism. That relationship, when it exists at all, must always be played out in the realm of history, not in the realm of metaphysics.[41]

"Be there one Marx or two," I just wrote. And for a reason. Althusser, who maintains there were two, points up the logic of both positions vis-à-vis atheism and religion:

> *Atheism* is a *religious* ideology (atheism as a theoretical system), hence Marxism is not an *atheism* (in that specific sense). It is no accident that the avant-garde theologians at Vatican II were deeply considerate of atheism, since they realized that there is no conflict *in principle* between religion and atheism. (As I have defined it, atheism as a theoretical system is always a *humanism*, and every humanism is an essentially religious ideology.) . . . Marxism is not an atheism, just as modern physics is not an anti-Aristotelian physics. The lunar and sublunar world mattered little to Aristotle; the categories of modern physics are not defined *in opposition to*, i.e., *on the basis of*, the categories of Aristotelian physics. . . . Marxism deals with religion, theism, and atheism in the same way that modern physics deals with Aristotelian physics. It fights them theoretically *when* they constitute a theoretical obstacle; it fights them ideologically and politically *when* they constitute an ideological and political obstacle.[42]

Some readers might say that Althusser's tone is disdainful or subtly ironic, with its allusions to the past. But what does that matter when our author makes the necessary specifications, eliminates misunderstandings, and ends up his discussion with his feet on the ground!

NOTES

1. See Note 25 of Chapter VII, p. 198.

2. Karl Marx, *Economic and Philosophical Manuscripts (1844), Early Writings*, Eng. trans. (New York: Vintage Books, 1975), p. 381.

3. Note that the human being *already* possesses those values. As in the case of religion, so here we should not assume that a human being (without values) adheres to a philosophy because of its intrinsic "truth" value and then appeals to it to find out what values he or she should pursue. The intervention of values in declaring a philosophy true or false is obvious. Perhaps nowhere is it more obvious than in Marxism's refutation of idealism and its vindication of *praxis* as the crucial criterion in deciding the issue. See my comments on the verifiability of philosophy further on in this chapter.

4. Nicholas Berdyaev, *Cinq méditations sur l'existence: Solitude, société et communauté*, French trans. (Paris: Montaigne, 1936), p. 35.

5. Karel Kosík, *Dialéctica de lo concreto*, Spanish trans. (Mexico City: Grijalbo, 1967), pp. 263-64.

6. As people discovered that some of that data was really *immanent* in human experience rather than transcendent, and hence subject to empirical verification, fresh

branches fell from the tree of philosophy and became *sciences* in the strict sense, and they were accepted as such.

7. Althusser's hypothesis is that young Marx (who wrote the phrase cited) thought that philosophy terminated with him and his system. The mature Marx, by contrast, replaced idealist philosophy with *the* scientific philosophy. But Althusser does not tell us clearly what the latter might be precisely, or by what criteria it is assumed to be the only one. Does he mean the only true one, the only one that does not use transcendent data, or the only fruitful one in advancing a revolutionary praxis and its concomitant science?

8. Actually Althusser comes out for science against any philosophy. Philosophy would always be "ideological" in some sort of pejorative sense, even in a classless society. At least it would be by comparison with science, which supposedly is not ideological because it is verifiable.

9. Here we might add a third opposition in which the word "materialism" would have a more precise reference: *materialism versus formalism*. Taking the latter term as a synonym for a tendency towards abstraction, we can say that materialism could, and in technical language often does, signify a desire for "concreteness." At least it opts for concreteness as its starting point, so as to avoid the deviations peculiar to abstract constructions. This understanding of the term would certainly apply to Marx's thought. The only problem is that there is no possibility of it dovetailing with what Marx wanted to put in the term, historically speaking. The fact remains that the founders of historical and dialectical materialism felt it was correct to replace the word "realism" with the word "materialism." This shows up clearly in countless passages of their works. Consider this example from Engels: "We comprehended the ideas in our heads *materialistically* again—as *reflections of real things* instead of regarding the real things as reflections of this or that stage of the absolute idea" [my italics] (Friedrich Engels, *Ludwig Feuerbach and the End of Classical German Philosophy*, Eng. trans. [Peking: Foreign Languages Press, 1976], p. 40).

10. "It was known to Newton that there are certain 'irregularities' in the observed motions of the planets which he could not explain in terms of his law of gravitation. In other words, their actual motions diverged very slightly from what they should be as calculated by his law. Moreover if these irregularities were cumulative, they would in the course of time pile up to such great deviations that they would upset the whole balance of the solar system. The planets would either dive into the sun or break loose from its control and rush off into outer space. Why is it that this does not happen? Newton could think of only one explanation. It must be that from time to time God intervenes and puts the errant planets back on their proper paths. This is noteworthy as being, so far as I know, the last historical occasion on which a great scientist was willing to give supernatural intervention as a cause of an observed phenomenon" (Walter T. Stace, *Religion and the Modern Mind* [Philadelphia: Lippincott, 1952], p. 70).

11. G. Lukács, *History and Class Consciousness: Studies in Marxist Dialectics*, Eng. trans. (Cambridge, Mass.: MIT Press, 1971), p. 1. The point is so important to Lukács that he quotes this 1919 passage in his "Preface to the New Edition (1967)." See Chapter VIII, Note 1 above.

12. Ibid., p. 2.

13. On the use of these terms by Marx, Erich Fromm writes: "In fact, Marx never used the terms 'historical materialism' or 'dialectic materialism'; he did speak of his own 'dialectical method' in contrast with that of Hegel and of its 'materialistic basis,'

by which he simply referred to the fundamental conditions of human existence" (E. Fromm, *Marx's Concept of Man* [New York: Frederick Ungar, 1961], p. 9).

14. Jean-Paul Sartre, *Being and Nothingness*, Eng. trans. (New York: Washington Square Press/Pocket Book, 1966), p. 5.

15. "That comes down to saying that neither absolute realism nor absolute rationalism exists for scientific philosophy, and that one need not start from some general philosophical outlook to judge scientific thinking" (Gaston Bachelard, *Le nouvel esprit scientifique* [Paris: PUF, 1975], p. 6). A little further on Bachelard notes again "the curious ambiguity which demands that all scientific thought be interpreted simultaneously in realist language and in rationalist language" (ibid., p. 7).

I might point out that Bachelard talks about the intervention of "objective" and "subjective" factors in scientific cognition. Hence we would be more than justified in replacing his term "rationalism" with the word "idealism." The latter is more common in the history of philosophy for designating the predominance of creative subjectivity in cognition. To justify this substitution, I need only point out that many French thinkers trace idealism back, not to Kant, but to Descartes, regarding it as a continuation of Cartesian rationalism.

16. Marx himself describes the idealist dialectic of Hegel as follows in *The Holy Family*: "*Hegel's* conception of history presupposes an *Abstract* or *Absolute Spirit* which develops in such a way that mankind is a mere *mass* that bears the Spirit with a varying degree of consciousness or unconsciousness. Within *empirical*, exoteric history, therefore, Hegel makes a *speculative*, esoteric history develop. The history of mankind becomes the history of the *Abstract Spirit* of mankind, hence a *spirit far removed* from the real man" (Marx and Engels, *The Holy Family, or Critique of Critical Criticism*, Eng. trans. [Moscow: Progress Publishers, 1975], p. 100).

17. Lukács, *History and Class Consciousness*, p. 68. In the next section Lukács confirms what I have been saying when he explains why only the proletariat can be decisive—because it alone can get away from a particularistic (i.e., nondialectical) knowledge of history: "Naturally we do not wish to deny that the proletariat must proceed from the facts of a given situation. But it is to be distinguished from other classes by the fact that it goes beyond the contingencies of history; far from being driven forward by them, it is itself their driving force and impinges centrally upon the process of social change" (ibid.).

To be sure, this is not a mere statement of fact but a declaration of an ought-to-be. Nevertheless this "ought-to-be" points up a possibility specific to the proletariat.

18. Ibid., p. 48.

19. On this essence of the dialectic according to Lukács, see Chapter VIII, Section I, pp. 201-6 in this volume.

20. Lukács, *History and Class Consciousness*, p. 51; see also pp. 73 and 76.

21. "The dispute over the reality or non-reality of thinking that is isolated from practice is a purely *scholastic* question" (Marx, *Thesis II Concerning Feuerbach*, in *Early Writings*, Eng. trans., p. 422).

Thus A. Schaff is quite logical and right about Marx when he writes that from the standpoint of epistemology and the whole controversy between realism and idealism Marx is simply *realist*, not materialist. His materialism would be a stance *in ontology*, in what deals with being in general. I shall consider that point further on. Here the point to note is that idealism presented itself in the history of philosophy as a solution to epistemology. Hence one deliberately misunderstands the issue if one sets up an opposition between materialism and idealism insofar as Marx is concerned. Recall the text of Engels cited in Note 9 above.

22. The post-Hegelian origin of Feuerbach's materialism explains why he was first praised, then rejected, by Marx.

23. See Chapter IV, p. 100 in this volume.

24. Marx and Engels, *The German Ideology*, Eng. trans. (New York: International Publishers, 1970), p. 42.

25. L. Althusser, *For Marx*, Eng. trans. (London: Verso Editions, 1979), p. 241. To be perfectly logical, then, one should not say that atheism or any other *a priori* critique of some *faith* is a part of Marxism so conceived. A consistent materialism of that sort must *prescind* from the ontological question, to the extent that it claims to be scientific and empirically verifiable. For further comments on this point see Althusser's remarks on "real humanism," *For Marx*, pp. 244–47. For the correct "materialist" response both to atheism and religion, see Althusser's comment at the end of this chapter (p. 242).

26. Marx, *Early Writings*, p. 421. "Marx actually took a firm position *against* a philosophical materialism which was current among many of the most progressive thinkers (especially natural scientists) of his time. This materialism claimed that 'the' substratum of all mental and spiritual phenomena was to be found in matter and material processes. In its most vulgar and superficial form, this kind of materialism taught that feelings and ideas are sufficiently explained as results of chemical bodily processes, and 'thought is to the brain what urine is to the kidneys' " (Erich Fromm, *Marx's Concept of Man*, p. 9).

27. As Fromm rightly points out, this starting point has nothing psychologically "materialist" about it. Quite the contrary is true: "But it hardly needs such proof from Marx's psychological ideas to show that the popular assumption about Marx's materialism is utterly wrong. Marx's whole criticism of capitalism is exactly that it has made interest in money and material gain the main motive in man, and his concept of socialism is precisely that of a society in which this material interest would cease to be the dominant one" (Fromm, *Marx's Concept of Man*, p. 14).

See my discussion of the difference between the "economic structure" and the "economic factor" in Chapter VII, p. 192.

28. Note that we are talking about a *past* version of materialism or, if you will, a version surpassed by more recent developments in the sciences of physics and chemistry. It could be said that the current trend in these sciences does not permit us to picture matter, even inert matter, in terms of *simplistic* processes that would *reduce* the complexity of "spiritual" or higher phenomena to a simplistic mechanical process that would be totally determined. A Spanish manual on quantum mechanics (T. Bense and R. Sosa Sánchez, *Introducción a la mecánica cuántica* [Montevideo, 1976]), begins with this quote from the well-known scientist Louis de Broglie (*Matter and Light*): "The more we descend into the lowest structures of matter, the more we realize that the concepts forged by our mind in the course of daily experience, especially the concepts of space and time, are powerless to enable us to describe the new worlds into which we are penetrating. One could say, if you will excuse the expression, that the contour of our concepts must progressively grow blurred to allow for their possible application to realities at the subatomic level."

However, we must not confuse the extraordinary complexity of our *access to knowledge* of matter and its mechanisms with the increasing objective complexity it takes on as it moves toward life, the learning apprenticeship of living beings, and the different degrees of this apprenticeship as we get to the so-called "higher" animals. It should also be remembered that when I talk about Marx's "materialism" here insofar as it is related to the sciences of matter, I am talking about the state of the sciences in his day.

29. Fromm, *Marx's Concept of Man*, p. 40.

30. See Althusser, *For Marx*, p. 229.

31. See ibid., "Introduction: Today," pp. 21–39.

32. Here one would have to explore the arguments offered in the debate. Lukács, Schaff, and Fromm, along with many others, defend the unity of Marx's thought throughout his life and present arguments in support of that position. For example, see Fromm, *Marx's Concept of Man*, pp. 1–83, especially the section entitled "The Continuity in Marx's Thought," ibid., pp. 69–79.

33. Insofar as Marx's anti-*idealism* is concerned, note that the term "idealism" here does not relate to "ideal" (i.e., a value or an ought-to-be) but to "idea" (i.e., knowledge which allegedly creates its object). Althusser, who advocates discontinuity in Marx's thought, sums up his youthful humanism as follows: "History is the alienation and production of reason in unreason, of the true man in the alienated man. Without knowing it, man realizes the essence of man in the alienated products of his labour (commodities, State, religion). The loss of man that produces history and man must presuppose a definite pre-existing essence. At the end of history, this man, having become inhuman objectively, has merely to re-grasp as subject his own essence alienated in property, religion, and the State to become total man, true man" (*For Marx*, p. 226).

34. Marx, *Economic and Philosophical Manuscripts (1844)*, in *Early Writings*, p. 354.

35. See Erich Fromm, *Marx's Concept of Man*. Most of these expressions come from the *Economic and Philosophical Manuscripts (1844)*. But it is possible to show that the mature Marx, using different language (e.g., alienation and fetishism), continues the same line of concepts.

36. Note this interesting observation by Schaff: "It is surprising that nothing is made of the analogy existing between the status of normative propositions which enunciate social content (and form part of ideology) and the status of normative propositions which enunciate natural content (and form part of technology or medicine, for example). . . . It is easy to see the difficulties resulting from such a comparison. The fact is that no one would deny the statement that reasoning about the necessity of the socialist revolution is part of the realm of ideology. But if that conclusion is based solely on the normative character of such propositions and a proper conception of their relationship to descriptive propositions, what are we to do with technology and its recommendations about the way to construct a bridge?. . . . In this way we have suppressed the only factor that distinguishes ideology from science" (Adam Schaff, "La objetividad del conocimiento a la luz de la sociología del conocimiento y del análisis del lenguaje," Spanish translation in the anthology edited by Eliseo Verón, *El proceso ideológico* [Buenos Aires: Ed. Tempo Contemporáneo, 1973], pp. 74–75).

37. Marx, *Early Writings*, p. 423.

38. Discussing the idea of the human being and humanism in *The German Ideology*, Marx points out that the idea of human nature, of a human essence, entails a two-edged value-judgment. The two poles are *human* and *inhuman*. Althusser re-

marks: "In *The German Ideology* Marx commented that the idea of human nature, or of the essence of man, concealed a *coupled value-judgment*, to be precise, the couple human/inhuman; and he wrote: 'the *inhuman* as much as the *human* is a product of present conditions; it is their negative side.' The couple human/inhuman is the *hidden* [my italics] principle of all humanism" (Althusser, *For Marx*, pp. 236-37).

I would add here that any effort to suppress this hidden principle, instead of explaining it, by shifting from humanism to "science" displays the very naiveté denounced by Adam Schaff in the passage cited in Note 36 above.

39. "Of course, Marx was never tempted to assume that 'human nature' was identical with that particular expression of human nature prevalent in his own society. In arguing against Bentham, Marx said: 'To know what is useful for a dog, one must study dog nature. This nature itself is not to be deduced from the principle of utility. Applying this to man, he that would criticize all human acts, movements, relations, etc., by the principle of utility, *must first deal with human nature in general, and then with human nature as modified in each historical epoch*'" (Fromm, *Marx's Concept of Man*, pp. 24-25).

40. Adam Schaff seems more honest and clearsighted on this matter. On the basis of his experience at Jelonki (see Chapter I, Note 5, p. 29 in this volume) he admits that he had neglected questions concerning "ethics" and the "meaning of life" for the sake of "ideological questions." He did so in particular because he felt the solution did not lie in looking somewhere (certainly not in science) for a response, but rather in spelling out the basic value-judgments which were already *implicit* in the ideology that was accepted and utilized. He goes on to say: "Up to then I have always rejected such questions outright as so much nonsense. I think that right there I was to be convinced of their coherence, or at least of my need to examine them and offer an answer as *a Marxist starting off from Marxist positions*" [my italics] (Schaff, *La filosofía del hombre*, Spanish trans. [Buenos Aires: Lautaro, 1964], p. 69; see also pp. 35, 65, etc.).

41. For one typical example of this approach among many, note the following "reason" for atheism offered by Marx in the *Economic and Philosophical Manuscripts (1844):* "A *being* sees himself as independent only when he stands on his own feet, and he only stands on his own feet when he owes his *existence* to himself. A man who lives by the grace of another regards himself as a dependent being. But I live completely by the grace of another if I owe him not only the maintenance of my life but also its *creation*, if he is the *source* of my life. My life is necessarily grounded outside itself if it is not my own creation" (Marx, *Early Writings*, p. 356).

42. Louis Althusser et al., *Polémica sobre Marxismo y humanismo*, Spanish trans. (Mexico City: Siglo XXI, 1968), pp. 198-99.

B. *The Dense Complexity of Historical Reality*

CHAPTER X

Means and Ends:
Industrially Developed Countries

So far we have been passing in review some important and perhaps crucial data of our culture. We have found misunderstandings and clichés that will not survive critical analysis. They fade before an appeal to method for which we need only a modicum of objectivity and common sense. Yet these hollow and even mistaken commonplaces continue to exert incredibly strong and persistent influence on the conduct of individuals, groups, and classes in society. Forces destined by their very nature to meet and complement each other prove to be victims of these clichés and end up as mortal enemies. Meanwhile the real adversaries are regarded as coreligionists. I would not hesitate to say that many of us find this to be one of our bitterest personal experiences. Somehow we find it impossible to put order and rational content into the historic struggles of our time and place.

I am afraid, however, that my "review" might well have come across as excessively abstract to many readers. This may be particularly true for those who have been compelled, by circumstances and by their concrete commitments to the people of Latin America today, to make life-and-death decisions and burn their bridges behind them insofar as my areas of discussion are concerned.

Hence I now want to call a halt to the theoretical journey I have been on. I would like to examine the implications of all that has been said so far, this time without appealing to weighty erudition and closely reasoned arguments. I would like my discussion to shed some light on our real life and activity, on our inner thinking and feeling, on our hopes and disappointments, on our thoughts and value-judgments, and on our affiliations and disaffiliations. For my reflections, despite appearances, are *situated* in time and space, even though I have not yet expressly alluded to Latin America in the third quarter of the twentieth century.

My seeming disregard for our concrete situation as a starting point had its reasons. Too often we overestimate the value, for committed reflection, of starting with problems as they present themselves concretely and consciously in the life and practice of human beings. We tend to forget that emotional involvement and concrete detail often prevent us from grasping or discussing the larger dimensions that are at stake.

That is why I have taken a different approach up to now. It has its advantages, provided one condition is met. In his book entitled *El hombre*, Ernest Hello shrewdly points out that the mediocre individual "sometimes acknowledges an idea but does not follow it through in its applications; if you pursue it to its conclusions, he or she will tell you that you are exaggerating." Mediocre people tend to be frightened when they perceive the concrete consequences of principles that they accepted on a more abstract level. So they go back to the principles to see if they can find some way to deny them and hence escape their consequences. It should be obvious that my reflections in this chapter are offered on the assumption that my readers are not people of that type.

I. The Death of Ideologies?

Between 1950 and 1975, to specify a concrete period, a large number of Latin Americans, young people in particular, went through a series of sharply traumatic experiences. Obviously there were many different tendencies at work, but I would characterize the whole experience briefly as follows. Starting out with the impression that there was much which urgently needed to be done, they gradually came to the disillusioned realization that the major means for accomplishing the desired transformations had somehow slipped through their fingers. At the start of the period in question, the various hopes emerging on the horizon clashed with a certain degree of ferocity; by the end of the period, there was a converging sense of despair, a feeling that all roads had been cut off.

Now despite certain significant similarities, we must clearly distinguish that problem-set from the one which was being faced simultaneously by people living in the developed capitalist and socialist countries. In those countries there was endless talk about the "death of ideologies." The phrase had a very specific import, which I must spell out more clearly. To many it seemed that even though political options continued to clash in the old "ideological" terms of right and left (roughly equivalent to capitalism and socialism respectively), the real human problems were being played out elsewhere. This surprising and disorienting statement of the problem must be analyzed in the light of what we have seen so far.

To begin with, this view assumes, not without some reason, that the humanist "faith" behind the two models is fundamentally the same, that there is really no black and white opposition involved. It also suggests that the costs involved, i.e., the dehumanizing results of the two systems of realization, or the two "ideologies," end up looking more and more alike.

Such a view will seem untenable at the outset to anyone who systematically confuses or equates faith and ideology. Such people will tend to regard the inhuman results of one or the other system—depending on their own stance—as the "values" around which the ideology of the particular system is built. From the standpoint of the left (the socialist camp), capitalism shows up as a system that values unlimited profit plus certain individual liberties that are to be enjoyed by a privileged minority who reap this profit. From the standpoint of the right (the capitalist camp), socialism shows up as a system that values a certain economic levelling, but the levelling is intrinsically bound up with the repression of all imbalancing factors, i.e., of all those factors associated with creativity and competition on the level of individuals or groups.

I am not suggesting that the above formulation means that the two projects for human society end up in a tie before the bar of objective reason. My point here is to point up one of the most typical "ideological" (in the pejorative sense) mechanisms used by people in the face of two different systems. They tend to go in for a lame comparison, pitting the *faith* of their system against the *ideology* of the other system. Thus they analyze their own thinking in terms of meaning and values and the thinking of their opponent in terms of the costs required to put that thinking into practice.

Similarities in the Faith of Liberal Capitalism and Socialist Marxism

Back in Chapter I of this book I pointed out that all historical criticism must take due account of both dimensions; otherwise it will succumb to one-dimensional dehumanization. So we must always compare the corresponding dimensions of two different thought-systems.

Many readers may well be surprised, and indeed a little suspicious, when I suggest that the ideal conception of the human being differs little in the two systems under discussion here: i.e., capitalist liberalism and socialist Marxism. Opposed as these two systems may be, they do bear witness to the fact that their anthropological and social conceptions stem from a common trunk.[1]

We know that the model of capitalist liberalism was grounded on the credible historical possibility of "perfect competition" between human beings. But even granting the viability of such a system, why should people assume that a society offering that type of productive competition would provide humanity and individual human beings the best chance for satisfaction and happiness? Here we find coming into play a whole series of ideas conveyed by countless "referential witnesses" of European culture. One crucial witness emphasizes the fulfillment of the human being in his or her work, in the domination and transformation of nature. Perfect competition is thus the supposedly ideal condition permitting work and its product to be something truly human, something that is possessed by the worker as his or her own and that promises fulfillment.

There is an additional point here. The result of human labor will not truly belong to the human being unless labor is undertaken freely, unless it is creation, unless it is assumed as a vocation. Less than perfect competition, on the other hand, imposes a certain kind of labor on a human being from outside. Such imposed work will never bring fulfillment to human beings even though the product of work, economically speaking, may remain in the hands of the worker.

Thus "perfect competition" implies that we will not introduce into the market such things as interventions by the social authority or structural imbalances. For those things oblige people, *de jure* or *de facto*, to opt for a nonvocational kind of work. They must then accept work for some reason quite independent of their free choice: e.g., survival. And the outcome of their work cannot help but be an impersonal commodity. Moreover, another assumption is required in this model, with its perfectly balanced market. The assumption is that society can and must keep deriving from that market all the goods it needs for life and for the continuance and progress of creative work by all its members. Hence, as Hinkelammert describes it: "The result of the model is curious. Balance occurs only if one assumes the complete mobility of all the factors of production [precondition for vocational work by all] and perfect foresight of everything happening in the entire market [precondition for a sufficient and satisfactory production]."[2]

Now let us try a curious experiment. Let us set over against the above model the following description of the human being in the ideal society:

In . . . society, where nobody has one exclusive sphere of activity but each can become accomplished in any branch he wishes, society regulates the general production and thus makes it possible for me to do one thing today and another tomorrow, to hunt in the morning, fish in the afternoon, rear cattle in the evening, criticise after dinner, just as I have a mind, without ever becoming hunter, fisherman, shepherd or critic.[3]

The experiment is curious because the above passage derives from the "faith" which is supposed to be the contrary of that of liberal capitalism. It is Karl Marx's description in *The German Ideology* of the ultimate stage of communist society.

Some readers might object that there is no mention of the societal factor in the capitalist view, that society does not assume responsibility for regulating anything. That is a very superficial view. The very notion of a total market in liberal capitalism is equivalent to the notion of society. And the society which seeks to regulate production in the communist system has features very much like those of the capitalist market with its perfect competition; it will not be a social *institution* endowed with powers of coercion.[4]

In the liberal model, the marketplace with its perfect competition will not be guided by any social authority but rather by an "invisible hand." The invisible hand will make sure that vocational work and the satisfaction of basic needs dovetail. In the finished socialist or communist model, the State will no longer exist. The necessary production for all will be regulated in some mysterious way by the aptitudes of all; it will be the result of an "association of free producers."[5]

The division of labor was not an evil in itself, insofar as Marx was concerned. Nor was it evil because it made some people dependent on other people insofar as their work and whole life were concerned. The division of labor became a source of bondage when it took on its own institutional life independently of human beings and over them, forcing them to accept unwanted work and turning the product of that work into an impersonal commodity. In the Marxian scheme, then, an association of free producers is the opposite of an institutionalization of the division of labor. It thus performs a function parallel to that of the invisible hand in the capitalist scheme. It makes the inevitable division of labor coincide with the free vocation of each individual.[6]

Problems of Efficacy

It is not the discovery of such unexpected similarities between the two systems that could prompt the "death of ideologies" or statements about the futility of conflict between them. As soon as we move away from these two types of "faith," so similiar in the abstract, and consider their realization in systems of efficacy (i.e., "ideologies"), however, we find that the latter are not only different but truly opposed. The fact is, to keep to my terminology here, that the faith embodied in both capitalist liberalism and Marxist socialism can be determined specifically only through the ideologies which implement it in history. This necessary and intrinsic complementarity holds true, as we have seen, both in the cognitive and the practical order. In short, we have to see values *realized* in some way and to some extent in order to be able to "believe" in their possibilities for providing satisfaction.

Marx devoted the final stage of his life and his later works to a critique of political economy. His precise aim was to show, by way of logical coherence (logical incoherence, to be more exact), that each step taken or envisioned for the sake of "perfect competition" only tends to unbalance the latter even more. The one-sided gains of some *increase* rather than disappear. The ideal value of the model is only a *pretext* for those who implement the means designed to achieve that model; it is not what they really are pursuing. If Marx's critique is correct, what they are in fact pursuing is profit, and the latter is placed above human freedom and human creativity.

Obviously Marx did not have a similar chance to apply his critical method to the historical realization of his socialist "faith." Playing a central mediational role in that process, as he saw it, was the transition to collective ownership of the means of production. Unfortunately, however, the implementation of this means seems to contain a parallel logical incoherence vis-à-vis the anti-institutional model. While the various reasons behind this incoherence may be more accidental than those accounting for the incoherence in the capitalist model, the fact remains that collectivization of the means of production only seems to accentuate the need of institutional controls. What stands out clearly in socialist countries is the intervention of the most powerful social institution of all: the State or government. Even if that intervention is not growing, it is ongoing and heavy-handed. Far from disappearing gradually, in more highly developed countries the State needs a strong-armed bureaucracy and harsh repression to promote and distribute the results of production. And it must repress, as dangers to the progress of the socialist project, the very things which constitute its goal: initiative, participatory democracy, and criticism—in a word, individual freedom. The vocational dimension of labor for each human being thus seems to be subordinated indefinitely to the abstract institutionalization which prevails and which is centered around the maximization of production rather than the agreement of free producers.

To repeat once again, I do not mean to suggest that these criticisms lead to a tie between the two systems. It seems to me that the critique of the capitalist ideology is much more solidly grounded and goes much more to the very heart of the system. But that is not the point I am trying to bring out here. Right now I am simply trying to trace back to its roots the hypothesis known as the "death of ideologies."

One of the most subtle and convincing advocates of this European hypothesis is Raymond Aron. Here is how he puts it in one of his works:

> Here is the problem which serves as my starting point. Let us grant that in today's societies, be they Soviet or Western, we find one major fact: the application of science to industry. This brings with it an increase in productivity and resources for the whole society and on a per capita basis. Now what are the consequences of this for the social order? . . . *This question is a way of avoiding the opposition, socialism versus capitalism, as a point of departure.* It permits us to view them as two species of *one and the same genus: industrial society.* My trip to Asia convinced me that the major concept of our time is the concept of industrial society. Seen from Asia, Europe is not composed of two basically heterogenous worlds: the Soviet world and the Western world. It is made up of one single reality: industrial civilization. The Soviet societies and the capitalist societies are merely two species of one genus, two forms of one and the same social type: progress-oriented industrial society [my italics].[7]

It comes as a surprise to no one that the conceptual elaboration of both the capitalist and the Marxist ideologies was more or less contemporaneous with what is known as the "industrial revolution." Much of the two ideologies, both in their *positive* and *negative* aspects, was intimately bound up with the mode of production existing at the time they arose. That, after all, is one of the most basic tenets of historical materialism, isn't it?

We have already seen that a *positive* element of the industrial revolution figured in the ideal models of both liberalism and socialism: i.e., the possibility, for the first time in the history of civilized humanity, that production would be sufficient to give to everyone according to his or her needs. Both systems viewed this new possibility as basic and fundamental. Up to now it has been compromised or blocked by some accidental or structural flaw in the process of competition in the marketplace. Both systems also agree that there is no turning back from what has been achieved so far by the industrial revolution. Hence, as Aron tells us, the industrial revolution has "advanced" or moved ahead indefinitely in both systems.

That is clear in liberal capitalism. It is due not so much perhaps to the internal logic of the system as to the fact that this progress constitutes a more or less rationalized justification of the existing mode of production.[8] The situation is a bit more complicated in Marxism. For one thing, Marx's criticism of the inhuman nature of the industrial revolution, and its more remote origin in the specialization and institutionalization of the division of labor, would seem to oblige him to date his communist model back to some sort of society that is clearly preindustrial. That shows up clearly enough in the passage cited above from *The German Ideology*, where he talks about the possibility of hunting, fishing, rearing cattle, and engaging in criticism on one and the same day. Would it make sense to talk about a similar kind of choice in an industrial society? Could one be engineer and electronics expert, foundry worker and actor, for example?

Moreover, only the introduction of complex, specialized techniques can provide the general run of human beings with the material goods they need to free themselves from unwanted work that is prolonged far beyond the limits compatible with freedom and vocational choice. In Marx's eyes, communism could only follow developed capitalism. Why? Because capitalism would produce its own contrary, a pauperized proletariat, and, even more importantly, because capitalism would make possible a sufficient production, on which the new substitute model would be grounded.[9]

Enter at this point the hypothesis known as the "death of ideologies." It would say that the type of human (or better, inhuman) relations created by industrial society and inseparable from it change the picture. Granted those relations, the fact that the means of production are or are not owned by individuals *loses importance*.[10]

As we saw above, both models attach great relevance to the fact that production work be identical with the "vocation" of the individual. In other words, it should be the fruit of personal choice, and the individual should be able to see a close connection between that work and the implementation of his or her values. Once we reach a certain stage of industrial development, however, it seems that work is irrevocably detached from what we might call its "human" dimension. The mathematical rationalization of advancing industrial development introduces impersonality into human labor—irreversibly.

Now if that is the case, there is no use at all in trying to fashion an "industrial'' socialism; such a socialism would have little to do with Marx's humanism. The motivations underlying work in such a society could not change radically. There would always have to be an appeal to egotism and profit. Hence the allegation is that it is futile to oppose socialism to liberalism as if they were antagonists. If the two are translated into an industrial society, both will ultimately force human beings to continue selling their labor as an impersonal commodity.[11]

Aron himself offers this disillusioned comment: "Political theorists of the past considered that a good society was one in which human beings were virtuous. Today's sociologist tends to think that a good society is one which utilizes individual vices to serve the common good."[12] If that is the case, how far the "common good" has dropped in value! In Aron's supposedly realistic disillusionment we see the seedbed of the "death of ideologies." It is a big "What for?" or "What's the point?" raised in the midst of efforts to transform social life in what seems to be radical ways.

There can be no doubt that this argument is deliberately used as a blind by conservative factions, particularly when it is voiced in underdeveloped countries which are nowhere near the take-off point for large-scale industrialization. But does this twisted use prove that the whole issue itself should be disregarded? Here I want to delve into its more convincing human arguments, even though they apply more to developed countries and have little to do with today's Latin America.

Aron himself points up one of the major problems. It is a universal one, but it is greatly accentuated and intensified by an "advanced industrial" type of society. It has to do with the compatibility of government and democracy. Combining close observation and a surprising dose of cynicism, Aron notes:

> There is a contradiction in this twofold exigency: that rulers be wise and that they act in accordance with the wishes of the ruled. . . . No political system has ever found a definitive solution for the contradiction between a wise government and a government by consensus; all existing regimes represent some possible compromise between the two principles.[13]

Aron points out the fact that no civilized nation resorts to a popular plebiscite or referendum every time it has to make complex decisions whose effects on the masses will be visible only in the long run. Public responsibility itself prohibits that. If such a course is regarded as fatal,[14] it is because the whole population cannot be expected to possess enough complex, specialized knowledge-data to make a sound judgment on such issues. The question which few people ask themselves is whether it wasn't really fatal that society arrived at such questions. Once society arrives at that point, however, the people must delegate, i.e., *give up*, the solution of such issues to *representatives* who are supposedly qualified to do that and who are popularly elected; the latter then go to work without consulting their electors.

Now advanced industrial society renders this relationship between electors and elected officials ever more remote and fortuitous.[15] On their own, the electors can no longer judge to what extent their elected representatives are heeding the common good when they make decisions whose components and results escape the understanding of the average citizen more and more. The best we can get from that point on is an apparent democracy: "one which has found a way to give the common people the impression that the rulers are executing the general will, when in fact it permits the rulers to find some way to make wisdom prevail [over the general will]."[16]

Obviously this tension between government wisdom and real democracy is intensified when a government does not even try very hard to get across the "impression" of which Aron speaks. In such a case there will necessarily arise conflicts between the political handling of affairs and the (anthropological) faith which the citizens seek to convey through their social community, between political obligations stemming from external orders and ethical obligations stemming from within the citizen.

A notorious example of that very problem was what went on in the socialist countries of Europe, satellites of Moscow to a greater or lesser extent, during the Stalinist era. Writes Adam Schaff: "I have in mind a particular type of situation, one which gave rise to profound moral upsets among wide segments of the populace during the years 1955 to 1957. Even today it causes concern to large segments. I am referring to the sense of moral responsibility stemming from *political* activities which are carried out in situations that can give rise to *conflicts of conscience*. . . ."[17]

If the mentors of socialist society can forget that the great problem of the "meaning of life"[18] and its ethical implications lies hidden behind "ideological questions," then Marcuse's diagnosis of "one-dimensional man" cannot be restricted offhandedly to capitalist industrial society.[19] So people do have a point when they stress the basic connection of this whole problem-complex with the dimensions of "advanced industrial society." To be sure, one can abuse the argument and use it to relativize the choice between capitalism and socialism, thus leading people to conservative stances. But that does not mean that the basic problem ceases to exist.

The Scale of Means and the Ecological Crisis

There is another point, very important for my analysis, which must be noted here. It has to do with a cliché bandied about in our time and in our Western culture. It suggests that the societies stemming from Marxism practice an ethical aberration: i.e., they proclaim and implement the principle that "the end justifies the means." That actually is far from the truth, in my opinion. I would maintain that the ethical crises noted by Schaff stem precisely from the fact that the dimensions of "advanced industrial society" have rendered impossible what should be possible: i.e., that the end justifies the means. Let us look at this issue.

In another book I sought to prove that the principle, "the end justifies the means," constitutes the most obvious moral maxim.[20] Common sense tells anyone of sound judgment that a means, precisely because it is a *means* or is viewed as such (i.e., as an *instrument for*), acquires its only possible justification from the ends or values that it serves.

Let's look at it from a slightly different angle. What different justification could there be for the morality or immorality of something that is a means or instrument? Obviously it would be the fact that the moral laws were dictated to me from *outside* myself, by someone who had other ends than mine. In that case the means would still be justified by the ends. But since those ends are not mine, we would have means that would seem to possess a morality in themselves, a morality independent of the end that I could impose or understand. That heteronomous type of morality would still sustain the basic principle cited above, but it would make me realize that I am not to rely on *my* ends when I make ethical judgments.

In Chapter I of this book I ruled out the possibility of a values-structure, a meaning-system, a faith, being dictated to me from outside.[21] Ideology, on the other hand, is subject to two criteria, one of which is always external to me. On the one hand I must maintain consistency between ideology and the values it is called upon to realize: the end justifies the means which really lead to it. On the other hand an ideology must respect the "physical" or objective laws which ensure efficacy and which stem from the reality confronting me rather than from my values.

The danger in the hasty or indiscriminate use of the maxim, "the end justifies the means," lies in the fact that objective reality is often more complicated than it seems. At first sight I may judge something to be effective for my ends or goals, but in the long run it may actually pose obstacles to my ends or destroy them completely. To love each other more deeply, a husband and wife might decide it would be better to isolate themselves from social problems. They might see this as the most appropriate and effective line of conduct for their goal. Later, however, they might discover that this isolation from society was radically undermining or even destroying their love.[22]

Now how does this point relate to "industrial society"? Let me cite an example from the interesting and documented work by E. F. Schumacher, *Small Is Beautiful.* In a chapter entitled "The Proper Use of Land," Schumacher writes:

> These questions suggest that "The Proper Use of Land" poses, not a technical nor an economic, but primarily a metaphysical problem. . . . There are always some things which we do for their own sakes, and there are other things which we do for some other purpose. One of the most important tasks for any society is to distinguish between ends and means-to-ends, and to have some sort of cohesive view and agreement about this. Is the land merely a means of production or is it something more, something that is an end in itself? And when I say "land," I

include the creatures upon it. . . . There is no escape from this confusion as long as the land and the creatures upon it are looked upon as *nothing but* "factors of production." They are, of course, factors of production, that is to say, means-to-ends, but this is their secondary, not their primary, nature. Before everything else, they are ends-in-themselves; they are meta-economic, and it is therefore rationally justifiable to say, as a statement of fact, that they are in a certain sense sacred.[23]

Here let me quickly bypass one difficulty, already indicated above. Once a society goes beyond a certain scale, it would find it very difficult to achieve the *consensus* which Schumacher deems essential. Such a consensus could only come from a real democracy, which is rendered impossible when certain dimensions of complexity, scope, and specialization are reached. But let us get to the core of Schumacher's argument.

While one may disagree with the terminology used by Schumacher, the point of his warning is clear enough: once we persuade ourselves that things are means, and nothing more than means, we begin to manipulate them in such a way that we end up destroying them.[24] And we end up destroying even the most essential means, the ones which are means needed for any end. On the terminological level I am not satisfied with Schumacher's notion that the land or earth is an "end-in-itself." But his basic point is clear enough: the earth is a means so vital to *all* human ends that we must be extremely cautious about its rational use. Such is always the case when we face things which we know will affect the ends we are pursuing in a direct and crucial way.

Now this argument is closely bound up with the *scale* of means, instruments, and manipulations that are part and parcel of industrial society. In past times the energy available to human beings did not permit them to seriously jeopardize the equilibrium of those universal means which, as such, would almost deserve to be characterized as ends. Today the situation has changed greatly for that sorcerer's apprentice known as *homo*. On many levels of existence, and particularly in the developed countries, human beings are being urgently summoned to correct the notion of "mere means" which they have been applying to contexts and complexes of extraordinary complexity and importance.

Let us get back to Schumacher's example, the use of land. Here the problem of *ecology* confronts us in crucial terms. Ecology tells us

that an environmental setting developed over millions of years must be considered to have some merit. Anything so complicated as a planet, inhabited by more than a million and a half species of plants and animals, all of them living together in a more or less balanced equilibrium in which they continuously use and re-use the same molecules of the soil and air, cannot be improved by aimless and uninformed tinkering. All changes in a complex mechanism involve some risk and should be undertaken only after careful study of all the facts available. Changes should be made on a *small scale* first so as to provide a test before they are widely applied. When information is incomplete, changes should stay close to the natural processes which have in their favor the indisputable evidence of having supported life for a very long time [my italics].[25]

Perhaps my readers may now see the fundamental unity of the topic I have been discussing. Once industrial production, be it capitalist or socialist, reaches certain dimensions, humanity enters a profound crisis. I began by pointing out that the calculations needed to increase such industrial production ruled out work as a vocation. It also worked against any form of democratic and representative government based on the decisions of the common people. I then went on to show that humanity was confronted with an ever-growing ethical crisis. Probing deeper, we saw that this crisis did not stem from using the principle that the end justifies the means. It stemmed instead from the fact that the scale of means employed made it impossible for us to decide exactly what ends they were really serving. The ability to compare the means with the end, and hence to decide whether they were in harmony or not, has somehow been slipping through our fingers.

II. The Problem of Means

The above reflections arose in the *developed* countries, of course, and only when people began to feel the devastating effects of that development. It is also clear that the vast majority of people in those countries are still hoping for some magical ecological formula which will enable them to go on enjoying the benefits of those resources at the expense of the rest of the planet. Our problems in Latin America are different in that respect, to be sure. But before I proceed to deal with Latin American problems in the next chapter, I want to explore and clarify something else in the issue discussed above. My hope is that it will serve as a better introduction to our own Latin American problematic, our own "death of ideologies."

That particular expression, in the context studied so far in this chapter, gives rise to two misunderstandings which must be cleared up. First of all, from the standpoint of my own terminology and the terminology in current use, it is important to realize that ideologies are not dying in the sense that they are disappearing or giving way to something else that is no longer ideological. It is not as if human beings no longer had anything to discuss in that area. At most the death of ideologies would mean that the classic ideologies, such as those of the political left and right, were being replaced by others which probed deeper and touched on more fundamental problems, whether they had a name of their own or not.

Second, I noted above that some people seek to turn the alleged death of ideologies into an ideological weapon. The intention of minimizing the alternative between capitalism and socialism was explicit in Aron's work, for example, with all its implicit conservative consequences. Hence it is all the more interesting to read what Schumacher has to say on this score. While he does attack both capitalist and socialist industrial society, he also points up the ideological danger of his argument. Capitalism, he feels, has little possibility of posing the problems of industrial society seriously and hence solving them. Socialism, on the other hand, is capable in principle of doing so:

> But it is also necessary to recognize that private ownership of the means of production is severely limited in its freedom of choice of objectives, because it is compelled to be profit-seeking, and *tends* to take a narrow and selfish view of things. Public ownership gives *complete* freedom in the choice of objectives and can therefore be used for any purpose that may be chosen. While private ownership is an instrument that by itself largely determines the ends for which it can be employed, public ownership is an instrument the ends of which *are undetermined and need to be consciously chosen* [my italics].[26]

Having jumped that hurdle, we may now examine where the arguments of the previous section are leading us. Recall my basic terminology, faith and ideology, and my stress on the complementarity of these two human dimensions. It should then be obvious that the arguments in the previous section of this chapter point up *both the necessity and the unsuspected complexity of the complementarity existing between faith and ideology*.

We discover at our own expense the dense complexity of reality. We run head on into the complexity that awaits us when we seek naively to place reality in the service of our values. At every turn reality seems to take its revenge on us when we, using great means, seek to make it dovetail with the meaning we wish to give to our individual and social life as human beings.

Science is not of much help to us here. Indeed science itself, with its potent and almost imperious technical applications to nature and society, is partially responsible for the problem we face. It is science that continually creates more and greater *means*, means whose dimensions undermine the equilibrium of the human groups who seek to use them for their own *ends*.

Machoveč: Socialist Eschatology and Socialist Means

Let us stop and focus on this precise point. As we all know, "advanced industrial society" arose in the liberal, capitalist culture of the West. Due to the very same cultural roots, however, the creators of a new model of social life, the socialist model, were insensitive or at least unwary in the face of the very same dangers. Thus large-scale manipulation of things and of human beings invaded a system which claimed to restore the universe to the human being and thus create a new human being.

Milan Machoveč uses the term "eschatology" to describe the latter claim or goal: i.e., the *end* of all the old to establish the *new* and definitive human being, world, and society:

> On the one hand, Marxism had "something to show" as it transformed a once backward agricultural country into a world power, and thus demonstrated that it was not simply "utopian." But there was another side to the question. Millions of men in these countries underwent painful human tragedies, ranging from judicial errors to the simplest sufferings caused by illness or human shipwreck because of unrequited love, failure, misunderstanding by one's comrades, etc., and in view of this one can and must correct certain "paradisiac" ideas which had been typical of the founding fathers and of the majority of pre-revolutionary socialists. Early socialism had the concept of a totally different, incomparably "other" future. It was thus "radically eschatological" and much closer in mentality to some of the prophetic figures of the biblical tradition than anyone in the nineteenth century, Marxist or Christian, was prepared to admit.[27]

But what results ensued from the *means* employed? Machoveč goes on to say:

> But it is very difficult to go on "waiting" with such intense concentration and in so "eschatological" a way fifty years *after* a Marxist revolution; and it is difficult to believe that the expropriation of private property, given the correction of a number of faults that happen to have been made *en route*, will eventually have such wonderful consequences as to bring about an "absolutely different" form of life and soon put within everyone's grasp all possible beauty and pleasure.[28]

The *means* in question, from which Marx may have expected too much, was "the expropriation of private property," as Machoveč puts it. But the dense complexity of human reality soon made clear that this powerful means of social engineering was not the open sesame to the gates of paradise.

Moreover, the Marxist goal was to effect a revolution in a complex social mechanism. Reducing that revolution almost exclusively to that *means* bears a certain resemblance to the manipulation on an excessive scale which seems to be part and parcel of industrial society. It would take no little dose of violence to begin to apply that means generally and then maintain it, however provisional and temporary people might imagine the use of violence. This dose of violence, some will say, was part of the calculation. However, Machoveč points out that this calculation did not take into account another kind of insidious and persistent violence. The latter goes on after the revolution, manifesting itself "ambiguously" in the countless self-interested ways in which people adhere to the installed system.[29]

In other words, the *assumption* was that any initial violence would end when the achieved values had demonstrated their effect. But the means, by virtue of its proportions, seems to go its own way in the whole process. An effort to alter the sphere of meaning and values is much more complicated, long-term, and increasingly expensive than is the continued use of an "apparatus" which "wins" adhesion by fear and convenience. It is here that "industrial society" fits like a glove. For it is a society which takes advantage of the vices of the old human being for the sake of the common good instead of achieving the latter through the creation of a new human being. Writes Machoveč:

> When in the final analysis it is lasting progress and systematic activity which are at stake, force ought to be only a momentary, a fringe form, not the principal form, of this activity, and it must later be replaced by other motivations which are compatible with humanism. Thus Marxists too begin to wonder whether the pacifism characteristic not only of the Sermon on the Mount but of Jesus' entire ministry could not be joined perfectly harmoniously to the most rigorous forms of Marxist commitment to progress.[30]

For the moment let us leave aside his reference to the religious aspect, which I shall examine later. The point I want to bring out here is that Machoveč is saying something akin to what Schumacher said about "the proper use of land" (see pages 258–59): some things must be shifted from the category of mere means to one closer to that of ends-in-themselves. In our case here, we are talking about the use of persons in the process of social engineering. That is why, says Machoveč, in socialist society "the moral factor will play an increasingly greater role as the years go by."[31] In other words, there will be an increasingly greater role for a type of knowledge concerned with the realm of life's meaning and meaningfulness.

Bateson: The Human Factor and the Need for Grace

I think we are seeing a necessary shift in emphasis today from the realm of means to the realm of ends, from the pole I have called "ideology" to the pole I have called "faith." If that is true, Gregory Bateson can be of special service to us, for he has devoted almost all of his scientific work to the elucidation of that very problem. And his work is of particular use to us because he did not focus so much on the external conditioning factor at work: the excessive magnitude of the *instruments* used. Instead Bateson focused on an explicitly anthropological factor, on the inner disposition of the human being. To be more specific, he focused on human perception and valuation of means and ends.[32]

For Bateson the central anthropological problem is that of *grace*. He was not a religious thinker in the traditional sense of the word, but in this matter he followed the thinking of Aldous Huxley, who was even less traditionally religious. As Bateson puts it:

Aldous Huxley used to say that the central problem for humanity is the quest for *grace*. This word he used in what he thought was the sense in which it is used in the New Testament. He explained the word, however, in his own terms. He argued—like Walt Whitman—that the communication and behavior of animals has a naiveté, a simplicity, which man has lost. Man's behavior is corrupted by deceit—even self-deceit—by purpose, and by self-consciousness. As Aldous saw the matter, man has lost the "grace" which animals still have.[33]

This line of thought may well strike us as a bit paradoxical. In order to link it up more easily with my terms, faith and ideology, let me continue Bateson's remarks:

> I shall argue that the problem of grace is fundamentally a problem of *integration* and that what is to be integrated is the diverse parts of the mind—especially those *multiple levels* of which one extreme is called "consciousness" and the other the "unconscious."[34] For the attainment of grace, the *reasons of the heart* must be integrated with the *reasons of the reason* [my italics].[35]

Recall Bateson's talk about partially self-validating premises. There he was obviously alluding to the reasons of the heart, the level which I call faith. It is the level of meaning and values, which cannot get some further rational explanation. By "reasons of the reason" in the above quote Bateson is obviously referring to premises that are rationally checked by experience, to the systems of efficacy which human beings recognize and use to achieve their "purposes." Now in a later section of the same paper Bateson discusses "the corrective nature of art." He says:

> The point . . . which I am trying to make in this paper is not an attack on medical science but a demonstration of an inevitable fact: that mere purposive rationality unaided by such phenomena as *art, religion, dream,* and the like, is necessarily *pathogenic* and destructive of life; and that its virulence springs specifically from the circumstance that life depends upon *interlocking circuits* of contingency, while consciousness can see only such *short arcs* of such circuits as human purpose may direct [my italics].[36]

Here I am not interested in reiterating or exploring criticisms which were analyzed earlier in this book. Instead I want to examine the epistemological alternative, the new way of knowing, which Bateson proposes as a complement or replacement for "purposive rationality." Note that the passage just cited above dealt with artistic knowledge, to which Bateson added the types of knowledge which derive from religion and dreams. We shall soon see why. In another article Bateson comments on a paper by his ex-wife, the noted anthropologist Margaret Mead. He felt that Margaret Mead had been able "to transcend the habits of thought current in her own culture." And he summarized her view as follows:

> Before we apply social science to our own national affairs, we must re-examine and change our habits of thought on the subject of means and ends. We have learnt, in our cultural setting, to classify behavior into "means" and "ends" and if we go on defining ends as separate from means *and* apply the social sciences as crudely instrumental means, using the recipes of science to manipulate people, we shall arrive at a totalitarian rather than a democratic system of life.

Bateson immediately adds his own comment here:

> The solution which she offers is that we look for the "directions" and "values" *implicit in the means*, rather than looking ahead to a blue-printed goal and thinking of this goal as justifying or not justifying manipulative means [my italics].[37]

Though Bateson's terminology is different, he is obviously dealing with the same epistemological problem that has occupied us in this chapter: i.e., establishing closer ties between the consideration of means, the more central means at least, and the whole realm of ends.[38] If we now ask Bateson to tell us what type of knowledge, what way of approaching reality, might serve as the basis for the attitude he is urging upon us, we find his answer couched once again in quasi-religious terms:

> We are now . . . in a position to examine Dr. Mead's proposal in some-what more concrete terms. She advises that when we apply the social sciences we look for "direction" and "value" in our very acts, rather than orient ourselves to some blueprinted goal. . . . She would be the first to disparage any suggestion that fear (even enjoyed fear) should be our basis for assigning value to our acts. Rather, as I understand it, that basis should be *some sort of hope*—not looking to some far-off future,[39] but still *some sort of hope or optimism*. . . . And I think that what Dr. Mead is urging us toward might be defined . . . as a habit of rote sequences *inspired by a thrilling sense of ever-imminent but undefined reward* [my italics].[40]

From this statement it is clear that when Bateson advocates the kinds of knowledge provided by art, religion, and dreams, it is the second kind that is fundamental; the other two serve as introduction or reinforcement.

What in fact does Bateson mean by *religion*, then? When he talks about a hope which avoids a total dissociation between ends and means, and hence the manipulation of the latter, he is implicitly but necessarily alluding to *transcendent data*, the first element we came across when defining or describing an anthropological faith that might be properly called "religious" as well.

With this *in mind*, let us go back to other views we met in this chapter. Remember how Schumacher talked about the proper use of land, and how we should avoid viewing it a "mere means." He pointed out that this was not just a technical or economic problem but a *metaphysical* one. Its solution, in other words, is not verifiable by experience. The secret, he suggested, was to consider certain global means as "in a certain sense *sacred*" (my italics; see p. 259). Here again we find a religious allusion. Metaphysics, as we saw, is a species of secular religion. And Schumacher's religious allusion might be viewed as a reference to crucial *transcendent data* in the realm of values-in-themselves, in which he wants us to include that "means" which is the earth and the creatures on it.

Machoveč, for his part, writes about the Christian conception of non-violence. In other words, he too writes about a *transcendent datum* conveyed by a religious tradition, about a value-in-itself which is crucial to the moral factor that "will play an increasingly greater role as the years go by" (see p. 263).

Now let us get back to Bateson and the hope or optimism which he feels will help us to choose and use means conducive to our ends. Let us try to explore his thinking more deeply, reviewing what we saw in Chapter IV in the process.

Remember that my term "faith" is synonymous with Bateson's "ontological and epistemological premises," which he views as "partially self-validating."[41] Ontological premises are self-validating because the value-in-itself, that which is not justified as a means for something higher, cannot be the result of a reasoning process validated by empirical reality. Indeed it is the source of lines of reasoning which enable us to judge reality and reconcile it with what we think it ought to be. These premises are also self-validating in another sense, as we saw in discussing Bateson. Curiously enough, perceived reality rarely checkmates them; instead it seems to confirm them. Thus the premises are not only ontological but also "epistemological." They are a sort of code we use to perceive and decipher reality in a certain way. Using that code, we interpret reality and find orientation in it. We recognize certain reiterated sequences even though the flow of events seems chaotic at first glance. Our premises function akin to a grammar. They divide or "punctuate" the flux of reality into meaningful segments or phrases.

We then asked how one ended up an optimist or a pessimist. The optimist, we saw, uses his or her ontological premises to identify what is good for him or her and then, *in addition*, punctuates events in such a way that the recognizable sequences always end with a happy or satisfying event. Even though the optimist may have the same ontological premises as the pessimist, the former puts the punctuation after the agreeable event and will be inclined to view the next sad event as the start of a new sequence that will also end happily. Even though pessimists may be seeking the same values, their "episte-mological" premises incline them to punctuate the sequence of events after something sad or disagreeable has occurred. Such is the differing "syntax" of optimist and pessimist, both of whom feel that "experience teaches" their lesson.

That brings us to an important question. If both optimist and pessimist are dealing with identical values and events, what crucial importance can there be in punctuating events one way or the other? Why does Bateson seem to stress optimism as of capital importance for an appropriate anthropological rela-tionship between means and ends?

Let us try to understand his point here. In varying degrees all of us human beings are seeking far-off ends or values. And we know that before we achieve them in any broadly satisfying way we will have to go through media-tions that will not always be agreeable. At the very least we can describe them as a curious mixture of pain and pleasure.

Here a relatively spontaneous tendency comes into play. Bateson would call it "unconscious" and talk about the "reasons of the heart." Our ten-dency is to choose means which bear at least some resemblance to the ends we have in mind, which have at least some minimal particle of the satisfaction we are expecting to find at the end of our journey or as we draw nearer to our goal. If we value friendship, for example, it is more likely that we will choose mediations based on friendship or friendliness. Now to the extent that expe-rience "seems" to offer us these little doses of satisfaction after we use means analogous to the ends we seek,[42] we will not be strongly tempted to make complicated rationalistic calculations about the possible effectiveness of means that "in themselves" are contrary to our goal: e.g., terrorism to obtain a just peace. We will not be inclined to carom to our goal by taking the opposite approach or direction first. To stick with our example of friendship: so long as friendly means seem to provide satisfaction, we will not be inclined to do serious harm to some person in secret so that we can then present our-selves as his or her savior and thus win his or her friendship.

Here is the value of learning to punctuate events in an optimistic manner. We may do so by natural disposition, after a process of learning or re-education, or through a process of cultural revolution (see Part Three, Sec-tion C further on). If we succeed in punctuating events in such a way that the use of means analogous to the ends brings satisfaction, or if we become op-timistic or hopeful in that direction, *we will give a more important place to the reasons of the heart in the discernment of means.* And remember that the heart can only appreciate the analogy of means to end through satisfac-tion.

What happens in the case of the pessimist? Punctuating the sequence of events in just the opposite way, pessimists get used to the idea that "expe-rience" almost systematically gives the lie to the satisfaction that might be expected from the analogy or likeness of means to end. *To that same extent pessimists will tend to rely on calculating, manipulative reason to discover more efficacious means, even though the latter may not bear any likeness to the goal.*

I think this little example makes the point clearly enough, but I would like to add one more. It is human labor or work, and in fact Schumacher has much to say about that in *Small Is Beautiful*. Let me combine his ideas with Bateson here. Let us say that it makes a big difference whether workers make a whole product or just some part of it. Let us say that they will be more or less "optimists" or "pessimists" depending on which they do. In the first case (making a whole product), workers will tend to picture the end of their work, to punctuate events, in terms of a finished object. And along with that will go an appreciation of its form and characteristics; an assurance about its usefulness; pride in the craftsmanship which produced it; a feeling for all the interpersonal relations involved among fellow workers, bosses, and clients; and so forth. In the second case (making some part of a product), and assuming the same basic working conditions, workers will tend to picture their work in terms of weariness, monotony, bossism, etc.

To bring in Bateson's ideas here, let us say that in the second case there will be an *increased* tendency towards "rational" manipulation. Workers will be interested in their work ending—not by some *result* or product being completed but simply by work being *called to a halt*. Thus work-as-means will be much more dissociated from any satisfaction. The start of satisfaction will come when one has one's paycheck in hand and leisure time to spend it. The relationship between activity and satisfaction will be set by the "reasons of the reason," not by the "reasons of the heart."

Here we see surfacing the great anthropological danger noted by Margaret Mead and Gregory Bateson. It is the danger of establishing means which have no likeness to the ends and of doing this with "reasons" which embrace only "short arcs" of the "interlocking circuits" of reality (see p. 264 above). The conditioning influence of "industrial society" simply augments the scope and the potential danger of such "rational" means or arcs.

Note that I speak of a "danger."[43] The fact is that no human being can avoid using means unrelated or even opposed to his or her goals on countless occasions. Consider our "optimistic" worker, for example. He or she may sometimes have to work in ill health, or for a salary that does not cover basic needs. During such a period he or she will probably lose the ability to see "analogies" between the means and ends of work. Only reason will be able to link the two. Or think of someone interested in achieving general social peace. He or she will have to *fight* against those whose interests are opposed to the establishment of such peace. And if "fighting" means anything at all, it means doing harm to one's adversary in the short run—enough harm to stop that adversary from opposing peace. Until that is achieved, the *only means* to the goal will have been the one which is least analogous to the goal itself.[44]

What, then, goes on in the case of Bateson's "optimist" or "hopeful" person? Recall Machoveč's discouraged comment about force, which was to be "only a momentary, a fringe form" (see p. 263), becoming permanent. Well, if what we have said so far makes sense, then hope will prompt the optimist to use means different from the ends only when there is no other recourse. Logically, thanks to the "reasons of the heart," the optimist will be alert and ready to change those means as soon as they are no longer necessary.[45]

The Possibility of Nurturing Hope and Optimism

And so we come to the big question: Is it possible to *educate* people in that sort of "optimism" or "hope"? Does there exist a psychological therapy, an educational method, a set of spiritual exercises, or a cultural revolution which, on their respective planes, will furnish the *transcendent data* that form the basis for such an attitude and differentiate it from the opposite attitude?

We have already seen that this state of "grace" cannot derive from rationally controlled or verified experience. The course is just the opposite, as Bateson points out. Without saying so explicitly, Machoveč sought those transcendent data, so basic to his hope and the hope of thousands more, in the Judeo-Christian or biblical tradition: the Psalms, the passion and resurrection of Jesus, etc.[46] And Schumacher looked to the religious tradition of Buddhism to find principles of hope and optimism that would narrow the distance between means and ends.[47]

To go back to Bateson, he is content "to mention some of the factors which may act as correctives—areas of human action which are not limited by the narrow distortions of coupling through conscious purpose and where wisdom can obtain." He specifies four basic ones:

> *a*. Of these, undoubtedly the most important is love. . . .
>
> *b*. The arts, poetry, music, and the humanities similarly are areas in which more of the mind is active than mere consciousness would admit. . . .
>
> *c*. Contact between man and animals and between man and the natural world. . . .
>
> *d*. There is religion.[48]

From the anthropological standpoint, and from what has been said above, it is easy to see the *common* elements in those four factors. However, from a sociopolitical standpoint, from the standpoint of some possible global reeducation of hope in the use of means and ends, there is a *difference* between the fourth factor and the other three. That difference has not escaped Machoveč or Schumacher. The "wisdom" that may come from the first three factors depends on a venture which begins from scratch with each generation. The fourth area, religion, is constituted by a *tradition*. To put the latter point another way, a certain memory of the human species traverses generations and communicates, through interconnected referential witnesses, something that is simultaneously the transcendent data and the human experiences in which they were found.[49]

Further on we shall examine the fourth factor a bit more closely. Here I simply want to offer a brief summary of this chapter. We have been considering the anthropological problem highlighted by the so-called "death of ideologies" in the developed countries. That led us to examine the relationship between means and ends, and we found it to be much more complicated than it might seem at first glance. The solutions suggested by various people have clearly pointed us in the direction of those elements of anthropological faith which shape a "religious faith" in the stricter sense of the term.

NOTES

1. That trunk could be called "Western" or "European" and "Christian" if we are careful to add that no value-judgment (not even a religious one) is implied. It is simply a general indication of overall historical and cultural origins. But even then it is not a pure origin, as the Renaissance period suggests, for links were also forged with pre-Christian classical culture.

2. Franz Hinkelammert, *Ideologías del desarrollo y dialéctica de la historia* (Buenos Aires: Nueva Universidad/Paidós, 1970), p. 24. It is obvious that there is a *transcendent datum* in this "faith": "The mathematical model is *metaphysical*, and methodologically it is what Kant calls a *transcendental* ideal or thing-in-itself. As a naive concept, on the other hand, it is a *myth*" (my italics; ibid., p. 25). Note the convergence of terms coming from "religion" ("myth") and from "religion brought into thought" ("metaphysical" and "transcendental").

3. Marx and Engels, *The German Ideology*, Eng. trans. (New York: International Publishers, 1970), p. 53.

4. On the anti-institutional nature of this regulation of production and the basic question it raises, see the dialogue in Leonov's *Doroga na Okean*, cited in Note 17 of Chapter IV, pp. 114–15, above.

5. See the following passage in *Capital* by the mature Marx: "Let us finally imagine, for a change, an association of free men, working with the means of production held in common, and expending their many different forms of labour-power in full self-awareness as one single social labour force. All the characteristics of Robinson's labour are repeated here, but with the difference that they are social instead of individual. All Robinson's products were exclusively the result of his own personal labour and they were therefore directly objects of utility for him personally. The total product of our imagined association is a social product. . . . The social relations of the individual producers, both towards their labour and the products of their labour, are here transparent in their simplicity, in production as well as in distribution" (*Capital*, Volume One, Book I, Chapter 1, Section 4; Eng. trans. [New York: Vintage Books, 1977], pp. 171–72).

Robinson Crusoe, shed of his solitude, was the symbol of a man related intimately and freely (to some extent, of course) with his work in the liberalist outlook. Yet despite Marx's criticism of the "robinsonades" of his adversaries, the anti-institutional ideal of a Robinson Crusoe remained a key element in Marx's system.

6. Hence Hinkelammert rightly reiterates here what he had to say about liberal-

ism: "The goal of total revolution and communism is revealed to be a limit-concept or a transcendental idea in the sense of Kant's thing-in-itself" (*Ideologías del desarrollo*, p. 78). As in the first case, we could also say that as a theoretical formulation it is a *metaphysical* principle, and that as a naive concept it is a *myth*. In short, it is a *transcendent datum*.

7. Raymond Aron, *Dix-huit leçons sur la société industrielle* (Paris: Gallimard, 1962), pp. 49–50.

8. Paradoxical as it may seem, the anti-institutional and hence anti-industrial character of liberal capitalism continues to exert more influence than people tend to think. Hence the "robinsonades" mentioned above: i.e., the ideal image that each individual is to be a Robinson Crusoe, i.e., a nonindustrial producer by definition.

9. See for example Karl Marx, *The Poverty of Philosophy*, Chapter II, Eng. trans. (New York: International Publishers, 1963), pp. 103–75.

10. In *Capital* (Volume III, Chapter XLVIII), Marx himself seems to go against his model of communist society and allow for something much more modest. Contrary to his revolutionary forecasts, the following would not go beyond reformism applied to capitalist society: "Freedom in this field can only consist in socialised man, the associated producers, rationally regulating their interchange with Nature, bringing it under their common control, instead of being ruled by it as by the blind forces of Nature; and achieving this with the least expenditure of energy and under conditions most favourable to, and worthy of, their human nature. But it nonetheless still remains a realm of necessity. Beyond it begins that development of human energy which is an end in itself, the true realm of freedom, which, however, can blossom forth only with this realm of necessity as its basis. The shortening of the working-day is its basic prerequisite" (Eng. trans., [New York: International Publishers, 1967], p. 820).

11. We will consider the fundamental flaw in this argument further on in this chapter (see p. 261). But that does not mean it does not conceal a deeper, underlying problem.

12. Aron, *Dix-huit leçons*, pp. 123–24. Also see the passage from Keynes cited below in Note 31 of this chapter.

13. Aron, *Dix-huit leçons*, pp. 88–89

14. Ortega y Gasset offered this observation: "If we observe the public life of countries where the triumph of the masses has made most advance . . . we are surprised to find that politically they are living from day to day. . . . Public authority . . . exists from hand to mouth. . . . Its activities are reduced to dodging the difficulties of the hour; not solving them, but escaping from them for the time being, employing any methods whatsoever, even at the cost of accumulating thereby still greater difficulties for the hour which follows" (*The Revolt of the Masses*, Eng. trans. [New York: W. W. Norton, 1932], p. 13).

15. Only small-scale countries, and ones determined to keep curbs on advanced industrial society, such as Switzerland, manage to escape this antidemocratic tendency to some extent.

16. Aron, *Dix-huit leçons*, pp. 88–89. Except that there is reason to doubt this "wisdom" of government authorities. Indeed insofar as the relationship between industrial society and democracy is concerned, there is another element which deserves our special attention in Latin America. A progressively industrialized society is also an ever increasingly militarized society. First, because of its growing vulnerability insofar as individual citizens have at their disposal instruments of increasingly greater power. Second, because it is so easy and convenient to pass from civilian industry to the weapons industry. Third, because of the need to maintain more and more controls

over what are regarded as vital industrial secrets; thus there is a temptation to use the inherent power of the whole industrial complex for repression (see Aron, ibid., p. 90).

17. Adam Schaff, *La filosofía del hombre*, Spanish trans. (Buenos Aires: Lautaro, 1964), p. 96. The most powerful, though tendentious, literary characterization of this problem is to be found in Arthur Koestler's *Darkness at Noon*. The novel's main character is immersed in this kind of conflict when he is judged by the kind of human being which he, as a revolutionary, declared necessary and helped to shape: " 'You brute,' he thought again. 'Yet it is just such a generation of brutes that we need now' " (Eng. trans., [New York: Macmillan, 1941], p. 187).

18. "Careful analysis will reveal that there are two major types of problems worthy of special attention: (a) personal responsibility for one's actions, in the political arena as well, and particularly in situations which entail the clash of differing moral principles; (b) the position and role of the individual in the world, a question vaguely described as having to do with problems concerning the 'meaning of life.' The two groups of problems are part of a broadly conceived science of morality. Unfortunately, however, they did not occupy any place in the traditional development of Marxist ethics" (Schaff, *La filosofía del hombre*, p. 32).

19. Despite his sympathy with Marxism, Marcuse himself recognizes this. By the same token, the intrinsic relationship between democracy and ethics is facing a crisis in formally democratic societies. After all, what can the ethics of individuals say and do in a marketplace dominated to a large extent by multinational companies? On this problem see Richard Barnet and Richard Muller, eds., *Global Reach* (New York: Simon & Schuster, 1974), especially Part I.

20. See J. L. Segundo, *The Liberation of Theology*, Eng. trans. (Maryknoll, N.Y.: Orbis Books, 1976), Chapter VI, pp. 170f.

21. For Adam Schaff, a religious morality is synonymous with a heteronomous morality dictated from outside: "Once again we must first distinguish the secular viewpoint from the religious viewpoint. Besides being different, they correspond to two totally different mental habits. If we accept the thesis of faith, here again we can solve the question in a simple and 'easy' way: people are exempted from the necessity of thinking because they are obligated to observe heteronomous norms dictated from outside themselves by God; they owe obedience to those norms. The latter assign only one end to the human being: to live worthily. In short, they inform him or her of the meaning of life within the context that concerns us here. And with that the question is closed. No problem remains except the exegesis of the divine norms which are the product of revelation. And that exegesis seeks better understanding of the norms enunciated in it" (Schaff, *La filosofía del hombre*, p. 76).

22. Here I shall disregard one case which is much clearer, the case where one applies the designation "end" to an intermediate value which is, in turn, a means to another "higher" end. We can readily imagine that the means justified by the secondary end could be opposed to the principal end. The internal equilibrium of a family can be an end, ordained in turn to something larger such as the solidarity of a whole society. The means justified by the former end could obviously be fatal to the achievement of the latter end. That does not prove that the end does not justify the means, however. It merely proves that we must include in our dictum a *scale* of values, a *hierarchy* of ends.

23. E. F. Schumacher, *Small Is Beautiful: Economics as if People Mattered* (New York: Harper & Row/Perennial Library, 1975), pp. 104-7.

24. It is also practically inevitable that we will simultaneously and for the same

necessities plan for gigantic means of production and gigantic means of destruction (of our enemy). As an example, here is a comment taken at random from the West German press concerning the neutron bomb: "To those who are mainly concerned about matters of defense and *reject sentimentality and emotionalism*, the statements of the majority of parliament during the recent debate on defense policy are logical. . . . The federal ministry of defense furnished the defense committee with objective and convincing material concerning technical, military, strategic, and political matters. It was also able to demonstrate that if some such device was not approved, Western strategy would run a grave risk in the future. Everyone knows that the new weapon is 'inhuman.' The response of the minister of defense was: *'There are no humane weapons'* " (Excerpts from the *Stuttgarter Nachrichten*, September 10, 1977; Spanish trans. in the *Tribuna Alemana*, September 18, 1977).

The italics in the last quoted phrase are mine. Note that the remark seems to overlook the fact that the humaneness or inhumaneness of weapons depends, at least to a large extent, on their destructive capabilities.

25. Ralph and Mildred Buchsbaum, *Basic Ecology* (Pacific Grove, Calif.: Boxwood, 1957); cited by Schumacher, *Small Is Beautiful*, pp. 134–35.

26. Schumacher, *Small Is Beautiful*, p. 259.

27. Milan Machoveč, *A Marxist Looks at Jesus*, Eng. trans. (Philadelphia: Fortress Press, 1976), p. 26.

28. Ibid., pp. 26–27. There is, I think, a weak point in the parallel analysis of Adam Schaff, which should arrive at the same conclusions. It is the fact that Schaff does not seem to sense any flaw in the *social* dimension of the construction of socialism. However, he does feel keenly the fact that the *whole* human problematic is not on its way to a solution in socialism. There remains *the problems of the individual*. It is no accident that his later efforts focus on the integration of Marxism and *existentialism* (see his *La filosofía del hombre*), and that his most profound work is *Marxism and the Human Individual*, Eng. trans. (New York: McGraw-Hill, 1969).

29. Machoveč, *A Marxist Looks at Jesus*, pp. 28–29.

30. Ibid., p. 33.

31. Ibid., p. 28. Otherwise we could apply to it what Keynes once said (see Schumacher, *Small Is Beautiful*, p. 100): "For at least another hundred years we must pretend to ourselves and to every one that fair is foul and foul is fair; for foul is useful and fair is not. Avarice and usury and precaution must be our gods for a little longer still."

Keynes is talking about liberal capitalism. It would be generalized by various anthropological mechanisms triggered by the use of certain *means* in the building of socialism as well.

32. See Gregory Bateson, *Steps to an Ecology of Mind* (New York: Ballantine Books, 1972). The very title of his work indicates his intention to trace the external ecological problem back to its mental source. See Parts V and VI of the book: "Epistemology and Ecology" and "Crises in the Ecology of Mind."

33. Ibid., p. 128.

34. Means and ends are not separated in the unconscious. That is why Bateson regards the unconscious as usually "wiser" than consciousness. Of its very nature the unconscious is immune to the infirmity which Bateson, talking about Job, calls "purposiveness" (*Steps*, p. 447).

35. Ibid., p. 129.

36. Ibid., p. 146. Bateson proceeds to offer two examples. One is prehuman: the

armaments race of the dinosaurs, which wiped them off the face of the earth. The other is of more recent history: the use of DDT with its terrible ecological consequences. Then he offers this conclusion: "That is the sort of world we live in—a world of circuit structures—and love can survive only if wisdom (i.e., a sense or recognition of the fact of circuitry) has an effective voice" (*Steps*, p. 146).

37. Bateson, *Steps*, p. 160. The article of Margaret Mead's on which Bateson comments specifically contains the following passage noted by Bateson: "Those students who have devoted themselves to studying cultures as wholes, as systems of dynamic equilibrium, can make the following contributions: . . . (4) Implement plans for altering our present culture by recognizing the importance of including the social scientist *within* his experimental material, and by recognizing that by working toward defined *ends* we commit ourselves to the manipulation of persons, and therefore to the negation of democracy. Only by working in terms of values which are limited to defining a *direction* is it possible for us to use scientific methods in the control of the process without the negation of the moral autonomy of the human spirit" (Bateson, *Steps*, p. 159).

38. An example offered by Bateson confirms this: "But in social manipulation our tools are people, and people learn, and they acquire habits which are more subtle and pervasive than the tricks which the blueprinter teaches them. With the best intentions in the world, he may train children to spy upon their parents in order to eradicate some tendency prejudicial to the success of his blueprint, but because the children are people they will do more than learn this simple trick—they will build this experience into their whole philosophy of life; it will color all their future attitudes toward authority. Whenever they meet certain sorts of context, they will tend to see these contexts as structured on an earlier familiar pattern. The blueprinter may derive an initial advantage from the children's tricks; but the ultimate success of his blueprint may be destroyed by the habits of mind which were learned with the trick" (*Steps*, pp. 163–64).

39. If the hope is rendered *far-off*, that will again introduce a dissociation between the means and satisfaction, which is precisely what we are trying to avoid here.

40. Bateson, *Steps*, p. 175.

41. See Chapter IV, p. 91f., above.

42. In Bateson's scientific terminology, this is what is called "instrumental reward" (*Steps*, p. 175). We could define a pessimist as one whose "epistemological" premises do not permit him or her to experience "instrumental rewards." Since those rewards are a weighty factor in human conduct, their absence would also substantially alter that conduct.

43. This problem and its relationship to Freud's psychoanalysis was the subject of Herbert Marcuse's great work entitled *Eros and Civilization* (Boston: Beacon Press, 1955). But as far back as Marx himself, we have his comments on commodity *fetishism* and its concomitant human alienation, which dovetail with our analysis. The main difference is that Marx focuses on the conditioning which stems from the social structure. That is why Marx, seeking to destroy the conditioning, also envisioned the quick and inevitable destruction of the conditioned as well. However, when I say that the viewpoints of Bateson and Marcuse are anthropological, I do not mean to suggest that they are individualistic in orientation. They cover human relations with nature, other human beings, and society.

44. In estimating the harm one may be willing to cause an opponent in the immediate present, one must of course make a crucial comparison between it and the importance and complexity of one's goal. It is in making that estimate that the attitude

studied by Bateson comes into play. But that does not do away with the fact that we must frequently use means opposed to our ends in the short run, and that those means must therefore be justified rationally in terms of the goodness and importance of our ends.

45. That is the only sense there can be in Jesus' summons to *gratuitous* love—or nonviolent love, if you will, though the latter term is ambiguous. See Luke 6:27–35, with its triple allusion to the notion of grace or gratuitousness, which is a key notion for Bateson and Huxley. Jesus himself does not demand that people give up all violent means once and for all (See Segundo, *The Liberation of Theology*, pp. 154f.). Instead he asks that they begin to feel and experience the satisfaction of gratuitous action, to learn that "it is more blessed to give than to receive" (Acts 20:35).

46. Only in this way can we understand why he writes as follows: "However—and here the Christian suspects that we are reaching the heart of the matter—if thousands and hundreds of thousands of sincere socialists and Marxist intellectuals and even 'apparatchiks' should have so frequently and painfully lived through such experiences, then it is obvious that such men will no longer believe eschatologically that a 'wholly different' life is just round the next corner. Their experience will make them appreciate certain situations which are described in the Bible and which centre on the figure of Jesus. The European Marxist of the twentieth century can find no models or clear indications in earlier Marxism either for *spiritual aspirations* in a sated consumer society or for the trampling on human dignity in the world of industry or for the painful moral conflicts already mentioned or for the better understanding of *other* intellectual *traditions* and their *way to humanity and fulfillment*. The situation impels the Marxist to take a fresh look at other positions. Although this does not mean that he is on the point of becoming a Christian, it would be difficult for him to *ignore the fact that the Judaeo-Christian tradition has been concerned with these problems and contributed certain models towards their solution* [my italics] (Machoveč, *A Marxist Looks at Jesus*, p. 29).

My only query would be: What does Machoveč mean by the phrase, "becoming a Christian"? Does he mean it in one of those distorted senses which cause so much confusion in our culture and which I have been trying to clear up and rectify in my own work?

47. One whole chapter, and one of the best, is entitled: "Buddhist Economics" (*Small Is Beautiful*, pp. 53–62). Schumacher also offers an interesting *economic* "translation" of the Gospel Beatitudes (ibid., pp. 156–57).

48. Bateson, *Steps*, pp. 446–47.

49. Art might seem to bear some resemblance to the tradition of religious faith. In art, however, there is a much greater distance between the tradition of artistic *instruments* and *procedures* on the one hand and the esthetic satisfaction in contemplating *masterpieces* on the other. With the possible exception of poetry, the latter masterpieces do not often express the concrete life-context in which they arose. Reducing all those *distances* is basic to the goal Bateson seeks. And the fact is that authentic religious faith (as I defined it in Chapter III) reduces those distances to a minimum for the sake of "instrumental rewards."

CHAPTER XI

Means and Ends:
Our Latin America

As I noted already, a very different situation was experienced by Latin Americans in the quarter of a century from 1950 to 1975. The situation itself affected everyone in Latin America, but here I want to pay particular attention to the young people of Latin America because their human adventure was centered in this period.

My hope is that the anthropological elements already studied in this book, even when they relate to situations different from ours, will have a little or even much to offer the youth of Latin America. And when they are combined with the remarks which follow in these last three chapters, I hope they will serve as a rough sketch or approximation of a Latin American anthropology. Specifically, I hope they will suggest ways in which we can truly live our present and make it better.

By way of introduction I would suggest that human beings in Latin America lived through three successive crises in the period under study here (1950–1975). It was an intense and wide-ranging experience, and the common denominator in the crises might well be described as desperation or despair. In the first stage desperation surfaced and grew, in the second stage it led to desperate actions, and in the third stage it gave way to despairing passivity.

Latin America is a mosaic of differing realities, of course, and some areas contrast sharply with others. So the crises did not everywhere have the same shape, the same rhythm, the same content, or the same intensity. A handful of Latin American countries seemed to be atypical or to constitute exceptions to the general rule. Besides this geographical differentiation, there were also differences in the magnitude of the crises and the human depths which they plumbed.

One question which might be raised here is: did the situation affect only a small minority of the people, those who were more clear-eyed, idealistic, and impatient? My hypothesis, which I hope to substantiate in this chapter, is this: although the effects were always more visible in that particular minority, the anthropological factors brought into play reached the vast majority of our young people; through them, with the passage of time, those factors also touched the adult population and the whole society.

A continentwide phenomenon of the sort under study here presents itself as a political phenomenon at first glance, but that is not my focus here. I am interested in it as an anthropological phenomenon. By that I do not mean to make it a private matter or to depoliticize it. Rather, I mean to go to its roots and take its true and complete measure.

Despair—lack of hope, if you prefer a less dramatic term—is not simply a state of mind or heart. As we just saw in the previous chapter, it is an "epistemological premise" which is "partially self-validating." And it is the direct opposite of the personal experiencing of an "instrumental reward," which Bateson tells us should be almost a rote experience. Now since the human being is a political creature, that premise will serve as the basis for manipulating typically political means in certain ways. It will serve as the basis for attitudes which, if what we have already seen is correct, would be incomprehensible to us if we chose to analyze them solely in terms of their political rationale.

I. The Period of Consciousness-Raising

In 1950 it was no secret to anyone that the vast majority of Latin American countries, if not all of them, were an underdeveloped world from the economic standpoint. One could debate endlessly about what constituted development and what criteria enabled us to recognize it, but it was obvious that no such criteria were to be found in our Latin American countries.

Countless theories of development and concomitant strategies were formulated, and some even got to the initial stage of implementation. There was an avid search, first in theory and then in practice, for the take-off point. Once that economic take-off point was reached, it was claimed, backward countries could eventually catch up if they pushed ahead at a steady clip. There was talk about all sorts of steps: industrialization; the mental and technical modernization of backward sectors; a Latin American common market; the massive infusion of capital, from the multinationals in particular; and agrarian reform entailing both technological modernization and more profitable distribution of property.

There is no point in recounting the history of those theories and efforts, nor the story of their successive failures. The thing I want to point up here is the movement of growing awareness which, for obvious reasons, was concentrated among university students at first. They constituted an intellectual elite. Not yet forcibly integrated into the system, in most Latin American countries they enjoyed university autonomy vis-à-vis government pressure and government activity. It was they who would shift the whole debate on development from the economic to the political arena. Here their role was much greater than that of workers themselves, even though the latter directly suffered the consequences of the economic process and the failures of various developmentalist policies, and even though they were often members of powerful labor organizations.

The Lie and the Growth of Suspicion

In my opinion, the chief object of this growing consciousness was not injustice itself. It was something on a level which could already be called anthropological: i.e., *the lie*. The first discovery was an intellectual one, so to speak, with all the ambiguity entailed. And in most cases the discovery provoked *suspicion* rather than indignation.

In the vast majority of Latin American countries, domestic injustice was too obvious to be camouflaged or silenced. Moreover, there were constant references to it in political life. What people now began to suspect and discover was the lie which surrounded and perpetuated the injustice, even in circles quite unselfishly seeking to eradicate that injustice.

The discovery in question affected first intellectual circles and then the most varied circles among the populace: members of labor unions, professional people, politicians, church personnel, and so forth. Gradually they came to notice that all the magical formulas for development, which supposedly would put an end to the more basic injustice, were running up against the *structural*, *systematic* character of that injustice.[1] So they began to think that the planners, who could not possibly be unaware of those conditioning factors, were either very stupid themselves or, much more likely, were setting traps for numbskulls.

This awareness of a systematic lie began to spread and become general. It was not the monopoly of any one ideology, though some were more inclined or prepared for such a discovery.

People perceived that transformative political activity was confined to a very, very narrow margin of operation. Of this there could be no doubt. It would have to stay within those narrow limits if it did not wish to clash, at its own expense, with the rules of foreign trade; with the credit-granting powers; with the affluence and permanence of private sources of capital; with multinational producers or middlemen; and, beyond the economic sector, with barefaced political and military intervention in one form or another. After the Cuban missile crisis especially, Latin America had lost any real chance of dickering with the two dominant international blocs.[2]

Two important observations will help to dispel a tenacious misunderstanding about this new and growing awareness of insurmountable structural obstacles to development and the elimination of injustice in Latin America. That misunderstanding, by the way, was often conveyed and utilized with deliberate intent.

Mass Movements and Third-Way Approaches

The *first* observation has to do with the scope of the "awareness" I am talking about. I said that it began to take a clearly formulated shape, and I traced its source back to university circles. However, *that does not mean I am attributing the role of political vanguard to that intellectual minority*. The fact is that in the period under review there already existed large popular movements which were fighting against the unjust structures of society in one way or another, even though they may have been less clear about the systemic character of the problem.

In some countries there obviously existed a politics of the left, associated more or less closely with Marxism and its theoretical systemization. It naturally organized popular movements or political parties, and its "doctrine" naturally stressed the structural character of the problem no matter what the degree of awareness may have been on the grass-roots level.

Here I am interested in a much broader phenomenon, however. When did the new awareness become a major fact embracing practically the whole Latin American continent? It did so during the period under study *once* broad popular movements became interested in some alleged approach to development that would avoid the reefs of the older disjunction: capitalism *or* socialism. One way to avoid the old alternative, at least in theory, was to make a political search for some *third-way approach*. Openly proclaimed as such, it was to be an alternative to the two opposed systems. The political movements which arose out of this search got their chance. At some point they came to power in most of the countries of Latin America.

These "third-way" movements took two or three main forms. One form, the vaguest in terms of political doctrine but the most strongly supported by the common people, was represented by Peronism in Argentina and similar contemporary movements in Colombia and other parts of Latin America. A second form, more structured politically and intellectually, was represented by Christian Democracy, particularly in Chile and Venezuela. The third form resembled the first insofar as it arose out of a military revolution. Its most clear representative in recent years is the government of Peru. It differs from Peronism most clearly in the fact that government power has remained with the original military organization. Supposedly "of the people," power has not passed to grass-roots political movements of a popular character. Military rule is regarded as a surer defense against domestic and foreign pressures.

The vicissitudes of these "third-way"[3] governments might well have induced many people to think that these regimes could constitute a valid alternative if their course were not interrupted in one way or another. It is here where the new consciousness or awareness intervened in a decisive way. It made it clear that all of these well-intentioned and enthusiastic initiatives fell prey to an ironclad system which they were unwilling or unable to replace, however good they might seem on the surface. The new awareness made clear that halfhearted capitalism is not possible in today's world, at least not on the impoverished periphery of the great international economic powers.

Once the industrial revolution began, capital began to impoverish the domestic proletariat in an impersonal way through the ground rules of the market economy. This went on until political and/or economic impoverishment threatened the very existence of capital or its profits. Much the same thing is being done by the nations which now act out the role of capital in the international market. Using the rules of the international market for their own benefit, those countries are now impoverishing the poor countries on the periphery of the system. The latter serve as a foreign or external proletariat. And the former countries will keep doing this so long as they do not see economic or political danger to themselves.

To be sure, isolated (and ineffective) forms of development may show up here and there. For example, industrial complexes may be moved to countries where cheap manual labor reduces the cost of their products and hence enhances their competitiveness. Some people might naively imagine that the government of the cheap-labor countries could step in and do something at that point. If those governments are truly interested in development, they could presumably increase their national product and also fashion a better tax system to distribute the national product more equitably through their society. Why is such a view naive? First, because it assumes that the tax system can be freely controlled by the government. It is through tax concessions and tax breaks that capital is attracted to the country and kept there. Then there is a more long-term problem. The growth and more equitable distribution of the national product will eliminate the advantage which attracts industrial capital to the periphery and induces it to risk settlement there: i.e., the cheapness of manual labor.

More important still is the fact that the international capital market is definitely not apolitical. When a substantial source of capital moves from one country to another, it does not do so without forming political forces of its own. Those forces are supported economically by the foreign capital interests. In turn, they give the latter the strong arm it needs to discourage temptations to nationalization, sabotage, effective domestic control, excessive taxation, and so forth.

That is just one example of the whole process. The point here is that the door was closed to any and all third-way approaches in Latin America, just as it had been closed earlier to those countries who wanted to practice some brand of "orthodox" capitalism.

Structural Failure as a Fact

My *second* observation is not unconnected with what we have just seen: this *structural* failure or collapse on the road to development is not a "theory," as is often presumed;[4] still less is it a Marxist dogma, though it is often depicted as such by all those who attack the new awareness for one reason or another. In the course of numerous initiatives over a twenty-five-year period, everyone had an opportunity to realize that the truth was much simpler. Structural failure was much more than a theory of oppression or imperialism; it was a *fact*.

The developed countries themselves are the first to realize this full well. Otherwise, why is there so much talk in the non-Marxist West about the creation of a *new* international economic *order?* What is North-South dialogue all about? Let me cite one random passage from a recent article in the West German press, which hardly was inspired by communist Marxism:

> The core of the Genscher plan, the German model for a *new order* in regulating the world economy, is economic growth. Without growth it will be impossible to overcome the North-South conflict. To overcome that conflict, there must be stable growth. In other words, growth must be stabilized in the industrialized countries, because only in that way can we get a *disproportionately* higher growth in the developing countries. That economic growth in the Third World is to *accelerate far more than it will in the developed countries* is an important *concession* to the developing nations. . . . But *the Third World will harbor doubts* as to whether the ruling forces in the world economy will *ever* permit them equal opportunity [my italics].[5]

So after more than twenty-five years we still have this legitimate doubt, and we still have an admitted need for a new international order. Only the latter, it is said, can clear the way for development in the poor countries of the capitalist area, which would include the countries of Latin America. All this merely proves, if proof were necessary, that the situation described above is a plain and simple fact, not the theoretical formulation of people who hold a particular ideology.

Everyone knows that the Marxist ideology applied its scheme of interpretation to our situation from the very beginning; that was perfectly logical. It foresaw and tried to explain the facts. Nor should it surprise anyone that the Marxist view would be influential in spreading awareness of the systematic nature of the problem, which is now universally admitted. But a fact is a fact, no matter who points it out. And the fact is that every possible political approach to development has been tried over the past twenty-five years, and that at the end of that time—a whole human generation—we are farther away from the goal than when we started. This fact has enormous anthropological significance. Since it is not noticed by everyone, I think it deserves our attention and study here.

In line with what we saw in the previous chapter, there has been a growing accumulation of frustration in all those sectors of the population which do not profit from underdevelopment and which advocate political activity in favor of any people caught in an inhuman situation.

The word "accumulation" here is not meant as a mere metaphor. I am talking about a sense of frustration that has grown and turned into a *premise*. As everyone knows, the lines of communication on our continent have grown increasingly closer. Every major political project is known and lived beyond its own specific area of application, and every "model" is expected to do something more than solve the problems of one single country. By the same token, every failure has wide repercussions and is added on to the sum of previous failures.

To put the matter in Bateson's terms, I would say that our Latin American experience of life and political activity over the past twenty-five years has led to a growing *emotional dissociation of means and ends*. Hence it has led to an increasingly disaffected rationality when it comes to justifying the means by the ends. Politics has been increasingly stripped of any "instrumental reward" in the form of human values. Less and less do we feel any "ever-imminent but undefined" hope that we are building something worthwhile. Horizons were closed off, silencing the "reasons of the heart" in many people and unleashing the unbalanced "reasons of the reason." And there has been a resultant loss of "wisdom" and "grace."

In short, as a consequence of all that, we have witnessed a tremendous "ecological" destruction in Latin America over the past quarter of a century. To be specific, we have witnessed the destruction of the *social* ecology.

II. The Period of Violent Action

It is now time to analyze the period of desperate violent action through which the whole continent has gone, or is still going. That is not easy to do with impartiality, or at least with the moderation that guarantees profundity. We are too close to the events in question, and they have had a sharp impact on our sensibilities, fears, projects, and hopes. But someone, indeed many people, must make the effort, and the sooner the better.

One of the major difficulties in dealing with the problem as objectively as possible and making our situation comprehensible to all is a concrete fact. The fact is that the phase under study here coincided with the appearance of subversive or revolutionary violence. This may pose two problems of unfairness, or at least two serious inconveniences that cannot go unnoticed.

The *first* problem is that our starting point seems to disregard the *cause* of the subversive or revolutionary violence: i.e., the violence that had already been institutionalized for years or for centuries. Even in merely quantitative terms that institutionalized violence has been much more inhuman and death-dealing than the violence I intend to study here. Moreover, it is a well-known ideological technique to present violence as *suddenly* arising in a social context where no violence was present before.

The *second* problem in associating the start of the violent stage with "subversion" is that we may lose sight of the fact that the violence subsequently practiced to repress the subversion, the violence of repression, was immensely greater in physical terms, more thoroughgoing in its disturbing effects on the social ecology, and more inhuman in its use of the "reasons of the reason" at the expense of the "reasons of the heart."

Granting all that, I think it is fair to say that the problem of violence pushed its way into our continent on the heels of political pessimism. People had the feeling that they were caught in a vicious circle. Continuing and growing feelings of frustration met them at every turn on the road towards justice.

Medellín and the Temptation to Violence

It is not my purpose here to pinpoint responsibility or blame. If it were, I would have to say that those who provoked the violence were far more culpable than those who actually practiced it. Medellín's final document on "Peace" had this to say among other things (MED II: 78):

As the Christian believes in the productiveness of peace in order to achieve justice, he also believes that justice is a prerequisite for peace. He recognizes that in many instances Latin America finds itself faced with a situation of injustice that can be called institutionalized violence. . . . We should not be surprised, therefore, that the "temptation to violence" is surfacing in Latin America. One should not abuse the patience of a people that for years has borne a situation that would not be acceptable to anyone with any degree of awareness of human rights [n. 16].

The two separate passages just quoted from the Medellín document on "Peace" (n. 16), deserve a brief commentary. Note first the reference in the second part to people who would step in and have the injustice stopped if they were its victims. That is obviously an allusion to more developed classes or peoples. In their case legal justice and its attendant police forces would step in to fight for their rights, using the armed violence of the police to restrain and coerce the miscreants. Obviously, then, those who possess a solid awareness of their human rights employ violence by *proxy* or *power of attorney*. Though they may not bear and use weapons, they organize and pay armed and "violent" corps to serve their supposed rights. In line with the Medellín text, then, we can say that no one should be surprised or scandalized to see a "volunteer" armed corps in the service of justice arise when the paid violence is actually in the service of the evildoers, when it is the institutionalized violence mentioned earlier in the same section of the Medellín document.[6]

However, the second part of the section quoted above suggests an important difference between "the patience of a people" and those "with any degree of awareness of human rights." The "patience" of the people may be nurtured by *ideology* in the pejorative sense of the term (see Chapter IV, Section II, above). In other words, a situation which is the *violent* result of selfish interests and acquired advantages may be camouflaged or justified as being "natural." Critical-minded awareness, by contrast, is the work of *reason*. In this case it is reason unmasking illusions and fighting to destroy them as it seeks justice and truth and proclaims that reality can be changed.

Why, then, does Medellín talk about a "temptation to violence"? Wouldn't violence be the logical and rational response to the already existing institutionalized violence, which is now being uncovered and denounced in all its scope and severity? Why is there a seeming preference for patience on the part of the people rather than impatience in the face of the systematic injustice of which they are the victims?

It must be noted that on this point Medellín had to take into account a reply which had just been suggested, if not imposed, by Pope Paul VI. In his opening address to the Medellín Conference he said: "Violence is neither Christian nor evangelical."

Such an assertion is new in Catholic theology. The latter canonized warrior saints and inquisitors, and for centuries it debated the conditions for a *just* war. Of course it was not then able to take into account the terrible nuclear connotations of the word "war." Moreover, the assertion was also new in the teaching of Paul VI himself. In *Populorum progressio* he had pointed out the causes that might justify violence in specific political situations.[7]

In another book I dealt with that issue from the standpoint of moral theology.[8] Here I want to focus the attention of my readers on the *ecological* side of the same issue.

From the vantage point of what we saw in the last chapter, we can see a "temptation to violence" in another sense. There is such a temptation to the extent that one loses sight of the fact that even the institutionalized violence of years and centuries has ended up constituting a certain *social* ecology. That does not justify it, of course. We have the right and even the duty to change it if, as in this case, we are convinced that its foundation rests on injustice. But changing a whole ecology is not like changing a tire. The possible temptation lies in the fact that we may decide to change the ecology in any way we can, even if we have to *do violence to it*.

In the previous section we saw how such a decision was gradually gestating in Latin America. People encountered systematic political failure in their efforts to end underdevelopment by improving various sectors of reality. And they found it impossible to effect the political mobilization of the masses who could only benefit from a change in the system.

Thus the "patience of the people" surfaced as the great rational scandal, much in the same way that "religion" did for Marx in his day. For him it was a factor inducing patience where it did not make rational sense.

Now this explanation is not meant to justify the unjustifiable or to foster acceptance of the unacceptable. Its potential value for us here is in pointing up the unsuspected density and complexity of our Latin American reality, a reality which we, with the best intentions in the world, had pictured as being much simpler than it was.

Let us start with a hypothesis, even though distinctions made in the early chapters of this book suggest that it is oversimplified. Let us assume that religion here does play a negative role, inculcating illusion and evasion in the face of the central problems of justice and injustice in societal life. From an anthropological standpoint, however, that illusion and evasion are never merely negative or neutral. The stores of energy displaced from what we consider essential are transposed to other fields where they fulfill important functions. For example, it has often been observed that people in a situation of dire poverty seem more capable than others of expressing joy about the positive aspects of life. Even when those positive aspects are meager, they know how to express their individual and collective joy over them.

We talk about certain virtues frequently being found among the common people: e.g., hospitality, extended family ties, ease in interpersonal and group communications, loyalty, and friendship. And we notice that such virtues often tend to disappear when we get a more just social structure in which the social product is distributed more equitably.

To state this is not to succumb to romantic conservatism, though the latter certainly does use the point for ideological purposes. My assertion here has to do with a point fundamental to anthropology: even unjust societies constitute *ecologies* in the long run. They constitute social systems with a complicated equilibrium, and hence they must be changed *as such*.

Marxism in its most authentic form was extraordinarily well equipped to reflect on this point, thanks to the overall social vision implied in both historical and dialectical materialism. It is one of the sad paradoxes of history, therefore, that it lost sight of this key point.[9] One historical explanation for this fact, already suggested earlier, is the dependence of original Marxism on the nineteenth-century version of the Enlightenment and its apotheosis of rationalism. Another explanation, which hits closer to home for us Latin Americans, is the fact that the early stages of the Latin American process described above were characterized by an activist "urgency." This urgent activism was closely associated with political pessimism which, perhaps unconsciously, had become systematic.

In this atmosphere of assumed urgency, all complex reflection or attention to complexities gave way to action, the latter being expected to produce results in the short run. It was a stage marked by reflective impoverishment, rationalist simplification, and emotional activism. Faith and ideology—be it Christianity, Marxism, liberalism, or fascism—were lived in a spontaneous way. Creative thought and reflection were sacrificed on the altar of activism, which was felt to be urgent and crucial. Herein lies the paradox for Marxism, if my comments in Chapters VII, VIII, and IX were correct. Marxism should have been open and alive to the complexity of the real. In fact, however, it was employed in its most simplistic and oversimplifying versions.

How, then, did the "reasons of the reason" operate in the quest for a more just and humane society? Once again I must point out that it is difficult to talk dispassionately and critically about an idealistic venture which mobilized the better part of the Latin American continent in terms of its intentions, if not in terms of its methods. Once again I must say that any criticism of the means employed would go double for the irreparable destruction of the social ecology caused by the efforts to repress the sedition. The repression instituted in the various countries of Latin America, far from being a defense of the earlier existing ecology (however unjust), was really its death blow. In short, the repression did not even succeed in being *conservative*.

The Destruction of the Social Ecology

As my readers know, by "ecology" I mean the whole system of relations existing between human beings and their context or environment. There is a *biological* ecology because human beings live in a context which relates them to the problems of the vegetable and animal world. There is a *social* ecology because they likewise live in a context of social relationships. But the term "ecology" also suggests the unsuspected complexity of humans' relationships with their environment. And if the word has become fashionable today, there is a reason for it. While human beings may have recognized this complexity in theory, in practice they have tried to improve their situation as if that sort of conditioning did not exist. So the means employed by human beings, however simple and logical they may have seemed, have produced unexpected chain reactions far beyond the concrete, simple intentions of the people employing them. Indeed the reactions have gone so far as to obstruct and destroy those intentions.

In the past, a *conventional* war did not always provoke ecological destruction. A war of subversion or guerrilla tactics does not differ in intent from a conventional war. And if it succeeds or fails quickly, it has an even greater resemblance to a limited war. The "cause" supported, akin to patriotism in a conventional war, will begin by dividing the two enemy camps; within the two camps the rules of the game and loyalties will continue to function for the most part. In this case, however, the enemy is "internal" or "domestic." So if the guerrilla war is prolonged, and if the prospects of victory grow remote, the differences between such a war and a conventional war will become increasingly obvious.

All that remains of war, in fact, is the rationalist factor: i.e., that the "cause" in question justifies the destruction of persons. In guerrilla war, however, those prepared to do this destruction will keep on using the social relations of a normal context with those who are to be destroyed. Such relations as family, friendship, and hospitality would be inhibited vis-à-vis a known and declared enemy, for example. But they are necessarily operative vis-à-vis an unknown or secret enemy. The latter does violence to those relationships at their very core: i.e., trust. The incognito enemy wittingly compromises and involves those who establish or maintain basic social relationships with him or her or with the causes the latter has espoused. And because people did maintain such relationships with the enemy, they may later be outraged, imprisoned, tortured, or killed.

Once again I remind you that I am not discussing the morality of an isolated case, nor am I raising any doubt about the end generally justifying the means. I am simply pointing out that a morality which appeals to such a principle should be able to maintain control over the means used and recognize their scope. It cannot remain blithely unaware of their ecological effects, of their mounting destruction of basic social ties.

The first to suffer the impact of such falsified human relations are the "high priests" of the guerrilla movement, if you will pardon the term. Why? Because for them, too, normal human relationships in the social context were, and remain, basic. The destruction of those relationships cannot be replaced, or physically compensated for, by mere comradeship or the activism of armed combat. In the long run, as many have learned, there must be repeated recourse to the psychologist or to suicide in the guise of desperate guerrilla actions.

It does not always reach such extremes, to be sure. When it comes to ecology, much depends on the length of time in which a disturbing factor is operative. But some effects are visible even in the short run.

One factor of particular relevance is the destruction of the meaning and purpose of many social institutions. A secret war, precisely because it is secret, uses those institutions for ends for which they were not made. In a declared war a captured soldier is viewed as having a specific status. Whether that status is respected or violated, the normal institutions stay on course. In the case of guerrilla warfare, such as that in Latin America, matters are very different. A prisoner is viewed not as a soldier but rather as a criminal; he or she is to be judged individually by the system of justice, be it civil or military depending on the nature and gravity of the case. The prisoner becomes part of that game, though in an ambiguous and disorienting way. Notice what happens.

In the case of an ordinary criminal, only help with criminal intent will normally be prosecuted and punished as complicity. And from time immemorial the ordinary criminal has enjoyed certain supports which to some extent balance off his or her inferiority vis-à-vis the armed force of society as a whole. Hence, without there being any intention to "whitewash" crime, there have always been social institutions offering special protection to the criminal.

Traditionally, for example, respect was shown for the asylum offered by religious authorities or institutions. The difficulties placed in the way of extraditing ordinary criminals from one country to another do not exemplify mere exaggerations of nationalistic pride. They bear witness to a human fact: i.e., in case of doubt or ignorance one should protect the weak, even if that entails the risk of sheltering a guilty party. And both national and international institutions work to promote respect for legal mechanisms in criminal proceedings and to help convicts who have served their sentences—even offering them financial help.

Other recognized mechanisms of protection are operative for an accused person in normal times. Professional secrecy is one important basis of social coexistence. Lawyers, psychologists, priests, and medical doctors are thus not regarded as accomplices of criminals when they offer them professional help or advice. It is also generally understood and accepted that neighbors, relatives, and friends will not denounce a criminal even when they know of their crime. And a spouse is not regarded as an accomplice when he or she refuses to testify in court.

Notice what happens in a prolonged clandestine war, however. Even though its protagonists may have no such intention, that kind of war undermines those basic rules of human and social coexistence. The soldier in that war hides himself by acting like a plain citizen. Thus all the people who protect him, knowing what he is really, necessarily become possessors of "military" secrets that are vital to the other side.

Examples abound. Doctors who treat a guerrilla soldier without betraying him are regarded as "safe" by the guerrilla organization. Their names are passed on to other guerrillas, and indeed they may be extorted into giving even greater and more crucial help. A lawyer or a relative of a captured prisoner might pass along a message or carry out some action as a normal favor to the prisoner. Later the act might turn out to have had strategic importance. Someone may seek hospitality on a purely human basis and end up expressing thanks in the name of the organization he or she serves.

Obviously the whole situation becomes more complicated and acute when repression begins on a truly large scale. For then the forces of repression will try to detect and destroy this *new* kind of complicity.

There is another matter of the utmost importance, and it has to do with the political arena specifically. Just as basic social relationships are enormously disrupted, so are all the institutions of political expression.

The secret warfare has political goals which parallel those of certain political parties that are using perfectly legal methods. For example, socialism may find embodiment in a clandestine armed force on the one hand, and in legal political parties on the other—which is not to say that the two necessarily share all the same views. The same can be said for the forces of repression.

In some instances it has been claimed that the clandestine armed forces constitute the "strong arm" of corresponding political parties. In fact, that sort of hierarchical subordination has rarely, if ever, been the case. What we find instead is frank opposition with regard to means, even though the latter may be viewed as aiming for the same ends or goals. It is also obvious that if an armed revolution had imposed socialism, socialist political parties would not have renounced socialism because of the way it came about. On the other hand we must not minimize the "political" importance of the difference over means. The fact is that one system of means does not necessarily agree with others because the end is the same.

During election time, of course, these differences may be passed over in silence. The citizen who is a clandestine soldier will vote just like other people, and he or she will carry on similar political activities in broad daylight. When the secret war begins again, however, the situation changes.

To begin with, some of those captured or killed in the warfare will be known to have had certain political affiliations. Naturally enough of this will raise some doubts about the "electoral" sincerity of the parties which sheltered and used those people, whether the parties were aware of their true intentions and activities or not. It is easy to assume some sort of complicity, especially when one wants to make such an assumption.

Then there is the treatment of prisoners of war. When that treatment does not measure up to the legal or constitutional guarantees provided for peacetime, or even for wartime, as is the case today, then logically the more closely related political parties will be in the forefront of the fight to get those rights respected. Other parties will prefer to ignore such violations and occupy themselves with other matters. This only bolsters the impression that there is some complicity between certain legal political parties and the clandestine warfare. Added to this, of course, is the force of deliberately hostile propaganda, which is backed up by all the power of the government.

So we come to an undeniable fact. Wittingly or unwittingly the guerrillas destroyed the political future of the parties which were seeking the same end through legal means. They left a good portion of the population, young people in particular, without any possibility of political expression or activity. And that always and necessarily entails an enormous ecological destruction.

The same holds true for other legal pressure groups: e.g., labor unions, the press, the mass media. Undermining their operativeness also entails enormous ecological destruction.

III. From Liberalism to Repression

What I have said above is only the beginning, however. So far I have only been focusing on the ecological destruction caused by the Left and its allies, so to speak.

The impact was much more general. A people or nation can maintain its coherence and some minimum of comprehensible institutions when it is attacked by an identifiable enemy. The identification may be due to a difference in nationality, race, or language, for example.[10] The problem immediately becomes more complicated, even when the battle is armed and visible, when it takes place between fellow citizens divided by antagonistic political ideologies. In that case there is every reason to assume there will be infiltration behind the lines of open warfare. "Fifth columns" of unidentifiable enemies will presumably be lurking around. But there still remains some minimal basis of reference and understanding: such things are bound to happen in war. In a clandestine war, however, one of the things most difficult to comprehend is the creation of a war atmosphere among the civilian population which is living in peace and does not want to give up peace.

The Shift of the Middle Classes

This problem has been framed in the following terms: how is it that the middle classes shift from liberalism to fascism? As I hope to make clear, no merely political interpretation is really capable of providing a plausible explanation.

The middle classes are the front-line defenders of the rules of the game which permitted them to move up and retain their position. When only small groups have used this mechanism successfully, one might reasonably fear that they would close the door to new competitors after obtaining their objective in free competition. But when the process is more or less permanent and ongoing, the new ascending strata prevent any blocking or backsliding. They uphold and maintain a liberal-democratic ideal which at first glance might seem to be consubstantial with the whole middle class. Indeed one might even say it is alluring to a good portion of the lower classes, who feel they can take the same route and arrive at the same destination over a longer or shorter period of time.

Now what did the Left in our countries do when they saw the first signs that the middle classes, in the face of rebellious activities, were beginning to disregard the rules of the democratic game and call for more repression than such rules would permit? The Left immediately began to talk about Nazi or fascist infiltration. That explanation was as superficial as it was ineffective. Insofar as Nazism went, for example, it was obvious that the Latin American middle classes did not hold any such elaborate ideology, particularly one rooted in some foreign version of nationalism. The accusation of fascism was ineffective because people lacked the political education and memory to even see the point of such a charge. In fact, the mechanism was much simpler and more home-grown. If the diagnosis of fascism hit closer to home it was because the Latin American phenomenon, like that of fascism, drew its strength from an emotional reaction by an upset, insecure middle class.

Aside from that, however, the phenomenon in Latin America did not derive from infiltration; nor could it be combatted with opprobrious name-calling. In my opinion, only very small and restricted circles sought ideological support in foreign movements of a bygone day. Even the various ideologies of *national security*, which were relatively more elaborate, won adherence in very restricted circles, though they may have been widely taught and held by those who truly exercised power.

If you look closely, you will find a political and sociological phenomenon of much greater magnitude and importance: i.e., the fact that the middle classes called for and supported the repression and even the destruction of democratic government *without consciously realizing they were abandoning the liberal, democratic ideology*.

This was the general phenomenon which the subversive side failed to estimate correctly. It did not hesitate to continue its struggle as the repression escalated. Already having failed to appreciate the magnitude of the ecological destruction so far, it assumed it could press a button and bring the middle class over to its side; for the liberal and democratic sensibilities of that class would presumably be outraged by the escalating repression. Many documents made public in some way by the subversive side at that point make it clear that the escalation of repressive measures was no unexpected surprise to it. The subversives saw such escalation as an additional factor helping them to win over the populace.

In other words, the Left assumed that the middle classes and a good portion of the lower classes had a definite and deeply rooted ideology. But rather than possessing any such ideology, the majority of the population, it turned out, had a great capacity to change its most basic attitudes unwittingly if some new factor seriously upset its calculations.

Why should that be the case? What I said earlier about the forces of subversion must now be applied and extended to a large part of the Latin American population. *Systematic pessimism exacerbates the use of rationality* in one's search for means, for solutions to a crisis. And this is done at the expense of ecological wisdom, of course.

People were experiencing basic insecurity in an ongoing and ubiquitous way. This led them to the "rationalist" solution of temporarily suspending liberal safeguards and guarantees. Later, no one knew exactly when, they would go back to real democracy. The "rational" button of repression was pushed, and the ecological destruction already under way went completely out of control.

Some readers will object here. It seems difficult to imagine that people could have recourse to ironclad dictatorships in order to maintain and preserve democracy. Indeed it seems totally ridiculous for such a dictatorship to demand nothing less than an oath of faith in the system of *representative, republican democracy* from anyone joining the administration, entering a university, or whatever. But, as Chesterton pointed out, fools do not lack the use of reason; they lack a sense of reality.

The Justification of Repressive Government

Here, then, we simply must go to the psychosocial roots of this curious phenomenon: the loss of the sense of reality. The best example I have to illustrate the matter is embodied in two memoranda written by the President of Uruguay, J. M. Bordaberry, a civilian elected at the beginning of 1971. Dated December 9,1975, and June 1,1976, the two memoranda were addressed to the commanders-in-chief of the armed forces. On the basis of these memoranda, they deposed the president and then had the memoranda published in the press.[11]

One major point of interest in the two documents is the despairing conclusion reached by the president: all the mechanisms of democracy breed its destruction. Even more interesting, perhaps, is the sincerity of his anguish. Here we have a man elevated to supreme authority by those very mechanisms which he now feels obliged to destroy, out of conviction. He must destroy democracy in order to preserve and maintain it: "This is quite clear, in my opinion. It becomes crystal-clear once one analyzes the present situation of the government in depth. But I must admit that this way of thinking involves such a profound change that it cannot be presented abruptly to public opinion. There is the danger that such a course would cause a trauma and, even worse, facilitate political exploitation of the situation by Marxism."

All elections are to be postponed indefinitely. Overlooking the fact that Uruguay is a nation exploited in international trade, President Bordaberry points out that electoral achievements can never measure up to, or compete with, utopian desires and promises. A focus on government and elections leads nowhere: "That will necessarily force us to try to compete with Marxism on the economic and labor fronts, pushing towards an increasingly accelerated pace of development under the hidden prick of communism and trying to prevent its takeover of labor organizations. But our recent history proves that in such a contest those who advocate utopias always prevail over those who have the responsibility of governing."

Political parties no longer merit any confidence, notes President Bordaberry, and he goes on to explain why: "Insofar as the takeover of government power becomes the primordial objective of the political parties, Marxist action is made all the easier. The takeover or retention of government power naturally impels them to indulge in demagoguery, or to place party interests before the general interest. . . . This fact limits or inhibits their ability to govern or to offer serious opposition, which is a serious matter. . . . Insofar as they are not able to take any effective public action, they only abet the activity of communism. . . .''

The same holds true for the liberties of the citizenry, the backbone of representative democracy: "Secondary individual rights, such as freedom of the press and freedom of association, are maintained over and above the primary rights of the human beings: e.g., to freedom, life, honor, and property. The maintenance of these secondary rights is also exploited by communism."

If communism takes advantage of a government-sponsored race for development, then the race must be slowed down or called off. Otherwise one is in danger of succumbing to an evil that is synonymous with communism: i.e., totalitarianism. Writes Bordaberry: "Goaded by the need for material achievements in order to combat Marxism, we would end up looking with disfavor on those who do not enter into our plans. We would impose indirect sanctions on them by excluding them from credit, tax exemptions, and the countless resources available to the government. So all private activity would have to become a part of the system, and thus a form of totalitarian government would take shape in this area as well."

Since there is no way out, one will reluctantly accept a totalitarian government, so long as it is not totalitarian in the one area where communism does not have an assured victory: i.e., the economic area. Bordaberry explains: "The common good and the national conscience, then, will be the objective and limit of the public government authority. For that to be the case today, the government authority must be strong and national; which is to say, it must be government power and it must be public. Hence only the armed forces, by their very nature and mission, should be its custodians today. That will prevent any one group from laying claim to it. For once a struggle to obtain it is triggered, Marxism will find some way to get it by and by. This is clear from our own experience and that of others."

So Bordaberry proposes a new type of government power. It entails no liberties, but it is limited by a national conscience imbedded in the military. What name is to be given to this sort of government? By definition it should be called "democracy," but that term is dangerous. After all, isn't it Marxism that "raises its voice in the alleged defense of democracy"? So we must make a distinction and talk about a new type of democracy: "This leads us to make a distinction between real democracy and formal democracy, between democracy as a form or philosophy of life and democracy as a form of government. Our conclusion is that in no circumstances can the latter prevail over and against the former. What is more important, democracy exists under different forms of government, and it is not specifically identified with any one of them so long as its real essence is maintained: i.e., liberty."

My readers may wonder what sort of liberty he is talking about. It is the only one that remains in reality: the liberty of private initiative in the market-place. That is what is deemed to be the essential form of life insofar as democracy is concerned. That is the thing for which everything else must be sacrificed in circumstances like the present, the thing which can perdure under different forms of government.

Here we have an example of terrible ideological confusion. But it is not an example of sheer cynicism, in my opinion, as are so many public statements deliberately designed to plug the dike with a sieve. Remember that these were secret memoranda in which President Bordaberry expressed his thoughts to the heads of the armed forces. And in them he accused the latter of not seeing the danger involved in their talk about a return to the democratic system of government, even at some vague and remote date. What shines through in these documents, in my opinion, is all the anguish and despairing "rationalism" of the middle class. Sadness, not ambition, is clearly the prevailing tone. Writing of communist aggression, Bordaberry remarks: "If that aggression makes use of the traditional forms of democracy, then the latter cannot continue to exist—*not because they are not effective for the happiness of human beings*, but because they are not effective for the national defense" (my italics).[12]

The relevance and importance of my example, as I said earlier, lies in the exceptional circumstances surrounding the two documents. They were addressed to the chiefs of the armed forces by no one less than the president of the country, and they were issued in secret, though that secrecy was later violated. They attest to a middle class expressing its desperation and despair over the collapse and presumable defeat of the classic mechanisms of democratic coexistence and suggesting the "rational" means which must be taken. One can hardly imagine those two things being expressed in normal everyday life without triggering violent attacks.

Speaking from a strictly political standpoint, one might object that no military dictatorship erected to repress guerrilla warfare can claim to represent the people or, more specifically, the middle class. I think we do well to take a close look at that argument. I hope to point up its falseness, or at least its inadequacy from the sociological standpoint. And I hope to show what we have here is a destruction of the social ecology much greater than if some armed band, akin to an army of occupation, had taken over a country whose outlook it did not share at all.

The Practice of Repressive Government

Repressive governments arose in Latin America with varying degrees of speed, depending on local circumstances. They imposed their role as a military response to some war, the latter being no less real for being hidden. Where such warfare did not yet exist, in Brazil and Chile for example, the government alluded to a war which hidden forces were plotting to unleash.

Now one interesting point deserves mention here. It is very difficult, if not impossible, for a legal government to declare that a civil war exists in its territory unless it has the consent of a good portion of the population, and of the middle class in particular, in favor of such a declaration. Even if it is assumed that such a declaration would make clear the true situation of society, the government will generally delay a long time before making such a declaration—if it ever does at all. There are Latin American countries where guerrilla warfare and a *de jure* government of laws have coexisted for years.

The difficulty of such a declaration of war is rooted in many factors connected with our discussion here. First of all, it is difficult to get a popularly elected parliament to declare such a state of internal war. That would come down to parliament imposing limitations on itself, if not abolishing itself. Parliament would have to be pushed mightily to do this, not only by all sorts of normal pressures but also by the weight of a broad grass-roots consensus.

Even rulers who can do without parliamentary approval have difficulty in placing a whole country in a state of war. Such a move distorts the domestic economy greatly, leading to the automatic inflation of military appropriations and damage to other production sectors. Then there is the international economic factor, as foreign investments needed for development are reduced or withdrawn completely.

There are even deeper reasons working against such a declaration. For the latter entails going down a road from which there is no easy way out. A government at war must be able to say whether it is winning or losing, especially after "operations" have been going on for awhile. Quite aside from the fact that it is always difficult to estimate the strength of clandestine forces, winning the war would mean not only popularity but also returning to legal forms of rule. Military prisoners would have to be turned over to the civil courts, defense appropriations would have to be reduced, and the military would have to surrender control over the government. By the same token, it is scarcely honorable or popular to keep maintaining, year after year, that the war is still going on as it was at first. That would mean admitting the ineffectiveness of the means employed and the failure of the armed forces against groups which must be assumed to be less numerous, less well organized, and less well equipped.

It is not surprising, then, that the dominant theme of such regimes gradually changes, though there are occasional reversions as well. The focus on war shifts to a focus on *development*. This is meant to maintain a bridge between the government and those sectors of the population which supported it at the start. For those groups would gradually grow weary of a costly war from which there was no way out.

One point must be remembered. The ambition of praetorian groups was not the only factor leading to the establishment of most of the repressive military regimes in Latin America. Perhaps even more important was the pressure, passive consent, and even plotting of the middle class. Their rationality had been exasperated by systematic desperation resulting from the combined impact of economic crisis and political subversion.

My explanation does not propose to place responsibility or blame on anyone. It is offered as an explanation of a historical phenomenon which became general on our continent. If it is valid and deep enough, it will be important for our future. In society as in nature, ecological crises develop in this way. Wittingly or unwittingly, step by step, people move down the fatal path towards disaster.

Of course, as we know from experience, the middle classes soon weary of their cozy complicity with the repressive governments they once supported and applauded. Or perhaps I should have said that they are driven to desperation. The reason is not simply the one offered by a simplistic brand of Marxism. It is not just that the repressive governments turn their backs on the people, succumb to international economic pressures, and totally fail to rationalize the economic sector.

People quickly begin to notice what I have been calling the destruction of the social ecology, and they realize that it is a far more serious threat to their security than is the party of subversion. Unlike the military, the middle class cannot so easily continue to delude itself. For it does not possess that spontaneous sense of operational infallibility enjoyed by people who are armed and used to giving orders.

We do well here to examine briefly the process whereby the middle class ceases to be deluded about the situation. Let us focus on three major areas of social life: the administration of justice, intercommunication, and cultural life in general.

Feeling anxious and hopeless over the progress of Marxism, the middle class cheerfully sacrifices the classic judicial guarantees. They are followed by a large portion of the lower class, for whom those guarantees never existed in reality. It is assumed that the mechanisms of repression, inhuman as they may be, will pounce on the enemy. So people shut their eyes and ears to the judicial methods of repression: e.g., kidnapping, physical and moral torture, improper jailing, arbitrary dismissals, long terms of imprisonment, and executions. But they cannot do so for long. One reason is that such things are repugnant to the middle class, particularly when they are continued for a long period and then become habitual. Other reasons are even more important since they hit home to the middle class.

When the judicial apparatus loses its independence and its control over police procedures, it generates a much more generalized brand of repression than the middle class had thought to tolerate or ignore. Though there is a stubborn effort to conceal police activities on the international level, outside pressure forces the government to provide a great deal of data, however doctored it may be. Since groups are trying to establish the facts one way or another, the government has to provide a great deal of information about the harrassment of men and women, of the innocent and the guilty. Now combined with this is another fact on the domestic front, which might seem contradictory at first glance. It is the use of intimidation to discourage both physical and ideological resistance. While torture and executions are concealed on the one hand, they are also unofficially made known to large segments of the population. There are many ways to do that. One of the more common ways is to attribute deeds to so-called rightist guerrillas who systematically escape government control and investigation.

Two other facts help to make the police repression more general, so that it exceeds the boundaries of the domestic war and unexpectedly affects large segments of the middle class itself.

The first fact is that the practice of repressive procedures proves to be clearly advantageous in trying to obtain information. It is not surprising, then, that the government moves from crimes of subversion to real or alleged economic crimes. One of the main justifications for the imposition of military government is the desire to impose honesty and thus rebuild the country. Thus well known and distinguished members of the middle class personally experience the treatment they had allowed or demanded for others, and they talk about their experiences.

The second fact is that the majority of the subversive elements belong to the middle class, too. So when repression grows general, its brutal methods are unleashed directly or indirectly on whole families, however much individual members may have disagreed with subversive relatives. Discovering the whereabouts of the latter when they are captured or killed, suffering the indignities of surveillance when one tries to visit them, having to spend the savings of a lifetime to win their release: all these things bring home the reality of repression to each family. Such is the real face of the repression which once seemed to be the *rational* means to regain the security and tranquillity which had been lost!

Worse still, insecurity now begins to touch zones which had never been affected before. Legality was always one of the basic pillars of middle-class life. But a judicial system in the service of repression establishes new crimes and, what is more, makes them retroactive. What was once a duty performed in full compliance with the legal rules of the game can suddenly become a crime already committed. Without knowledge or intent, one did something that benefited the enemy; now one must pay for that crime.

The fight against a subversive movement which operated under legal forms also undermines legally authorized guarantees. Thus the guarantees of civil service employment and even private labor contracts disappear. A veteran member of the civil service could not be summarily dismissed unless charges were proved against him; now, in some Latin American countries, he can be dismissed to "improve service" no matter what his age or length of service. Naturally department heads will use this technique to purify the ideological atmosphere. But once the need for legal proof is dropped, what is to stop bosses from firing people out of envy and hatred or from blackmailing them? Once again this procedure hits a large part of the middle class, who never imagined they would have to pay such a high price in insecurity for the security they were supposed to be getting.

Many other items could be added here. Official blacklists prevail even in private employment; certain employees and workers must be overlooked or dismissed, though no reason may be given. Moreover, as we can glean from the comments of former president Bordaberry above, one omnipotent group, whether economically corrupt or not, will accept and grant favors of all sorts. Is it any wonder, then, that the vast majority of the population should come to feel that the measures designed to provide greater societal security have actually undermined the foundations of any and all security? The hope was to exorcise one evil. Now another and worse evil of the same stripe has been introduced in its place.

The functioning of the justice system is fundamental, of course, and many of its effects are permanent. But it operates in a more limited and less ubiquitous way than do interpersonal relations within the societal context. This second area of study is not even protected by the prestige of so-called "human rights."[13]

These relationships surround and make the human being. Day-to-day life becomes tolerable only insofar as those relationships are maintained at an acceptable level of understanding and sympathy. Hence, as Bateson points out (see p. 135), the falsification of the data that links us with the attitudes of our neighbors, through communication, quickly becomes *pathogenic*.

Bateson does assure us that the pathology can never be total. Our communications with our fellows, the iconic communications at least, have largely been withdrawn from our conscious control. In our daily life it saves us a great deal of energy to know that the truth escapes through unguarded gestures, tones of voice, and mechanical attitudes in certain circumstances. As the Latin proverb puts it: *in vino veritas*. So the real attitudes of others come through to us no matter how much they may be falsified by the content of what they literally say to us.

But there is another side to the coin. First of all, even iconic language cannot remain immune to the impact of repression over a long period of time. Though only a superb actor can voluntarily control his or her gestures, the rest of us can render ourselves largely expressionless after prolonged effort. We can invest as much voluntarism as possible even into our involuntary language so that it does not communicate or betray who we really are or what we really think.

Now if that is true for our largely involuntary forms of social communication, imagine what is the case with our digital language, which corresponds to our conscious plans and projects. It is seriously drained and voided by the impact of repression.

Why can't digital language adapt itself effectively to this situation of general repression? Here we come to one of the most profound effects of the destruction of the social ecology. No one can feel secure, even when he or she is expounding the topics most favored by the government or even when he or she is repeating statements made by government rulers. What has happened? As we noted above, the regime is driven to despair by the enemy's use of any and every social institution. It is led to suspect that the subversive front is also utilizing the vocabulary of those values that are most widely accepted.

Let me give one example here. In some countries people must swear an oath of loyalty to the democratic, representative, republican system. Now the government system itself knows very well that it is not democratic or republican in any real sense, much less representative. So what exactly is it to think of those people who swear that they are true democrats, republicans, and partisans of a representative government? It is wiser to be suspicious and to keep a close eye on them.

To manifest one's loyalty to the regime, one must sing the national anthem louder and more often than ever before. But the national anthem may contain some such phrase as: "Tremble, tyrants!" What are people thinking, then, when they sing the anthem with all their heart and soul? Are they thinking of the government in power or of the Marxists who might have come to power? One no longer knows what words means. They no longer identify friends or enemies.

Nor is it possible to know who are our friends and who are our enemies on the international front. Perhaps the real enemies are those diehard anticommunist countries who are trying to urge a democratic government on us. After all, experience shows that such a government only paves the way for a communist takeover! And what about those who criticize ideologies condemned by the regime? Depending on the intelligence or temperament of the listening censor or official, the criticism may seem to be on target, or too weak, or just a bit overdone.

And what about the great national heroes? Even though the government may still go through the motions of honoring them, it might doubt that they are still proper heroes and models. In their day they were what the guerrilla fighters are today. Though they called themselves Christians, they must not have been. After all, they used violence, and we now know that violence is not Christian, and that it only leads to ever increasing violence. Is it cynical to feel that the only difference between them and today's guerrillas is the fact that the old heroes won their fight? Can their ideals still be proclaimed today, when subversives have made them their own and given them new life and pointedness?

Government panic about the great national heroes has risen to new heights. In some places there has been a thorough ideological purge of school teachers and professors. Even then their lectures are censored in advance. Indeed in some instances the government sends them speeches and lectures which are simply to be read to the audience, thus ruling out even the most timid effort to inject a critical-minded comment.

Governments have always issued enigmatic and even contradictory statements about problems that are difficult to face and solve. There have always been evasions, excuses, and flights of political cynicism. But it is one thing when such declarations can be subjected to public exegesis; it is something very different when the only proper response is silence. Front-page coverage, without editorial comment, must be given to exact quotations such as the following: "As much blood will flow as is necessary for national peace or security"; "The government will be returned to elected civilians, but power will not"; "The Armed forces are the proprietors of the process"; "Democracy is compatible with any form of government."

The danger is that all digital language in Latin America, if it is one remove from onomatopoeia, is going to drive humor out of our societal life. And humor is one of the most human features of social life among human beings. In more than one Latin American country humor has been turned out to other pastures. The political jokes that were once to be found in songs, plays, and sketches, must now be confined to circles of close friends. The element of the ridiculous in politics, present there as in every area of human activity, must now assume a solemn air.

All real communication is risky. When we don't know exactly whom we are talking to, it seems wiser not to talk, or to talk without really saying anything. Some individuals may have already nurtured a rich inner life. Some may have already formed solid circles of friendly and sincere communication over the course of years. For such people the situation is sad, but they are not forced to despair. But what about those who are still shaping their inner world or their circles of close and trusted friends? For them silence is asphyxiating. For youngsters it is pathogenic, indeed lethal.

Cultural Destruction

That brings us to a third area undergoing ecological destruction, one closely related to the two areas described above. Here the destruction of the social ecology is more measurable on the one hand and, curiously enough, less perceptible on the other. I am talking about the destruction of cultural life, its retreat and emigration.

The rationale of repression, because it is so deeply rooted in desperation, multiplies the sources of subversion. It obviously wants to be rid of *all* its enemies. And since the latter cannot exercise any physical power, the repressive mentality sees them incarnated in hidden cultural agents. A book, a good play, a highly regarded professor: all of them are potential enemies. If having ideas were the essential constituent of a race, a *genos*, the rationality of repression would not stop at genocide. As it sees the matter, a certain class of human beings ought to disappear from the scene because of their ideas, be the latter actual or potential, expressed or alleged.

Their disappearance is accomplished in many different ways, and the result unfortunately is cumulative. The forces of repression have never ceased to accuse the subversives of torturing, kidnapping, and killing, but the former have done far much more of all three. Repression also has its own peculiar way of eliminating people: exile. It has been accomplished by direct and indirect means, the latter including threats, persecution, and job deprivation. The exile *en masse* of Latin Americans is one of the most significant and tragic facts of our time.[14] There are Latin American countries, relatively underpopulated to begin with, which have lost up to ten percent of their population in recent years! There are Latin American countries which hold the sorry record of possessing the highest number of political prisoners in the world, relatively speaking. And that would include the communist world! Of those prisoners a goodly number, if not the majority, can be described as people who had been agents of culture and who are now condemned to inactivity.

How are we to grasp the cultural impact of this outpouring, this hemorrhaging, of human beings! Can we say anything definite about the cultural values and qualities of the many people who have been forced to emigrate? And what is the case with the population that remains behind?

Let us start with the biological supposition that the intelligence and capacity to create culture are distributed evenly throughout the entire population. Hence we should find those factors, in germ at least, distributed over the whole political spectrum.

Well, the fact is that we cannot really get very far if we follow the route of that supposition. We will soon notice a close relationship between nonconformity and the creation of culture on the one hand, and repression and the absence of culture on the other hand. I am not suggesting we entertain delusions about the intellectual and moral equilibrium of all those nonconformists who emigrate. But it is hard to believe we will see cultural ferment where everything is measured by one and the same standard, where people are discouraged from contact even with cultural revolutions of the past.

On the outside no one may notice the purging of curricula, professors, and libraries; the elimination of any and all organs of critical opinion; and the definitive departure from a country of its best professionals, teachers, and researchers. Indeed, in the face of a chaos of ideas, one's first sensation might be one of peace and constructive progress. But the fact is that culture has been undermined at its very ecological roots.

The Destructiveness of One-Sided Ideologies

As I reach the end of this chapter, I realize that some readers might not see clearly the relevance of the points made in it to the context of this work and its overall purpose. So let me briefly summarize the points made in Part Three of this book up to now before we move on to Section C and try to draw some more positive and creative conclusions.

We began with the fact that some very familiar ideologies claim to prescind from any and every type of faith, be it religious or anthropological. Having already seen the dubiousness of such a claim in Part Two, we first explored the bases of such a view in Marxism, one of the most articulate ideologies of that stripe. My aim was to subject Marxism to logical analysis and delimit its *proper* and *positive* dimensions. Those who see Marxism as their be-all and end-all, and who refuse to analyze it from a critical and historical perspective, will tend to see my approach as an attack on Marxism, but that cannot be helped. Nor can I help the fact that those who view Marxism as the worst of evils will regard my treatment as support for Marxism.

In Section B of Part Three, I moved on to a historical confirmation of earlier assertions. I hope I have shown that Marxism and liberalism are one-sided ideologies insofar as they disregard their own flaws, the complexity of reality, and the possibility of their claims being compatible with anthropological faith, indeed with a specific faith. However fine its aim or purpose, any large-scale effort steeped in one-sidedness will end up destroying the basic relationship between human beings and their biological or social environment. Hence it is absolutely necessary to relate ideology to ecology, to link up ideology with the ecological dimension that is part and parcel of any ideology.

Since this book is addressed particularly to a generation of Latin Americans who personally have felt the impact of that ecological destruction, I also wanted to offer a brief analysis of what has happened on our continent over the past quarter of a century. My effort may be premature, but I have tried to add needed precisions and connotations. And I think it is enough to show that the whole continent was in fact affected by what happened.

Faced with that picture, I think it would be childish and extremely dangerous to accept the outlook of those who nurture simplistic dreams. It is not enough to hope merely for a return to representative democracy, an end to repression, and the recovery of respect for those human rights which were in force in better days. There are much more more basic things that have to be reconstructed. Otherwise the cycle of desperation, subversion, and repression will surface again, sinking its teeth deeper into an increasingly weaker and sicker continent. What we need is the creative "wisdom" to rebuild human beings and society from the roots of their relational base up.

That does not mean that the major ideologies of our time are dead. Nor does it even mean that they have been displaced. Sooner or later circumstances will permit us to go out in search of a real future. When that time comes, we will have to choose the societal models we want to build from among those ideologies. In so doing, however, we will have to consider the "ecological" state of the human beings who are part of that societal model and who will introduce their own basic features and network of relationships into it.

Nor do I mean to suggest that the past violations of ecology prove that conversions of the heart are more urgent and decisive today than structural changes. I am not siding with this view, which stands in opposition to the claims of the most widely held ideologies. Both things are intimately related and cannot be separated, and that will continue to remain true. What ecology adds to these conflicting ideologies is a more profound and overall appreciation of human conditionings.

So is it a matter of having better ideologies? Do we need more scientific ideologies, since ecology is a science in the last analysis? And what does that have to do with faith? Such is the sort of question that will occupy us in Section C, the final two chapters of this book.

NOTES

1. It is called "institutionalized violence" by Medellín. See its final document on "Peace," n. 16: MED II: 78. In general terms the same idea found acceptance among

economic experts, though they may have used different terminology. See the many documents issued by CEPAL, for example.

2. Hence the deceitfulness in the terms most generally and widely used to designate the countries of Latin America: "developing countries," when they were moving further and further away from developmentalist models; "Third World," when in fact they had no chance at all to bargain or operate autonomously because they constituted the poor periphery of the First World.

3. This term, like "reformism," is frequently used with a pejorative connotation. Nevertheless it was the explicit aim of those governments to try some middle road, some third way, between socialism and capitalism. I should also point out that the Peruvian revolution did not consider itself a third-way approach, at least at the start. It used the term "socialism." Nevertheless the term "third way" is applicable to it, not only because of the way it went but also because of the capitalist "reformism" which characterized its measures from the very start.

4. In the frequent attacks on liberation theology and movements stemming from it, we often find talk of the "*theory* of oppression" or the "*theory* of dependence." The implication is that liberation theology is based on something unproven or open to scholarly debate. The misunderstanding here, be it deliberate or not, lies in not appreciating that dependence and oppression are facts, major facts for our continent. That does not mean that they explain everything, or that the elimination of those two problems would automatically usher us into paradise.

5. The article appeared in the *Hannoversche Allgemeine* on September 30,1977; Spanish translation in *Tribuna Alemana*, Montevideo, October 9,1977. It is no accident that the latter paper reprinted another article on the same subject the following week. This article originally appeared in the *Süddeutsche Zeitung*, October 1,1977, and it said: "When all is said and done, even the Third World knows that the Bonn government will play the role of conservative 'bridler' as soon as the market economy seems to be jeopardized."

6. It is obvious that there does not enter into this characterization any blithe reference to *terrorism* properly speaking. In Latin America it has been an ideological habit to denigrate subversion by calling it "terrorism." I think that term should be reserved for the use, by both sides, of *indiscriminate* terror, for violent action which makes no distinction between innocent and guilty people. Not all subversion in our countries is, or was, terrorist. As I see it, terrorism is the rationalist extreme of hopelessness: i.e., the most thorough possible separation between the ends one is seeking and the means one employs. Obviously the temptation to resort to terrorism grows as victory for the subversive side becomes increasingly difficult.

7. Medellín picked up the description of such situations which had been made pointedly by Paul VI in *Populorum progressio* (n. 30): "The injustice of certain situations cries out for God's attention. Lacking the bare necessities of life, whole nations are under the thumb of others; they cannot act on their own initiative; they cannot exercise personal responsibility; they cannot work toward a higher degree of cultural refinement or a greater participation in social and public life. They are sorely tempted to redress these insults to their human nature by violent means" (Eng. trans., *The Pope Speaks* 12 [Spring 1967]:154).

Deciding whether such situations exist or never exist will depend on whether one sticks to the letter or the spirit of the pope's description.

8. See J. L. Segundo, *The Liberation of Theology*, Eng. trans. (Maryknoll, N.Y.: Orbis Books,1976), Chapter Six, pp. 154f.

9. Some might point out that official Marxism of the Moscow stripe did not inspire or encourage the subversive venture in Latin America. And everyone knows that there were differences and frictions between Moscow and Havana on this matter. But it is also clear that the subversive movement in Latin America found its inspiration somehow in Marxism in most instances. The most plausible explanation of this phenomenon is that the position of official Marxism was not regarded as a doctrine but as a tactic dictated by the balance of international forces. Perhaps there was more to it than that. In any case, official Marxism let its position be portrayed in that light, rather than as somehow bound up with the essence of its ideological system.

10. Consider another clandestine war: the French Resistance. Though we should not minimize its ecological effects, it had nowhere near the impact of the Spanish Civil War—to cite another European example. With good reason one can say that the reconstruction of Spain's social ecology required more than one human generation.

11. See, for example, *El País*, Montevideo, June 10,1976. Subsequent events tend to confirm the impression that the publication of those memoranda was a political tactic designed to explain the removal of the president, that it did not signal a change in direction or the use of a spare political theory.

12. The problem was perceived as a continent-wide one, rather than as one confined to a single country. This is evident at the end of the second memorandum, though the remarks are rather pretentious considering the minor importance of the country on the international front. Bordaberry writes: "It is worth glancing around and noticing that throughout America political situations similar to ours are arising spontaneously. Having arisen with the same *naturalness*, they consecrate the same general principles of public law without there having existed any prior agreement on that. And it is worth realizing the fact that all those in charge of those processes face the same alternative we do. We hear voices talking about a return to the prior state of affairs at some hazy point when 'conditions are right' or 'the objectives have been achieved.' Sooner or later they will realize what the real alternative is: i.e., the one I pose to the Uruguayan armed forces today. Hence I think it is not only proper that we be the first to offer a juridical formulation of the present situation, but that this step will enable Uruguay to maintain its traditional role as the vanguard of democracy in America. We will thus avoid being accused of following the lead of other countries."

13. There is a sad irony here that only contributes to the general confusion. What are called "human rights" are certain freedoms particularly useful to the middle classes. And they have been defended by the very people who have generated poverty and misery in the past and the present—even if only by their own consumption. By creating this situation of misery, democratic institutions drain away their own substance (since it benefits only small minorities in the end) and give rise to subversive movements. Moreover, ever-increasing degrees of repression are needed to make the people and nations in poverty accept institutionalized violence without muttering. See J. L. Segundo, "Direitos humanos, Evangelização e ideologia," *Revista Eclesiástica Brasileira* 37 (March 1977): 91–105.

14. Consider this significant and almost unbelievable fact. At Christmas the bishops of Chile addressed a pastoral letter "to Chileans outside the country" (see *Mensaje* 266 [January-February 1978], p. 84).

C. Towards a New Culture
in Latin America

CHAPTER XII

Ideology, Faith,
and Historical Flexibility

We have examined our present situation in Latin America. We find that we face the task of reconstructing a society from the foundations up, but at a point in time when there seems to be room only for despairing passivity. The majority of us are used to the political means associated with democratic freedoms, and so our impression is that we can no longer build anything, anything of social significance in any case. We stand on the sidelines and observe the decisions of others, or else we simply hope that the situation will change by itself.

But we cannot rest content with that, for several reasons. The most compelling reason is that new generations continue to follow behind us and are preparing to take their place in society. We cannot abandon them to a hollow destiny merely because we lack certain means which, when all is said and done, are fairly recent in the history of humanity and have their limits.

A second reason is that we should be able to offer effective help to that small proportion of the idealistic population which needs it most. I refer to those in prison, in exile, or under close surveillance, who have nothing on which to rely but their human nature as they seek to survive, to uphold their dignity, to contemplate a future, and to hope against hope. With only the most basic human resources at their disposal, they are already trying to prepare the kind of future to which every human being has a right. Though it may take a long time, some day that future will actually be feasible.

The third reason is that we must look inside ourselves to find new creative possibilities, however limited they may seem to us and however limited our customary resources may actually have proved to be. Suppose, for example, we can no longer simply entrust the moral structuring of young generations to the school system, because of the repression. In that case we will have to assign a new function to family life: its relationships, tempo, lifestyle, and economic resources. It must be turned once again into a creative element, a

305

transmitter of values, and a locus of profound dialogue. If society, with its disordered ecology, has grounded itself in the false support of consumption, then we will have to show fresh imagination and define consumption in terms of human relationships that are more enriching and amicable rather than vice versa.

We are in the same position as the prisoners in jail. Like them, we must work within our limited living space to survive as human beings and to help others do the same. We can do much more than we think. But for that to be really possible, we must recover a hope, a "premise," about all our successful little efforts to remain human in a dehumanizing world. We must see and feel them to be important contributions to the future society that will one day rise on the ashes of the present. We must stop viewing those little efforts and achievements as failures simply because at present they cannot be politically implemented as structural changes. In short, we must work to re-form things without turning into mere reformers.

I am not suggesting that we give up the idea of making the major changes necessary. I am simply saying that we must try to carry them out on the scale that is possible for us, thus preparing ourselves more fully for the time when conditions make them truly feasible. We must work for liberation from our situation of captivity.

The term "captivity" strikes me as unsuitable from the anthropological standpoint, however, if my comments in the previous chapter are correct. It is a poor image that does not faithfully reflect our reality. We are immersed in a process. In the broadest terms, we are immersed in the process of universal evolution. In narrower terms, we are immersed in that specifically human process of evolution known as history.

What is happening to us becomes comprehensible in that perspective. People in prison may see themselves immobilized on the margin of society and history. That is not true in our case since the mechanisms of evolution continue to operate. But how? On us? To destroy us? Even if that were the case, knowing those mechanisms would offer us the most realistic hope of escaping that fate.

This chapter will be dedicated to that topic. I will use many elements already familiar to my readers, linking them up with our central focus on faith and ideology. I believe this will provide us with a deeper and more correct picture of our concrete position in history and the field of operations open to us.

I. Two Different Views of the Evolutionary Process

From the very start of discussions about evolution, the central problem posed was this: how, in the general line leading towards perfection, did qualities acquired by living beings in the struggle for existence become hereditary, i.e., genetic?[1]

Heredity and Repetition

It was a one-sided formulation of the question, to which two extreme and unsatisfactory answers were given. One answer said that useful modifications in living beings became routine and eventually were transmitted to the genes. The other answer stressed competition in the struggle for existence; this competition actually eliminated those individuals who did not possess the useful characteristics. Left unanswered in this theory was the question as to how one eventually arrived at genetically formed species. While the importance of the environmental context was underlined, one still had to explain how the survival of the fittest was converted into genetic heritage.

The solution of that problem, which remains obscure, does not concern us here. The point I want to make now is that both solutions presupposed the very same thing: i.e., that evolution was achieved when the useful qualities acquired by some individuals of a species became hereditary in one way or another.

Let me give an example. Whatever may have been the cause or mechanism behind the exceptional development of the brain in some prehominids, the assumption is that the decisive evolution took place when practically all the individuals of the species were born with such a developed brain, thanks to biological heredity and the mechanism of the genes. In other words, the decisive phase of human evolution began when the individual, thanks to genetics, began from a certain point of development which had been achieved by the species and which, in fact, surpassed that of all other mammals. And the same would hold true for the location of the thumb on the hand or any other feature that has benefited human development.

Now my readers might logically conclude that within the human sphere evolution should consist in something parallel. In other words, useful qualities discovered and achieved at some point by an individual or a small group ought to become instinctive and hereditary; that would be the key to progress. As a result of such progress every human individual, when confronted with a given situation or problem, could say almost automatically: "This is how I must act." Much energy would be saved insofar as individuals would not have to go through the work of judging the pros and cons of their choice.

Remember the old joke about the British during the days of their imperial rule. It was said that they donned their dinner jackets to dine even in the midst of the jungle. That would be an example of the same process in the realm of human culture. In a different way, of course, we would get the same result. Certain acquired characteristics would become inherited cultural qualities.

In this view, therefore, the indefinite and compulsive repetition of certain actions or attitudes vis-à-vis reality would bear the weight of evolution in human culture. Freud himself entered into this conception with his theory of the social "superego," which becomes largely instinctive. Biological instincts are intermingled with those acquired by the individual, resulting in what might be called the "evolutionary memory" of the whole human species or some subgroup within it.

Homeostasis and Flexibility

But there is a second and very different view of human evolution, to which I also alluded earlier. If we look at the chain of evolution, we notice that the characteristic feature of the higher animals is the fact that they have fewer established instinctive instructions than do the lower animals. They are superior, however much they may seem to be dullards to us at times. And the reason seems to be that they are more exposed to error.

If the human being is the social and political animal *par excellence*, it is not just because *homo* "takes" to it. More than any other creature, the human being must go to the society of its kind to ask for the information it needs to get its bearings, to make up for its lack of hereditary instructions. But of course society cannot serve as a straight substitute for inherited instinct, as we can see right away.

A question arises at this point in evolution, which can be pushed back prior to the appearance of *homo*. What mechanisms compensate for the loss or absence of instinctual or genetic inheritance? ("Instinct" is a very unscientific term we use to designate features determined by genetics.) Put in scientific terms, the answer is: homeostatic mechanisms. In plain terms that means all the mechanisms which utilize and recapitulate experience.[2]

Household thermostats are good examples of homeostatic mechanisms. They are designed to maintain a constant temperature within certain limits. The characteristic feature of such an apparatus is that it does not exert constant pressure on the variable it has to specify: temperature in this case. Instead we could say that the thermostat exposes itself to variations in the variable. It confronts the new and the unexpected in a way which merely genetic information could never do. In the face of the new and unexpected, the homeostatic mechanism goes through experiences of trial, error, and correction. When the temperature in a tank of hot water loses heat or drops, when it becomes "erroneous" insofar as the aims of the apparatus are concerned, the thermostat lights the heating device. When the temperature rises above a certain point, again becoming "erroneous," the thermostat turns off the heating device.

All the products of cybernetics, the real robots, are homeostatic mechanisms. After all, the model for all of them is the most complicated and perfect homeostatic mechanism: the human mind. That is why scientists frequently use the word "mind" with reference to anything that displays the characteristics of a homeostatic mechanism: i.e., the basic ability to learn by going through experiences of error and its correction.

Here I use the word "error" in the broad sense, of course, referring to everything that does not suit the entity in question. Because of the way it is constructed, a thermostat knows that a temperature higher than seventy-five degrees or lower than seventy degrees does not suit the tank of hot water. When either of those limits is passed, the thermostat notes the "error" and corrects it, turning on or off the heating device which warms the water.

As I noted above, homeostatic mechanisms began long before human beings appeared in the course of evolution. They continue to operate in the evolutionary process and are extended in many of humanity's products and artifacts. But it is obvious that not all these mechanisms have the degree of consciousness, willfulness, and systematization that is typical of the human mind. Those kinds of mechanisms which are more conscious, deliberative, and systematic are what human beings refer to as "reason" in themselves.

Now let us go back to the general theme of evolution. It would seem that the preferences were not always clearcut. Some lean towards the security of genetic heredity. For others the advantage seems to lie with homeostatic mechanisms and their exposure to error.

If we consider the matter from one angle, it would seem great if the whole of mathematics could be incorporated into our genetic heredity. Algebra and the multiplication tables would flow out of human beings as surely as the ability to build a nest flows from a bird. Mathematics would come as easily and unconsciously as muscular movement in the process of respiration.

On the other hand we have that great cultural movement known as the Enlightenment, which was characterized by the opposite preference. It wanted to introduce conscious awareness, deliberation, and choice—homeostatic mechanisms—into areas where things seemed to function almost automatically and unconsciously (as if by genetic inheritance). It wanted to expose what had been going on uncritically and unexamined for generations to critical examination and the possibility of error. Freud's exploration of the unconscious and the whole psychoanalytic movement is one example of this thrust. Marxism is another.

So which way should we lean? Advances in the theory of the evolution suggest that we should not lean either way. To put it better: we should not favor one side a priori, without taking into account surrounding conditions.

Bateson wisely points out that evolution as such does not consist in the difficult becoming easy or the higher replacing the lower. The chief quality pervading the whole process and keeping it going is *flexibility*. And the latter quality can be threatened by both tendencies: the tendency to turn all useful qualities into genetic ones, and the tendency to replace genetic inheritance completely with homeostatic mechanisms of a more mental or rational stripe.

This view is grounded in the laws of thermodynamics. Evolution does not have an unlimited supply of energy at its disposal. Nor can it even count on new supplies of energy as it progresses. Having a constant supply of energy at its disposal, the evolutionary process is faced with the crucial question of *how it is to make use of that energy*. Being *flexible* really means having energy at one's disposal and thus being able to confront the problems which crop up. We could say that evolution has moved along by following the best energy calculus. That comes down to saving energy when it can be done without danger in order to invest it where it might produce better results.

Now genetic heredity is the supreme energy-saving process. It gives us things ready-made and done, but its importance does not lie in that convenience. Its importance lies in the fact that it frees energy for use in other activities. Contrast this fact with the reality of homeostatic mechanisms. Although they can confront larger problems because they are exposed to error and the unexpected, they are costly processes in terms of energy expenditure.

When we say that a friend overburdened with problems is likely to get an ulcer, we are alluding to this necessary energy equilibrium. Having many problems means setting many homeostatic mechanisms in motion. (Note that "problems" solved by genetics do not usually show up as problems exactly.) To overload those homeostatic mechanisms with supplies of costly energy is akin to writing a check on an overdrawn account. We are actually making a dent in our savings, and it is not surprising that the bodily functions carried out by genetic instructions should be impaired.

Something analogous can be said of the opposite approach. If we manage to routinize large areas of life and solve problems that way, we will store up large quantities of available energy. Habit serves as a quasi-genetic mechanism. The main problem here is that we may have sacrificed *too much* the possibility of confronting new challenges, exercising critical judgment, and creatively solving problems. In that case our energy savings are enough to buy us a gold-plated Cadillac—for use in a desert.

These considerations add needed refinements to overly simplistic philosophies. If the supreme evolutionary quality is flexibility in the face of environmental challenges, such flexibility obviously comes from maintaining a proper balance between genetic inheritance and homeostatic mechanisms. That balance must be kept under control at all times.

Depending on how you take the matter, you may regard the point as an obvious cliché or as an important scientific point which holds true in many areas besides the biological realm. In energy terms, flexibility does not depend on delivering all qualities useful in the past by making them hereditary. In the face of new and unexpected challenges, that magnificent tradition-bound mechanism would break down and be useless. But neither does flexibility entail liberating more and more homeostatic or "mental" mechanisms to replace hereditary ones. The ever-increasing number of urgent problems could overwhelm the system and render it equally incapable of solving them.

The course of evolution has been more intelligent in its quest for flexibility. It has selected certain problems to be solved by one mechanism and others to be solved by the other mechanism. If the most serious problems of survival are also more or less constant, solving them by genetic inheritance will ensure an economy of energy and also provide for flexibility. For then homeostatic circuits are set free to tackle problems that are variable and unforeseeable.

Insofar as human life and culture are concerned, human beings and society must engage in the same selection of problems and mechanisms in order to continue and direct the further course of evolution. The two extreme tendencies, which might be called Darwinian and Lamarckian, would only undermine flexibility in the long run if they were applied absolutely.

II. Political Analogies

I assume my readers have followed the thread of my argument so far in this chapter and this book. So they will readily see the *political* analogies and conclusions to be drawn from my comments in the previous section of this chapter.

Legislation, Rights, and the Conservation of Energy

Bateson himself makes a point about this matter. While every society, like every living being, combines procedures akin to those of genetic inheritance and homeostatic mechanisms, more emphasis may be placed on one or the other factor. Indeed this may be done to the point where the evolutionary process is blocked, as the extinction of certain species attests. Bateson suggests that on the human level it is societal *legislation* that is most akin to genetic inheritance.[3] I would like to add two points to complete the analogy and make it more precise.

The first point is that the *freedoms* granted by legislation as lawful rights play the role of homeostatic mechanisms in society. They offer people the possibility of learning something new through their experience of error and its correction.

The second point has to do with what is legislated in a society. In many cases, and particularly in our countries today, legislation is not just what is established in the constitution. The decrees and repressive measures of an authoritarian or totalitarian government, be they legitimate or not, expand the area of imposed things and thus shrink the realm of liberty. Thus they constitute an expansion of processes akin to genetic inheritance at the expense of homeostatic mechanisms in society. The latter are restricted to the small group of political rulers and decision-makers—aside from the private homeostatic circuits of individuals which no amount of repression can wholly or effectively control.

One important conclusion remains to be drawn. In the sociopolitical realm, as in the biological realm, it does not matter very much what response is given to abstract discussions about human rights or the legitimacy of this or that kind of government. Such discussions do not take into account the context of energy-related problems and challenges which different societies must face. In most cases, therefore, such discussions are merely a trap laid for the weak by the strong, on the pretext of teaching the weak how they ought to organize themselves.[4]

Take the case of the United States or the countries in the European Common Market, for example. If it is fully democratic mechanisms that are going to decide whether a country which represents 6 percent of the world's population (the United States) is going to go on consuming more than 40 percent of the world's production, then it is futile to expect that the error will be noticed through the use of those mechanisms (analogous to homeostatic mechanisms). It is futile to hope that the direct and indirect ecological destruction discussed in the last two chapters will be avoided. So long as that type of society continues the tragedy of its mistakes beyond its frontiers, which are also the frontiers of its democratic sensitivity, its homeostatic mechanisms will not detect the mistake until it is incurable, until in the end it becomes noticeably intolerable even for those who have committed it. The *de facto inflexibility* of one of the most seemingly flexible societies in the world is one of the tragic dramas of our time.

Equally tragic, though in a very different way, is the behavior of totalitarian or repressive regimes. The tragedy is not that they violate "human rights." Those who are motivated by something more than personal ambition usually start off from an obvious fact that has struck home to them. It is a realization centered in the middle class: i.e., that if the country is to survive, it is necessary to increase the communal reserves of energy. Those reserves are meager in poor countries, and they are undermined when homeostatic mechanisms get overloaded. All that people can see, in fact, are overloaded mechanisms of that sort: interminable parliamentary debates; phony political campaigns; the ongoing pursuit of votes at the expense of administrative efficiency; labor-union demands which pay no regard to the overall economic context; student criticism and violence; university protests; overemphasis upon judicial procedural technicalities in trials; and so forth.

Not without reason, then, representatives of the repressive regime get the idea that they should implement more social mechanisms which, as Bateson puts it, simulate Lamarckian inheritance. This, they feel, will enable the country to move out of domestic chaos and confront the growing challenges of foreign pressure with fresh reserves of energy. Certain attitudes and patterns of behavior must become automatic and compulsory—quasi-genetic—instead of being left to the free choice of individuals as they were in the past. They can no longer be left to homeostatic mechanisms.

The tragedy lies in the fact that such governments seem to remain systematically ignorant about one thing: what is to be done with the "cheap" energy thus acquired? It obviously cannot be invested in culture, in the creation of culture at least. For the savings of energy have come at the expense of homeostatic (i.e., creative) mechanisms. The repressive governments are uncontrolled by any outside opinion and devoid of critical-mindedness or creativity. All those elements have been sacrificed to achieve survival at first and easy authoritarianism later. So those governments seem incapable of finding any goal other than that of some sort of material "development."

Now in the global context it is obvious that only certain intermediate goals are viable. Far more important, however, is the fact that the final goal would be achieved only with the complete destruction of the social ecology. Hence it would be achieved for creatures who were no longer "political human be-ings," complete human beings bound together by real social ties. Yet only such human beings could possess and enjoy that "development." In this case, too, *flexibility* has been left by the wayside.

The Role of Faith and Ideologies

The dense complexity of political reality, perhaps unsuspected by us at the start, forces us to go even deeper into the basic anthropological dimensions which have been our theme. We cannot help but ask: what role do *faith* and *ideologies* play vis-à-vis the flexibility of the social human being?

As we saw in Section I of this chapter, needed flexibility called for a certain balance between genetic mechanisms and homeostatic mechanisms. Here it should be obvious that there is a certain analogy: between faith and the re-serve store of energy embodied in genetic inheritance on the one hand; and between ideologies and homeostatic mechanisms on the other.

Human beings must explore the possibilities which reality offers them to achieve their ends. They must try creatively to make reality malleable, without overloading their exploratory mechanisms and overdrawing their supply of energy. Hence they need a store of energy-savings akin to that supplied by genetic inheritance.

Bateson rightly suggests that *legislation* fulfills this role in society, saving up precious energy to ensure the flexibility of individuals and society as a whole. But legislation is only one example, and it does not tell the whole story. That particular energy-saving comes from the social roots of the hu-man being. A far deeper and more significant social source of energy-saving is what I have been calling anthropological faith.

Basic anthropological faith is social in two senses. We do well to recall them here so that we can better appreciate the role of faith. First, faith is social because human beings must depend on referential witnesses provided by society in order to create their own world of meaning and values (see Chapter I). But if the social function of faith were limited to that, faith could hardly be considered analogous to genetic inheritance insofar as storing up energy is concerned. It must do something more than drop a wide range of potential referential witnesses on the doorstep so that the individual may pick and choose and test different combinations. The energy-saving of heredity derives from the fact that genetic inheritance *imposes* rather than merely proposing.

Bateson makes a useful observation in this regard. He points out how dangerous it might be if the pressure of imposition by heredity were to slacken, if changes could be introduced into it insofar as experience proved certain qualities to be useful. Even though the outside world might remain stable and nonthreatening, any genetic change would entail readjusting the whole system of homeostatic mechanisms to the new *premise*. Every such system would have to learn all over in a world that had become new, even though the world itself might not have changed at all. Only if such changes were imposed slowly and gradually could one avoid the danger mentioned earlier with respect to changes in the outside context.

For example, suppose an elephant acquired the neck of a giraffe. Even though it remained in its usual environment, most of its mental mechanisms would have to focus on the adventure of living in a new world. The elephant would have to carefully relearn most of the things it knew, moving slowly and step by step. And if the next day its trunk was replaced with the nose and mouth of a lion, the poor elephant would not know what to do. It would lie down and die without any external threat having appeared on the horizon.

As we saw, something similar happens to human beings when they are confronted with such drastic changes as those caused by the destruction of the social ecology. In general, however, human nature is wiser. Or at least it is just as wise as nonhuman nature. It not only proposes but to a large extent *imposes* meaning-systems. It not only proposes witnesses but chooses them within a certain framework of coherent meaningfulness. The human being chooses, but within channels which have been traced out for it to a large extent. We call those channels "cultural traditions."

So our question is: *what kind of cultural tradition* do we need to restore flexibility to our society? This important matter will be the subject of Section III.

III. The Nonneutrality of Society and Cultural Flexibility

The very posing of such a problem may be shocking to a secularist outlook, but here a distinction is in order between practical secularism and theoretical secularism. Practical secularism tends to do away with the dogmatic impositions of any and all public institutions, particularly of those institutions against which the human being is more defenseless: i.e., those which educate him or her in early childhood and youth. *Theoretical* secularism is closely associated with a liberal philosophy about the human being and with the ideals of the Enlightenment; it serves as the alleged basis for practical secularism.

The Career of Theoretical Secularism

Theoretical secularism, commonly known as philosophical liberalism, played a positive role in history as did the rest of the Enlightenment. It did so insofar as it corrected an existing one-sidedness—but with a one-sidedness of its own. Despite its characteristic faith in progress, theoretical secularism would have blocked human evolution if its proponents had managed to apply it consistently to life. It would be anachronistic, of course, to blame philosophical secularism and the Enlightenment for not knowing things which were discovered much later. But the fact remains that those movements did not picture the human being and society in terms of *flexibility*, in terms of an energy calculus. They tended to reject as undesirable anything that came to human beings without the latter being able to make it their own by rational criticism and a subsequent free choice.

Let us take a brief inventory of some of the general things which theoretical secularism wanted to reject on the above grounds, since that inventory would serve as the backdrop for practical secularism and its actions.

The most obvious and external impositions to be rejected by secularism were those imposed on the individual by external social institutions, and primarily the government, in an area where individuals ought to exercise critical judgment and freedom: i.e., the realm of values. Excluded from this ban as we shall see was the imposition of anything and everything regarded as *neutral*: e.g., science.

Another series of impositions hit the individual closer to home, though these impositions were also conveyed socially. They *dogmatically* impeded or undermined the mental processes of criticism and deliberation. Human thinking was not exposed to personal experiencing of reality and error. Instead it imposed a priori views on that experience. Thus secularism was strongly opposed to any and every transmission of religious faith that might entail pressure on individuals, particularly on more defenseless individuals such as young children and adolescents.

Now Marxism also came out of the Enlightenment, and we can say that it agreed with its postulates in general terms. That agreement was not destined to last, however, insofar as Marxism consistently applied one of its basic principles. Let us disregard here its ambiguity about the existence of a neutral science insofar as the nonhuman world is concerned. Let us also disregard the fact that Marxism became dogmatic as it became practical, thus locking up the critical mechanisms it was designed to set free. The important point here is that Marxism knew very well that a society transmits its structure from one generation to the next and that its structure is grounded in values centered around the satisfaction of the interests of those who dominate the structure and the disregard of other possible interests. Marxism and the later, even more universal, theory of ideology-in-the-service-of-interests pointed up the falseness of the alleged neutrality of civic morality. Marxism made clear that the adaptation of each generation of citizens to society cannot help but be the imposition of certain values on the citizenry by society. Those values, which are debatable, are presented to the citizens as beyond doubt or question.

Once that point was made clear, the clash between Marxism and secularism became an open one. We know for a fact that secularism, in the name of neutrality, proscribed the Marxist interpretation of society in the educational process. In turn, Marxism denounced secularism as merely an irrational imposition, under the guise of neutrality, of bourgeois morality. And it stressed that bourgeois morality embodied and suited the ruling interests of capitalist society.

If genetic manipulation were possible on a large scale in the near future, it is perfectly possible that secularism would be in favor of it if it thought that the criteria governing its implementation were scientific and neutral. Marxism, on the other hand, would point out that those criteria derived from the division of labor and hence served the interests of the ruling classes which stemmed from that same division of labor. This has been the most serious underlying reason for Marxist opposition to psychoanalysis and its manipulation of the human unconscious.

Be that as it may, I think I have shown in this book that human beings must willy-nilly entrust themselves to some meaning-orientation. The latter is not completely verifiable when they are young and inexperienced. And it is even less open to verification when they have burned their bridges behind them, chosen to follow a given path empirically, and hence closed themselves off to the authentic experiencing of other courses.

Now people who claim that they have mounted the shoulders of other human beings to see farther and reach higher must also admit that they have been carried by others. And that those others imposed many things on them: e.g., a superego; value-models inculcated by family, social class, school, propaganda, and patriotic sentiments; prescriptive legislation which enforces certain attitudes and values and prohibits others; iconic communication of certain ways of seeing and judging things, which appeals more to our sensibilities than to our reasons; and so forth. All these things are forms of pressure exerted on us by the past, and the most diehard secularism could not suppress them in order to "liberate" the human being or make individuals more rational. What is more, secularism itself is mounted on shoulders which it may not notice. Two examples are language and tradition, which we must now consider briefly.

Language and Tradition

Linguistics supports the view that the language we learn to speak as our native tongue does much to shape our outlook and view of the world. We don't think in a vacuum. Even when we are silent, we don't think without words or grammar. We think according to the rules and mechanisms of a particular language. The syntax of a language, for example, is closely associated with a certain way of perceiving reality, which highlights certain aspects and leaves others in the shadows. It establishes certain relationships but seems not to perceive others. What human being can first compare different languages and *then* decide which one seems the most suitable for him or her? What "neutral" arguments might be used in such a process?

We do not choose our language. We do not choose the classics of our language which are transmitted to us by the school system. Nor do we choose many other things which form a large part of our basic ontological and epistemological premises.

In another work I commented negatively on an incident which took place during a survey of rural life in my native country. When a peasant was asked what his religion was, he replied: "the local one." Here I am not interested in the caliber of a faith which purports to be authentically religious. In terms of our present topic, there is much common sense in the peasant's response. Adhesion to a tradition is the basis for saving energy so that the latter may be invested in more important tasks. No tradition could perform that function if its content were thoroughly foreign, so that people would have to stop and ask questions and make personal decisions with every step they took.

To be left without a tradition would be akin to being left without genetic instructions. In like manner, too complete or rapid change in traditions would overload our homeostatic mechanisms for dealing with the external world. Even if that world remained unchanged, we would be brought to a standstill as was our poor elephant.

We need complementary doses of both elements: what we receive ready-made or half-made from tradition and what we must pose to ourselves as problems. However, we cannot prescribe any precise dosage that would be universal and valid once and for all. The fact that we need a dose of tradition does not exempt us from the task of wisely criticizing the shoulders on which we are mounted. Evolution requires that we introduce alterations, perhaps even radical alterations, into the foundation prepared by earlier generations and other social models. But we must do this prudently, following a delicate energy calculus comparable to the types mentioned so far in this chapter.[5]

The human being is not a cultural being simply because it is given a ready-made culture as the launching pad for its own individual creation. It is a cultural being because its individual creation, in turn, leaves an imprint on that culture.

Schaff and Machoveč: The Search for Socialist Flexibility

My remarks so far in this chapter are part of our larger search for the preconditions which will ensure creative complementarity between faith and ideology, tradition and criticism, heritage and mental mechanisms. We are seeking a kind of complementarity that will allow us to re-create culture after the crisis we have suffered with regard to our social ecology. We are seeking a flexibility that we have lost.

Some light may be shed on our quest by the comments of Milan Machoveč and Adam Schaff, even though they were not discussing our situation in Latin America. Both of them were concerned with the achievement of social-ism, and both of them in their own way pointed to some strain of inflexibility that had blocked or impeded the development which was expected and hoped for. Even more significant is the fact that the two of them attributed the inflexibility to a certain lack of needed complementarity between faith and ideology, though they did not use the term "faith."

Let me summarize the problem posed by those two authors in the following terms of my own. Any faith (i.e., a particular system of meanings and values) gives rise to an ideology for its implementation in history. The specific merit of the ideology obviously lies in its effectiveness in inscribing those values in reality. That does not mean any and every type of efficacy will be valued, of course; nor will some type of efficacy vaguely related to the values in question suffice. In principle, the system of efficacy must be directly in line with the aim being pursued.

Now according to both Machoveč and Schaff, the ideology implemented by Marxist socialism has to some extent belied the hopes invested in it by the Marxist faith. This does not mean that the ideology has proved totally ineffective or nonviable. The establishment of a society without the classes generated by private ownership of the means of production has been carried through, and it was assumed that this would create a new human being. Some of the mechanisms and preconditions for such a new human have been dragged down from the realm of utopia and actually implanted in real life. But the new human being, for some reason, has not emerged, at least not on the scale which had been envisioned.

Note how Adam Schaff makes the same point indirectly in his comments. Marxism did indeed found a new society. But in its excessive preoccupation with "ideological" questions dealing with its realization in history, Marxism failed to elaborate an *ethics* consistent with the human destiny it sought to give that society. Thus the ideology has been realized in history, though ideological questions will always crop up. But even where it has been realized, the problem of human meaningfulness has not been solved. Its most conscious and sensitive supporters are now asking themselves, in all sincerity, what the meaning of life is.

Phrased in my terminology, then, the question is: how does one explain this gap or lack of it between faith and ideology, assuming that one does not simply take for granted that the whole project was mistaken from the start?

Interestingly enough, in diagnosing this somewhat unsatisfactory historical outcome, both Machoveč and Schaff clearly allude to phenomena of *inflexibility*. There has been some kind of ossification in a process which should have been able to develop much more, which supposedly would have kept creating new mechanisms as it proceeded.

From all that I have said so far, we would certainly be wrong in trying to attribute that inflexibility solely to the fact of political repression. Evolutionary flexibility is the product of an equation involving several factors. Two factors are internal to the individual or social organism: i.e., inheritance and homeostatic mechanisms. One factor is external: i.e., the problems or challenges provoked by the context.

When confronted with the fact of political repression, then, we must consider to what extent it is unnecessary and harmful. But in so doing, we must take into account the equation just mentioned. In different and more discreet terms Machoveč and Schaff suggest the same thing. We do well to examine their testimony here because it is more rewarding and profound than mere denunciations of repression, be the latter Stalinist or otherwise, which might still be found under socialist governments today. And I shall incorporate our new-found terminology into my description of their positions.

Schaff[6] tells us that in the effort to protect the socialist "inheritance," socialist governments have gone too far in obstructing "homeostatic mechanisms." Obstruction consists in denying the existence of problems perceived by young people and leaving no room for discussion of such problems. The latter problems derived from philosophies which generally were incompatible with Marxism. To be specific, they derived from existentialist formulations concerning ethics and the meaning of life. To re-establish the flexibility equation, Schaff attempts to prove two basic things: (1) that the external danger is minute; (2) that the application of mental mechanisms to such problems can enrich and deepen the values upheld by the Marxist heritage. For although the Marxist heritage does advocate those values, it does so in a way that is excessively unconscious (hereditary) and insufficiently explicit (mental). Thus the Marxist heritage becomes a factor of inflexibility insofar as it ignores the benefits to be derived from discreet exposure to trial-and-error mechanisms.

At first glance Machoveč[7] seems to be saying almost exactly the same thing. But instead of focusing on problems posed by atheistic existentialisms, this atheist focuses on things to be found in the great spiritual traditions of the West—particularly in the Bible. He, too, makes clear that there is no (external) danger that recourse to the Bible or Jesus will undermine the socialist heritage, given the present state of affairs and the present stage of exegesis. Machoveč, too, insists that such recourse can enrich and deepen the Marxist heritage. If the latter is not willing to risk such a venture, it may all too easily end up promoting a superficial and automatic kind of adaptation.

But Machoveč goes further than does Schaff in his diagnosis of Marxist inflexibility. He goes so far as to accuse Marx of naiveté. Marx failed to take note of the many superficial and simplistic ways in which one might win over the human heart and soul to the side of a given kind of society, even a socialist one.

To phrase it in our new terminology, Marx's equation did not accord due importance to anthropological faith as a heritage to be transmitted. The values basic to his own thought did not figure in the social "genetics" he imagined.

Because Schaff and Machoveč differ somewhat in their diagnoses, their solutions to the problem of flexibility also differ. Schaff says that socialism must end the blockade against the mental mechanisms which deal with real, important philosophical issues, and derive the correct answers from the Marxist heritage. Machoveč says that socialism must nurture and transmit a richer faith, so that the ideology which built and maintains socialist society will not succumb to oversimplification, the easy way out, and inflexibility in various forms: consumptionism, servility, egotism, bureaucracy, etc.

Now these two witnesses or examples have not been drawn from Latin America or its real-life situation. Yet in one way or another we see both authors posing the same issue that I have raised with respect to our reality. It is also interesting to note that the complementarity between faith and ideology, heritage and mind, becomes so intimate that the two dimensions share something like a common ground. It is no longer a matter of merely juxtaposing two completely distinct functions in a coherent way. At this point we find that an inappropriate ideology degrades faith and that a faith which fails to recognize all its components leads to a counterproductive ideology.

We find the same thing in biological evolution, as a matter of fact. If heredity does not integrate all of a creature's potential for acting, it will obstruct mental mechanisms which are of great evolutionary value. And the obstruction of those mechanisms, in turn, will result in only one-sided qualities being incorporated into heredity. Those one-sided qualities will be closed off to complementary contributions of a precious sort.

Latin America: The Need to Create an Effective Cultural Tradition

This book does not propose to offer concrete solutions to problems which vary from place to place and from group to group on our continent. All readers can expect from my recourse to method here are general lines of orientation for the task we cannot postpone: i.e., laying the foundations for a culture that is truly our own, hence flexible as well.

We began this chapter with the situation analyzed in the previous chapter: the serious ecological destruction of our social life and the impossibility of tackling the problem with our customary political means.

It seems quite obvious that we face the task of creating or re-creating culture. Is it possible to do something worthwhile and decisive in that area, given our rarefied atmosphere of political repression?

A fairly classic response to the question focuses on the individual. When this approach is turned into an ideological principle and trap, it assumes that the first thing is to transform human beings so that structural changes will then be meaningful and effective.

There is no reason why we should go to that extreme. We can and must recognize the value of simply surviving and living through this period in a humane, hopeful, and critical-minded way. We may face a long period of passivity, imprisonment, exile, and repression. But living through it in the way just described offers the best guarantee of a future for our continent. We still retain some possibilities for reflecting on the human condition, correcting it, and immersing ourselves deeper in it. If thousands and thousands of people are placing those possibilities in the service of our future, that in itself represents a considerable coefficient of *flexibility*. And it is such flexibility that will give direction and impetus to the changes which somehow will be feasible, sooner or later, at some future date. And this equation is certainly political.

But my comments in this chapter take us further than that. Perhaps I can trace out the broad outlines of a task that has a more direct political impact. The task in question is the creation of an adequate cultural base there where the destruction of the social ecology reigns supreme today.

We cannot talk about a cultural base or foundation unless we have in mind the task of organizing the broad-scale transmission of values-structures and meaning-structures from one generation to the next. It is not enough for a number of individuals, no matter how large, to live in a truly human way in an inhuman society. That will not suffice to get us away from a destroyed social ecology and to fashion a vast, well-integrated social dimension. Personal witness is crucial, but we must also find the means to *transmit it*. So we face the problem of shaping an effective cultural *tradition*. We must make a certain basic values-structure almost automatic. On that quasi-automatic structure we can then build the needed political ideologies with a certain degree of ease insofar as the use of energy is concerned.

It must be admitted that we are not used to raising or tackling the broad problem of creating a culture. We create culture to some extent, perhaps, insofar as we exercise our ability and practice our professions. But in general we are more used to being borne along by our culture or to criticizing it as adults. It is hard for us to picture culture emerging fresh from the oven, still malleable, and ready to receive the molds of language, art, and thought.

In the next and final chapter of this book, I shall offer a brief panorama of the various general courses which lie open to us. I shall describe various possible approaches to our task and what each might or might not have to offer us.

NOTES

1. Insofar as the basic scientific and anthropological underpinnings of my comments in this chapter are concerned, I refer readers to a chapter in Bateson's book. I will not give detailed references to it as I go along. See the chapter entitled "The Role of Somatic Change in Evolution," in Gregory Bateson, *Steps to an Ecology of Mind*, (New York: Ballantine Books, 1972), pp. 346–63.

2. On the definition, function, and limits of "homeostatic mechanisms," see Bateson, *Steps*, pp. 315–20.

3. Ibid., p. 354.

4. Thus a political policy may hypocritically pretend it is not permitting or maintaining oppression, when in fact it wittingly or unwittingly is failing to take this energy calculus into account. Such would be the case if it claimed to authorize or defend human rights without providing the energy needed to put their defense on a stable, effective basis. On this point see J. L. Segundo, "Direitos humanos, Evangelização e ideologia," *Revista Eclesiástica Brasileira* 37 (March 1977): 91f.

5. "Such a change will, in the nature of the case, be achieved comparatively slowly and be comparatively irreversible. . . . Reversibility implies that the changed value of some variable is achieved by means of homeostatic, error-activated circuits" (Bateson, *Steps*, p. 352).

6. See Chapter IX, Note 40, p. 247, above.

7. See Chapter IV, p. 90f, above.

CHAPTER XIII

Ideology, Faith, and Cultural Evolution

It is time to call a halt to our study of an inexhaustible subject. By way of conclusion I want to bring back on stage various types of faith and their associated ideologies which have been discussed in this book. This time around, however, I want to focus particularly on the relative capacity of each one to become culture.

We have seen that faith is an anthropological dimension linking the human being to past and present society, whether that human being is a religious believer, an agnostic, or an atheist. This dimension of faith is rooted in the need of human beings to rely on transcendent data if they want to structure a world of meaning and values. The data are not transcendent solely when and if they have to do with God or the beyond. They are such because they transcend all possibility of empirical verification by the individual human being. Such *data* are indispensable if we wish to know what reality has to offer in the way of satisfaction, and they can readily be tracked down and found in the conduct of any human being. Moreover, they are supplied to us *socially*, which is to say, by other human beings. However independent of his or her milieu a human being may claim to be, we find that person's data to have roots buried in some more or less remote past: i.e., *tradition*.

Please note what I mean by "tradition" here. The word is often used in a clearly political, indeed reactionary, sense. But, etymologically speaking, "tradition" comes from the Latin verb *tradere*, and it signifies the act of handing something down or over, as well as the end product of such a process. I start with that etymological meaning, but I mean to be more specific. In the realm of culture we do not use the term "tradition" for any and every type of individual, contingent, episodic transmission. If the transmission of something is to be regarded as tradition in the cultural sense, its content must somehow become stable and homogeneous so that we can recognize it coursing through time and human generations. We must be able to pinpoint it through history.

Tradition, in other words, is that which every society deliberately relegates to the heredity side of the energy equation discussed in the previous chapter (see Section I). Energy is thus stored up for other mental operations which seem more useful and important in the light of the surrounding context and its challenges.

Here, then, I want to take another look at the different types of faith to which I have alluded frequently in this book. I want to *situate them* one by one along a continuous spectrum, rating them on the basis of their capacity for cultural transmission. We should be able to draw some general conclusions about each one, and those conclusions would have to be taken into account when we formulate our own energy equation for the social task ahead of us. Our aim, of course, would be to expend our energy as wisely as possible in our efforts to construct or reconstruct the social organism.

I. Faith-Ideology Interaction: Two Extremes

Since it suits our purposes here, we take a civilized society as our field of observation. We notice right away that one extreme or end of our spectrum would be represented by the transmission of extremely simplistic and superficial values.

Some readers might cringe at such a judgmental statement. We all know it is not easy to talk precisely about the realm of meaning. My statement seems to suggest that I have already taken some unspecified stand and that I am condemning certain values in themselves before I even begin. As if I had not warned readers about doing that very thing! So let me explain myself.

Simplistic and Superficial Values

What do I mean when I talk about simplistic and superficial values? My point should be clear from everything I have said so far in this book. Certain values-systems focus on satisfactions of a clearly defined type which can be isolated from all the rest. They are *simplistic* in that sense. They can cause the importance of all the rest to fade from the horizon of our concern and preoccupation, along with the complexity that would be entailed in trying to incorporate them all in an effective, harmonious way.

And why do I refer to them as *superficial*? The first answer which may come to mind is that such satisfactions, insofar as they can be recognized and isolated from the rest, must be rather closely bound up with the material realm: money, sex, physical well-being, and so forth. However, I don't want to get involved in unnecessary disputes here; nor do I want to get caught up in commonplace misunderstandings. So I prefer to offer one observation which can be readily verified.

Let us say that some people can simplify and isolate the particular satisfaction to which they entrust the meaning and purpose of their existence. Now if they manage to do that in the sense meant here, they will do so with a very limited gamut of the mental or homeostatic mechanisms which confront reality and try to solve its challenges in meaningful terms. In general human terms, the array of homeostatic mechanisms used will be very unsophisticated as well as very limited. Many of their mental mechanisms, particularly the more complicated ones, will become atrophied. The calculations of their human computer will be performed on a very small set of variables. That is why I talk about superficiality here.

Viewed in this light, we are not so surprised by the furious invective which Miguel de Unamuno hurls at Don Juan Tenorio, that great hero of Spanish literature. Unamuno regards him as a silly fool, who is superficially active and creative in one line only and woefully passive in everything else: "It cannot be said that he was a biblical, Shakesperian, or Ibsenian sinner—that blustering jerk, Don Juan Tenorio. He was an out-and-out dunce. And if the ghost of the commander had not whisked him away in time, you would have seen him a respectable old graybeard—defending order, the venerable traditions of our elders, liberty in the right sense, and the 'bread and catechism,' and piously attending the solemn rites of his confraternity. His sheepish intelligence was not up to more."[1]

Insofar as the formation or deformation of a culture is concerned, simplistic and superficial meaning-structures of that sort can be transmitted without major difficulties. Indeed they do not even need the literary trappings of a Don Juan.

For example, consider propaganda which points to consumption as the supreme value or, if not that directly, as the undeniable key which unlocks the door to the supreme value: e.g., prestige, power, the good life. Such a line of propaganda greatly simplifies any human constellation of values and makes it superficial. In so doing, it decreases the cost in energy terms and renders its transmission easier.

Serious Philosophy and the Meaning of Life

At the other end of the spectrum I would place the anthropological and ethical reflection of *philosophy* in its quest for a satisfactory meaning in life.

As we have seen, there are two essential characteristics required for any values-system to merit the label of philosophy—which is not to say that the two are logically consistent. The first feature is the one which makes philosophy look like a religion in disguise: i.e., its rich store of transcendent data, almost to the exclusion of anything else. The second feature is what constitutes the disguise: the intent of philosophy not to accept that data as mere tradition, but rather to subject it to the critical examination of reason and a carefully reasoned process.[2]

These two features, paradoxical as they may seem, are to be found together in philosophical thought. Only when we recognize that can we appreciate the strange fascination which philosophy has continued to exert, on small groups of people at least, in the midst of a world increasingly built around technology.

Kant pointed out that philosophy did not display the continuing progress evidenced by science. He sought to remedy that situation but he did not succeed. Despite hesitation and mistakes, science does seem to move from one achievement to the next on the basis of past successes. But methodology dictates that every philosopher start all over and build his edifice from the ground up. If he did not do that, he could hardly claim the title of philosopher. Every philosophy appeals to experience, of course, but experience is unable to resolve disputes between different philosophies. The empirical data are elaborated on the basis of different premises, and the latter keep the data above and beyond empirical control or verification.[3]

Now let us turn our attention from philosophy's method of obtaining transcendent data to the quality of that data. We notice right away that we are at the other end of the spectrum, far from meaning-structures of an excessively simplistic and superficial sort. Every important philosophy deals with complex and profound values, even though it may not be able to integrate all values and may show some inconsistencies. In other words, it opens up its mental or homeostatic mechanisms to a huge multiplicity of factors conditioning the meaning of human existence.

The meaning-systems elaborated in philosophical activity are therefore complex and profound. But this is accompanied by a limitation as well. Philosophical activity *as such* is the very opposite of tradition. Even though traditional elements filter through inevitably, philosophy painstakingly tries to avoid that; indeed it sees that effort as its justification. Imagine how scandalous it would be for a philosophy to try to impose itself on people through songs or rituals, to spare people the work of logically and rationally thinking out each step involved in organizing their mental life. One conspicuous exception only confirms the general rule. Auguste Comte tried unsuccessfully to remedy the inherent cultural weakness of philosophy by establishing a positivist cult.

There is no doubt that some philosophies have exercised a cultural influence, but only insofar as they were transposed to other cultural levels endowed with very different means of transmission. One could say that philosophical pragmatism had much to do with the increasingly pragmatic culture of the industrialized West. But insofar as this "religious" influence in disguise is concerned, we must realize that philosophical pragmatism was more the product than the creator of that culture. The same could be said for many other cases. In some instances, Greece for example, we can talk about a more creative influence being exerted by philosophy. But we must not forget that the most important portion of that influence was translated into legislation, and legislation, as a technique of transmission, is quite the opposite of philosophical reflection itself.

So at this other end of our spectrum we find great complexity and depth of meaning. But since philosophy seeks to exercise rational control from start to finish, it denies itself the means of transmission which a cultural tradition has. If the latter lacked such means of transmission, then everyone who wanted the same sort of richness and depth would have to become a philosopher. Some individuals might succeed, but most people would probably lose their bearings altogether. I am reminded of the comments made by one character in Joyce Cary's novel entitled *To Be a Pilgrim* (1942). He remarks that there seemed to be more common sense in the air once upon a time. It was not that people were born with more common sense, but that it seemed easier for people to be sensible. Today, by contrast, people have to discover everything for themselves, and they are old before they learn anything important.

The two extremes examined so far are the purest examples of the two one-sided views of evolution which I discussed in the previous chapter. One exemplifies the Lamarckian view, the other the Darwinian view. And both overlook the supreme evolutionary quality: flexibility.

Such evolutionary strategies could be justified only in rare contexts. We can scarcely imagine such contexts, which could hardly last for very long in any case. Thus the urgency of a total threat might offer some justification for simplistic and superficial valuations, and the security of unalterable prosperity and abundance might justify a serious philosophical approach.

II. Faith-Ideology Interaction: Three Familiar Instances

The most interesting cases of faith-ideology interaction examined in this book do not occupy such extreme points on our spectrum. Here I want to go back over three familiar cases which, in their own different ways, do combine the two internal dimensions to some extent. I would like to suggest how they might be related to culture.

Religion

In the early chapters of this book I discussed what goes by the label "religion" in sociological terms. I pointed out that "religion" in that sense is not primarily some basic anthropological faith that has reached or crossed a certain threshold. Instead it is a belief in a set of nonscientific instruments which are imposed as rituals or moral regulations from the outside, endowed with an authority which is assumed to be sacred, and hence effective for realizing certain values whose attraction derives from other sources.[4]

Here we run into a persistent and tenacious misunderstanding that is encouraged by ecclesiastical authorities. They may do this for impartial or self-serving reasons, depending on their particular conception of faith and its necessities. They tend to insist that this *ideological* system, because it is "religion," comes under the jurisdiction and responsibility of the Church. They make this claim even when they may not go so far as to say that the system is the authentic faith which serves as the foundation of the Church, which must be preserved at all costs, and to which every other function of the Church must be subordinated. In fact, however, we are dealing with a *cultural* phenomenon. The instrumental system, in other words, is much more closely bound up with the rest of the culture than with any strictly or properly religious faith. Its values—its "faith"—are those conveyed by the culture itself, and they will not be separated from the culture no matter how many changes the ecclesiastical authorities may make in dogmas, rites, and moral precepts.

This also explains the extraordinary isolated resistance of traditional religion in the midst of governments which inaugurate traditions and appeal to new values. Indeed such religious traditions may not even see in the new values a challenge to participate in building a new society, even if in a critical-minded way. They are simply cultural driftwood.

The fact is that important and complicated problems—moral and political ones, for example—may be solved down to their last details by way of tradition and heritage combined with the prestige of the sacred. And note what this means, at least on our Latin American continent: if repressive governments want to ensure themselves solid cultural grounding in their own nation's past, they will successfully resort to "religious" support. It does not matter a bit that those who presumably legislate on religious matters may try to discredit or rule out that support. Oddly enough, the civil authorities carry more weight in this area. It is not just because they have means of coercion at their disposal. It is because they hold the culture as a whole in their hands.

All this points up how close such religio-cultural traditions are to the first extreme case examined in Section I of this chapter. This form of transmitting values is far better equipped than other forms for iconically transmitting a certain meaning-world, so long as that meaning-world remains fairly simplistic and superficial.

The iconic richness of popular religion is a well-recognized fact. What is not recognized so well is the simplistic and superficial quality of the values-world it can transmit.

When people talk about richness and depth in popular religion, they are confusing things. The richness lies in the abundance and variety of the means employed in its transmission of values, but that tells us nothing about the quality of the values transmitted. The depth lies in the fact that those religious elements are solidly bound up with the whole of the culture, even with its most profane elements. But if we examine the mental mechanisms which are triggered or obstructed by this type of heritage, we find ourselves compelled to echo Unamuno's critique of Don Juan. The only difference is that we may be compelled to stress the uncreative features which he saw in that phony hero, and which he, not without reason and not simply because he was writing in Spain, associated with certain religious positions.[5]

That brings us to another consideration which merits attention. In the previous chapter I wrote about the one-sidedness of secularism as a theory. Here I must rehabilitate it, at least to some extent, in practice. Its fight to free mental mechanisms from the pressure of religio-cultural traditions, such as the ones under discussion here, helped a great deal to restore balance to an energy equation which had become inflexible because of its proximity to the simplistic end of the spectrum. In other words, secularism helped insofar as it pointed towards a more complex equation, though it did not resolve the issue or result from such an equation.

One final observation. I just indicated that a certain dose of practical secularism freed many mental mechanisms by breaking with tradition and preventing the latter from conveying certain kinds of values or ideologies in a hereditary, ready-made way. But there was something in those traditions, too, which helped this liberation along.

Here I do not intend to pass judgment on the process of cultural osmosis which fixed the religious traditions of Latin America. Many geographic and human variables went into that process and made it diverse. The point here is that elements of what could be called an authentic Christian faith also were part of the mix. These elements had been elaborated and transmitted, well or badly, for centuries in the West.

Take the Prologue of Saint John's Gospel, for example. The reading of that prologue was used as a remedy for certain accidents or illnesses. In the vast majority of cases, to be sure, this magical use completely vitiated one of the loftiest expressions of content achieved by the Christian faith, one which in and of itself would bring into play complex and profound mental mechanisms. But this reading went on repeatedly. So reckoning by the law of probability, we can assume that such readings would sometimes trigger the functioning of the mental mechanisms for which it was intended.

The morality brought to Latin America may have been too complex, insofar as it was elaborated by and for Christian societies in Europe. But any relatively complex morality, even when grasped and revered in an extrinsic, quasi-magical way, obligates people to hold certain attitudes. And the meaning and import of those attitudes will be perceived now and then at least.

Then there are the saints, among whom popular piety includes the figure of Jesus himself. I do not mean to suggest that the officially recognized saints are always paragons of well-balanced humanity, particularly when they are taken out of context. Nor do I want to minimize the fact that they were "used" magically rather than being appreciated in terms of their real human problems and even their holiness. But even that "use" would have some relation to their lives, with which the common people were familiar to some extent. Here again these referential witnesses offered by the culture lived and spoke of values which went so far as to call into question the very traditions which were also served by the witnesses. Thus the saints stood within those traditions and outside them at the same time.

It makes sense that the saints have almost always worried a religious institution which tried to ground itself more on cultural traditions than on an authentic faith. The comments of one of Bernanos's characters in another context might well be echoed here: "God save us from the saints! . . . All too often they have been a problem for the Church before becoming its glory. And I'm not even considering all those half-way or failed saints who swarm around the real ones and . . . are more of a hindrance than a help."[6]

All these observations on the symbiosis of religion and culture tend to point up that here again there is an area where the clearcut boundaries between faith and ideology disappear. Christianity can be turned into a repressive tradition, and it can generate simplistic and superficial values. It can foster domestication, offering a heritage closed to critical mechanisms and profound problem-posing. But even in that case the elements transmitted by it cannot be wholly isolated from a much richer and more complex faith. Hence it often fails to live up to the expectations invested in it by the forces of repression.

Marxism

Marxism obviously holds a special place among those entities which ordinary language confusedly labels as "ideologies." I have already made clear that Marxism, like liberalism for example, combines a system of meaning and values (a faith) with a more or less scientific system designed to build a society that accords with those values (an ideology).[7] But I would be closing my eyes to reality if I did not admit that the relationship between the two dimensions poses special difficulties in Marxism.

It is pointless to try to impose one's terminology on people, so we will not worry about the fact that Marxism does not use the term "faith" for itself insofar as it is a system of human values aimed at building a society. The use of my term can be justified only through analyzing a dimension of human action that is not explicit. Moreover, Marxism has traditionally been adverse to anything that sounded like religion. What is surprising, however, is that doubts and debates have arisen within Marxism as to whether it should be called a philosophy, an ideology, a science, a theory, or even *the* Theory (as Althusser would have it).[8]

These matters are symptomatic of an underlying difficulty which is more serious and practical in nature, and which I have been analyzing in this book. How does Marxism view the social complementarity between heritage and mental mechanisms, which it then proposes to put into practice? What things will a society based on Marxism entrust to tradition and what things will it leave open to experimentation, not only in the realm of legislation but also in the realm of culture and its instruments? If something such as "Eurocommunism" does exist, for example, it is precisely because Marxism has *in fact* faced up to this problem.

At first glance this might seem to be a valid question only where a socialist society is actually being fashioned. But actually the question surfaces as soon as Marxism proposes its vision of a new society to masses living under a different system. This *proposal* entails a problem, and certainly a cultural problem, as we Latin Americans know from actual experience. In our midst Marxism is proscribed and violently persecuted as *foreign*, as alien and opposed to our cultural ethos.

It is so easy to unmask the cynicism of that accusation in its more explicit forms that we are forced to consider this problem seriously. Why is it that

Marxism lends itself to that sort of propaganda? Why do the largest and most important segments of our population fall for that propaganda even when they have nothing to gain from what is presented as native and homegrown? The fact is that propagandists appeal to our own native traditions against Marxism. They appeal to our own ethos and "lifestyle," and the appeal works.

Let us consider the two chief alternative hypotheses. Suppose that Marxism is *merely* a formulation of scientific socialism, the programmatic realization of a society in which the means of production are not the private property of a few people. In that case we would have to say that the "scientific capitalism" which prevails in our countries is much more foreign. If we hearken back to the earlier customs of our peoples, then socialism would be a much more natural approach to modernity for us than is capitalism.

Moreover, science as such knows no frontiers. No one in our countries has opposed Newtonian physics because the law of gravity occurred to him on English soil, after he allegedly saw an apple falling from an English tree.

Applied science, on the other hand, does indeed have nationality. Its nationality is that of the people who control the economic, military, and political mechanisms which science places at their disposal. Everyone knows very well that the decisions which have the weightiest impact on us are decisions which we ourselves do not make. Yet for some reason Latin Americans are still swayed by the accusation that Marxism is foreign!

Is it correct to say that our ethos or lifestyle would change a great deal with the advent of socialism? To begin with, the most obviously vexatious aspects of a change in our lifestyle would be perceived only by a small minority of our people. In the economic area they would be felt by the small minority of those who own the means of production and by those patriarchs who are anxious to keep their large inheritance in their own nuclear family. But in the general culture, insofar as the vast majority of our people are concerned, what change would there be? We already have loads of things that are not to the liking of Latin Americans, from censorship to concentration camps: all imposed in the name of combatting socialism! It seems to me that the general atmosphere would be very different under socialism. Imposed restrictions would be borne with much more naturalness and good humor since people would feel that this was the way to greater and more equitable opportunities for all in jobs, education, and so forth.

The second hypothesis brings us much closer to reality. According to it, the accusation that Marxism is foreign has substance insofar as Marxism poses as *something more* than the science for building socialism. This does raise a serious and important question, one which I have tried to tackle in this book: how close and intimate is the relationship in Marxism between "philosophical" elements and its "scientific socialism"?

Once again it is hard to see why any *philosophy* should be particularly foreign to us. Marxism is not even an oriental philosophy. It is a European philosophy of German vintage. In general, our Hispanic countries have not been creators of the philosophies we espouse. No one has been scandalized by the fact that foreign philosophies are taught in our universities. Judeo-Christian thought itself can make no greater claims to being indigenous, quite aside from the fact that it has been handed down in the molds of European philosophies from which we have borrowed the higher forms of our culture.

But there is another problem here, which brings us to the doorstep of the *cultural* issue. The very term Marxist "philosophy" is awfully ambiguous. Here I need hardly go back over the preliminaries,[9] nor repeat the observations about Machoveč and Schaff made in the previous chapter. Instead let us first consider the *method* of thinking entailed in any system which claims to be a "philosophy" and then the *content* of that thinking.

In Section I of this chapter we saw that philosophy occupies one extreme of the spectrum under consideration: the extreme which has the minimum potential for becoming tradition and which makes maximum use of digital language. It is the digital language characteristic of mental mechanisms using their capacity for abstraction to the utmost, even though their aim may be to arrive at knowledge of the concrete. Philosophy also makes maximum use of reason for checking out every step of the thinking process, whether it is focusing on a conception of the universe or on concrete political strategies.

We have already considered the cultural implications of all this in countries where Marxism has managed to establish a society in line with its philosophy. Here we are focusing on another version of the same problem. We want to see what happens when Marxism is merely being proposed in a country or area, as is the case in our Latin America.

Remember our second hypothesis: i.e., that Marxism is not only a socio-economic science but a philosophy as well. Now if that is the case, then Marxism would be the one and only political ideology requiring people to cross the threshold of philosophical adherence, to adopt a specific way of thinking about the world, human beings, and their values.[10]

Some might object here that the same thing happens with all other political ideologies, only it is done less consciously and reflectively. My reply is that it is precisely that degree of consciousness and reflection that constitutes the cultural problem we are trying to pose.

Note that there is a very clear and crucial dividing line between the leadership and the masses insofar as Marxism is concerned. If one wants to comprehend and enter the control level, where political decisions are made in the name of Marxism, one has to penetrate an unknown, foreign, esoteric world. One must talk a new language. One must acquire Marxist "culture."

This is not just the customary esotericism of any science. It is not just that one must move from popular language to more precise operational concepts and calculations. Here, in addition, one must accept a particular conception of the world, a whole series of different premises about the functioning of thought and about the real import of the most accepted values in one's cultural tradition.

Anyone can apply the label "Marxist" to himself or others. It is happening all the time. But the power and ability to really be a Marxist entails something else. It entails, for example, having criteria for discussing which is the course authorized by the materialist dialectic and which is the "opportunistic" course to take in making a given political decision. At the same level one would also debate to what extent certain values of a petty bourgeois cast may have a revolutionary impact at times.

Let's go one step further. Consider a book expounding capitalist economics. Aside from the difficulty inherent in any scientific terminology, the arguments will be left to the reader's judgment. It will not make authoritarian references to certain documents (by Smith and Ricardo, for example) which fix and decide orthodoxy. Now consider a book dealing with the right policy to adopt in a given situation from the Marxist standpoint. Right away there will be references to texts of Marx, Engels, Lenin, and perhaps even Mao Tse-tung. In most instances those references will be explicit and abundant.

So what? some readers will answer. There is a Marxist "Bible" just as there is a Christian Bible, and someone like Lenin is no more foreign than someone like Jeremiah. But the resemblance is very superficial, I would say. Quite aside from the fact that the Christian Bible is linked to our cultural tradition in countless ways whereas the Bible of Marxist masters is not, the *mode of transmission* is very different.

Insofar as popular Christianity, the average Christian, and even religious authorities are concerned, one need only believe in the Christian Bible. Whether one uses that Bible or not has no decisive importance for one's status as a Christian believer. By contrast, no Marxist would admit that he or she "believes" in Marx, much less that he or she would entrust political leadership to someone who merely "believes" in Marx. Moreover the authoritative Marxist text is a philosophical text, according to my second hypothesis. By its very nature, then, it occupies the opposite end of the spectrum from tradition. That raises various cultural problems insofar as the accusation of foreignness is concerned.

The first problem, as I noted above, is that this esoteric world of Marxism does not constitute a mechanism of cultural *tradition* despite its allusions to texts from the past. Hence it does not offer any way of that sort to gradually replace one tradition with another. That problem has already surfaced consciously in Marxist countries, as the comments of Schaff and Machoveč indicate. Even more important is the fact that the transmission of a philosophy is the very opposite of creating cultural traditions. Each individual must invest a serious amount of energy in order to penetrate this new world, comprehend its structures, and find the correct applications. He or she must give up a "naive" or "bourgeois" conception of the world and adhere to a very different conception. Even if the teaching of the new philosophy were obligatory in the schools, the old values criticized by it would not disappear from the culture insofar as they were not attacked in cultural terms. Should that be the case, or has Marxism needlessly paid too high a price in taking that route? Readers must form their own judgment in the light of my discussion in Part

Three of this book. But I hope the above remarks give a first indication as to what the adjective "foreign" might mean, especially since it has been used so successfully against Marxism in our countries.

The second problem has to do with the cultural situation of a multitude of people who adhere to Marxism. They broadly identify with the ideals of greater social justice and feel that Marxism is the most effective way to achieve socialism. They have not made, nor are they capable of making, the expenditure of energy required to penetrate the esoteric realm of Marxist theories and thus gain access to the small nucleus of Marxists who make decisions. Now this two-edged situation may be common to all political ideologies to some extent, but the problem is obviously accentuated in the case of Marxism.

On the one hand the cultural traditions of this multitude remain unchanged, the same as everyone else's, because Marxism does not have the means of cultural transmission. Not surprisingly, then, there is a heightened impression that the multitude, who are still wedded to received cultural traditions, are being manipulated by a small elite. The latter are operating with a different line of thought. One is inclined to think that if they won power, they would impose a very different cultural heritage. Any other course would seem to be suicidal for them. And their would-be heritage seems all the more alien insofar as known examples of it go very much against the grain of our culture: e.g., antireligious propaganda and prohibitions against the reading of literary classics, such as those by Dostoyevsky.

Marxism seems to establish watertight compartments separating the masses from the ruling "philosophic" nucleus. Even Stalin, for example, dealt with questions of a philosophic nature. In cultural terms that sort of compartmentalized structure is not a relic from the time of Stalin or Lenin. It is a problem arising out of the fact that Marxism has not sufficiently clarified the relationship between faith and ideology in its system.[11] Insofar as Marxism has proposed its ideas here in Latin America, it clearly has not tried to ascertain whether any elements in our transmitted culture might serve to express the most important points of its ideology in our own cultural language. We have our own native expressions of value and our own referential witnesses to the meaning of life, which should not be overlooked or shunted aside. Marxism has paid a high price for doing precisely that. It is one more reason why Marxism finds itself so easily a prey to the accusation of foreignness.

The third problem is closely associated with the second, but it touches upon the *content* of Marxist philosophy as well as its method. It has to do with the relationship of Marxism to Christianity, insofar as the latter is part of our culture.

As I noted earlier in this book, there are certain weak spots in Marxism which seem to have something to do with the nineteenth-century world in which it arose. Certain contentual elements continue to be advocated stubbornly as intrinsic elements of Marxism, when such a view is questionable:

e.g., a deterministic brand of materialism, atheism, the assumption that historical materialism rules out any kind of faith and prohibits values prior to the classless society, and so forth.[12] At the same time, however, we find a strange phenomenon in many parts of Europe. Marxists seem quite ready to abandon other elements which seem to be much more intimately bound up with Marx's original thought: e.g., the necessity of the dictatorship of the proletariat as a stage in the establishment of socialism. They are quite willing to challenge such ideas as the latter, but they are reluctant to give up the former set of ideas. And the first set of ideas are far more clearly and forcefully in conflict with the cultural traditions of millions of human beings.

In the previous section we saw that simplistic and superficial values run deep, not because they are profound, but because they are very difficult to uproot. One example was a religion consubstantial with the culture and wielding instruments of a sacred character. We also noted, however, that even a religion of that type in Latin America is connected up with the great spiritual traditions of the West through Scripture, certain precepts, and saintly heroes. Hence it can give rise to something very different than what now exists. It can prompt a solidly different faith that may turn into a cultural force. And even though that faith may be a minority one, it may be a powerful cultural force.

Curiously enough, Marxism typically ignores this latter phenomenon, even though it does not escape the notice of international security mechanisms. Marxism lumps the phenomenon with the concept of "religion." Insofar as Marxism rightly or wrongly views itself as a philosophy that is to be implemented politically—and every philosophy is a complete system—it has nothing to offer anything that is "religion" except "freedom of worship." It does not consider the caliber of thought in any religion, and the freedom of worship is ambiguous and dubious at best. Religion and faith are conceded the rights of an alien or foreigner by Marxism. The latter does not expect or value any doctrinal contribution from faith as a corrective or complement to its own thought. Here we have another feature which underlines the "foreign" cast of Marxism. Marxism is foreign when it does not rule, and it turns all others into foreigners when it does rule.

Such are the negative aspects I wanted to mention. Readers must judge for themselves whether they stem from misconceptions which have come to be taken for granted by both Marxists and anti-Marxists. To be specific, I mean misconceptions about the nature of faith, ideology, and the complementary relationship between them. It seems to me that there are such misconceptions and short circuits and that they render inflexible the equation between heritage and mental mechanisms on the cultural level.

The Christian Faith

In the early chapters I tried to describe authentic religious faith. Now I must try to position it on the spectrum we have been considering. I fully admit that authentic types of religious faith can exist outside Christianity, but my concern here is to position the *Christian* faith on our spectrum, if only for practical reasons.

In our Latin American culture, adherence to a non-Christian religious faith would substantially alter the energy equation which underlies the following considerations. Assuming that religious faith is of equal complexity, we know that adherence to it would entail a considerably greater expenditure of energy insofar as it was not transmitted in and through one's own culture. While we would not equate that process with the transmission of a philosophy, we know it would be closer to it on the spectrum. The believer would have to start from scratch in building this new meaning-world. Scriptures, rites, and practices would have to be explored and learned well enough to ensure a gratifying result. So I focus on the Christian faith here because it is related, however confusedly and ambiguously, with the actual cultural traditions of our Latin American countries.

The first point I want to make here holds true for all the cases examined in this chapter. But it is in more urgent need of emphasis at this point because many serious misunderstandings prevail in this particular area. Some traditions, particularly in a given context, can have clearcut cultural advantages. But that need not mean that it is to the advantage of *each and every individual* to incorporate them. The energy equations which are the best for a society as a whole are not necessarily the best for a goodly number of the persons in that society. Indeed they often may not be.

A simple example will illustrate this point perfectly, though it may seem silly and pointless at first glance. Learning a foreign language has become a cultural tradition in our Latin American countries, at least in certain levels of society. The foreign language may even be Spanish, when the students are native Indians or Brazilians. The energy presumably acquired from that study derives from the contact one makes with important cultures which are not accessible to us, beyond a certain quantitative or qualitative point, except in their own languages.

For example, sure and accurate access to the fonts of Western philosophy will call for more than middling knowledge of Greek. Similar access to the golden age of philosophical Idealism will call for more than middling knowledge of German. But the whole process must be reconsidered in the case of a given individual. That person needs the ability to learn a foreign language satisfactorily and the ability to take proper advantage of the philosophical data thus acquired. If both abilities are present, the effort might well be worthwhile; if neither is present, it would not be. Difficulties arise when people possess one ability but not the other in sufficient degree. Suppose a person has great creative ability in philosophizing but very poor ability in learning foreign languages. In such a case the energy cost in exploring Greek or German philosophy in the original language would probably be too high. Such a person would do just as well to concentrate on those works which have already been translated into his or her native language.

Often it is not easy for individuals to calculate this equation on their own, particularly if they are youngsters. They will have to keep taking stock as they go along. They cannot make a final decision after studying the foreign language for only two months or after one course in philosophy. Yet somehow, with the help of others, this sort of vital calculation must always be made whenever and wherever one begins to lay hold of tradition as a problem in need of resolution.

On the individual level religious traditions certainly do not escape this problematic status. I think it is time that religious authorities stopped assuming automatically that the problem has been solved in principle.

Leaving the problem of the individual aside, it would seem that a religious faith such as the Christian one would occupy a central point on our spectrum. It combines optimum possibilities for cultural transmission with a rich store of profound experiences and reflections on ethics and the meaning of life. That store has been accumulated by human beings over the course of many centuries.

If my above observations are true, however, that position on the spectrum can never become a fixed, assured one. It is continually and seriously threatened from both ends of the spectrum. Only resolute combat against the two polar types of conditioning will ensure it the possibilities that it seems to possess in principle.

Remember that we are talking here about an authentically religious faith, such as the one described in the case of Jesus. That sort of religious faith seems to be more in opposition to, than in continuity with, religious traditions which have become culture. Religious faith is a prolongation of anthropological faith. It makes use of transcendent data provided by a body of testimony concerning meaning and values. The testimony is incarnated in a series of witnesses linked together by their common quest.[13] This approach leads people to *first* accept certain human values and *then* recognize their sacred or absolute sense. Religious traditions transmitted as culture represent a very different approach. First it seeks to recognize the sacred as such, i.e., as something supernaturally effective; only then, and usually indirectly, does it propose to adopt the values implicit in that sacred set of instruments.

As we noted in the case of Jesus himself, however, the instruments of transmission are basically the same in both cases: a Scripture which can be rightly or wrongly understood; certain rites which can be interpreted and lived out rightly or wrongly; and a morality which may or may not be glimpsed at its essential core and wellsprings.

Basic to my whole method and approach in this book is the fact that *Jesus founded a community on this very distinction*. Granting that there are historical and exegetical problems with the term, I shall call that community "Church" here. No Christian Church would have come into existence if the distinction noted here had not come across, first to Jesus and then to the apostolic community, as sound enough to effect a radical rupture and a new beginning.

Now if that is the case, then the cultural traditions which are called "Christian" today do not belong to the Church either. In other words, they do not represent the Church, and they do not fall under the Church's embrace or jurisdiction. The Church cannot isolate them from their overall context and roots, and thus effectively control them. The Church cannot acknowledge them as its own, despite surface affinities. Nor can the Church hide a basic opposition to them by virtue of its very institution, on the false pretext that one and the same faith can have different motivations and hence different levels of quality.[14]

On the other hand we cannot deny that the Christian faith and Christian community necessarily uses traditional elements which are partly similar to, and partly identical with, those belonging to religious cultural traditions: e.g., Scriptures, sacraments, lives of the saints, dogmas, and basic moral precepts. Indeed it is precisely its critical-minded use of the traditional that gives Christian faith and Christian community the place it ought to have on our hypothetical spectrum.

Here I would simply like to take a quick look at the two basic conditions that will permit the Christian faith to occupy and hold this central position on the spectrum. I have already pinpointed them in the course of this work. I bring them up again here because their importance will now be seen to be related to the problem of flexibility. *Only these two conditions can ensure that Christianity will retain or regain its true character as a factor fostering cultural flexibility.*

Let us consider the first condition, which is connected with the threat of oversimplified and superficial cultural traditions. As I indicated earlier, the danger of such easily transmitted traditions lies in the secure certainty with which they offer solutions to problems which, given sufficient energy, ought to be posed in more complex terms and explored by higher mental mechanisms. That this occurs with religious traditions is only too obvious. Religious traditions are presented as clear and indisputable (sacred) answers to moral and social problems which should be tackled by mental mechanisms, the latter utilizing data more in line with the complexity of human problem-posing and problem-solving.

By way of contrast, consider what Paul called "Christian liberty." That liberty or freedom remained associated with the biblical tradition which it had received and continued to work with. But it so destroyed the religious security of Paul's contemporaries and fellow believers that many of them preferred to return to the bondage of the law. The new "liberty" forced them to think about things for which they had previously had prefabricated answers. One of Paul's assertions illustrates this point very well: "Think before you do anything—hold to what is good" (1 Thess. 5:20). Notice that the reaction of Paul's contemporaries would be imitated by many people today who regard themselves as Christians by virtue of cultural heritage. Paul would say that Christ lived and died to no purpose in the case of those who do not comprehend or accept the new human situation and its problematic. If you stick to the old approach, "Christ will be of no advantage to you" (Gal. 5:2; see also Gal. 2:21; 3:4; 4:11).

Such a viewpoint must be silenced by a Church which seeks to represent the people rather than serve them. It must assume its religious traditions without any radical criticism, taking them as they are understood and lived by the people in accordance with the culture as a whole. Without ceasing to be a "people," it cannot derive from that heritage the elements that would unlock mental mechanisms, liberate thinking, and thus gradually transform tradition itself and return it to the people in the form of richer energy equations.

How, then, can Christian tradition be simultaneously normative and liberative as it passes through the ecclesial community? Certainly not by offering us an inherited set of ready-made answers. It must assume tradition to be a process of *learning to learn*.[15] Each bit of transcendent data which comes into play here serves as a launching pad: the more solid it is, the deeper and further the problems we may explore.

That brings us to the other threat and our second condition. Insofar as the official Church tends to succumb to the first tendency, to show no critical distancing from "Christian" cultural traditions, many Christians tend in the opposite direction as they grow more consciously aware. The Church's uncritical stance has certain consequences insofar as religious assertions, social effects, and political commitments are concerned. More aware Christians will despise those consequences and tend to reject the elements that turn Christianity into a cultural tradition. Alienated from an uncritical, tradition-bound Church, aware of other exigencies and possibilities for Christianity, these Christians move towards the "philosophical" end of our spectrum.

Many Christian communities now focus on an exploratory process involving complex mental mechanisms, rejecting elements which even a purified Christianity must receive and transmit culturally: Scriptures, rites, celebrations, and formulas to convey the transcendent data which provide the meaning-structure of Christianity. In this case, then, Christianity takes on the complexity of a philosophy insofar as energy is concerned. One starts from scratch because one mistrusts all the simpler means of transmission. And the result is a situation akin to the one depicted by the character in Joyce Cary's novel (see p. 326). Clearly a difficult balance must be maintained if Christianity is to be a factor fostering human and cultural *flexibility*.

III. Unfinished Business

My comments in this final chapter would be of little use unless the problems posed by them shed light on the themes treated throughout this book; I hope these problems were clarified by the latter as well. My aim has been to indicate a bit more concretely what was at stake in some of the issues posed earlier.

I make no pretense of offering clear solutions to specific problems. I have merely tried to analyze two basic human dimensions, using as rigorous as possible a method in the process. I was not trying to scratch an intellectual itch. I was trying to remove accumulated misconceptions that surround and obscure problems which are real and important to human beings.

I suppose there is no point in saying that this book, despite its many references to religious themes, was meant to be accessible to the perusal and judgment of all, whether they hold religious beliefs or not. Indeed one of its chief aims was to make people see that the problems of both groups are essentially the same: i.e., the meaning of human life and possible approaches to responding to this elementary challenge.

Readers who have no religion may find too many references to religion in this book. Those who have a religious faith, on the other hand, may feel that the significance of religious faith as such is not dealt with adequately or in sufficient detail.

What does it mean to have faith in God? What does it mean to have faith in Jesus? I intend to deal specifically with those two questions in subsequent volumes. The questions are obviously framed in Christian terms, but I hope that even readers who do not believe in Jesus will find my treatment open to them and their questions.

NOTES

1. Miguel de Unamuno, *Ensayos* (Madrid: Aguilar, 1967), 2: 418.

2. See Chapter IX, pp. 226f. above.

3. See the earlier discussion of ontological epistemological premises in Chapter IV, pp. 91f.

4. See Chapter II, pp. 37f, above.

5. See the Unamuno quote on p. 324.

6. Georges Bernanos, *Journal d'un curé de campagne* (Paris: Plon, 1952), p. 83; Eng. trans., *Diary of a Country Priest* (New York: Macmillan, 1962).

7. See Chapter IV, pp. 88f, above.

8. See Chapter IX, p. 229, above. "This terminology, distinguishing between (ideological) philosophy and Theory (or Marxist philosophy constituted in rupture with philosophical ideology) is authorized by several passages from the works of Marx and Engels. In *The German Ideology*, Marx always uses philosophy to mean ideology pure and simple. And Engels writes, in the earlier preface to his *Anti-Dühring*, 'If theoreticians are semi-initiates in the sphere of natural science, then natural scientists today are actually just as much so in *the sphere of theory, in the sphere of what hitherto was called philosophy.*' This remark proves that Engels felt the need to encapsulate the difference between ideological philosophies and Marx's absolutely new philosophical project in a terminological distinction. He proposed to register this difference by designating Marxist philosophy by the term *theory*. However, the fact that a new terminology is well-founded does not mean that it can really be manipulated and diffused. It seems difficult to go against familiar usage by designating the *scientific* [my italics] philosophy founded by Marx as Theory" (Louis Althusser, *For Marx*, Eng. trans. [London: Verso Editions, 1979], p. 162).

9. See Chapter IX, above.

10. This is what Machoveč seems to assume when he says that a soundly Marxist historical method would tend to rule out belief in Jesus. See Chapter V, pp. 131f, above.

11. This phenomenon, I think, is based on the "new task" which Lenin saw vis-à-vis Marx. As Lenin indicated, it was forced on Marxists by the "mass movements." The latter made it necessary to entrust mass manipulation to the apparatus of the revolutionary party. It is hard to get away from this mechanism once you latch on to it. But the whole issue is now coming in for debate, even in circles which have not yet explicitly given up the idea of the dictatorship of the proletariat. See, for example, the article by an interim minister of Hungary who is a member of the Central Committee of the Hungarian Communist Party: György Aczél. He wrote an article on "The Socialist State and the Church" in the Hungarian journal *Világosság* (October 1976). One section entitled "Unity, Not Homogeneity" is particularly interesting. There is an Italian translation in *Il Regno/13. 77' Documenti*, No. 356, 22 (July 1, 1977): 321–25.

12. It is paradoxical that some Communist Parties have found it easier to dissociate themselves from elements much closer to the core of the Marxist "ideology" (e.g., the dictatorship of the proletariat), than from hazy and obscure elements loosely caught up in the general philosophic context of the nineteenth century (e.g., determinism and atheism).

13. See Chapter III, pp. 72–78, above.

14. For example, note the contradiction between the following two statements of the Medellín conference. In the final document on "Pastoral Care of the Masses" (n. 6), we read: "Men adhere to the faith and participate in the Church at different levels. And while one may not presume on the existence of the faith behind all apparently Christian religious expressions, neither may one arbitrarily deny the character of true belief and of real ecclesial participation, no matter how weak, to every action which manifests spurious motives or temporal motivations, even selfish ones" (MED II: 124). This view essentially contradicts the following statement in the final document on "Education" (n. 9): "Therefore, all 'growth in humanity' brings us closer to 're-producing the image of the Son so that He will be the firstborn among many brothers' " (MED II: 101).

I find it very hard to see how "temporal motivations, even selfish ones," could be considered "growth in humanity" which reproduces "the image of the Son."

15. See Chapter III, pp. 75–76, above.

Index

Compiled by James Sullivan